Prentice Hall Realidades 2

Teacher's Resource Book
Para empezar–Tema 4

PEARSON

Boston, Massachusetts   Chandler, Arizona   Glenview, Illinois   Upper Saddle River, New Jersey

Acknowledgements for *Lecturas Teacher's Guide*

Bernadette M. Reynolds
Montbello High School
Denver, CO

Carol Eubanks Wargin

Rudolf L. Schonfeld
Parsippany High School
Parsippany, NJ

PEARSON

ISBN-13: 978-0-13-320376-9
ISBN-10:   0-13-320376-X
2 3 4 5 6 7 8 9 10   V056   16 15 14 13

Table of Contents

Welcome to *Realidades!*

Realidades is based upon the belief that the purpose of learning Spanish is to communicate with people who speak it and to understand their cultures. Across the different levels, *Realidades* offers you and your students a variety of print and digital tools that get them communicating from the first day!

Overview of the *Teacher's Resource Book*

This *Teacher's Resource Book* provides detailed support for teaching with *Realidades*. The introductory section gives an overview of different program components and teaching tips for using many of them in your classroom. The remaining section provides chapter-by-chapter support including answer keys, scripts, and blackline masters. All pages in this book are available digitally in the Interactive Teacher's Edition and Resource Library DVD and in **realidades.com** in the Teacher eText. For additional teaching support, we invite you to read the front matter articles in the Teacher's Edition and to visit MyPearsonTraining.com for training on using the digital components.

Program Components

The following charts highlight the program components. They provide a brief description of the component and indicate the different formats and locations of each component across our print and digital resources.

Legend:
Audio: Audio Program
EV: ExamView® Assessment Suite CD-ROM
IWB: Activities and Tools for Interactive Whiteboards DVD
PE: PresentationExpress™ Premium DVD
PV: *¡Pura vida!* DVD
TE: Interactive Teacher's Edition and Resource Library DVD
TRB: Teacher's Resource Book
VC: *Videocultura* DVD
VM: *Videomodelos* DVD
VP: Video Program DVD

Student Editions

The *Realidades* Student Editions are available in three formats: online, DVD, and print. The eText (on DVD and online within **realidades.com**) contains all the content from the print Student Edition plus embedded audio and video files, flashcards, and study tools. Individual eText activities are also available as assignable assets within the Course Content on **realidades.com**. For details on using the *Realidades* eText, visit the training modules on MyPearsonTraining.com.

In addition to the *Realidades* eText, **realidades.com** contains the eText edition of the highly acclaimed DK Spanish-English Bilingual Visual Dictionary. This resource gives students access to over 6,000 vocabulary words with audio support. The eText and individual visuals are also available on the Spanish Activities and Tools for Interactive Whiteboards DVD. For schools wanting the print edition of the DK dictionary, it can be purchased separately through PearsonSchool.com or your Pearson representative.

Component	realidades.com	DVD	Print
Student Edition Core instructional tool organized around thematic chapters	eText Course Content	eText	✓
DK Spanish-English Bilingual Visual Dictionary 6,000+ vocabulary words organized by topics	eText	IWB	✓

Workbooks

Realidades provides a variety of differentiated workbooks available in three formats: online, DVD, and print. The workbook activities available within the Course Content on **realidades.com** can be assigned and graded online. For details on assigning and grading within **realidades.com**, visit the training modules on MyPearsonTraining.com.

Component	realidades.com	DVD	Print
Leveled Vocabulary and Grammar Workbook Guided and core practice for new vocabulary and grammar plus puzzles and organizers	Course Content	TE	✓
Communication Workbook with Test Preparation Worksheets for audio and video activities plus reading skills worksheets, reading tests, and Integrated Performance Assessments	Course Content	TE	✓
Realidades para hispanohablantes All-Spanish companion worktext for heritage learners	Teacher eText Lesson Plans	TE	✓

Video, Multimedia, Audio, and Transparencies

Realidades features an outstanding selection of video, multimedia, and audio files accessible to both teachers and students. Resources available in the **realidades.com** Course Content can be assigned to students. Students can also access these resources through their Home Page.

Component	realidades.com	DVD/CD	Print
Video Program Contains the following video segments: • *Videohistoria* • *GramActiva* • *¿Eres tú, María?* (Levels A/B-1) • *En busca de la verdad* (Level 2)	eText Course Content	VP	n/a
Tutorial Videos Detailed grammar explanations; often include comparison of English and Spanish grammar	eText Course Content Tools	n/a	n/a
Videocultura Culture videos per theme in English or Spanish; activities online (Levels A/B-1 and 2)	Course Content	VC	n/a
Videomodelos Short videos of chapter speaking tasks modeled by teens from the Spanish-speaking world	eText Course Content	VM	n/a
¡Pura vida! Storyline video filmed in Costa Rica (Level 3); activities online	Course Content	PV	n/a
Animated Grammar Animations of verb conjugations	Course Content	PE	n/a
Canciones de hip hop Songs to teach new vocabulary and grammar	Course Content	n/a	n/a
Audio Program Audio for Student Edition, *Communication Workbook*, and Assessment Program	eText Course Content	AP	n/a
Transparencies All transparencies are online and on DVD; for vocabulary, grammar, fine art, maps, graphic organizers, and answers	Teacher eText	TE PE	n/a

Geography and Global Positioning

Realidades offers interactive KMZ files that transport students to locations in the Spanish-speaking world using global positioning technology. For details on using KMZ files, visit the training module on MyPearsonTraining.com.

Component	realidades.com	DVD/CD	Print
Mapa global interactivo Downloadable KMZ files with links to locations in Spanish-speaking world and accompanying culture notes and activities	eText Content Library	n/a	n/a
DK Reference Atlas Links to information on the various Spanish-speaking countries	Tools	n/a	n/a

Reading and Common Core

Realidades provides extensive support for helping students learn and apply reading skills and strategies. In addition to the reading support within the Student Edition, the program offers additional resources. For a correlation between *Realidades* and the Common Core English Language Arts Standards, visit PearsonSchool.com/Realidades2014.

Component	realidades.com	DVD/CD	Print
Lecturas Sixteen selections with comprehension questions	Teacher eText	TE	✓
Lecturas Teacher's Guide Answers and discussion questions	Teacher eText	TE	✓
Reading Skills Worksheets that practice essential reading strategies; found in the *Communication Workbook with Test Preparation*	Course Content	TE	✓

Grammar

The Grammar Study Guides are a popular "grammar at a glance" study tool. The three-ring punched laminated guides are ideal for placing in binders.

Component	realidades.com	DVD/CD	Print
Grammar Study Guides • Levels 1–2 • Levels 3–4	n/a	n/a	✓

Assessment

The program provides a variety of leveled assessment options available in multiple formats: online, DVD, and print. Assessments available in Course Content can be assigned to students and graded online.

Component	realidades.com	DVD/CD	Print
Instant Checks Auto-graded activities that quickly check for comprehension of new vocabulary and grammar	Course Content	n/a	n/a
Self-test End-of-chapter multiple-choice test	Course Content	n/a	n/a
Pruebas Assignable, auto-graded vocabulary recognition quizzes	Course Content	n/a	✓
Pruebas with Study Plans Assignable vocabulary production quizzes and all grammar quizzes; includes auto-assigned remediation and retesting	Course Content	n/a	✓
Examen del capítulo, Examen cumulativo, Placement Test Chapter, cumulative, and placement tests (online includes RealTalk!)	Course Content	TE	✓
Assessment Program Front matter, quizzes, tests, rubrics, answer keys, scripts	Teacher eText	TE	✓
Alternate Assessment Program Adapted chapter tests based upon core assessment; ideal for students needing extra help	Lesson Plans Teacher eText	TE	✓
Assessment Program: *Realidades para hispanohablantes* All-Spanish assessment for heritage learners	Lesson Plans Teacher eText	TE	✓
Integrated Performance Assessments Integrated assessments in the test practice section of the *Communication Workbook*	Course Content	TE	✓
Practice Tests Spanish or English readings with multiple-choice responses in the test practice section of the *Communication Workbook*	Course Content	TE	✓

ExamView® Assessment Suite Differentiated test banks per chapter with powerful editing and customization tools	Custom Content (test banks only)	EV	n/a

Planning and Presentation

With *Realidades*, you have variety of planning and presentation tools in multiple formats: online, DVD, and print. For details on using many of these planning and presentation tools, visit the training modules on MyPearsonTraining.com.

Component	realidades.com	DVD/CD	Print
Interactive Teacher's Edition and Resource Library Teacher's Edition with embedded links to resources; PDF files of program print resources and transparencies	Teacher eText	TE	n/a
PresentationExpress™ Premium Presentational tool for vocabulary, grammar, and review: audio, video, clip art, photo gallery, maps, self-tests, transparencies	n/a	PE	n/a
Activities and Tools for Interactive Whiteboards Activities written in SMART Notebook Express software for practicing new vocabulary and grammar; includes DK Bilingual Visual Dictionary eText, visuals with embedded audio in Image Gallery	Teacher Resources Folder	IWB	n/a
Teacher's Resource Book Provides program overview and key resources in print format	Teacher eText	TE	✓
Transparencies All transparencies are online and on DVD	Teacher eText	TE PE	n/a
Pre-AP* Resource Book Suggestions and activities for preparing students for the AP® Spanish Language and Culture Exam	Teacher eText	TE	✓
TPR Stories Suggestions and activities for integrating TPRS; written by Karen Rowan	Teacher eText	TE	✓

Component	realidades.com	DVD/CD	Print
ExamView® Assessment Suite Differentiated test banks per chapter with powerful editing and customization tools	Custom Content (test banks only)	EV	n/a

Planning and Presentation

With **Realidades**, you have variety of planning and presentation tools in multiple formats: online, DVD, and print. For details on using many of these planning and presentation tools, visit the training modules on MyPearsonTraining.com.

Component	realidades.com	DVD/CD	Print
Interactive Teacher's Edition and Resource Library Teacher's Edition with embedded links to resources; PDF files of program print resources and transparencies	Teacher eText	TE	n/a
PresentationExpress™ Premium Presentational tool for vocabulary, grammar, and review; audio, video, clip art, photo gallery, maps, self-tests, transparencies	n/a	PE	n/a
Activities and Tools for Interactive Whiteboards Activities written in SMART Notebook Express software for practicing new vocabulary and grammar; includes DK Bilingual Visual Dictionary eText, visuals with embedded audio in Image Gallery	Teacher Resources Folder	IWB	n/a
Teacher's Resource Book Provides program overview and key resources in print format	Teacher eText	TE	✓
Transparencies All transparencies are online and on DVD	Teacher eText	TE PE	n/a
Pre-AP® Resource Book Suggestions and activities for preparing students for the AP® Spanish Language and Culture Exam	Teacher eText	TE	✓
TPR Stories Suggestions and activities for integrating TPRS, written by Karen Rowan	Teacher eText	TE	✓

Integrating Technology in the *Realidades* Classroom

Realidades offers teachers and students a wide range of technology tools to plan, teach, practice, explore, assess, and remediate.

Student Technology on realidades.com

Students using *Realidades* have access to a wide range of digital tools on **realidades.com**. These tools include:

- *Realidades* eText with embedded audio and video
- *Realidades* eText for mobile devices
- *DK Spanish-English Bilingual Visual Dictionary* eText with embedded audio
- Course Content (assignable content)
  - eText activities with embedded audio and video*
  - RealTalk! activities*
  - Leveled Vocabulary and Grammar Workbook*
  - Communication Workbook with Test Preparation*
  - *Mapa global interactivo**
  - *Canciones de hip hop*
  - Animated Grammar
  - Videos: *Videocultura, Videohistoria, Videomodelos, GramActiva, Videomisterio, Videodocumentario, Pura vida,* Tutorial
  - Flashcards
  - Instant Checks*
  - Culture reading tasks*
  - Games and puzzles*
  - Self-test
  - *Pruebas* (with and without Study Plans)*
  - Integrated Performance Assessments*
  - *Examen del capítulo* *

  * Indicates activities that require computer or teacher grading and must be assigned by the teacher. The scoring feeds into the Gradebook.

For details on using **realidades.com** with students, visit MyPearsonTraining.com under the SuccessNet Plus tab. You will also find important information for using **realidades. com** on home computers and mobile devices.

Teacher Technology on realidades.com

Getting Started on realidades.com

To get started, teachers need to create an account on SuccessNet Plus, the learning management system that serves as the platform for **realidades.com**. Use the following self-registration process to accomplish this:

1. Go to **realidades.com** and register as a new user.
2. Request and/or enter the School Code.
3. Continue self-registration by providing the requested information. Create a unique username and a password.
4. Once your account has been set up, log in using the username and password.
5. Use the provided link to check your computer for compatible browsers, software, etc.
6. Go to MyPearsonTraining.com to learn more details on how to add products, create classes and calendars, and enroll students. You will find extensive resources for teachers, students, and parents related to using **realidades.com** and the many digital tools that come with *Realidades*.

Management and Instructional Tools

SuccessNet Plus and **realidades.com** offer teachers powerful management, reporting, and customization tools. In **realidades.com**, teachers can:

- Register and create a Home Page
- Add product, create classes, set up calendars, and enroll students
- Assign activities with or without Due Dates
- Personalize and differentiate assignments to individual or groups of students

- Set Preferences such as customizing the grade schema, determining when assignments are due, and setting the number of attempts for an activity
- Assess vocabulary and grammar as well as listening, speaking (using RealTalk!), reading, and writing
- Communicate with students
- Create a wide range of Reports
- Add, Customize, and Create Content

For in-depth training on how to get started and use the many teacher tools on **realidades.com**, visit MyPearsonTraining. com to view the many SuccessNet Plus and *Realidades* Video Modules.

Using realidades.com for Assessment

There are a variety of ways to use the content and tools on **realidades.com** for assessment. The assessments listed below are all assignable through the Course Content. For details, see the information in Program Components. In addition, **realidades.com** offers a variety of assessment templates in the Custom Content: Add Content section.

Formative assessment
- Instant Checks
- *Pruebas* (vocabulary recognition)
- *Pruebas* with Study Plans (vocabulary production and grammar)

Summative assessment
- *Examen del capítulo* (vocabulary, grammar, listening, speaking, reading, writing, and culture)
- *Examen cumulativo* (vocabulary, grammar, listening, speaking, reading, writing, and culture)
- Placement Tests (listening, speaking, reading, writing)

Performance assessment
- Integrated Performance Assessment
- *Presentación escrita*
- RealTalk! *Presentación oral*
- RealTalk! Communicative Pair Activities
- RealTalk! Situation Cards

Teacher Resources Within Pearson Content

Teachers using **realidades.com** have access to same Course Content listed previously in the Student Technology section. Teachers can preview, assign, and customize any of the Pearson Content.

From the teacher Home Page within **realidades.com**, teachers have additional teaching resources in the Pearson Content link. These resources include:
- Teacher eText: includes Student Edition plus all the PDF files found on the Interactive Teacher's Edition and Resource Library DVD. Teachers can link to program resources.
- Teacher Resources Folder that contains:
  - Lesson Plans
  - Teacher's Resource Book
  - Answer Keys: Student Textbook, Core Workbook, Guided Practice Workbook, Assessment Program
  - Vocabulary and Grammar Transparencies
  - Pre-AP* Resource Book
  - *Videomisterio* Teacher's Guide (Levels 1 and 2)
  - Spanish Interactive Whiteboard Teaching Tools
  - *Mapa global interactivo*

Using the *Mapa global interactivo* Files

The *Mapa global interactivo* files uses global positioning technology that enables students to zoom in on the places they are studying across the Spanish-speaking world. To access these files, you need to download them to your computer from the Teacher Resources Folder and use them with third-party global positioning software. For in-depth training on using this technology, visit MyPearsonTraining.com to see the module under *Realidades* ©2014.

Using Activities and Tools for Interactive Whiteboards

The Activities and Tools for Interactive Whiteboards component is available both as downloadable files within **realidades. com** and on a separate DVD. You will find a variety of activities per chapter that provide practice for the new vocabulary and grammar. The activities are written in SMART Notebook Express but can be used on most interactive whiteboards. For detailed information on how to use these activities, please read the information provided within the **realidades. com** folder or on the DVD.

Teaching Support in the *Teacher's Resource Book*

This *Teacher's Resource Book* is divided into two volumes. Volume I contains the teaching resources to supplement the preliminary chapter, called *Para empezar*, and *Temas* 1–4. Volume 2 includes the resources needed for *Temas* 5–9. For your convenience, both volumes are also provided digitally on the Interactive Teacher's Edition and Resource Library DVD and within **realidades.com** in the Teacher eText.

The following resources are provided for each chapter in *Realidades.*

Theme Project

Each *Tema* has a classroom theme project. These projects span the two chapters within the *Tema* and encourage students to prepare products and presentations directly related to the *Tema* subject matter. These projects help students internalize both vocabulary and grammar, and allow them to apply the language in a performance-based task. The blackline masters in this section introduce students to the theme project and contain instructions for preparing the project. A rubric is also provided for students so that they will understand how the project and

presentation will be evaluated. Each project is accompanied by suggestions for integrating 21st Century Skills, including digital tools, into the project. A second rubric has been provided to assess 21st Century Skills. Feel free to integrate these skills into the project as appropriate.

School-to-Home Connection Letter

Parental involvement plays an integral part in student success and in supporting language learning at home. To that end, we provide a model letter for each chapter that you can either photocopy or personalize and send home to parents or guardians.

Videocultura Scripts

This section contains the complete video script in English and Spanish for the *Videocultura* segments. Use these scripts to complement the accompanying video program or as a student comprehension aid in class. You might want to use them to familiarize yourself with the videos before using them in class.

A primera vista Input Scripts

Each chapter of *Realidades* has a language input section called *A primera vista: Vocabulario en contexto* that introduces vocabulary and lexical uses of grammatical structures to students. The Input Scripts offer a step-by-step approach to presenting the new terms in a contextualized manner that engages students, yet requires minimal production on the learner's part. They can be followed in their entirety or they can be used as a resource for ideas to supplement the suggestions found in the Teacher's Edition. The Input Scripts are based on the theory of comprehensible input as a teaching tool. (For more information on how to use the Input Scripts, see the discussion under Teaching with Input Scripts on p. xvi.)

Audio Scripts

This section contains the complete script for Student Edition audio including vocabulary, activities, pronunciation, end-of-chapter

vocabulary, and *Preparación para el examen*. It also includes the script for the audio activities in the *Communication Workbook with Test Preparation*. The scripts for the listening associated with the chapter tests can be found in the Assessment Program.

Video Scripts

The *Realidades* program has a comprehensive video component to support each chapter. The captivating input video for the *A primera vista: Vocabulario en contexto* section, corresponding to the *Videohistoria*, was shot on location in Spain, Mexico, Costa Rica, and Texas, and integrates culture and vocabulary with real-life, often humorous, situational interactions. In addition, *Realidades* offers the unique *GramActiva* Videos that explain and practice grammar structures in high-energy, entertaining segments that complement the *Gramática* sections within each chapter. Finally, in Temas 3 to 7, a third video component further engages student interest by means of a suspense-filled mystery story called *En busca de la verdad*. In some cases, you may want to provide copies of the video scripts to students as an aid to comprehension when they view the videos. You may also want to use them to identify specific vocabulary and grammar structures that you want to focus on in the videos before you show videos in class.

Communicative Pair Activities

These Communicative Pair Activities blackline masters focus on student-to-student involvement where students have some control over the communicative elements. They allow for personalization and individualization, and often allow students to share real information. They practice communication and help students become comfortable interacting in a second language. Although a given activity may focus on particular vocabulary or structures, the emphasis is always on using language to give

or obtain information. These activities have been designed to complement the ones found within *Realidades* and are meant to help students develop better communicative skills. (For more information on these blackline masters and how to use them, see Teaching with Communicative Pair Activities on p. xvi.)

You also have the option to record the Communicative Pair Activities within **realidades.com** using RealTalk! Each Communicative Pair Activity can be assigned from the Course Content (located in the *¡Adelante!* folder). Students can open the activity and print off the PDF for *Estudiante A* and *Estudiante B*. The PDF is identical to the copy in this *Teacher's Resource Book*. This gives you the option of printing it yourself for students, or having them print it in preparation for completing the activity. Students record their conversation and send it to you for evaluation. For details on using RealTalk!, visit MyPearsonTraining.com and view the video module.

Situation Cards

The Situation Cards blackline masters are designed to help students build confidence and develop skills as they work toward the goal of communicative proficiency. These guided conversations will provide your students with the opportunity to complete real-life tasks in Spanish. They will build confidence in even the most uncertain or reluctant students, and will enable more talented students to be truly creative with the language. There are a total of 38 pairs of Situation Cards, two per chapter. (For more information on these blackline masters and how to use them, see the section Teaching with Situation Cards on p. xvii.)

You also have the option to record the Situation Cards within **realidades.com** using RealTalk! The activity can be assigned from the Course Content (located in the *¡Adelante!* folder). Students can open the activity and print off the PDF for *Estudiante A* and

Estudiante B. The PDF is identical to the copy in this *Teacher's Resource Book*. This gives you the option of printing it yourself for students, or having them print it in preparation for completing the activity. Students record their conversation and send it to you for evaluation. For details on using RealTalk!, visit MyPearsonTraining.com and view the video module.

GramActiva Blackline Masters

The *GramActiva* reproducible masters are templates and graphic organizers to be used in conjunction with specific hands-on activities in the Student Edition. These blackline masters require students to create products or to use charts, graphs, and other visual aids such as Venn diagrams, word webs, and surveys. They are referenced at point of use in the Teacher's Edition. Depending on the activity, you may want to pass these out the day before so students can fill them in or otherwise prepare for using them.

Vocabulary Clip Art

The Vocabulary Clip Art offers reproducible images of the visualized vocabulary in each chapter of *Realidades*. These visuals can be used in a variety of ways to provide students with a hands-on opportunity to work with the new vocabulary. Engaging students in activities in which they "see, hear, say, and do" will help more students learn the new words and phrases. The Clip Art is available online. You can also access digital images of this vocabulary through the Interactive Teacher's Edition and Resource Library DVD. You will find this visualized vocabulary used through the program:

- PresentationExpress™ Premium DVD
- Flashcards (eText)
- Leveled Vocabulary and Grammar Workbook: Guided Practice

Leveled Vocabulary and Grammar Workbook

Answer Key: Core Practice

The Answer Key for the *Core Practice* activities allows you to quickly check the answers so students can have quick feedback. You may wish to reproduce these as a classroom set that you keep in a resource center or hand out so students can check their own work. You can also access pages with the answers displayed on the PresentationExpress™ Premium DVD.

Answer Key: Guided Practice

These are reduced pages of the *Leveled Vocabulary and Grammar Workbook: Guided Practice*. You can use them yourself to check work, or reproduce them in booklet form or on overheads so that students can check their own work. You can also access these pages on the PresentationExpress™ Premium DVD.

Communication Workbook with Test Preparation

Answer Key: Writing, Audio & Video Activities

These are reduced pages of the Writing, Audio & Video Activities with the answers printed on them. You can use them yourself to check work, or reproduce them in booklet form or on overheads so that students can check their own work. You can also access pages with the answers displayed on the PresentationExpress™ Premium DVD.

Answer Key: Test Preparation

This page provides answers for the Reading Skills worksheets and the Practice Test. Please note that answers to the Integrated Performance Assessments will always vary. The rubrics that you can use to assess student performance are given right on the student's page so that the students can see how they are to be evaluated.

Teaching Tips for the *Teacher's Resource Book*

Teaching with Input Scripts

The Input Scripts are based on the notion of comprehensible input. Rather than putting pressure on students to produce complex sentences with their newly acquired vocabulary and structures, they are given opportunities to show their comprehension through minimal responses. These responses range from physical responses (such as pointing to images in their textbook or manipulating the Vocabulary Clip Art images found in this *Teacher's Resource Book*) to short verbal responses (such as answering yes-no questions or questions with a choice of two answers) to short, structured conversations.

Input Vocabulary: This section provides a script for presenting the vocabulary in *Vocabulario en contexto*. The vocabulary from both pages may be presented at once, or it may be broken up into two presentations. For example, in the *A primera vista* for *Capítulo 2A*, a boy's daily routine is presented on one page, while a girl's daily routine is presented on the facing page. In this case, the Input Scripts present the two sets of vocabulary separately. The emphasis in this section is on presenting the new terms in a creative fashion.

Input Dialogue/Monologue: In the *A primera vista*, grammatical structures are presented in context through dialogues and monologues. Although they are quite short, many key concepts are embedded in the dialogues. The goal of this section of the Input Scripts is to help you present the dialogues in manageable sections that allow you to stop and ask students minimal-response questions that target the key grammatical concepts.

Comprehension Check: This section provides additional activities to help you gauge how well students understand the vocabulary and grammatical structures presented. Additionally, this section reinforces learning through high-interest games and other activities.

Teaching with Communicative Pair Activities

Learning a foreign language does involve learning important linguistic skills, such as grammar, syntax, and spelling, but also involves developing communicative skills, such as the ability to carry on a conversation in the target language, the ability to make a brief oral presentation, and the ability to communicate through written language.

These communicative activities focus primarily on listening and speaking skills—those skills that are more difficult to acquire outside of the classroom. Most of the activities are completed in pairs. One type of activity (*Actividades en grupo*) is intended for small groups of students. Students must communicate with each other to complete the activities. They ask and answer questions, role-play different scenes, share opinions on a variety of topics, and exchange real, but limited, information. In short, they use language in realistic situations that do not involve the teacher or a recording.

Activity Types: There are nine basic types of communicative activities included in this book: *Con otro(a) estudiante* (Partner Practice), *Descubrir …* (Discovery), *Diagramas* (Diagrams), *Entrevista* (Interview), *Hacer un papel* (Role-Play), *Opiniones* (Opinions), *Opiniones y reacciones* (Opinions and Reactions), and *Tres en raya* (Tic-Tac-Toe).

General Guidelines: Because most true communication takes place between two people or in small groups, most of the activities are to be used by pairs of students. You will want to determine the assignment of partners for the activities to be completed by student pairs. Also, you will want to have partners for a week or more, but partners

should change at least once a month. Working together for several activities helps students get to know each other and learn to work together; changing partners at least once a month prevents students from getting too comfortable and wasting time. Reassign partners if a partnership simply doesn't work out, for whatever reason. Before students begin an activity, check to make sure that everyone understands the directions. As students complete these activities, keep in mind that most conversation, even in one's native language, involves hesitation, mispronunciation, and errors. These will occur more frequently while learning a second language. Remember that these activities are not intended as grammar practice, but are designed as conversational activities to practice communication. If you notice consistent errors while students are working, make brief notes and review the relevant structures after the activity has been completed. Although difficult, it is best not to comment on errors while students are completing the activities. Students should be focusing on communication, not on structure.

Teaching with Situation Cards

The Situation Cards are designed to focus on the chapter's communicative objectives while integrating the vocabulary and grammar. In addition, they guide an exchange between two students, in which Student A initiates the conversation and Student B responds (both students know what the general topic is, but neither knows exactly what the other one's instructions are). Finally, they provide a structured role-play with opportunities for personalization and open-ended conversation.

Using the Situation Cards: The Situation Cards are most successful when students have already worked with the vocabulary and grammar. You will see the cards referenced in the *Repaso del capítulo* section of the *Teacher's*

Edition. There are a variety of ways to use the Situation Cards. You can photocopy them, cut them out, and paste them on 3 x 5 cards. Some teachers copy them directly onto colored paper and use a different color for each level. Other teachers laminate them for use as class sets. Use the cards for extended oral practice at the beginning of the class, as a warm-up, as practice for the speaking section of the *Examen del capítulo* (found in the Assessment Program book that is also part of the *Realidades* ancillary program), as informal speaking practice, or as the chapter's formal assessment for speaking proficiency. The Situation Cards also work well as a review for an end-of-quarter or final exam or at the beginning of the following year.

Directions:

1. Organize the students in pairs.

2. Distribute the cards. You can give each pair both situations to work on or you can give one situation to a pair of students and then have them exchange with another pair when completed.

3. Quickly brainstorm vocabulary and expressions that might be helpful in completing the tasks on the Situation Cards.

4. Start the activity. Remember that Student A will always initiate the conversation. Keep the activity within reasonable time limits. Three to seven minutes is ideal.

5. Circulate to verify that students are on task. This is also a good moment to informally assess students' level of comfort with the vocabulary and the speaking task, and to decide whether any reteaching is necessary. Do not correct errors at this point.

6. Signal when students should stop. You may ask them to reverse roles. Or you may devise a "traffic pattern" in which each pair of students puts their two cards together and exchanges them with another pair of students.

Assessment for Situation Cards: The Situation Cards can be used as a tool for informal or formal assessment. Students can act out the conversation with the partner with whom they practiced, with an assigned partner, or with the teacher.

Assessment can be based on a single criterion or on several different ones. For informal assessment, you might want to choose from any of the following criteria: completion of the task, appropriateness, comprehensibility, originality, quality above and beyond base expectations, individual improvement, group improvement, accuracy, or fluency. For a more formal assessment tool, see the *Scale for Evaluating Writing/Speaking Proficiency*, found in the *To the Teacher* section, pp. T1–T9, of the Assessment Program book. Whatever system you use, be sure to share it with your students before the assessment begins so that they will understand how they are to be graded.

Finally, once students have become accustomed to the Situation Cards, you might encourage them to write their own.

The use of these Situation Cards is a motivating and effective tool for guiding students to a level of increased comfort and confidence, and to a quality performance in the very challenging process of developing speaking proficiency.

Teaching with the Vocabulary Clip Art

The following ideas for using the Vocabulary Clip Art are only a sample of the many ways in which it can be used. You will probably devise additional ways to get students physically involved with learning and practicing new vocabulary. You will need to make copies of the art for each student to participate in these activities. You may wish to laminate one or two complete sets for permanent classroom use.

Homework Assignment: Have students use the visuals to create flashcards. They can cut and paste the visuals on cards and write the

Spanish word on the back of the card.

Picture Dictionary: Have students write the Spanish word for each picture on photocopies of pages as art of a "picture dictionary." These pages can be kept in a notebook that can be used as a valuable reference or review tool for students.

Assess Listening Comprehension: Begin by simply identifying a word on a page and by having students identify objects. Describe an object and have students point to it. Tell a story using the visual and have students point to vocabulary words in the story or indicate the sequencing through drawing lines or arrows. You might want to make an overhead transparency so that you (or a student) can be at the overhead doing both activities at the same time.

Additional Assessment of Listening Comprehension: Have students work in pairs to use the ideas in the prior bullet item. Circulate to keep the students on task and assess pronunciation and comprehension. Do not correct errors at this point; rather, use this time to determine areas needing further work.

Individual Images: Have students cut out the individual pictures and keep them in their notebook in a large zippered freezer bag that is three-hole punched. Here are some ideas for using the individual images:

1. Repeat the activities in "Assess Listening Comprehension" section above, and have students sort through the individual images to indicate comprehension. For example: If you say the word *lápiz*, students should place the picture for "pencil" in the center of their desks and then continue to add the pictures for objects you call out. Cut up the overhead transparency of the vocabulary art so that you (or a student) are at the overhead manipulating the image simultaneously with the students.

2. Have students work with each other saying the vocabulary words, telling stories, and

asking questions. For example, a student might say, *"Dame el libro."* The partner should use the visuals to perform the action. Getting each student to manipulate the vocabulary images is an excellent way to assist learning.

3. Have students draw a background for the visuals, such as a classroom. Have them sit back-to-back, and have one student arrange objects in a certain order. He or she then tells the partner where each item is located. For example, one student can tell the partner, *La silla está delante de la mesa*. The other student can ask questions, but should not see the layout of the objects until he or she thinks the placement is correct. Students can then compare layouts.

4. Encourage students to color in the pictures or personalize them and use them to decorate their compositions.

5. Have students create their own Bingo cards using the visuals. Have each student create a grid of five down and five across. Students then place 25 visuals in any order. Have one student be the "caller" and call out different vocabulary words. Students turn the words over on their grids until one has five down, across, or diagonally. The winning student names the vocabulary pieces he or she turned over and becomes the next "caller."

6. Use the individual pictures as an oral vocabulary quiz. Have students name each image as he or she lays them on the desk in front of you. Students who do not feel confident with all the chapter's vocabulary may select a handful of images and name those visuals for you.

Teaching Tips for the Test Preparation Section of the *Communication Workbook with Test Preparation*

The Test Preparation section reinforces the language arts skills and test-taking strategies needed for success on high-stakes exams. The activities in this section practice these key skills and strategies while building proficiency in Spanish.

Reading Skills Worksheets

For each chapter, you will find two worksheets that focus on core reading skills. Each activity allows students to practice the reading skill with existing activities from the corresponding *Realidades* chapter. These are important worksheets to use if you want to emphasize teaching students to read or if your school or district has an initiative to support reading across the curriculum or support for the Common Core. The Reading Skills worksheets can be completed in the print *Communication Workbook with Test Preparation*. In addition, all worksheets can be assigned to students within the Course Content in **realidades.com** and graded online.

Practice Tests

To further reinforce reading skills, the Test Preparation section of the *Communication Workbook* provides a reading passage for each chapter followed by three question types: multiple choice, short response, extended response. Each Practice Test can be completed in the print *Communication Workbook with Test Preparation*. In addition, all Practice Tests can be assigned to students within the Course Content in **realidades.com** and graded online.

Multiple Choice Multiple choice questions always have four answer choices. Students pick the one that is the best answer. Answers to the multiple choice questions are included in this *Teacher's Resource Book*.

Short Response This symbol appears next to questions that require short written answers:

This symbol appears next to questions requiring short written answers that are a creative extension based on the reading:

It is suggested that students take approximately 3 to 5 minutes to answer a Short Response question. These types of questions are called "performance tasks" and require that students read all parts of the question carefully, plan their answer, and then write the answer in their own words. A complete answer to a Short Response question is worth 2 points. A partial answer is worth 1 point or 0 points. The Short Response questions on the student test preparation pages are written in either English or Spanish. Students are instructed to respond in English when the question is in English and in Spanish when the question is in Spanish. Sample top-score Short Response answers are included in this *Teacher's Resource Book*.

Extended Response This symbol appears next to questions requiring longer written answers based on information that can be inferred from the reading:

This symbol appears next to questions requiring longer written answers that are a creative extension based on the reading:

It is suggested that students take about 5 to 15 minutes to answer an Extended Response question. These types of questions are also called "performance tasks" because they require that students read all parts of the question carefully, plan their answer, and then write the answer in their own words. A complete answer to an Extended Response question is worth 4 points. A partial answer is worth 3, 2, 1, or 0 points. The Extended Response questions on the student test preparation pages are written in either English or Spanish. Students are instructed to respond in English when the question is in English and in Spanish when the question is in Spanish. Sample top-score Extended Response answers are included in this *Teacher's Resource Book.*

How the Test Will Be Scored

Multiple Choice Questions
Multiple choice answers are either right or wrong. Students receive 1 point if the correct answer is selected.

Performance-Based Questions (Short Response and Extended Response)
Short Response and Extended Response questions, which are called "performance tasks," are often scored with rubrics. Sample rubrics follow. These rubrics describe a range of performance and students receive credit for how close their answers come to the anticipated response.

Rubric for Short Response Questions

2 points The response indicates that the student has a complete understanding of the reading concept embodied in the task. The student has provided a response that is accurate, complete, and fulfills all the requirements of the task. Necessary support and/or examples are included, and the information given is clearly text-based. Any extensions beyond the text are relevant to the task.

1 point The response indicates that the student has a partial understanding of the reading concept embodied in the task. The student has provided a response that may include information that is essentially correct and text-based, but the information is too general or too simplistic. Some of the support and/or examples may be incomplete or omitted.

0 points The response is inaccurate, confused, and/or irrelevant, or the student has failed to respond to the task.

Teaching Tips for the Communication Workbook with Test Preparation **xxi**

Rubric for Extended Response Questions

4 points   The response indicates that the student has
a thorough understanding of the reading
concept embodied in the task. The student has
provided a response that is accurate, complete,
and fulfills all the requirements of the task.
Necessary support and/or examples are
included, and the information given is clearly
text-based. Any extensions beyond the text are
relevant to the task.

3 points   The response indicates that the student has
an understanding of the reading concept
embodied in the task. The student has provided
a response that is accurate and fulfills all the
requirements of the task, but the required
support and/or details are not complete or
clearly text-based.

2 points   The response indicates that the student has a
partial understanding of the reading concept
embodied in the task. The student has provided
a response that may include information that
is essentially correct and text-based, but the
information is too general or too simplistic.
Some of the support and/or examples and
requirements of the task may be incomplete or
omitted.

1 point   The response indicates that the student has
very limited understanding of the reading
concept embodied in the task. The response is
incomplete, may exhibit many flaws, and may
not address all the requirements of the task.

0 points   The response is inaccurate, confused, and/or
irrelevant, or the student has failed to respond
to the task.

Using the Practice Tests

Practice Test and Answer Key Format

There is one Practice Test for each *tema* in Level 2. For each test, you will find three parts:
- reading selection
- questions
- response sheet

The student tests for *Communication Workbook with Test Preparation* are not reproduced in this *Teacher's Resource Book*. You will need to refer to the student workbook for copies of the tests. Answers to each test for *Temas* 1–4 appear in this *Teacher's Resource Book*.

Practice Tests

There is one reading per *tema*. This reading incorporates the themes and content of each *tema* (e.g., school, shopping, leisure activities).

The readings incorporate the chapter vocabulary and grammar and are most useful after completion of the *temas* for which they were written. Of course, these selections add the challenge of reading in Spanish to the other strategies used on reading tests. Encourage students to employ the same strategies used when reading in English (see "Tips for Improving Your Score" on pp. 204–207 of the Introduction to the *Communication Workbook with Test Preparation*). You will notice that the multiple choice questions are written in English. This practice is supported by research stating that students can demonstrate reading comprehension more effectively when the follow-up questions are in English and they are allowed to respond in English. The Short Response and Extended Response questions are generally written in English prompting an English response. Responses in English again allow students to demonstrate comprehension and allow them to practice reading skills, such as comparing and contrasting, recognizing cause and effect, and identifying author's purpose, required for success with standardized tests. This practice recognizes that beginning-level students do not have the proficiency in Spanish to respond to such in-depth questions.

Integrating the Practice Tests with Instruction

Decide when you want to use a practice test within your lesson plan. You can use the tests during class time or as homework assignments. Be sure to review with students how the test questions will be scored, including how the rubric is used. Students have a copy of the rubrics on pp. 207–208 of their workbook. Allow approximately 25 minutes for students to take the test. Grade the multiple choice questions as a whole-class activity and discuss the correct responses, or collect the papers and grade them on your own. The answers are provided in this *Teacher's Resource Book*. However, to grade the Short or Extended Response questions, it is suggested that you collect the papers and grade them using the rubrics and the sample top-score responses provided in this *Teacher's Resource Book*. When you return the tests to the students, you might want to share the sample top-score responses and discuss how they could best construct a response that earns the highest score on the rubric.

Preparing Students for Standardized Tests

Teaching Students to be Good Test-Takers

Many students are not successful on standardized tests because they lack the skills and strategies employed by good test-takers. You can use the strategies found on pp. 204–207 of the Introduction to the *Communication Workbook with Test Preparation* to review with students prior to administering the first practice test. It is helpful to remind students of these strategies each time that they take a practice test.

Success for ALL Students

Helping Students Raise Their Test Scores

The *Communication Workbook with Test Preparation* provides each teacher with complete support to prepare students for success on standardized tests. Students learn valuable test-taking tips, practice taking tests and responding to various types of questions, learn why a response was correct, and learn how to better shape their responses in the future. Over time, they will become more comfortable with taking standardized tests. In addition, the high-interest readings will enable students to expand their knowledge and understanding of the cultures of the Spanish-speaking world while building important reading and writing skills.

Teaching Tips for *Lecturas*

The *Lecturas* reader contains a variety of reading selections that are interesting, age-appropriate, and accessible to students at varying proficiency levels. The selections progress from less difficult to more difficult, thereby allowing students to sample material that gradually becomes more challenging lexically and syntactically. The answers to the *Lecturas* questions are found at the end of the *Teacher's Resource Book,* Volume 1.

Each of the reading selections is accompanied by one or more prereading questions; two or more postreading questions, which appear in the section called *¿De qué se trata?*; and in a vocabulary section called *¿Qué quiere decir?*

The prereading questions are designed to help set the scene so that students can focus on the material that follows. They have been personalized to draw students into the reading.

Some unfamiliar words, expressions, and grammatical structures have been incorporated into each reading selection. Many are cognates or other easily decodable words, and therefore, have not been glossed. A limited number of unfamiliar words, expressions, and grammatical structures that students may not so readily understand are explained at the end of each reading in the section called *¿Qué quiere decir?*

When one asks students to respond to questions about a reading, three different kinds of information may be requested: factual, inferential, or information that requires some kind of personal application. In order to test students' comprehension of the selections, you may prefer to ask (or have students ask) some factual questions first and then proceed with the question in the *¿De qué se trata?* section. You may use the additional questions provided in the Teacher's Guide as time permits to elicit more in-depth discussion of the readings.

Realidades 2

Para empezar

Table of Contents

Theme Project

Para empezar
¿Quién soy yo?

Overview:

You will create a four-page "Who am I?" booklet. You will write two sentences per page to describe yourself and your activities without revealing your identity. On the last page, you will use the verb *ser* to identify yourself. After you have completed the "book," you can share it with your class members and try to guess the author of each one.

Resources:

Digital or print photos, page layout/word processing software and/or construction paper, markers, photos, glue or tape, scissors

Sequence:

STEP 1. Review the instructions with your teacher.

STEP 2. Submit a rough sketch of each page of your "book."
Work with a partner and present your drafts to each other.

STEP 3. Create layouts leaving room for photos and descriptions.

STEP 4. Submit a draft of each page of the book.

STEP 5. Share your book with other members of the class. Try to guess the author of each book before you reach the last page.

Assessment:

Your teacher will provide you with a rubric to assess this project.

Para empezar Project: ¿Quién soy yo?

Project Assessment Rubric

RUBRIC	Score 1	Score 3	Score 5
Evidence of Planning	No written draft or page layouts provided.	Draft was written and layout created, but not corrected.	Evidence of corrected draft and layout.
Use of Illustrations	No photos/visuals included.	Very few photos/visuals included.	Several photos/visuals included.
Presentation	Contains details that develop characters.	Contains one sentence per page.	Contains two or more sentences per page.

21st Century Skills Rubric: Foster Social and Cross-Cultural Skills

RUBRIC	Score 1	Score 3	Score 5
Preparing for the interview	Is unable to find student(s) to interview	Relies on teacher assistance in finding student(s) to interview	Does not rely on teacher to find student(s) to interview
Preparing questions	Does not prepare questions in advance of interview	Prepares questions but none ask about cultural differences	Prepares questions in advance including some that ask about cultural differences
Interaction skills	Does not react to or follow up on responses	Has minimal interaction; asks some follow-up questions	Interacts extensively and asks several follow-up questions

Realidades ❷

Para empezar

School-to-Home Connection

Dear Parent or Guardian,

Thank you for taking the time to review what your child is learning in his or her Spanish class. You can play an integral role in your child's acquisition of Spanish by staying informed of what is being taught in class and supporting language learning at home.

Realidades, your child's Spanish textbook, is designed to promote both written and oral communication. Each theme-based chapter includes vocabulary in context, grammar, and cultural lessons. Also included are pronunciation exercises, detailed language studies, and ways to recognize and use Spanish outside of the classroom.

In this chapter, students will be reviewing some things that were learned last year:

- talking about what they and other people are like
- talking about where they and other people are from
- talking about what they and other people do
- talking about how often they do certain things

To reinforce and enhance learning, students can access a wide range of online resources on **realidades.com**, the personalized learning management system that accompanies the print and online Student Edition. Resources include the eText, textbook and workbook activities, audio files, videos, animations, songs, self-study tools, interactive maps, voice recording (RealTalk!), assessments, and other digital resources. Many learning tools can be accessed through the student Home Page on **realidades.com**. Other activities, specifically those that require grading, are assigned by the teacher and linked on the student Home Page within the calendar or the Assignments tab.

You will find specifications and guidelines for accessing **realidades.com** on home computers and mobile devices on MyPearsonTraining.com under the SuccessNet Plus tab.

Check it out! Have your child review the vocabulary in this chapter by describing two friends and what they like to do in their free time.

Sincerely,

realidades.com ⓥ

For: Tips to Parents
Visit: www.realidades.com
Web Code: jce-0010

Para empezar

Input Script

Presentation: ¿Cómo eres tú?

Input Vocabulary: Distribute copies of the Vocabulary Clip Art from Level 1, Capítulo 1B, and have students cut them into individual images. Act out the various personality traits and have students hold up the Clip Art image and name the personality trait. Then call out the names of celebrities and/or teachers at your school and have students hold up the Clip Art image and name the personality trait they believe each person has.

Input Dialogues: Two days before the presentation, tell students to bring an old, clean sock to class. The day before the presentation, assign the roles of Gloria, Enrique, Sonia, Alicia, and Felipe to students and have them make a sock puppet for their character. Have them use markers to draw the facial features, and glue on yarn for hair. The day of the presentation, pair the "Glorias" with the "Enriques," and make groups with a "Sonia," an "Alicia," and a "Felipe." Have the students practice their conversations and then perform the conversations with their sock puppets.

Presentation: ¿Qué haces?

Input Vocabulary: Tape the Vocabulary Clip Art from Level 1, Capítulo 1A, that shows the four activities pictured on p. 8 on the chalkboard, upside down and backward, so that the images can be flipped up. Also write the names of the activities on the same size paper and tape them on the chalkboard upside down and backward, too. Number the pieces of paper from 1 to 8. Have students try to match the name with the activity by calling out two numbers at a time in Spanish. Flip the numbers for them to show whether they have made a match. Remove the matched images and words.

Input Dialogue: Have pairs of students guess what Pepe and Paula might be saying and write a dialogue based on the images they see. Have volunteers perform their dialogues. Then have volunteers read the dialogue in the textbook. Then discuss with students if they are more like Pepe or Paula, and what other activities they like to do in winter and summer.

Comprehension Check

- Have students choose the personality trait that best describes themselves and the one that is least descriptive of themselves and tape each one to the front of their shirt. Have students circulate around the room and ask each other about the traits they see taped to their classmates.

- Write the words for personality traits and activities on slips of paper and place them in a bag. Divide the class into teams. Have one member of a team at a time draw one of the personality traits from the bag. Give the student one minute to draw the trait on the chalkboard for his or her team members to guess.

6 *Para empezar* ▬ *Input Script*

Realidades 2

Para empezar

Audio Script

Audio DVD, Para empezar

Track 01: *¿Cómo eres tú?*, Student Book, p. 2

Lee en tu libro mientras escuchas los diálogos.

TEEN FEMALE 1: Oye, Enrique, ¿eres artístico?

TEEN MALE 1: Sí, según mis amigos soy muy artístico y estudioso. También dicen que soy reservado. Y Gloria, ¿cómo eres tú?

TEEN FEMALE 1: Bueno… mis amigos dicen que soy paciente y trabajadora. Pero según mi hermanito, ¡soy impaciente y perezosa!

TEEN MALE 2: ¡Hola, Sonia y Alicia! ¡Uy! ¡Qué deportistas son Uds.!

TEEN FEMALE 2: Sí, somos muy deportistas y también muy talentosas. ¿Te gusta hacer deportes, Felipe?

TEEN MALE 2: Pues, no. No soy nada deportista, pero me gusta pasar tiempo con mis amigos. Soy sociable y muy simpático.

Track 02: *¿Cómo eres tú?*, Act. 4, Student Book, p. 4

Dos jóvenes

Lee esta descripción de dos chicas latinoamericanas. Luego escribe los números del 1 al 6 en una hoja de papel. Escucha las frases y escribe C si la información es cierta y F si es falsa. Vas a escuchar las frases dos veces.

1. Alicia y Carmen tienen 18 años.
2. Alicia es de Puerto Rico, y Carmen es de Cuba.
3. Alicia es poeta.
4. Carmen es muy sociable.
5. A Carmen no le gusta escuchar los poemas de Alicia.
6. Los amigos de las jóvenes son negativos y serios.

Track 03: Audio Act. 1, Writing, Audio & Video Workbook, p. 1

As an icebreaker for the first week of school, a teacher asks his students to draw a poster that describes him or her. Listen as each student describes him or herself and match each description to one of the bio-posters below. Write the corresponding number underneath the poster. You will hear each description twice.

1. Yo soy muy trabajadora. Después de mis clases, trabajo en un restaurante hasta las nueve de la noche. Luego estudio por dos horas.
2. Mi madre dice que soy muy desordenado. Siempre busco mis libros o mi cuaderno.
3. Me gusta mucho practicar deportes. Voy al gimnasio todos los días. Soy muy deportista.
4. Yo tengo muchas amigas. Siempre hablo con ellas después de las clases. Soy muy sociable.
5. No entiendo bien las matemáticas, pero soy un estudiante muy serio. Estudio mucho y saco buenas notas.

Track 04: Audio Act. 2, Writing, Audio & Video Workbook, p. 1

As a second-year Spanish student, David is helping in the school counselor's office during the first week of school. As Spanish-speaking students enroll, he asks their name and nationality. Listen to each conversation, then circle the native country of the Spanish-speaking student. You will hear each conversation twice.

1. **TEEN MALE 1:** Hola. Bienvenido. ¿Cómo se llama Ud.?
   TEEN MALE 2: Me llamo Martín. Soy de América del Sur.
   TEEN MALE 1: ¿Es Ud. boliviano?
   TEEN MALE 2: No. Soy chileno.
2. **TEEN MALE 1:** Hola. Me llamo David. ¿Cómo se llaman Uds.?
   TEEN FEMALE 1: Me llamo Marta.
   TEEN FEMALE 2: Y yo me llamo Vanesa.
   TEEN MALE 1: ¿De dónde son Uds.?
   TEEN FEMALE 1: Somos uruguayas.
3. **TEEN MALE 1:** Hola. Bienvenidos. ¿Cómo se llaman?
   TEEN MALE 3: Hola. Me llamo Arturo y mi hermano se llama Ricardo. Somos hondureños. Es nuestro primer día aquí.
   TEEN MALE 1: Mucho gusto de conocerlos.
4. **TEEN MALE 1:** Hola. Me llamo David. Eres puertorriqueña, ¿no? ¿Cómo te llamas?
   TEEN FEMALE 2: Soy Natalia. Sí, soy puertorriqueña. ¿Es Ud. puertorriqueño también?
   TEEN MALE 1: Sí. Encantado de conocerte.
5. **TEEN MALE 1:** Buenos días. ¿De dónde es Ud.?
   TEEN MALE 4: Soy Samuel. Soy dominicano.
   TEEN MALE 1: Bienvenido a nuestra escuela.

Track 05: *¿Qué haces?*, Student Book, p. 8

Lee en tu libro mientras escuchas el diálogo.

TEEN MALE: ¡Uy! No me gusta nada el invierno. Paula, ¿qué te gusta hacer en el invierno?

TEEN FEMALE: Pues, paso tiempo con mis amigos: escuchamos música, cantamos y por la noche bailamos. Lo que más me gusta hacer es practicar deportes.

TEEN MALE: ¿Qué deportes practicas?

TEEN FEMALE: Monto en bicicleta o corro todos los días para hacer ejercicio. Practico deportes todo el año. ¿Y tú, Pepe?

TEEN MALE: No soy muy deportista. A veces nado, por eso me encanta el verano. Generalmente tomo el sol y leo. ¿Qué haces en tus vacaciones de verano?

TEEN FEMALE: En el verano a veces patino y también monto en monopatín con mis amigos.

Track 06: *¿Qué haces?*, Act. 13, Student Book, p. 8

Paula y Pepe

Divide una hoja de papel en dos columnas. En la primera columna escribe *Paula*, y en la segunda escribe *Pepe*. Escucha una lista de actividades. Si Paula hace la actividad, escribe el número de la actividad debajo de *Paula*. Si Pepe la hace, escribe el número debajo de *Pepe*. Usa las fotos para ayudarte. Vas a escuchar las palabras o frases dos veces.

1. bailar
2. leer
3. escuchar música
4. montar en bicicleta
5. tocar la guitarra
6. nadar
7. correr
8. escribir canciones

Track 07: Audio Act. 3, Writing, Audio & Video Workbook, p. 2

After Alicia enrolls at the counselor's office, David offers to show her to her first class. As he walks her to class, he points out his friends to her and tells her what each is doing. Match the pictures with each description of his friends. You will hear each description twice.

1. Aquí está Ana. Ella siempre habla por teléfono con sus amigos. Es muy sociable.
2. Miguel y Luis siempre llegan temprano a la clase y terminan su tarea antes de la clase. Están allí en la clase de inglés.
3. Anita siempre saca fotos de los estudiantes. Ella trabaja en el periódico de la escuela.
4. Allí está mi amiga Luisa. Come su desayuno en la cafetería porque siempre sale tarde de su casa.
5. Luis siempre lee revistas en la biblioteca. No es muy sociable y prefiere estar solo.

Realidades 2

Para empezar

Nombre _____

Fecha _____

Communicative Pair Activity **P-1**

Estudiantes **A y B**

¿Cómo eres tú? Answer the following questions about your personality, likes, and dislikes. Record your answers in the spaces provided. Examples: *Soy estudiosa. Me gusta la música.*

1. ¿Eres estudioso(a) o perezoso(a)? _____

2. ¿Eres serio(a) o gracioso(a)? _____

3. ¿Eres deportista? ¿Qué deportes te gustan/no te gustan?

_____

4. ¿Te gusta la música? ¿Qué tipo de música te gusta/no te gusta?

_____

5. ¿Eres artístico(a)? _____

6. ¿Te gusta hablar por teléfono? _____

7. ¿Eres sociable? ¿Te gusta pasar tiempo con tus amigos?

_____

8. ¿Eres paciente o impaciente? _____

9. ¿Eres ordenado(a) o desordenado(a)? _____

10. ¿Eres reservado(a)? _____

¿Cómo es tu compañero(a)? Ask your partner six (6) of the questions above about his or her personality, likes, and dislikes. Record his or her answers in the spaces provided below. Examples: *Ella es estudiosa. Le gusta la música.*

1. _____

2. _____

3. _____

4. _____

5. _____

6. _____

Realidades ②

Para empezar

Nombre _____

Fecha _____

Communicative Pair Activity **P-2**

Estudiantes **A y B**

¿Qué haces? What do you do in your free time? Choose five activities from your routine from the list below and write them on the lines *JUEGO UNO*. For example: *En mi tiempo libre, paso tiempo con mis amigos.* Take turns with a partner asking questions to try to be the first to discover the other person's five activities. Record your partner's answers by writing *Sí* or *No* on the blank space corresponding to each game next to the listed items. Answer your partner's questions in complete sentences. Use the expressions listed under *PALABRAS ÚTILES* in your answers. For *JUEGO DOS,* choose five activities you never do or that you only do sometimes.

1   **2**

_____ _____ comer

_____ _____ bailar

_____ _____ caminar

_____ _____ cantar

_____ _____ correr

_____ _____ esquiar

_____ _____ patinar

_____ _____ dibujar

_____ _____ tomar el sol

_____ _____ montar en bicicleta

_____ _____ leer revistas

_____ _____ nadar

_____ _____ escuchar música

_____ _____ usar la computadora

_____ _____ escribir cuentos

_____ _____ hablar por teléfono

JUEGO UNO

_____

_____

_____

_____

_____

JUEGO DOS

_____

_____

_____

_____

_____

PALABRAS ÚTILES:

a veces
a menudo
los fines de semana
después de
antes de
nunca
todos los días

Realidades ❷

Para empezar

Nombre _____

Fecha _____

Communicative Pair Activity **P-3**

Estudiantes **A y B**

¿Qué haces en tu tiempo libre? Answer the following questions about your activities in your free time at different times of the year. Record your answers in the spaces provided. Examples: *Por las tardes leo revistas.*

1. ¿Qué haces durante los fines de semana? _____

2. ¿Qué haces cuando estás de vacaciones? _____

3. ¿Qué haces en el invierno? _____

4. ¿Qué no haces en el invierno? _____

5. ¿Qué haces en el verano? _____

6. ¿Qué no haces en el verano? _____

7. ¿Qué haces en el otoño? _____

8. ¿Qué no haces en el otoño? _____

9. ¿Qué haces en la primavera? _____

10. ¿Qué no haces en la primavera? _____

¿Qué hace tu compañero(a) en su tiempo libre? Ask your partner six (6) of the questions above about his or her activities in his or her free time at different times of the year. Record his or her answers in the spaces provided below. Example: *Ella lee revistas por las tardes.*

1. _____

2. _____

3. _____

4. _____

5. _____

6. _____

Situation Cards

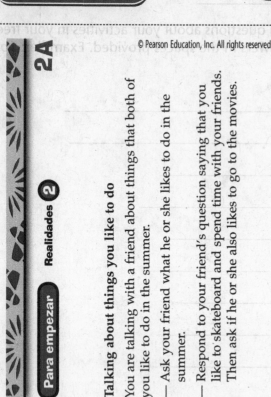
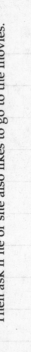

2A

Para empezar   Realidades **2**

Talking about things you like to do

You are talking with a friend about things that both of you like to do in the summer.

— Ask your friend what he or she likes to do in the summer.

— Respond to your friend's question saying that you like to skateboard and spend time with your friends. Then ask if he or she also likes to go to the movies.

2B

Para empezar   Realidades **2**

Talking about things you like to do

You are talking with a friend about things that both of you like to do in the summer.

— Respond to your friend's question saying that you like to read and that you ride your bicycle often.

— Ask him or her what he or she does in the summer.

— Respond to your friend's question.

1A

Para empezar   Realidades **2**

Talking about what you are like

You are describing yourself to a new friend at an international summer camp.

— Shake hands with your new friend as you tell him or her that you are Mexican. Then ask him or her where he or she is from.

— Respond to your partner's question saying that you are sporty/athletic and that you like to swim often. Ask him or her if he or she likes to swim.

1B

Para empezar   Realidades **2**

Talking about what you are like

You are talking with a new friend at an international summer camp.

— Shake hands with your new friend and respond that you are Puerto Rican.

— Tell your new friend that you are not very sporty/athletic and ask if he or she is.

— Answer the question by stating that you can swim, but not very well.

GramActiva

¿Qué haces?
Paula y Pepe, p. 8

Paula	Pepe

Core Practice Answers

P-1

A.

1. jóvenes
2. simpáticos
3. guapas
4. inteligentes
5. atrevidas

B.

Row 1: trabajadora
Row 2: deportista
Row 3: paciente
Row 4: alto
Row 5: vieja

C.

1. desordenado
2. ordenada
3. trabajadoras
4. serios

P-2

A.

Row 1: soy / somos
Row 2: eres
Row 3: es / son

B.

1. Isabel es inteligente.
2. Sara y Ana son estudiosas.
3. La señora García es sociable.
4. Los estudiantes son serios.
5. Mi familia y yo somos artísticos.
6. La chica es talentosa.
7. Nosotras somos jóvenes.
8. Tú eres bajo(a).
9. El profesor es gracioso.
10. Yo soy reservado(a).

P-3

1. Eres argentina.
2. Es puertorriqueño.
3. Somos dominicanos.
4. Son chilenas.
5. Soy mexicano.
6. Es guatemalteca.
7. Son panameños.
8. Es peruana.
9. Somos cubanos.
10. Eres colombiano.
11. Es costarricense.
12. Soy estadounidense.

P-4

A.

Paragraph 1: corro / vive / corro /
regreso / desayunamos
Paragraph 2: paso / practican /
toca / canto / Practicamos
practicamos
Paragraph 3: escucho / bailo /
leen / ven / monta

B.
Answers will vary.

These blank cards can be used to write and practice other Spanish vocabulary for the chapter.

Copy the word or phrase in the space provided. Be sure to include the article for each noun.

¿Quién(es)?

¿Cómo?

¿De dónde?

¿Quién(es)?

¿Cómo?

¿De dónde?

viejo, vieja

atrevido, atrevida

desordenado, desordenada

viejo

atrevido

desordenado

vieja

atrevida

desordenada

reservado, reservada

gracioso, graciosa

sociable

reservado

gracioso

reservada

graciosa

sociable

Sheet 1

Realidades 2

Para empezar

Nombre _____

Fecha _____

Hora _____

Vocabulary Check, Sheet 1

Tear out this page. Write the English words on the lines. Fold the paper along the dotted line to see the correct answers so you can check your work.

¿Cómo eres tú?	*What are you like?*
alto, alta	*tall*
atrevido, atrevida	*daring*
bajo, baja	*short*
desordenado, desordenada	*messy*
estudioso, estudiosa	*studious*
gracioso, graciosa	*funny*
guapo, guapa	*good-looking*
impaciente	*impatient*
inteligente	*intelligent*
ordenado, ordenada	*neat*
reservado, reservada	*reserved, shy*
sociable	*sociable*
trabajador, trabajadora	*hard-working*

Fold In ↓

Sheet 2

Realidades 2

Para empezar

Nombre _____

Fecha _____

Hora _____

Vocabulary Check, Sheet 2

Tear out this page. Write the Spanish words on the lines. Fold the paper along the dotted line to see the correct answers so you can check your work.

What are you like?	*¿Cómo eres tú?*
tall	*alto, alta*
daring	*atrevido, atrevida*
short	*bajo, baja*
messy	*desordenado, desordenada*
studious	*estudioso, estudiosa*
funny	*gracioso, graciosa*
good-looking	*guapo, guapa*
impatient	*impaciente*
intelligent	*inteligente*
neat	*ordenado, ordenada*
reserved, shy	*reservado, reservada*
sociable	*sociable*
hard-working	*trabajador, trabajadora*

Fold In ↓

Para empezar
Guided Practice Activities PE-2

Adjectives (continued)

• In Spanish, if the person, place, or thing is singular, the adjective that describes it must be singular.
Mi hermano es paciente. *My brother is patient.*

• If the person, place, or thing is plural, then the adjective is also plural.
Mis abuelos son pacientes. *My grandparents are patient.*

C. Circle the adjective that best completes the sentence. Use the underlined word to help you. Follow the model.

Modelo Mi <u>abuela</u> es (a.) graciosa.   b. graciosas.

1. Mis <u>hermanas</u> son   a. joven.   (b.) jóvenes.
2. <u>Pedro</u> es   (a.) guapo.   b. guapos.
3. <u>Los niños</u> son   (a.) serios.   b. serio.
4. <u>Marta</u> es   a. trabajadoras.   (b.) trabajadora.
5. <u>Eduardo</u> es   a. altos.   (b.) alto.
6. <u>Nosotras</u> somos   (a.) desordenadas.   b. desordenada.

D. Look at each sentence below and write the correct ending in the space provided. Follow the model.

Modelo María y Anita son chicas muy simpátic **as**.

1. Tú no eres una chica ordenad **a**.
2. Mis primos son chicos gracios **os**.
3. Nosotros somos personas estudios **os**.
4. Tú y Pancho son estudiantes reservad **os**.
5. Mi padre es un hombre baj **o**.
6. Mis hermanos no son niños atrevid **os**.
7. Nacho es un chico sociabl **e**.

6 *Guided Practice Activities* — PE-2

Para empezar
Guided Practice Activities PE-1

Adjectives (p. 3)

• Remember that adjectives describe nouns: people, places, and things. The following is a list of some common adjectives in Spanish.

	Masculine		Feminine	
	Singular	**Plural**	**Singular**	**Plural**
	serio	serios	seria	serias
	deportista	deportistas	deportista	deportistas
	trabajador	trabajadores	trabajadora	trabajadoras
	paciente	pacientes	paciente	pacientes
	joven	jóvenes	joven	jóvenes

A. Read each sentence. Circle the adjective and underline the noun. Follow the model.

Modelo Enrique es un <u>joven</u> (serio).

1. Mi <u>primo</u> es (joven).
2. Mis hermanas son <u>chicas</u> (jóvenes).
3. Carlos y Pedro son <u>chicos</u> (deportistas).
4. Tú eres una <u>persona</u> (paciente).
5. Yo soy una <u>chica</u> (trabajadora).
6. Nosotras somos <u>estudiantes</u> (serias).

• In Spanish, if a person, place, or thing is masculine, the adjective that describes it must be masculine: **El chico es muy serio.** If it's feminine, then the adjective must be feminine: **María es muy seria.**

B. Find the noun in each sentence below. Determine whether each noun is masculine or feminine and write **M** for masculine and **F** for feminine in the first blank. Then, fill in the missing letter in each adjective: **-o** for masculine nouns and **-a** for feminine nouns. Follow the model.

Modelo **M** Ricardo es muy seri **o**.

1. **F** Mi amiga Karla es alt **a**.
2. **F** Mi tía es una mujer ordenad **a**.
3. **M** Mi abuelo es un hombre desordenad **o**.
4. **M** Ese chico es muy gracios **o**.

Guided Practice Activities — PE-1 **5**

Realidades 2

Para empezar

Nombre

Hora

Fecha

Vocabulary Flash Cards, Sheet 3

Copy the word or phrase in the space provided. Be sure to include the article for each noun.

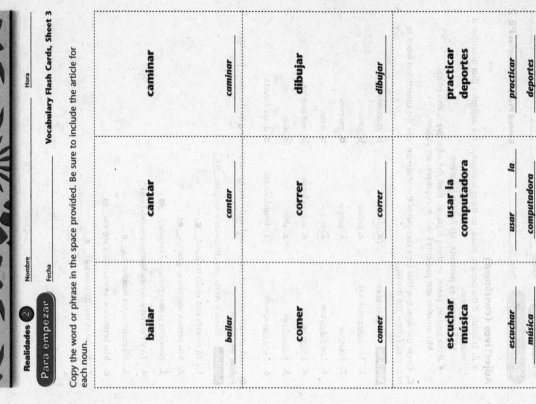

bailar	cantar	caminar
bailar	_cantar_	_caminar_

comer	correr	dibujar
comer	_correr_	_dibujar_

escuchar música	usar la computadora	practicar deportes
escuchar _música_	_usar_ _la_ _computadora_	_practicar_ _deportes_

Realidades 2

Para empezar

Nombre

Hora

Fecha

Guided Practice Activities PE-3

The verb ser (p. 5)

• **Ser** is an irregular verb and it means "to be." These are its present-tense forms:

yo	soy	I am	nosotros(as)	somos	We are
tú	eres	You are (fam.)	vosotros(as)	sois	You are (fam., pl.)
Ud./él/ella	es	He, she is; You are (form.)	Uds./ellos/ellas	son	They are; You are (form.)

• Remember that you can use **ser** with adjectives to tell what someone is like: **Esas chicas son altas.** *Those girls are tall.*

A. Choose the correct form of the verb **ser** in the word bank to complete the sentences. Follow the model.

eres	somos	soy	son	es

Modelo   Tú _eres_ reservado.

1. Yo _soy_ sociable.

2. Nosotros _somos_ deportistas.

3. Elena _es_ alta.

4. Tú _eres_ inteligente.

5. Ustedes _son_ trabajadores.

• To tell where someone is from, use **ser + de +** place: **Ricardo es de México.** *Ricardo is from México.*

B. Say where each of the people is from below based on their nationality. Follow the model.

Modelo   Linda: venezolana   Linda _es_ _de_ Venezuela.

1. Juan Carlos y Sofía: españoles   Ellos _son_ _de_ España.

2. Rosa: guatemalteca   Rosa _es_ _de_ Guatemala.

3. tú: mexicano   Tú _eres_ _de_ México.

4. Orlando: cubano   Orlando _es_ _de_ Cuba.

5. Luz y Marisol: colombianas   Ellas _son_ _de_ Colombia.

6. Mercedes y yo: panameñas   Nosotras _somos_ _de_ Panamá.

realidades.com
• Web Code: jdd-0002

Sheet 4 (right page)

Tear out this page. Write the Spanish words on the lines. Fold the paper along the dotted line so you can check your work.

- Fold In ↓

to play sports	*practicar deportes*
to dance	*bailar*
to walk	*caminar*
to sing	*cantar*
to eat	*comer*
to draw	*dibujar*
to swim	*nadar*
to use the computer	*usar la computadora*
music	*música*
often	*a menudo*
sometimes	*a veces*
never	*nunca*
always	*siempre*
afterwards, after	*después (de)*

To hear a complete list of the vocabulary for this chapter,
go to www.realidades.com and type in the Web Code jdd-0099.
Then click on **Repaso del capítulo.**

Sheet 3 (left page)

Tear out this page. Write the English words on the lines. Fold the paper along the dotted line so you can check your work.

practicar deportes	*to play sports*
bailar	*to dance*
caminar	*to walk*
cantar	*to sing*
comer	*to eat*
dibujar	*to draw*
nadar	*to swim*
usar la computadora	*to use the computer*
música	*music*
a menudo	*often*
a veces	*sometimes*
nunca	*never*
siempre	*always*
después (de)	*afterwards, after*

- Fold In ↓

Present tense of regular verbs (p. 9)

• **Hablar** (*to talk*), **comer** (*to eat*), and **vivir** (*to live*) are regular verbs. To form the present tense, drop the **-ar, -er,** or **-ir** endings and add the present-tense endings.

	hablar	comer	vivir
yo	hablo	como	vivo
tú	hablas	comes	vives
usted/él/ella	habla	come	vive
nosotros/nosotras	hablamos	comemos	vivimos
vosotros/vosotras	habláis	coméis	vivís
ustedes/ellos/ellas	hablan	comen	viven

A. Circle the present-tense verb form in each sentence.

Modelo   Nosotros (corremos) en el parque.

1. Mis amigas (viven) en Nueva York.

2. Carlos (come) en casa a las seis.

3. Yo (escribo) mi tarea en el cuaderno.

4. Ustedes (hablan) inglés y español.

B. Look at the drawings below. Complete each description by circling the correct form of the verb using the subject pronouns given.

Modelo

Él (escuchan / (escucha)) la radio.

1.

Andrea (escribimos / (escribe)) cuentos.

2.

Tú (usa / (usas)) la computadora.

Present tense of regular verbs (*continued*)

3. Nosotras (comes / (comemos)).

4. Marta ((toca) / tocamos) la guitarra.

5. Ustedes ((cantan) / canto) muy bien.

C. Choose the correct ending for each incomplete verb and draw a line beneath your choice. Follow the model.

Modelo   Ana camin(**-a** / -e) a la escuela.

1. Tomás escrib(-a / **-e**) cuentos fantásticos.

2. Nosotros practic(**-amos** / -emos) muchos deportes.

3. Yo escuch(-a / **-o**) la música clásica.

4. Juan y Lola le(**-en** / -an) novelas de horror.

D. Write the correct form of each verb in the space provided.

Modelo   Luis ___**nada**___ (nadar) en la piscina.

1. Lolis ___**corre**___ (correr) en el parque todos los días.

2. ¿Tú ___**montas**___ (montar) en monopatín?

3. Vicente y yo ___**comemos**___ (comer) en el restaurante mexicano.

4. Tú y Rodrigo ___**viven (vivís)**___ (vivir) en el mismo pueblo.

5. Yo ___**saco**___ (sacar) la basura.

Page PE-6

Presentación escrita (continued)

D. Circle the activities in the box that you like to do and complete the sentence below with those activities. **Answers will vary.**

bailo	canto	camino	dibujo
leo revistas	monto en bicicleta	uso la computadora	escucho música

Todos los días yo _____ , _____ y _____ .

E. Which of the activities in **part D** do you like to do with friends? Complete the sentence below using three of those activities. **Answers will vary.**

En el verano, mis amigos y yo _____ , _____ y _____ .

F. Complete the sentence below with two activities you never do. **Answers will vary.**

Nunca _____ ni _____ .

G. Finally, use your answers from parts **B** through **F** to complete this poem in the shape of a diamond. **Answers will vary.**

Me llamo _____

No soy ni _____ ni _____

Soy _____ , _____ y _____

Todos los días yo _____ , _____ y _____

Mis amigos y yo _____ , _____ y _____

Nunca _____ ni _____

¡Así soy yo!

Page PE-5

Presentación escrita (p. 13)

Task: Write a poem in the shape of a diamond. The poem is going to describe you.

A. Look at the poem Linda has written about herself. Circle all the words she uses to say what she is or is not like (adjectives). Then, underline all the words that tell what Linda does or does not do (verbs). The first ones have been done for you.

Me llamo Linda.

No soy ni (seria) ni (vieja).

Soy (alta) (sociable) (estudiosa).

Todos los días yo escucho música, leo, corro, uso la computadora.

En el verano mis amigos y yo nadamos, cantamos, bailamos.

Nunca patino ni monto en bicicleta.

¡Así soy yo!

B. Look at the word list below and complete the sentence with two words from the list that do *not* describe you. Remember to use the *-o* ending if you are a boy and *-a* if you are a girl. And remember that **sociable** and **impaciente** don't change gender. Follow the model. **Answers will vary.**

alto, -a	atrevido, -a	desordenado, -a	estudioso, -a	gracioso, -a
ordenado, -a	reservado, -a	sociable	impaciente	

Modelo No soy ni _ordenada_ ni _sociable_

No soy ni _____ ni _____

C. Now, choose three words from the list in **part A** that describe you. Complete the sentence with those words. Be sure to use the appropriate endings on words you choose. **Answers will vary.**

Soy _____ , _____ y _____

Nombre _____ Hora _____

Fecha _____

Actividad 1

As an icebreaker for the first week of school, a teacher asks his students to draw a poster that describes him or her. Listen as each student describes him- or herself and match each description to one of the bio-posters below. Write the corresponding number underneath the poster. You will hear each description twice.

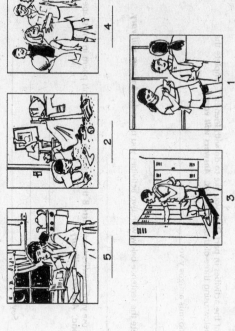

_____ 5 _____ 2 _____ 4

_____ 3 _____ 1

Actividad 2

As a second-year Spanish student, David is helping in the school counselor's office during the first week of school. As Spanish-speaking students enroll, he asks their name and nationality. Listen to each conversation, then circle the native country of the Spanish-speaking student. You will hear each conversation twice.

1. Bolivia, (Chile,) Uruguay

2. Argentina, Paraguay, (Uruguay)

3. (Honduras,) Panamá, Nicaragua

4. México, (Puerto Rico,) España

5. El Salvador, (República Dominicana,) Venezuela

Realidades 2

Nombre _____

Hora _____

Para empezar

Fecha _____

WRITING

Actividad 4

Look at the people pictured. Choose two adjectives from the box to describe each person or group of people and write them on the blanks provided. You may use each adjective more than once. Don't forget to change the adjective endings as necessary!

alto	guapo	paciente
atrevido	impaciente	reservado
bajo	inteligente	serio
deportista	joven	sociable
estudioso	ordenado	trabajador
gracioso		viejo

Answers will vary but should agree in gender with the subject.

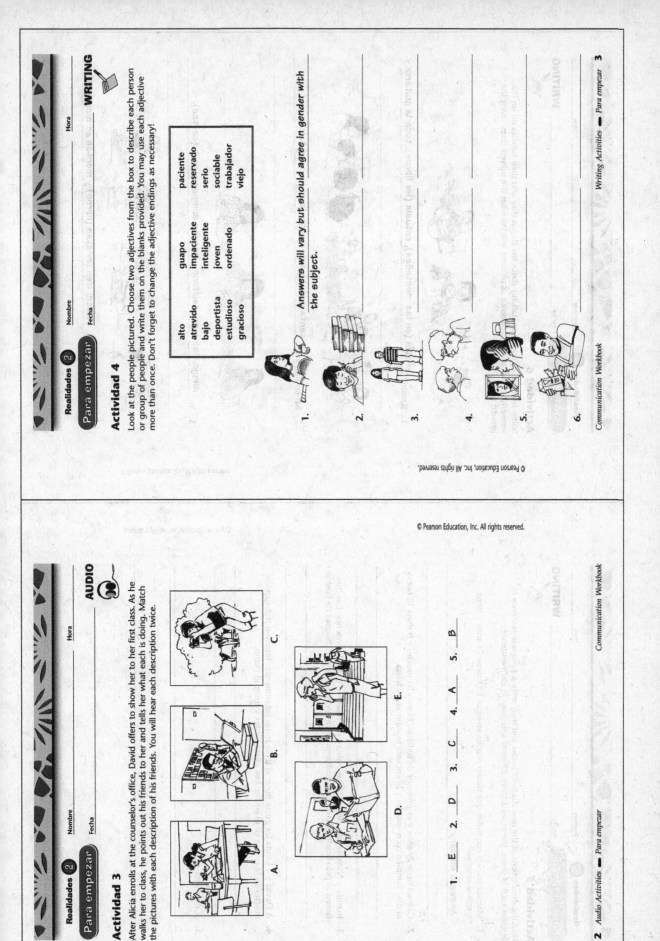

1. _____

2. _____

3. _____

4. _____

5. _____

6. _____

Realidades 2

Nombre _____

Hora _____

Para empezar

Fecha _____

AUDIO

Actividad 3

After Alicia enrolls at the counselor's office, David offers to show her to her first class. As he walks her to class, he points out his friends to her and tells her what each is doing. Match the pictures with each description of his friends. You will hear each description twice.

A.

B.

C.

D.

E.

1. __E__   2. __D__   3. __C__   4. __A__   5. __B__

Para empezar — Communication Workbook: WAVA Answers   **23**

Realidades 2

Nombre _____ Hora _____

Fecha _____ **WRITING**

Para empezar

Actividad 6

Some students at school are talking about the things they and their families do on the weekends. Look at each sequence of pictures and tell what the subject does, using the present tense.

1. Ramiro _esquía (en las montañas), estudia (lee libros), toca la guitarra y canta._

2. Mi familia y yo _cantamos, jugamos al tenis y vemos la tele._

3. Yo _dibujo, hablo por teléfono y escribo composiciones (cartas)._

4. Patricia y Chucho _corren, leen revistas (libros) y montan en monopatín._

Communication Workbook

Writing Activities ▬ Para empezar **5**

© Pearson Education, Inc. All rights reserved.

Realidades 2

Nombre _____ Hora _____

Fecha _____ **WRITING**

Para empezar

Actividad 5

Read the descriptions of the new students below and then write a complete sentence to describe each of them. Use at least three different adjectives in each sentence.

1. Marisol trabaja con niños que tienen mucha energía. Ella tiene 24 años y tiene muchos amigos.

   Answers will vary.

2. Gabriel tiene 29 años y es profesor de italiano. Él estudia mucho y trabaja 12 horas al día. También corre mucho y le encanta montar en bicicleta.

3. Juanita y Nicolita son amigas. Ellas hablan por teléfono todas las noches. Las dos tienen el pelo bonito y largo, y estudiaron en universidades muy buenas de Boston.

4. A David y a Linda les gusta jugar al tenis todas las semanas. También trabajan mucho en la casa y en el jardín. Les gusta pintar y tocar el piano.

5. ¿Cómo eres tú?

4 Writing Activities ▬ Para empezar

Communication Workbook

24 *Para empezar* ▬ *Communication Workbook: WAVA Answers*

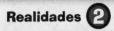

Table of Contents

Tema 1: Tu día escolar
Capítulo 1A: ¿Qué haces en la escuela?

Capítulo 1B: ¿Qué haces después de las clases?

Theme Project

Tu día escolar
Mi escuela: Una guía

Overview:

You will create a guide or brochure in which you describe your school for incoming students. In the brochure, you must compare your school, teams, and subject areas with those of other schools; describe the possible extracurricular activities your school offers; list the school rules. You can decorate the brochure with pictures or drawings and present it to the class.

Resources:

Electronic or print photos, image editing and page layout software and/or construction paper, markers, photos, glue or tape, scissors

Sequence:

STEP 1. Review instructions with your teacher.

STEP 2. Submit a rough draft of each page of the brochure. Work with a partner and present your drafts to each other.

STEP 3. Create layouts leaving room for photos and descriptions.

STEP 4. Submit a draft of the brochure.

STEP 5. Present the brochure to the class, explaining each page and describing selected pictures.

Assessment:

Your teacher will provide you with a rubric to assess this project.

Theme 1 Project: Mi escuela: Una guía

Project Assessment Rubric

RUBRIC	Score 1	Score 3	Score 5
Evidence of Planning	No written draft or sketch provided.	Draft was written and layout created, but not corrected.	Evidence of corrected draft and layout.
Use of Illustrations	No photos/visuals included.	Very few photos/visuals included.	Several photos/visuals included.
Presentation	Contains details that develop ideas about school.	Describes at least three rules, extracurricular activities, and comparisons.	Describes three or more rules, extracurricular activities, and comparisons.

21st Century Skills Rubric: Creativity and Innovation

RUBRIC	Score 1	Score 3	Score 5
Curiosity, inquisitiveness, and openness	Uninterested in looking for new solutions	Interested in new solutions but does not explore such ideas further	Motivated to find new solutions and explores new solutions
Flexibility and adaptability	Lacks flexibility, stubbornly maintains positions and points of view	Somewhat inflexible but can be guided to reconsider positions and points of view	Flexible, can independently monitor and adjust positions and points of view in response to change
Risk-taking	Unwilling to take a risk that might result in mistakes or failure	Hesitant to take a risk; considers carefully the odds of failure before taking on challenge	Willing to take risks and tackle challenges without obvious solutions; sees mistakes as learning opportunity

School-to-Home Connection

Dear Parent or Guardian,

The theme of our current unit is *Tu día escolar* (Your schoolday). This chapter is called *¿Qué haces en la escuela?* (What do you do in school?).

Upon completion of this chapter students will be able to:

- describe classroom objects and activities
- talk about classroom rules
- express affirmative and negative ideas
- compare the school rules and customs in other countries with those of their own school

Students will also explore:

- the correct pronunciation of the letters *b, v,* and *d*

Our textbook, *Realidades,* helps with the development of reading, writing, and speaking skills through the use of strategies, process speaking, and process writing. In this chapter, students will:

- read and understand an article about good study habits
- speak about school rules

To reinforce and enhance learning, students can access a wide range of online resources on **realidades.com**, the personalized learning management system that accompanies the print and online Student Edition. Resources include the eText, textbook and workbook activities, audio files, videos, animations, songs, self-study tools, interactive maps, voice recording (RealTalk!), assessments, and other digital resources. Many learning tools can be accessed through the student Home Page on **realidades.com**. Other activities, specifically those that require grading, are assigned by the teacher and linked on the student Home Page within the calendar or the Assignments tab.

You will find specifications and guidelines for accessing **realidades.com** on home computers and mobile devices on MyPearsonTraining.com under the SuccessNet Plus tab.

Check it out! At the end of the chapter, have your child use the new vocabulary from this chapter to tell you about five classroom rules. Then have him or her talk about three things he or she does in class.

Sincerely,

realidades.com ✔

For: Tips to Parents
Visit: www.realidades.com
Web Code: jce-0010

Videocultura Script

Vida escolar

Spanish version:

Argentina tiene un nivel muy alto de alfabetización. Es uno de los más altos del mundo. La educación en Argentina es gratuita.

En las escuelas se estudian materias como aritmética, español, historia, arte, idiomas.

El año escolar empieza en marzo, en el otoño, y se extiende hasta el mes de noviembre.

Los "bonaerenses" —como se les dice a los habitantes de Buenos Aires—, disfrutan de diferentes actividades fuera de la escuela. Ellos juegan al fútbol o van a los parques.

También van de compras a las tiendas de discos compactos.

Aunque pasan mucho tiempo estudiando, los estudiantes en Argentina se reparten su tiempo hacer sus actividades favoritas.

English version:

Education is a top priority throughout the Spanish-speaking world. For example, in Argentina, education is free from kindergarten through college. Because of this, Argentina enjoys one of the highest levels of literacy and education in Latin America.

Students in Argentina study a variety of subjects including mathematics, science, geography, Spanish language and literature, history, music, art, and foreign languages.

And because Argentina is in the southern hemisphere, the school year starts in March and ends in December.

When not in school, students in Buenos Aires, the capital, enjoy being outdoors as much as weather permits. They may spend time playing soccer or visiting the many parks around the city where there is always something going on.

Listening to music is also a very popular pastime among teenagers. They may visit a local music store or download songs from the Internet. Teens listen to a variety of music ranging from folk to rock to hip-hop.

Even with the strong emphasis on education, Argentine students balance their time between studying and other favorite activities.

Input Script

Presentation

Input Rules Vocabulary: Enter the classroom and announce to students that their regular Spanish teacher went to a teacher's workshop in Mazatlan, Mexico, and you will be their substitute teacher for the next month. (If you like, wear a disguise!) Distribute copies of the Vocabulary Clip Art and have students cut them into individual images. Place the overhead transparency with classroom rules on the screen. Go over the rules. Use props and gestures to convey the meaning of each rule. Then review the rules again and have students hold up the Clip Art image that corresponds to each rule.

Input Classroom Activities Vocabulary: Say: *¡Vamos a estar muy ocupados este mes! Vamos a ver lo que hacemos en la clase.* Place the transparency showing classroom activities on the screen. Point to the activities as you explain that they will repeat words, memorize vocabulary, discuss homework in the language lab, and write reports. Have students arrange the Clip Art of the activities on their desks in the order you mention them. Then announce: *Pero primero lo que vamos a hacer es un proyecto. Necesitamos los siguientes materiales: las tijeras, la grapadora, el papel, la cinta y un lápiz.* Hold up the objects as you mention them. Students will hold up the Clip Art images. Then lead students through a project using these materials, such as creating a bulletin board about classroom objects, or drawing and cutting out images of classroom objects to make a mobile. Or, if you chose to disguise yourself for the presentation, do a project that would lead students to discover your true identity. For example, you could call out the letters in your name in random order for them to write on scraps of paper and unscramble to find out who you are.

Work the other expressions from *A primera vista* into your description of the project. Tell students: *Para sacar una buena nota, tienen que prestar atención. Hay que pedir ayuda si no entienden. ¿Quieren hacer una pregunta? ¿No? Alguien debe tener una pregunta. ¿Ninguna persona quiere hacer una pregunta? Estoy aquí para contestar las preguntas.*

Comprehension Check

- Have volunteers sit in "detention" at the front of the classroom. Go to each one and ask them what they did to earn detention: *Se prohíbe almorzar en la sala de clases. Hay que traer los materiales a la clase.* Have the rest of the class hold up Clip Art to show the offenses their classmates committed.

- Give students choices between two assignments by saying the general assignments first (*¿Quieres escribir un informe o hacer un proyecto?*), letting them choose, and then giving the details (*El informe debe ser de 50 páginas; el proyecto se trata de almorzar con Ricky Martin y pedirle ayuda con el baile de la escuela.*).

Audio Script

Audio DVD, Capítulo 1A

Track 01: *A primera vista, ¿Qué haces en la escuela?*, Student Book, p. 18

Vocabulario y gramática en contexto
Lee en tu libro mientras escuchas la narración.

TEEN MALE: ¡Hola! Me llamo Miguel. En mi escuela siempre estamos muy ocupados. Vamos a ver lo que hacemos en las clases. Estos estudiantes discuten la tarea en el laboratorio. Estos estudiantes hacen un proyecto de arte. Marcos escribe un informe sobre la música latinoamericana. Victoria repite las palabras nuevas para aprender de memoria el vocabulario. La profesora le explica a Elena cómo usar la computadora.

Track 02: *A primera vista*, Student Book, p. 19

Vocabulario y gramática en contexto
Lee en tu libro mientras escuchas la narración.

ADULT MALE: La profesora de la Escuela Benito Juárez prepara un cartel con las reglas de la escuela. ¿Cuáles son las reglas?

ADULT FEMALE: Hay que… Hay que llevar el carnet de identidad. Hay que entregar la tarea a tiempo. Hay que pedir ayuda si no entiendes. Hay que traer los materiales a clase. Hay que estar en el asiento cuando la clase empieza. Se prohíbe… Se prohíbe ir al armario durante las clases. Se prohíbe almorzar en la sala de clases.

Vas a escuchar cada palabra o frase dos veces. Después de la primera vez hay una pausa para que puedas pronunciar la palabra o frase. Luego vas a escuchar de nuevo la palabra o frase.

contestar	las tijeras
hacer una pregunta	la grapadora
la cinta adhesiva	

Más vocabulario

alguien	ninguna
ningún	prestar atención
ninguno	respetar

Track 03: *A primera vista, Act. 1*, Student Book, p. 19

¿Qué hacen en la escuela?

Escucha lo que estos estudiantes hacen en la escuela y señala el dibujo correspondiente. Vas a escuchar las frases dos veces.

TEEN MALE 1: Tengo que escribir un informe esta noche.
TEEN FEMALE 1: Los estudiantes van a discutir la tarea.
TEEN MALE 2: Ellos hacen un proyecto de arte.
TEEN FEMALE 2: Yo siempre repito las palabras muchas veces.
TEEN FEMALE 3: La profesora explica el programa.

Track 04: *A primera vista, Act. 2*, Student Book, p. 19

¿Qué reglas tienes?

Escucha estas seis reglas. Si tienes la misma regla en tu clase de español, levanta una mano. Si no tienes la regla, levanta las dos manos. Vas a escuchar las frases dos veces.

TEEN FEMALE 1: Hay que llevar el carnet de identidad.
TEEN MALE 1: Hay que traer la grapadora a la clase de español.
TEEN FEMALE 2: Hay que estar en el asiento cuando la clase empieza.
TEEN MALE 2: Hay que ir al armario durante las clases.
TEEN FEMALE 3: Hay que entregar la tarea a tiempo.
TEEN MALE 3: Hay que aprender el vocabulario de memoria.

Track 05: *A primera vista, Videohistoria*, Student Book, pp. 20–21

La clase de Esteban
¿Qué pasa con Esteban el primer día de clases? Lee la historia.
Lee en tu libro mientras escuchas la *Videohistoria*.

See Student Book pages 20–21 for script.

Track 06: Audio Act. 5, Writing, Audio & Video Workbook, p. 9

Listen to these teachers welcoming their students to the first day of class. The pictures below correspond to things that the students must and cannot do in their classes. In the boxes under each teacher's name, write the letters of the pictures that correspond to what you must and cannot do in his or her class. There should only be one letter per box. You will hear each set of statements twice.

ADULT FEMALE 1: Buenos días. Soy la señorita Arcos, su profesora para esta clase de español. No se permite ni dormir ni hacer la tarea de otra clase aquí. Uds. tienen que aprender de memoria un poema de un poeta hispano cada semana. Empezamos con un poema de José Martí. La participación es muy importante en mi clase.

ADULT MALE 1: Bienvenidos a la clase de matemáticas. Soy el señor Cruz. Prestar atención es mi primera regla. Se prohíbe hablar cuando les explico algo a Uds. No es una clase difícil, pero cuando no entienden algo, hay que pedir ayuda.

ADULT FEMALE 2: Hola. Soy la señora Cazón y soy su profesora de biología. Primero, las reglas de mi clase. No se permite hablar con los amigos cuando la clase empieza a las nueve en punto. Hay que estar en el asiento con todos los materiales. Cuando vamos al laboratorio, hay que traer todos los materiales.

ADULT FEMALE 3: Buenas tardes. Soy la señora Rendón. Vamos a tener un semestre tremendo en la clase de arte. Como es el primer día del semestre, necesito decirles

mis reglas. Se prohíbe llevar sombreros o anteojos de sol en mi clase. ¡Uds. son tan guapos que necesito verlos bien! Al final del semestre hay que entregar un proyecto con cinco de sus mejores dibujos.

ADULT FEMALE 4: Bienvenidos a la clase de tecnología. Soy la señorita García. En mi clase no se permite ni beber ni comer. ¡Deben poner los refrescos en el armario antes de la clase! Ésta es una clase muy importante porque Uds. usan las computadoras en todas las clases de la escuela. Hay que dar un discurso al final del semestre que explica por qué las computadoras son importantes.

Track 07: Audio Act. 6, Writing, Audio & Video Workbook, p. 10

Listen as students talk about their classes this semester. Decide which class each one is describing and write the name of the class in the grid below. Then place a check mark in the box below the class name if the student likes the class, and an X if the student doesn't like the class. You will hear each set of statements twice.

TEEN FEMALE 1: Tengo miedo de esta clase de inglés porque hay que dar un discurso sobre nuestro autor favorito de literatura de Estados Unidos al final del semestre. Soy muy reservada y no me gusta hablar enfrente de un grupo. Me gusta leer novelas y poemas, pero ¿qué voy a hacer? ¡Quiero otra profesora de literatura porque necesito sacar una buena nota!

TEEN MALE 1: En mi clase de geometría no entiendo nada de los ángulos ni del área de los triángulos. Soy estudioso y mis notas me importan mucho. Tengo muchos problemas en esta clase y es difícil pedir ayuda. Quiero hablar con el profesor después de la clase.

TEEN FEMALE 2: Me interesa mucho mi clase de ciencias sociales. Este semestre estudiamos la historia moderna de los Estados Unidos. Para un proyecto hay que escribir un informe sobre uno de los presidentes modernos. Quiero estudiar más sobre estos presidentes.

TEEN MALE 2: Me interesa mucho mi clase de español. Mi familia va a visitar España en el verano y quiero hablar español allí. Después de estudiarlo por un año puedo entender mucho y ahora quiero aprender a contestar preguntas y discutir cosas interesantes.

TEEN FEMALE 3: ¡En mi clase de la biología necesito mucha ayuda! El profesor habla muy rápido y no entiendo mucho. Hay que trabajar en grupo en muchas actividades, pero no conozco a nadie en la clase. Todo eso del cuerpo humano no me interesa. Lo que quiero hacer es dibujar todo el día.

Track 08: *Pronunciación*, The letters *b*, *v*, and *d*, Student Book, p. 29

The letters *b* and *v* are both pronounced the same. When the *b* or *v* is the first letter of a word or follows an *m* or *n*, it is pronounced like the English letter *b*. Listen to and say these words:

You will hear each word twice. After the word is pronounced the first time, there will be a pause so you can pronounce it. Then you will hear the word a second time.

bien	también
vecinos	invierno

In all other positions, the letters *b* and *v* have a softer "b" sound. To produce it, put your lips close together (but no touching) and push the air through them. Listen to and say these words and sentences:

gustaba	árbol
jóvenes	devolver

Benito Vásquez era un hombre que viajaba en Brasil.
Mi novio vivía en el Caribe pero ahora vive en Buenos Aires.

Like the *b* and *v*, the Spanish *d* can have a hard or a soft sound. The *d* is hard at the beginning of a word or after *n* or *l*, like the *d* in the English word *dough*. Listen to and say these words:

donde	cuando
desfile	aprender
falda	

Otherwise the *d* is soft like English *th* in the English word *though*. Listen to the soft *d* in these words and repeat them:

ciudad	boda
moderno	ayudar
cuñado	

Repeat the following *refranes*. What do you think they mean?
Un hombre que sabe dos lenguas vale por dos.
Quien mucho vive, mucho ve.

Track 09: Audio Act. 7, Writing, Audio & Video Workbook, p. 10

Teachers and students all talk about their classes with their friends and family. Listen to snippets of their conversations to see if you can determine whether it is a teacher or a student who is talking about his or her classes. Write an X in the appropriate box in the grid. You will hear each set of statements twice.

1. **FEMALE 1:** Muchas veces repito las instrucciones porque algunos duermen en la clase. Es la primera hora, a las siete y media de la mañana, y algunos no pueden prestar atención porque tienen mucho sueño.

2. **MALE 1:** Ella nos pide hacer un proyecto cada mes. Pienso que este mes tenemos que buscar información sobre un poeta hispano. No puedo hacer eso. No sé nada sobre poesía. No quiero hacer el proyecto.

3. **FEMALE 2:** ¿Puede ayudarme? Ningún estudiante entiende la tarea. Empiezo a hacerla, pero no puedo entender las instrucciones. Es muy difícil. ¡Tomás y Sara no pueden entenderlas tampoco y ellos son muy inteligentes! No podemos hacer la tarea cuando no entendemos las instrucciones.

4. **MALE 2:** Ellos conocen las reglas, pero todavía llegan a clase sin libros. Les pido llevar sus libros y calculadoras a la clase cada día. En la escuela no se permite ir a los armarios durante la clase.

5. **FEMALE 3:** Siempre les digo que si ellos me piden ayuda, puedo ayudarlos después de las clases, a las tres y media de la tarde. Pero no me piden ayuda y nadie viene a las tres y media. Algunos sacan muy malas notas en los exámenes. Quiero ayudarlos.

6. **MALE 3:** Normalmente, cuando no entiendo algo en la clase le pido ayuda a otro estudiante, pero no conozco a nadie en esta clase. El profesor nos prohíbe trabajar con otro estudiante. ¡Es imposible! Al almuerzo puedo pedirles ayuda a mis amigos.

Track 10: Audio Act. 8, Writing, Audio & Video Workbook, p. 11

After listening to each of the following statements about school, decide whether it is *lógico* or *ilógico* and mark your answer on the grid. You will hear each statement twice. At the end of the exercise, you may want to compare your answers with those of a partner.

1. **MALE:** Nunca hay perros en las clases.
2. **FEMALE:** Algunos estudiantes prefieren estudiar en la cafetería.
3. **MALE:** No hay ningún libro en la biblioteca.
4. **FEMALE:** Los profesores nunca dan tarea a los estudiantes.
5. **MALE:** Algunos estudiantes almuerzan en la biblioteca.
6. **FEMALE:** Nadie baila en la clase de historia.
7. **MALE:** Es medianoche y algunos estudiantes almuerzan en la cafetería.
8. **FEMALE:** Algunos estudiantes sacan buenas notas en los exámenes.
9. **MALE:** No tenemos profesores en la escuela.
10. **FEMALE:** Hay algunos armarios en los baños de la escuela.

Track 11: Audio Act. 9, Writing, Audio & Video Workbook, p. 11

Listen as a reporter for the teen magazine *¿Qué hay?* talks to students about their "secrets" for doing well in school. Fill in the grid below with their secret for each category: 1) *La cosa más importante para sacar buenas notas;* 2) *El mejor lugar para estudiar;* 3) *Si es mejor estudiar solo(a) o con amigos.* You will hear each set of statements twice.

TEEN FEMALE 1: Pienso que la cosa más importante para sacar buenas notas es la organización. Algunos de mis amigos no pueden estudiar antes del examen porque no saben donde están sus apuntes ni su libro. Siempre tengo todas mis materias en mi carpeta de argollas o en mi escritorio. Estudio en la sala porque puedo concentrarme mejor allí. Prefiero no estudiar con nadie.

TEEN MALE 1: Para mí, la cosa más importante para sacar buenas notas es una profesora paciente que nos explica todo. Mi profesora de ciencias sociales es muy paciente y muy simpática. Normalmente estudio cada día en la biblioteca de la escuela con mis amigos. Es más divertido estudiar en grupo.

TEEN FEMALE 2: ¿Mi "secreto" para sacar buenas notas? Lo más importante es no tener televisor en mi dormitorio. ¡No puedo resistir las telenovelas! Algunas de mis amigas pueden hacer la tarea mientras miran su telenovela favorita, pero yo, no. ¡Tengo que estudiar en silencio en mi dormitorio! No puedo estudiar con mis amigas tampoco.

TEEN MALE 2: Para mí, la cosa más importante es dormir ocho horas cada noche. No puedes aprender nada si duermes en la clase. Siempre estudio en la cocina porque me da hambre cuando estudio. Puedo concentrarme mejor cuando como algo. Cuando tengo un examen, ¡como una pizza entera! Tengo clases bastante difíciles este año y por eso estudio solo.

Track 12: *Repaso del capítulo,* Student Book, p. 40

Vocabulario y gramática

Escucha las palabras y expresiones que has aprendido en este capítulo.

See Student Book page 40 for vocabulary list.

Track 13: *Preparación para el examen,* Student Book, p. 41

Escuchar

Practice task

Listen as two students compare their Spanish classes.
a) What are two things that students do in both classes?
b) What are two things that are different? c) Which class would you prefer? Why?

TEEN FEMALE 1: ¿Cómo es tu clase de español? En mi clase hay que entregar la tarea cada día y escribir un informe cada semana. También contestamos preguntas y hay que practicar en el laboratorio.

TEEN FEMALE 2: ¡Ay! ¿Mucho trabajo, no? En mi clase hay que prestar atención, pero no entregamos la tarea cada día. Practicamos y contestamos preguntas en el laboratorio. Discutimos algo de interés cada día en español y hacemos muchos proyectos.

Video Script

A primera vista: *La clase de Esteban*

ESTEBAN: Buenos días. Bienvenidos a la clase de historia. Algunos de Uds. ya me conocen. Soy el profesor Ríos.

PEDRO: Esteban, ¿qué es esto? ¿Tú eres el profesor? ¡Qué divertido!

ESTEBAN: ¿Cómo? ¿Qué dices? Y debes ser… Pedro Salazar.

PEDRO: Sí, señor. Ud. tiene razón.

ESTEBAN: Hay que estar en el asiento cuando la clase empieza. Pedro, ¡siéntate!

ESTEBAN: Ah, señoritas, ¿saben qué hora es?

ANGÉLICA: Hola Esteban. Son las nueve y seis.

ESTEBAN: Y la clase empieza a las nueve y cinco.

LISA: ¿Qué tal, Esteban? ¿Por qué estás delante de la clase? ¿Dónde está la profesora?

ESTEBAN: Yo soy el profesor. Y Uds., ¿por qué llegan tan tarde?

ANGÉLICA: Pues, Lisa y yo…

ESTEBAN: Pueden explicármelo todo más tarde. Tienen que quedarse aquí después de las clases, a las tres y media.

LISA: ¡Esteban! ¿Qué te pasa?

PEDRO: Piensa que es el profesor.

ESTEBAN: Y tú también, Pedro. Te veo a las tres y media.

ANGÉLICA: ¡Qué tonto es! Mi hermano—el profesor. ¡Ja!

ESTEBAN: Ahora, las reglas para mi clase.

LISA: Profesor Ríos…

ESTEBAN: ¿Quieres hacer una pregunta?

LISA: Ah, sí. A ver. Necesito ir al armario. No tengo el libro.

ESTEBAN: Lo siento. Pero se prohíbe ir al armario. Nadie tiene el libro. Es el primer día de clases.

LISA: Ah, necesito el cuaderno.

ESTEBAN: No.

LISA: ¿La carpeta?

ESTEBAN: No. Repito otra vez. No puedes ir al armario.

LISA: Está bien. No entiendo qué te pasa.

ESTEBAN: A repetir. Las reglas para mi clase… Uno… respetar a los demás…

MAMÁ: Una pregunta, una pregunta…

ESTEBAN: Mamá, ¿por qué estás aquí en mi clase…?

MAMÁ: No tengo idea. Es muy extraño, ¿no?

ESTEBAN: ¿Qué quieres…?

MAMÁ: ¿A qué hora llegas a casa después de las clases?

ESTEBAN: Mamá, ahorita no, por favor.

MAMA: Está bien, hijo mío. ¿Y qué vas a enseñar hoy?

ESTEBAN: Es la clase de historia. Pienso dar un discurso sobre todos los presidentes de los Estados Unidos.

MAMA: Y, ¿por qué no empiezas?

ESTEBAN: Gracias, mamá. El primer presidente de los Estados Unidos fue George Washington… Por favor. ¡Silencio! Hay que prestar atención al profesor. Silencio. ¡Hay que prestar atención…!

PEDRO: ¿Qué dices?

ESTEBAN: Nada.

ANGÉLICA: ¿Hay tarea para esta noche?

ESTEBAN: Sí, hay que aprender de memoria todos los presidentes de los Estados Unidos…

ESTEBAN: Un momento. Un momento. No se pueden ir todavía.

MAMÁ: Adiós, Esteban.

ESTEBAN: Hay que prestar atención. Silencio, silencio…

MAMÁ: Esteban. Esteban, ¡levántate! ¡Ya es tarde! Esteban, Esteban, ¡levántate!

ESTEBAN: ¿Qué pasa?

MAMÁ: ¡Levántate!

ESTEBAN: ¿Dónde estoy…? ¡Ay! Ay no, el primer día de clases…

GramActiva Videos
Stem-changing verbs

GIRL: Hello, today we're going to give you a quick refresher course on stem-changing verbs.

BOY: Ahhh! Stem-changing verbs.

GIRL: Remember, stem-changing verbs are nothing to worry about.

V.O.: The stem of a verb is the part that is left after you drop the *-ar, -er,* or *-ir* off the infinitive. Stem-changing verbs have a spelling change in certain forms. Check out how the *o* in *poder* changes to *ue,* and *pedir* gets its *e* changed to an *i.*

HOST: Just to be clear, let's do a run-through of these two verbs.

V.O.: *Poder,* "to be able."

HOST: Remember the stem-changing rule for this verb is pretty straightforward. The *o* in the stem changes to *ue* in all forms except *nosotros(as)* and *vosotros(as).*

V.O.: You should be an old pro at *poder,* "to be able."
Puedo. Puedes. Puede. Podemos. Podéis. Pueden.
And remember it's a boot verb.
To say what you are able to do, you use the infinitive after *poder:*
Puedo cantar. Podemos bailar.

HOST: Now it's time to ask for what you want. Oh, *gracias.*

V.O.: *Pedir,* "to ask for."
Pido. Pides. Pide. Pedimos. Pedís. Piden.
Ana pide mucha comida. Pides la cuenta.

HOST: Now it's your turn. Fill in the blank with the correct form of *poder* or *pedir.*

Quiz

V.O.: (poder) Tú _____ ir más tarde.
Tú puedes ir más tarde.
(poder) Nosotras _____ cocinar el pollo.
Nosotras podemos cocinar el pollo.
(pedir) Ella _____ un plato de paella.
Ella pide un plato de paella.
(pedir) Yo _____ su número de teléfono.
Yo pido su número de teléfono.

Affirmative and negative words

HOST: Every day, we use affirmative and negative words.

V.O.: Examples of affirmative words in English are: *some, someone, something, always,* and *also.* The Spanish equivalents are: *algunos, alguien, algo, siempre, también.*

GIRL: *Alguien va a escribirte.*

BOY: *Ella siempre presta atención.*

V.O.: And of course with the positive comes the negative. Examples of negative words and phrases are: *none, nobody, nothing, never,* and *neither.* In Spanish they are: *ninguna, ninguno, nadie, nada, nunca,* and *tampoco.*

FOOTBALL COACH: Now, if you're going to use negative and affirmative words, you've got to learn some rules!

V.O.: When using *alguno* and *ninguno* remember to match the gender (masculine or feminine) and number (singular, plural) of the noun they refer to.
Algunos muchachos juegan al básquetbol.

V.O.: How about a couple more examples?
Compré algunos libros.
[I bought some books.]
No tengo ninguna pregunta.
[I don't have any questions.]

COACH: And don't forget that when *alguno* and *ninguno* come before a masculine singular noun, they change to *algún* and *ningún.*

BOY 1: *¿Tienes algún libro sobre básquetbol?*

BOY 2: *No, no tengo ningún libro sobre básquetbol.*

HOST: OK, remember how to make a sentence negative in Spanish? That's right, you usually put *no* in front of the verb, as in *No voy al laboratorio por la mañana.* However, if the sentence begins with a negative word like *nunca* or *nadie,* you do not need to put *no* in front of it: *Nunca voy al laboratorio por la mañana. Nadie le presta atención al perro.*

COACH: OK, let's review!

COACH V.O.: The affirmative words for "some," *alguno,* as well as *ninguno,* match the number and gender of the noun they refer to.
Llaman a algunas amigas.
Escuchamos algunos programas.
No encuentro ninguna película.

V.O.: OK. It's your turn now. Fill in the blank with the correct negative or affirmative word.

Quiz

V.O.: (never) _____ hablo en el cine.
Nunca hablo en el cine.
(some) Pablo hace _____ proyectos en su clase de ciencias.
Pablo hace algunos proyectos en su clase de ciencias.
(none) No tengo _____ proyecto en mi clase de ciencias sociales.
No tengo ningún proyecto en mi clase de ciencias sociales.

Realidades 2

Capítulo 1A

Nombre _____

Fecha _____

Interview your partner about his or her class schedule and activities. You are curious to know about one activity that he or she does in each class, one activity someone else does, and one activity no one ever does. Using the chart below, complete as many statements as you can. Then ask your partner for the remaining answers. Ask your partner: *¿Qué tiene que hacer mi compañero(a) en la clase de biología? ¿Qué tienen que hacer algunos estudiantes? ¿Qué no tiene que hacer nadie?* Record your answers on the lines provided below the chart. Example: *Algunos estudiantes dan un discurso.*

	HISTORIA	QUÍMICA	ESPAÑOL	MATEMÁTICAS
Mi compañero(a)	pedir ayuda	llegar tarde		hacer un proyecto
Algunos estudiantes			aprender el vocabulario de memoria	
Nadie en la clase		hacer preguntas		entregar la tarea

1. En la clase de historia, mi compañero(a) _____ .

   Algunos estudiantes _____ .

   Nadie en la clase _____ .

2. En la clase de química, mi compañero(a) _____ .

   Algunos estudiantes _____ .

   Nadie en la clase _____ .

3. En la clase de español, mi compañero(a) _____ .

   Algunos estudiantes _____ .

   Nadie en la clase _____ .

4. En la clase de matemáticas, mi compañero(a) _____ .

   Algunos estudiantes _____ .

   Nadie en la clase _____ .

Realidades ②

Capítulo 1A

Nombre _____

Fecha _____

Communicative Pair Activity **1A-1**

Estudiante **B**

Interview your partner about his or her class schedule and activities. You are curious to know about one activity that he or she does in each class, one activity someone else does, and one activity no one ever does. Using the chart below, complete as many statements as you can. Then ask your partner for the remaining answers. Ask your partner: *¿Qué tiene que hacer mi compañero en la clase de biología? ¿Qué tienen que hacer algunos estudiantes? ¿Qué no tiene que hacer nadie?* Record your answers on the lines provided below the chart. Example: *Algunos estudiantes dan un discurso.*

	HISTORIA	QUÍMICA	ESPAÑOL	MATEMÁTICAS
Mi compañero(a)			sacar una buena nota	
Algunos estudiantes	entregar la tarea	hacer un proyecto		pedir ayuda
Nadie en la clase	ir al armario durante la clase		llegar tarde	

1. En la clase de historia, mi compañero(a) _____ .

    Algunos estudiantes _____ .

    Nadie en la clase _____ .

2. En la clase de química, mi compañero(a) _____ .

    Algunos estudiantes _____ .

    Nadie en la clase _____ .

3. En la clase de español, mi compañero(a) _____ .

    Algunos estudiantes _____ .

    Nadie en la clase _____ .

4. En la clase de matemáticas, mi compañero(a) _____ .

    Algunos estudiantes _____ .

    Nadie en la clase _____ .

Realidades 2

Capítulo 1A

Nombre _____

Fecha _____

Communicative Pair Activity **1A-2**

Estudiante **A**

In this activity, you and your partner take turns. You are **O** and he or she is **X.** Begin by having your partner choose a number from 1 to 9. Read the sentence in that box and wait for his or her answer. For each sentence, your partner must say the correct form of the verb. If your partner responds correctly, mark **X** in the box. If the response is incorrect, make no marks and do not tell the correct answer. Your partner may choose that number again later. During your turn, your partner will mark **O** in the appropriate box if your answer is correct. The first person to have three correct answers in a row is the winner.

En la escuela

1 Los profesores (*querer*) enseñar clases interesantes. (quieren)	**2** En la clase de matemáticas la profesora (*repetir*) las instrucciones. (repite)	**3** Yo (*entender*) las instrucciones del profesor. (entiendo)
4 Isabel y yo (*preferir*) la clase de español. (preferimos)	**5** Los estudiantes (*almorzar*) a las doce. (almuerzan)	**6** Nadie (*querer*) dar un discurso en la clase de álgebra. (quiere)
7 Algunos estudiantes (*pedir*) información. (piden)	**8** Ningún estudiante (*dormir*) en la clase de historia. (duerme)	**9** David y Cecilia (*jugar*) al tenis en la clase de educación física. (juegan)

Realidades 2

Capítulo 1A

Nombre _____

Fecha _____

Communicative Pair Activity **1A-2**

Estudiante **B**

In this activity, you and your partner take turns. You are **X** and he or she is **O.** You begin by choosing a number from 1 to 9. Listen to the sentence in that box as your partner reads it, and say the correct form of the verb. If you respond correctly, your partner will mark an **X** in the box. If the response is incorrect, the box will be left with no marks. You may choose that number again later. During your partner's turn, you will read the sentence that he or she chooses and will mark **O** in the appropriate box if the answer is correct. The first person to have three correct answers in a row is the winner.

La escuela

1 Luisa y Carmen (*estudiar*) la tecnología. (estudian)	2 Nosotros (*escuchar*) música en la clase de inglés. (escuchamos)	3 Tú (*pasar*) tiempo con amigos en el almuerzo. (pasas)
4 Maricarmen (*hablar*) mucho en la clase de arte. (habla)	5 Marco y yo (*bailar*) en la clase de educación física. (bailamos)	6 Yo (*trabajar*) mucho en la clase de ciencias naturales. (trabajo)
7 El profesor Rodríguez (*enseñar*) la clase de matemáticas. (enseña)	8 Los profesores (*usar*) la computadora en las clases difíciles. (usan)	9 Rita (*necesitar*) un diccionario para la clase de español. (necesita)

Situation Cards

2A

Capítulo 1A | **Realidades 2**

Talking about classroom rules using negative and affirmative words

You are talking with a teacher about rules everyone has to follow in class.

— Ask the teacher if he or she thinks the rules are very strict in school.

— Respond to the teacher's question with two rules no one likes. Then ask if he or she also dislikes them.

— Respond to your teacher's question.

2B

Capítulo 1A | **Realidades 2**

Talking about classroom rules using negative and affirmative words

You are a teacher talking with a student about rules everyone has to follow in class.

— Respond to your student's question negatively using a full sentence. Then ask what are two rules no one likes.

— Respond to your student's question. Then ask your student what rule he or she would change.

1A

Capítulo 1A | **Realidades 2**

Talking about what you do in class

You are talking with a new student in your school.

— Greet the new student and then introduce yourself.

— Name one of your favorite classes. Ask your partner if he or she enjoys it also.

— Respond to your partner's question. Ask which are two activities students do in his or her favorite class.

— Say goodbye to your partner.

1B

Capítulo 1A | **Realidades 2**

Talking about what you do in class

You are a new student in your new school talking with a student.

— Respond to your classmate with a greeting and your name.

— Answer the question by stating your favorite class. Ask your partner what he or she likes about his or her favorite class.

— Respond to your partner's question.

— Say goodbye to your partner.

GramActiva

¿Qué haces en la escuela?
Juego, p. 28

Vocabulary Clip Art

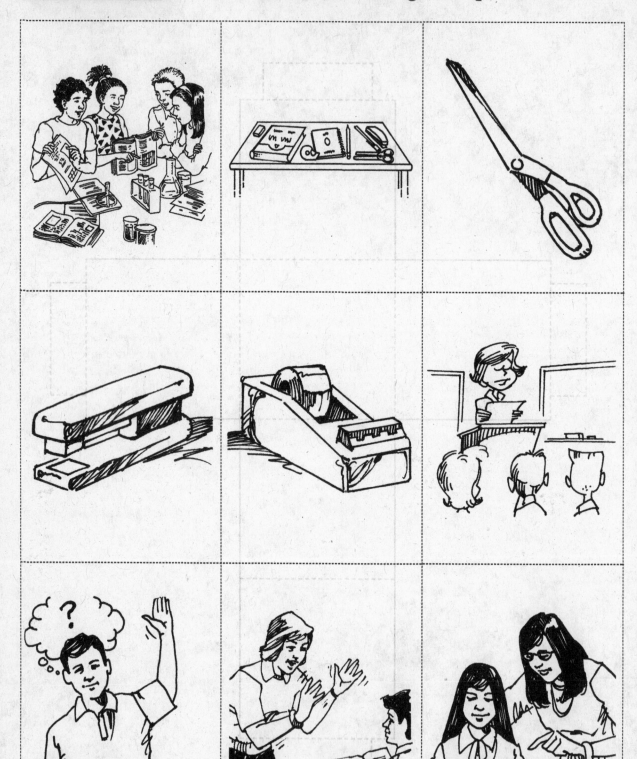

Vocabulary Clip Art

Vocabulary Clip Art

Core Practice Answers

1A-A

A.
1. carpeta de argollas
2. puerta
3. reloj
4. bolígrafo
5. cartel
6. diccionario

B.
1. la tecnología
2. el arte
3. las matemáticas
4. las ciencias naturales
5. la educación física
6. las ciencias sociales

1A-B

A.
1. Ellos tienen que comer.
2. Tú tienes que ir a la lección de piano.
3. Nosotros tenemos que ir a la escuela.
4. La profesora tiene que enseñar la clase.
5. Yo tengo que ir de compras.
6. Mis amigos tienen que beber leche.
7. Elena y yo tenemos que usar la computadora.

B.
1. traes, Traigo
2. haces, Hago
3. ponen, Ponemos
4. tienes, tengo
5. pone, Pongo

1A-1

A.
1. la cinta adhesiva
2. las tijeras
3. carnet de identidad
4. la grapadora
5. los materiales

B.
1. (Los estudiantes) prestan atención.
2. (Los estudiantes) hacen preguntas.
3. (Los estudiantes) piden ayuda.
4. (Los estudiantes) hacen un proyecto
5. (Los estudiantes) sacan buenas notas.

1A-2

A.
1. Se prohíbe
2. Hay que
3. Hay que
4. Se prohíbe
5. Hay que

B.
1. asientos
2. empieza
3. discutir
4. entiendo
5. explicar
6. aprendieron
7. repetir
8. palabra

1A-3

A.
1. conocer
2. tarde
3. armario
4. prohíbe
5. Nadie
6. asiento
7. laboratorio
8. discurso
9. proyecto

B.
Hay que prestarle atención al profesor.

1A-4
1. Elena Educada saca mejores notas.
2. Elena Educada contesta más preguntas.
3. Elena Educada. (Reasons will vary)
4. Elena Educada está en su asiento a las nueve y Teresa Traviesa llega a las nueve y cinco.
5. Elena Educada es la mejor estudiante... (Reasons will vary)

1A-5
1. repito
2. almuerzan
3. entiendes
4. prefiere
5. sirven
6. juega
7. empiezo
8. piensas
9. piden
10. dormimos
11. cuestan
12. quiero

1A-6

A.
1. ninguna
2. ningunas
3. ningún
4. Algunos
5. algunas
6. ninguno
7. algunas
8. algún

B.
1. No va nadie al laboratorio.
2. Ella no presta atención tampoco.
3. No aprenden nada de memoria.
4. No hay ninguna silla en la sala.
5. Nunca llevas el carnet de identidad.

1A-7
1. Los estudiantes no piden ayuda nunca.
2. Yo no quiero hacer el proyecto nunca.
3. Tú no quieres hacer el proyecto tampoco.
4. Nosotros no damos ningún discurso.
5. El profesor no repite ningunas instrucciones.
6. Los estudiantes siempre llegan tardee.
7. La profesora no conoce a ningunos estudiantes (de la clase).
8. Alguien va al armario cada dos minutos.
9. Mis amigos y yo siempre almorzamos en la clase.
10. Tú no traes los materiales a clase nunca.

Crucigrama (1A-8)

Horizontal:
2. contesta
6. grapadora
9. pide
10. cinta
12. conocen
13. prestar
15. nadie
17. tijeras
20. llega
21. discurso
22. proyecto

Vertical:
1. informe
3. saca
4. armario
5. asiento
7. palabra
8. memoria
9. pregunta
11. a tiempo
12. carnet
14. reglas
16. explicas
18. respetar
19. entregar

Organizer (1A-9)

I. Vocabulary Answers will vary.

II. Grammar

1.
Col. 1	Col. 2
puedo	podemos
puedes	podéis
puede	pueden

2.
Col. 1	Col. 2
pido	pedimos
pides	pedís
pide	piden

Negative Words
1. nadie
2. nada
3. ningún, ninguno(s), ninguna(s)
4. nunca
5. tampoco

Affirmative Words
1. alguien
2. algo
3. algún, alguno(s), alguna(s)
4. siempre
5. también

AVSR 1A-1

Realidades 2
Capítulo 1A

Nombre _____ Hora _____
Fecha _____ **AVSR 1A-1**

The verb *tener* (p. 15)

- Remember that *tener* means "to have." It is also used to tell how old you are (**tener años**), or to say that you're hungry (**tener hambre**), sleepy (**tener sueño**), or thirsty (**tener sed**).
- Here are the present-tense forms of *tener*:

yo	tengo	nosotros/nosotras	tenemos
tú	tienes	vosotros/vosotras	tenéis
usted/él/ella	tiene	ustedes/ellos/ellas	tienen

A. Circle the correct form of *tener* to complete each sentence.

Modelo Alicia ((tiene)/ tenemos) un reloj nuevo.

1. Yo no (tienes /(tengo)) los carteles.
2. Paco y Lulú (tenemos /(tienen)) hambre.
3. Nosotros ((tenemos)/ tienen) los bolígrafos.
4. Marco ((tiene)/ tienes) 14 años.
5. ¿Cuántos diccionarios (tiene /(tienes)) tú?
6. Alicia y tú no ((tienen)/ tienes) calculadoras, ¿verdad?

- To say that someone has to do something, use **tener + que + infinitive**.

Marta tiene que estudiar. *Marta has to study.*

B. Write the correct form of **tener + que** to tell what these people have to do.

Modelo Susana __tiene__ __que__ esquiar.

1. Yo __tengo__ __que__ practicar deportes.
2. Nosotros __tenemos__ __que__ comer a las 6.
3. Juana y Julio __tienen__ __que__ ir a clase.
4. Los estudiantes __tienen__ __que__ hacer la tarea.
5. Tú __tienes__ __que__ traer el libro a clase.

realidades.com
• Web Code: jdd-0101

AVSR 1A-2

Realidades 2
Capítulo 1A

Nombre _____ Hora _____
Fecha _____ **AVSR 1A-2**

Verbs with irregular *yo* forms

- The *yo* form of *tener* in the present tense is irregular. It ends in -go (**Yo tengo**).
- Other verbs that are irregular in the *yo* form are:

hacer (to do, to make)	hago
poner (to put)	pongo
traer (to bring)	traigo

C. Write the *yo* form of each verb in parentheses.

1. Yo (tener) __tengo__ un asiento.
2. Yo (poner) __pongo__ los cuadernos en la mesa.
3. Yo (hacer) __hago__ la tarea.
4. Yo (traer) __traigo__ la papelera.

D. Complete the sentences with forms of **traer, tener, poner,** or **hacer.** Follow the model.

Modelo (traer) Alejandro __trae__ su mochila a clase.

1. (tener) Raúl y yo __tenemos__ que estudiar.
2. (hacer) Yo __hago__ la tarea.
3. (poner) Juliana __pone__ sus libros en su mochila.
4. (hacer) Tú __haces__ un experimento en la clase de ciencias naturales.
5. (traer) Los estudiantes no __traen__ un sacapuntas a clase.
6. (poner) Yo __pongo__ una manzana en el escritorio del profesor.

realidades.com
• Web Code: jdd-0101

Nombre _____

Hora _____

Fecha _____

Vocabulary Flash Cards, Sheet 2

Write the Spanish vocabulary word or phrase below each picture. Be sure to include the article for each noun.

aprender _____

de _____ memoria

discutir _____

el _____ informe

prestar _____

atención _____

entregar _____

el _____ carnet

de _____ identidad

llegar _____

tarde _____

pedir _____

ayuda _____

el _____

asiento _____

18 Guided Practice Activities ━ Vocabulary Flash Cards 1A

Nombre _____

Hora _____

Fecha _____

Vocabulary Flash Cards, Sheet 1

Write the Spanish vocabulary word or phrase below each picture. Be sure to include the article for each noun.

las _____ tijeras

los _____ materiales

el _____ laboratorio

dar _____ un

discurso _____

la _____ cinta

adhesiva _____

la _____ grapadora

explicar _____

contestar _____

hacer _____ una

pregunta _____

Guided Practice Activities ━ Vocabulary Flash Cards 1A **17**

Sheet 4 (top half)

Realidades 2

Capítulo 1A

Nombre _____

Fecha _____

Hora _____

Vocabulary Flash Cards, Sheet 4

Copy the word or phrase in the space provided. Be sure to include the article for each noun.

se prohíbe...	alguien	algún, alguna, algunos, algunas
se prohíbe...	alguien	algún , alguna , algunos , algunas

nadie	ningún, ninguno, ninguna	almorzar
nadie	ningún , ninguno , ninguna	almorzar

empezar	entender	repetir
empezar	entender	repetir

Sheet 3 (bottom half)

Realidades 2

Capítulo 1A

Nombre _____

Fecha _____

Hora _____

Vocabulary Flash Cards, Sheet 3

Write the Spanish vocabulary word below each picture. If there is a word or phrase, copy it in the space provided. Be sure to include the article for each noun.

el armario	sacar una buena nota	a tiempo
el armario	sacar una buena nota	a tiempo

el proyecto	conocer	lo que
el proyecto	conocer	lo que

la palabra	la regla	respetar
la palabra	la regla	respetar

Nombre _____ Hora _____

Fecha _____ **Vocabulary Flash Cards, Sheet 6**

These blank cards can be used to write and practice other Spanish vocabulary for the chapter.

Nombre _____ Hora _____

Fecha _____ **Vocabulary Flash Cards, Sheet 5**

Copy the word or phrase in the space provided. These blank cards can be used to write and practice other Spanish vocabulary for the chapter.

sobre

sobre

Sheet 2 (page 24)

Tear out this page. Write the Spanish words on the lines. Fold the paper along the dotted line to see the correct answers so you can check your work.

- to pay attention — *prestar atención*
- it's forbidden… — *se prohíbe…*
- rule — *la regla*
- to respect — *respetar*
- to turn in — *entregar*
- to explain — *explicar*
- to ask for help — *pedir ayuda*
- report — *el informe*
- project — *el proyecto*
- someone, anyone — *alguien*
- no one, nobody — *nadie*
- to answer — *contestar*
- to discuss — *discutir*
- to ask a question — *hacer una pregunta*
- to arrive late — *llegar tarde*

Fold In ↓

Sheet 1 (page 23)

Tear out this page. Write the English words on the lines. Fold the paper along the dotted line to see the correct answers so you can check your work.

- prestar atención — *to pay attention*
- se prohíbe… — *it's forbidden…*
- la regla — *rule*
- respetar — *to respect*
- entregar — *to turn in*
- explicar — *to explain*
- pedir ayuda — *to ask for help*
- el informe — *report*
- el proyecto — *project*
- alguien — *someone, anyone*
- nadie — *no one, nobody*
- contestar — *to answer*
- discutir — *to discuss*
- hacer una pregunta — *to ask a question*
- llegar tarde — *to arrive late*

Fold In ↓

Sheet 4 (right side)

Tear out this page. Write the Spanish words on the lines. Fold the paper along the dotted line to see the correct answers so you can check your work.

Fold In ↓

to memorize	*aprender de memoria*
laboratory	*el laboratorio*
word	*la palabra*
to get a good grade	*sacar una buena nota*
on time	*a tiempo*
locker	*el armario*
seat	*el asiento*
I.D. card	*el carnet de identidad*
transparent tape	*la cinta adhesiva*
stapler	*la grapadora*
supplies, materials	*los materiales*
scissors	*las tijeras*

To hear a complete list of the vocabulary for this chapter, go to www.realidades.com and type in the Web Code jdd-0189. Then click on **Repaso del capítulo.**

Sheet 3 (left side)

Tear out this page. Write the English words on the lines. Fold the paper along the dotted line to see the correct answers so you can check your work.

Fold In ↓

aprender de memoria	*to memorize*
el laboratorio	*laboratory*
la palabra	*word*
sacar una buena nota	*to get a good grade*
a tiempo	*on time*
el armario	*locker*
el asiento	*seat*
el carnet de identidad	*I.D. card*
la cinta adhesiva	*transparent tape*
la grapadora	*stapler*
los materiales	*supplies, materials*
las tijeras	*scissors*

Stem-changing verbs (p. 27)

- Stem-changing verbs have one spelling change in their stem in the present tense: **almorzar → Yo almuerzo en la escuela.**
- The stem change, as seen in the verb chart below, resembles a shoe because the **nosotros(as)** and **vosotros(as)** forms do not change.

yo	**duermo**	nosotros/nosotras	dormimos
tú	**duermes**	vosotros/vosotras	dormís
usted/él/ella	**duerme**	ustedes/ellos/ellas	**duermen**

- Look at the **yo** form of the verbs in the chart below.

e → ie	o → ue	e → i	u → ue
empezar → empiezo	poder → puedo	pedir → pido	jugar → juego
entender → entiendo	almorzar → almuerzo	repetir → repito	
		servir → sirvo	

A. Look at the verbs below and connect the letter in each stem with the letters it changes to in the conjugated form. Follow the model.

Modelo empezar empiezo
1. poder puede
2. pedir pides
3. servir sirven
4. almorzar almuerzo
5. jugar juega
6. entender entienden

B. Fill in the blanks with the correct stem-change letters for each verb in the sentences below. Follow the model.

Modelo Miguel alm__u__ __e__rza en la cafetería.
1. Los chicos j__u__ __e__ gan al fútbol americano.
2. El camarero s__i__rve la comida a tiempo.
3. Yo p__i__do café con leche en el bar.
4. La clase emp__i__ __e__za a las cuatro y media.
5. La manzana c__u__ __e__sta veinticinco centavos.
6. Los estudiantes rep__i__ten lo que dice la profesora.

Stem-changing verbs (continued)

- Remember that the **nosotros** and **vosotros** forms do not change their stem.

C. Look at each pair of sentences below. In the space provided in the second sentence, write the **nosotros** form of the underlined verb from the first sentence to say that we don't do what the persons in the first sentence do. Follow the model.

Modelo Claudia empieza a hablar. Nosotros no _empezamos_ a hablar.
1. Tú juegas al fútbol. Nosotros no _jugamos_ al fútbol.
2. Jorge entiende la clase. Nosotros no _entendemos_ la clase.
3. Yo almuerzo con Juan y Rebeca. Nosotros no _almorzamos_ con Juan y Rebeca.
4. Rebeca pide una cinta adhesiva y una grapadora.
   Nosotros no _pedimos_ una cinta adhesiva y una grapadora.

D. Answer the following questions choosing the stem-changing verb that makes the most sense in the sentence. Once you have chosen a verb, write the correct form in the space provided. Follow the model.

Modelo Es el mediodía y tú tienes hambre. ¿Qué haces tú? (**almorzar** / entender) en la cafetería.
   Yo _almuerzo_ en la cafetería.
1. Son las diez de la noche y nosotras estamos cansadas. ¿Qué hacemos? (querer / **dormir**).
   Nosotras _dormimos_ (querer / dormir).
2. Juan y Felipe son camareros en un restaurante. ¿Qué hacen todos los días? (repetir / **servir**) la comida.
   Ellos _sirven_ la comida.
3. Tú sacas buenas notas en la clase de ciencias naturales. ¿Por qué? (**entender** / dormir) la información.
   Porque yo _entiendo_ la información.
4. Nosotros estamos en el equipo de vóleibol. ¿Qué hacemos? (**jugar** / almorzar) al vóleibol.
   Nosotros _jugamos_ al vóleibol.

Affirmative and negative words (p. 31)

• Affirmative and negative words are opposites.

• Affirmative words are used to say that something does exist, or that it does happen. Negative words are used to say that something doesn't exist, or that it doesn't happen.

• **Yo siempre hago preguntas** is an affirmative sentence. It means "I always ask questions."

• **Yo nunca hago preguntas** is a negative sentence. It means "I never ask questions."

Affirmative	Negative
alguien _someone, anyone_	**nadie** _no one, nobody_
algo _something_	**nada** _nothing_
algún _some, any_ **alguno(s)** **alguna(s)**	**ningún** _no, none, not any_ **ninguno** **ninguna**
siempre _always_	**nunca** _never_
también _also, too_	**tampoco** _neither, either_

A. Rubén and Nora are talking about a class. Look at the underlined affirmative or negative words in each sentence. Then, write + next to the sentence if the word is affirmative and — if the word is negative. The first one is done for you.

1. RUBÉN: ¿Por qué tú <u>siempre</u> haces preguntas en esa clase? __+__

   NORA: Porque yo <u>nunca</u> entiendo y me gusta entender. __—__

2. RUBÉN: ¿Conoces a Marina? A ella <u>también</u> le gusta hacer preguntas. ___+___

   NORA: ¡Sí! Ella <u>tampoco</u> entiende la clase. __—__

3. RUBÉN: Yo <u>siempre</u> te quiero ayudar. __+__

   NORA: Yo <u>también</u> quiero ayudar a Marina. ___+___

B. Each sentence below has an affirmative or negative word from the above chart. Find the word and circle it. Then, write its opposite in the blank. Follow the model.

Modelo Yo(siempre)respeto las reglas. ___siempre___

1. (Alguien)contesta la pregunta. ___Nadie___

2. Lucía(siempre)llega tarde. ___nunca___

3. Mis padres(nunca)dan un discurso. ___siempre___

Affirmative and negative words (continued)

4. Tú(también)haces tu proyecto. ___tampoco___

5. Marta y María(tampoco)piden ayuda. ___también___

6. Yo no tengo(ninguna)clase aburrida. ___alguna___

• When you want to say "some," change the ending of **alguno** so it matches what you're describing in gender (masculine or feminine) and number (singular or plural): **alguna chica, algunos libros, algunas chicas**. The same is true for **ninguno: ninguna clase**.

• Before a masculine singular noun, **alguno** and **ninguno** change to **algún** and **ningún**.

C. Look at the list of school supplies below. Is the word (or words) masculine or feminine, singular or plural? Circle the correct form of **alguno** or **ninguno** in parentheses.

1. (algunas /(algunos)) asientos

2. ((alguna)/ algunos) cinta adhesiva

3. (algunos /(algún)) armario

4. ((ningún)/ ninguna) libro

5. ((algunos)/ alguna) materiales

6. ((ninguna)/ ningún) grapadora

D. Circle the letter of the answer that best completes each sentence.

1. —¿Conoces a alguien en el laboratorio?
   —No, yo no conozco a _____
   a. alguien. (b) nadie.

2. —¿Va a comer algo Anita?
   —No, no va a comer _____
   a. algo. (b) nada.

3. —¿Conoce Sandra a alguien en el laboratorio?
   —Sí, ella conoce a _____
   (a) alguien. b. nadie.

4. —¿Conoce el maestro a alguien en el laboratorio?
   —No, el maestro no conoce a _____
   a. alguien. (b) nadie.

5. —¿Alfonso siempre llega a clase a tiempo?
   —Sí, él _____ llega a tiempo.
   (a) siempre b. nunca

Presentación oral (p. 37)

Task: You have been invited to be a school principal for a day. As principal, you will make new school rules and display them on a poster. Then, you will present your poster to a partner.

A. Think about what students will and will not be allowed to do in your school. Then list some phrases to describe these rules. A few phrases have been provided to get you started. ***Answers will vary.***

llegar a tiempo, hacer la tarea, conocer al director, _____

_____

B. Using the phrases from **part A**, complete the columns. In the **Hay que...** column, write three phrases to describe what students should do at your school. In the **Se prohíbe...** column, write three phrases to describe what should not be done at your school. One has been done for you. ***Answers will vary.***

Hay que...
1. _hacer la tarea_
2. _____
3. _____

Se prohíbe...
1. _____
2. _____
3. _____

C. On a piece of posterboard, write out complete sentences using your answers from part B. Leave space between each for your drawings. Follow the models.

Modelos Hay que _____ _hacer la tarea_ _____

Se prohíbe _llegar tarde a la clase_ _____

D. Now, illustrate each of your school rules on the poster.

E. Tell a partner about your school rules. Refer to the illustrations on your poster as you speak. Be sure to: ***Answers will vary.***
- include three things that students are allowed and three things that are not allowed
- use complete sentences
- speak clearly

Lectura: Para estudiar mejor... (pp. 34-35)

A. The reading in your textbook is an article about good study habits. First, look at the heads and subheads in the article. They can help you understand what the material will be about before you begin reading. Then, based on the information you read in the heads and subheads, list three things you would expect to find in this article.

1. ***Answers will vary.***
2. _____
3. _____

B. The following words are cognates from the reading. Remember that cognates are words that have similar spellings and meanings in English and Spanish. Write the letter of the English word that matches the Spanish word.

1. _a_ comprender   a. comprehend   b. communicate

2. _b_ clases   a. cases   b. classes

3. _b_ atención   a. attitude   b. attention

4. _a_ hábitos   a. habits   b. abilities

C. Read the following excerpt from the first section of the article in your textbook. Then, complete the chart below based on the excerpt. Write the answers in the space provided. The first one has been done for you.

¿Qué debes hacer a la hora de estudiar?

Para estudiar mejor necesitas una buena organización del trabajo y unos hábitos saludables. Siempre debes ser positivo. Repite frases como "yo puedo hacerlo" o soy capaz (capable) : Cuida (Take care of) tus libros y otros materiales.

Para estudiar mejor, necesitas...	Debes ser positivo(a) y usar frases como...	Debes cuidar...
una buena organización del trabajo	"yo puedo hacerlo"	tus libros
unos hábitos saludables	"soy capaz"	otros materiales

realidades.com
• Web Code jdd-0106

Realidades 2

Capítulo 1A

Nombre _____

Hora _____

Fecha _____

VIDEO

Antes de ver el video

Actividad 1

Imagine that you are a teacher and it is your first day of classes. Write four expressions you might use to address the class. The first one is done for you.

¡Buenos días!

Answers will vary.

_____

_____

_____

¿Comprendes?

Actividad 2

In the video, Esteban dreams he is a teacher. Circle the best choice to complete the sentences or answer the questions about his dream below.

1. En el video, Esteban es el profesor de

   a. matemáticas.

   b. español.

   c. ciencias sociales.

   d. historia.

2. ¿A qué hora empieza la clase de Esteban?

   a. a las diez y cinco

   b. a las nueve y seis

   c. a las nueve y cinco

   d. a las once y seis

Realidades 2

Capítulo 1A

Nombre _____

Hora _____

Fecha _____

VIDEO

3. En la clase de historia Esteban piensa dar un discurso sobre

   a. los verbos regulares en el presente.

   b. cómo hay que prestar atención al profesor.

   c. los presidentes de los Estados Unidos.

   d. la vida de George Washington.

4. Angélica y Lisa tienen que quedarse en la escuela después de las clases porque

   a. no tienen los libros.

   b. llegan tarde a la clase.

   c. hacen demasiadas preguntas.

   d. no saben qué hora es.

5. ¿Cuál *no* es una regla de la clase de Esteban?

   a. Los estudiantes tienen que estar en sus asientos cuando empieza la clase.

   b. Hay que respetar a los demás.

   c. Todos necesitan ir al armario.

   d. Hay que prestar atención al profesor.

Nombre _____ **Hora** _____

Capítulo 1A

Fecha _____ **AUDIO**

Actividad 5

Listen to these teachers welcoming their students to the first day of class. The pictures below correspond to things that the students must and cannot do in their classes. In the boxes under each teacher's name, write the letters of the pictures that correspond to what you must and cannot do in his or her class. There should only be one letter per box. You will hear each set of statements twice.

A. B. C. D.

E. F. G. H.

I. J.

	Srta. Arcos	Sr. Cruz	Sra. Cazón	Sra. Rendón	Srta. García
No se permite	G	A	C	J	H
Hay que	B	E	F	D	I

Nombre _____ **Hora** _____

Capítulo 1A

Fecha _____ **VIDEO**

Actividad 3

Identify the speaker of each of the following quotes from the video.

1. Mamá, ¿por qué estás aquí en la clase? Esteban

2. ¡Esteban! ¿Qué te pasa? Lisa

3. Señoritas, ¿saben qué hora es? Esteban

4. ¿Hay tarea esta noche? Angélica

5. ¿Por qué estás delante de la clase? Lisa

6. Lo siento. Pero se prohíbe ir al armario. Esteban

7. ¿A qué hora llegas a casa después de las clases? Mamá

8. Esteban, ¿qué es esto? ¿Tú eres profesor? Pedro

9. Soy el profesor Ríos. Esteban

10. ¿Qué pasa? ¿Dónde estoy...? Esteban

Y, ¿qué más?

Actividad 4

All teachers have rules for their students. We already know Esteban's rules. Imagine that you are Esteban and write three more rules for your class.

Answers will vary.

_____

_____

_____

Actividad 8

After listening to each of the following statements about school, decide whether it is **lógico** or **ilógico** and mark your answer on the grid. You will hear each statement twice. At the end of the exercise, you may want to compare your answers with those of a partner.

	1	2	3	4	5	6	7	8	9	10
Lógico	X	X				X		X		
Ilógico			X	X	X		X		X	X

Actividad 9

Listen as a reporter for the teen magazine *¿Qué hay?* talks to students about their "secrets" for doing well in school. Fill in the grid below with their secret for each category: 1) **La cosa más importante para sacar buenas notas** *(the most important factor in getting good grades)*; 2) **El mejor lugar para estudiar** *(the best place to study)*; 3) **Si es mejor estudiar solo(a) o con amigos** *(whether it's better to study alone or with friends)*. You will hear each set of statements twice.

	1	2	3	4
La cosa más importante para sacar buenas notas				
No tener televisor en el dormitorio			X	
Buena organización	X			
Dormir ocho horas				X
Tener un profesor paciente que explica todo		X		
El mejor lugar para estudiar				
La cocina				X
La biblioteca		X		
El dormitorio			X	
La sala	X			
¿Solo(a) o con amigos?				
Solo(a)	X		X	X
Con amigos		X		

Actividad 6

Listen as students talk about their classes this semester. Decide which class each one is describing and write the name of the class in the grid below. Then, place a check mark in the box below the class name if the student likes the class, and an X if the student doesn't like the class. You will hear each set of statements twice.

	1	2	3	4	5
Clase	literatura	geometría	ciencias sociales	español	biología
¿Le gusta (✓) o no le gusta (x)?	X	X	✓	✓	X

Answers may vary (for example, some students may write *literatura* and others might write *inglés* for #1).

Actividad 7

Teachers and students all talk about their classes with their friends and family. Listen to snippets of their conversations to see if you can determine whether it is a teacher or a student who is talking about his or her classes. Write an X in the appropriate box in the grid. You will hear each set of statements twice.

	1	2	3	4	5	6
Profesor(a)	X		X	X		
Estudiante		X	X		X	X

Actividad 11

Look at the pictures below and write two complete sentences to tell about what's happening in each one. Then, write one complete sentence that describes your experience or opinion about the activity indicated. Follow the model.

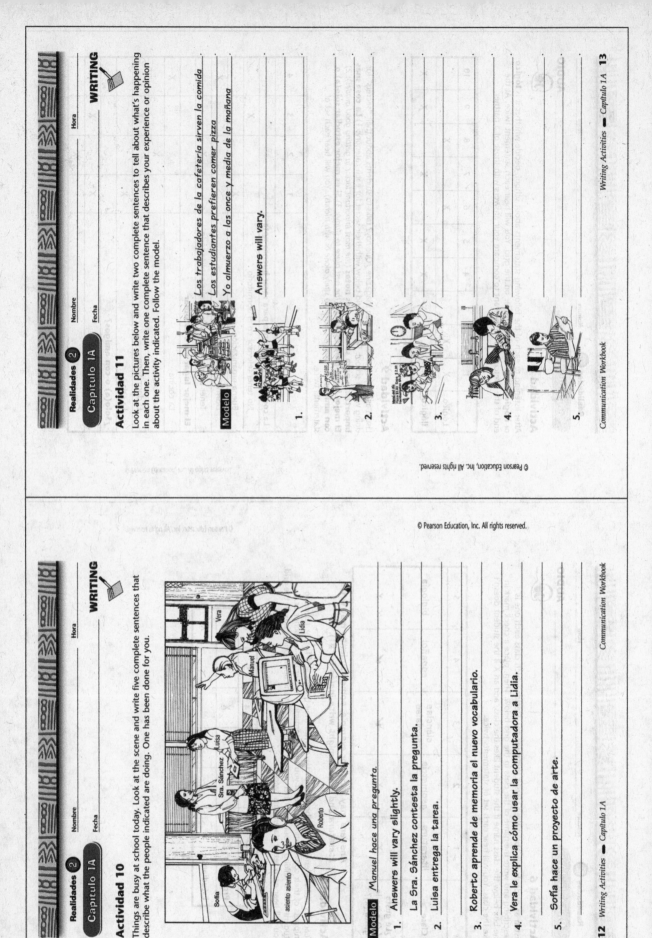

Modelo
Los trabajadores de la cafetería sirven la comida
Los estudiantes prefieren comer pizza
Yo almuerzo a las once y media de la mañana

1. Answers will vary.

2.

3.

4.

5.

Actividad 10

Things are busy at school today. Look at the scene and write five complete sentences that describe what the people indicated are doing. One has been done for you.

Modelo Manuel hace una pregunta.

1. Answers will vary slightly.

   La Sra. Sánchez contesta la pregunta.

2. Luisa entrega la tarea.

3. Roberto aprende de memoria el nuevo vocabulario.

4. Vera le explica cómo usar la computadora a Lidia.

5. Sofía hace un proyecto de arte.

Actividad 12

You are completing a survey about your life at school. Look at each of the statements in the survey. If you agree with the statement, put an X by it and write an explanation. If you disagree with the statement, rewrite it on the lines below, changing it to make it true for you and your experiences at school. Follow the model.

Modelo ___ Hay muchas escuelas con más reglas que nuestra escuela.
Hay algunas escuelas que tienen menos reglas, pero nuestra escuela
puede tener más.

___ 1. No conozco a nadie en mi escuela.
Answers will vary.
_____

___ 2. Nunca tenemos tarea los fines de semana.
_____
_____

___ 3. Siempre prestamos atención en la clase.
_____
_____

___ 4. Todos los estudiantes sacan buenas notas.
_____
_____

___ 5. En la clase de español hacemos un proyecto cada semana.
_____
_____

___ 6. La comida de la cafetería siempre es buena.
_____
_____

Communication Workbook

Actividad 13

A. Look at the picture below of Universidad Troyana. Based on the picture, circle the activities in the bank that people do there.

leer	estudiar	repetir	dormir
bailar	almorzar	pedir	poder
jugar	esquiar	servir	cocinar

Answers may vary.

B. Now, using the verbs above, complete the ad below that some students are writing to attract people to the Universidad Troyana.

¡La Universidad Troyana es la mejor! Aquí, nosotros...

Answers will vary, but will follow responses from Part A.

• _____
• _____
• _____
• _____

Para aprender más sobre nuestra universidad, lee lo que dice una de nuestras estudiantes:

"¡Hola! Yo soy Catalina, una estudiante de primer año aquí en la Universidad Troyana. Me encanta la vida aquí. Todos los días yo...

• _____
• _____
• _____
• _____

Realmente es la mejor universidad."

Communication Workbook

Test Preparation Answers

Reading Skills
p. 211   2. **C**
p. 212   2. **D**

**Integrated Performance
Assessment**
p. 213

Answers will vary.

School-to-Home Connection

Dear Parent or Guardian,

The theme of our current unit is *Tu día escolar* (Your school day). This chapter is called *¿Qué haces después de las clases?* (What do you do after school?).

Upon completion of this chapter students will be able to:

- talk about extracurricular activities
- compare people and things
- say what people know or what they know how to do; say what people are familiar with
- talk about knowing people
- understand cultural perspectives on extracurricular activities

Students will also explore:

- turning verbs into nouns

Our textbook, *Realidades,* helps with the development of reading, writing, and speaking skills through the use of strategies, process speaking, and process writing. In this chapter, students will:

- read a Web page about a dance school
- write about extracurricular activities

To reinforce and enhance learning, students can access a wide range of online resources on **realidades.com**, the personalized learning management system that accompanies the print and online Student Edition. Resources include the eText, textbook and workbook activities, audio files, videos, animations, songs, self-study tools, interactive maps, voice recording (RealTalk!), assessments, and other digital resources. Many learning tools can be accessed through the student Home Page on **realidades.com**. Other activities, specifically those that require grading, are assigned by the teacher and linked on the student Home Page within the calendar or the Assignments tab.

You will find specifications and guidelines for accessing **realidades.com** on home computers and mobile devices on MyPearsonTraining.com under the SuccessNet Plus tab.

realidades.com

For: Tips to Parents
Visit: www.realidades.com
Web Code: jce-0010

Check it out! At the end of the chapter, have your child talk about the extracurricular activities he or she is or wants to be involved in. If he or she is already involved in any, have him or her tell you since when.

Sincerely,

Videocultura Script

Vida escolar

Spanish version:

Argentina tiene un nivel muy alto de alfabetización. Es uno de los más altos del mundo. La educación en Argentina es gratuita.

En las escuelas se estudian materias como aritmética, español, historia, arte, idiomas.

El año escolar empieza en marzo, en el otoño, y se extiende hasta el mes de noviembre.

Los "bonaerenses" —como se les dice a los habitantes de Buenos Aires—, disfrutan de diferentes actividades fuera de la escuela. Ellos juegan al fútbol o van a los parques.

También van de compras a las tiendas de discos compactos.

Aunque pasan mucho tiempo estudiando, los estudiantes en Argentina se reparten su tiempo hacer sus actividades favoritas.

English version:

Education is a top priority throughout the Spanish-speaking world. For example, in Argentina, education is free from kindergarten through college. Because of this, Argentina enjoys one of the highest levels of literacy and education in Latin America.

Students in Argentina study a variety of subjects including mathematics, science, geography, Spanish language and literature, history, music, art, and foreign languages.

And because Argentina is in the southern hemisphere, the school year starts in March and ends in December.

When not in school, students in Buenos Aires, the capital, enjoy being outdoors as much as weather permits. They may spend time playing soccer or visiting the many parks around the city where there is always something going on.

Listening to music is also a very popular pastime among teenagers. They may visit a local music store or download songs from the Internet. Teens listen to a variety of music ranging from folk to rock to hip-hop.

Even with the strong emphasis on education, Argentine students balance their time between studying and other favorite activities.

Input Script

Presentation

Input Vocabulary and Expressions: Before class, assign your students to the clubs shown in *A primera vista* by making copies of the Vocabulary Clip Art and writing each student's name on one of the images that represents a club. Make some of the assignments unlikely or comical, for example, a student who is on the football team being assigned to the ballet club.

Place the transparency on the screen. Explain to students that they will be assigned to one of the clubs shown. Point to each club activity as you describe it. Ask students: *¿Tienes tú la oportunidad de participar en ____?* Have them give a "thumbs-up" or "thumbs-down" sign to show if they have the chance to participate in the activities you mention. Make statements about the clubs to present the expressions *conozco* and *tan… como.*

Then give students their club assignments by distributing the Clip Art images with students' names on them. Ask: *¿Quién participa en ____?* and have students raise the Clip Art image of their club when you ask about it. Next, tell students that they will be helping you create a video program about extracurricular activities to attract more students to your school. Each club will have a thirty-second segment in which to demonstrate their club's activities. The ballet club should perform pirouettes, the cheerleaders should come up with an original cheer for the school, and so forth. Give the clubs time to rehearse their segments in groups.

Begin "shooting" the video program. (If possible, have a student actually videotape it.) Read the first two paragraphs of *A primera vista*. Change *En mi escuela…* to *En nuestra escuela…* Then go to each club, describe the club's activities and have students perform their thirty-second demonstration. Use the *A primera vista* captions as the basis for your script (*Tienes que ir a los ensayos de la banda o a las prácticas del equipo de básquetbol para participar,* and so forth).

If you videotaped the presentation, distribute copies of the Vocabulary Clip Art and have students cut them into individual images. Play the video and have students hold up the Clip Art of each activity they see and identify the activity in Spanish.

If you did not videotape the presentation, tell students that if they would like to join a different club than the one you assigned them, they should draw a picture of the club they would prefer to join. Ask each student to hold up the Clip Art image or their drawing and say: *Me gusta el club de ____* or *Prefiero el club de ____.*

Comprehension Check

- Distribute copies of the Vocabulary Clip Art. Tell students that you are going to describe your high school classmates and the extracurricular activities they used to do. Students will write the names of your classmates by the activities they participated in.

- Write the words for the club activities on slips of paper and place them in a bag. Have a volunteer draw three activities. Give him or her one minute to act out the three activities for the rest of the class to guess. Repeat with other students.

Realidades 2

Capítulo 1B

Audio Script

Audio DVD, Capítulo 1B

Track 01: *A primera vista, ¿Qué haces después de las clases?*, **Student Book, p. 46**

Vocabulario y gramática en contexto
Lee en tu libro mientras escuchas la narración.

TEEN MALE: En mi escuela los estudiantes participan en muchas actividades extracurriculares. Les gusta practicar deportes o son miembros de algún club, como el club de computadoras. Éstas son algunas de las actividades más populares entre los jóvenes.

TEEN FEMALE: ¿Tienes tú la oportunidad de participar en muchas actividades? ¿Tiene tu escuela tantas actividades como mi escuela? ¿Cuánto tiempo hace que participas?

Vas a escuchar cada palabra o frase dos veces. Después de la primera vez hay una pausa para que puedas pronunciar la palabra o frase. Luego vas a escuchar de nuevo la palabra o frase.

el ajedrez	el músico
jugar a los bolos	la música
el animador	la banda
la animadora	el equipo

Lee en tu libro mientras escuchas la narración.

TEEN MALE: Tienes que ir a los ensayos de la banda o a las prácticas del equipo de básquetbol para participar.

Vas a escuchar cada palabra o frase dos veces. Después de la primera vez hay una pausa para que puedas pronunciar la palabra o frase. Luego vas a escuchar de nuevo la palabra o frase.

grabar una canción	el bailarín
la orquesta	la bailarina
la cantante	la fotógrafa
el coro	el fotógrafo
el cantante	

Lee en tu libro mientras escuchas la narración.

TEEN FEMALE: El coro y la orquesta están grabando una canción.

TEEN FEMALE: Los dos fotógrafos son miembros del club de fotografía. Hace dos años que son miembros del club.

Track 02: *A primera vista*, **Student Book, p. 47**

Vocabulario y gramática en contexto
Lee en tu libro mientras escuchas la narración.

TEEN MALE: Conozco a varios miembros del club de computadoras. Creo que este club es tan interesante como los otros clubes. En el club puedo… navegar en La Red… crear una página Web… hacer una búsqueda. Ramón está en línea. Le gusta visitar salones de chat.

Vas a escuchar cada palabra o frase dos veces. Después de la primera vez hay una pausa para que puedas pronunciar la palabra o frase. Luego vas a escuchar de nuevo la palabra o frase.

Me gusta ir al club atlético.
las artes marciales
el hockey
hacer gimnasia
la natación

Track 03: *A primera vista*, **Act. 1, Student Book, p. 47**

Unos estudiantes muy ocupados
Escucha a un estudiante que describe las actividades en su escuela. Señala cada actividad que él describe. Vas a escuchar las frases dos veces.

1. Hay dos músicos en la banda.
2. Hay un ensayo para la obra de teatro hoy.
3. Las animadoras del equipo de básquetbol son muy talentosas.
4. El coro va a grabar una canción esta tarde.
5. Me gusta mucho navegar en la Red.
6. Esteban tiene una página Web muy interesante.
7. Los bailarines y la orquesta practican todos los días.

Track 04: *A primera vista*, **Act. 2, Student Book, p. 47**

¿Sí o no?
Escucha las frases. Si lo que escuchas es lógico, señala con el pulgar hacia arriba. Si la respuesta no es lógica, señala con el pulgar hacia abajo. Vas a escuchar las frases dos veces.

1. El equipo de hockey va a grabar una canción.
2. Vamos a jugar a los bolos en el gimnasio.
3. Los fotógrafos sacan buenas fotografías.
4. Practicamos la artes marciales en el club atlético.
5. Hay un ensayo para la obra de teatro esta tarde.
6. Mis amigos van a jugar ajedrez en el salón de chat.

Track 05: *A primera vista*, **Videohistoria, Student Book, pp. 58–59**

Después de las clases
¿En qué actividades extracurriculares participan Esteban y sus amigos? Vamos a ver.

Lee en tu libro mientras escuchas la *Videohistoria*.

See Student Book pages 58–59 for script.

Track 06: *Manos a la obra*, **Act. 7, Student Book, p. 51**

Escucha y escribe
Escucha lo que dice una estudiante de Managua, Nicaragua, sobre las actividades extracurriculares allí. Escribe los números del 1 al 5 en una hoja de papel y escribe lo que escuchas. Después indica si estas actividades son populares entre los jóvenes de tu comunidad también. Vas a escuchar las frases dos veces.

1. Las clases de artes marciales son muy populares entre los jóvenes.
2. Muchos estudiantes tienen interés en el coro o la orquesta.

3. El club de ajedrez no es tan popular como el club de fotografía.
4. Visitamos salones de chat para conocer a otros jóvenes.
5. Mis amigos crean páginas Web o hacen búsquedas en la computadora.

Track 07: Audio Act. 5, Writing, Audio & Video Workbook, p. 18

As part of freshman orientation, students can go to the *Feria de clubes* to find the perfect club or activity for them. Write the number of the conversation next to the name of the corresponding club or activity that is being discussed by the two people. You will hear each conversation twice.

1. TEEN MALE: Tú dibujas muy bien. Tienes talento.
   TEEN FEMALE: Gracias. Mi madre es artista gráfica y me ayuda mucho.
   TEEN MALE: ¿Te gustaría saber más sobre nuestro club?
2. TEEN FEMALE: ¡Hola! ¿Sabes tocar un instrumento musical?
   TEEN MALE: Sí. Toco el violín.
   TEEN FEMALE: Bueno, necesitamos muchos violinistas. ¿Quieres ir conmigo?
   TEEN MALE: ¿Puedo ensayar hoy?
   TEEN FEMALE: ¡Por supuesto!
3. TEEN MALE 1: ¿Te gusta jugar el ajedrez?
   TEEN MALE 2: Sí. Hace cinco años que juego con mi padre.
   TEEN MALE 1: ¿Te interesa asistir a la reunión del club esta tarde?
4. TEEN FEMALE 1: Hola. Tú estás en mi clase de computadoras, ¿no?
   TEEN FEMALE 2: Sí. Me encanta navegar en la Red. Tengo mi propia página Web.
   TEEN FEMALE 1: ¿De veras? ¿Por qué no vas a la primera reunión de nuestro club?
5. TEEN MALE: ¡Qué cámara tan profesional!
   TEEN FEMALE: Sí. Es de mi padre, pero yo la uso cuando quiero.
   TEEN MALE: ¿Quieres ser miembro de nuestro club? A todos los miembros les gusta sacar fotos.
6. TEEN FEMALE: ¿Te gusta el karate?
   TEEN MALE: Sí. Participo en algunas competencias, pero no gano muchas.
   TEEN FEMALE: En nuestro club practicamos mucho. Hay oportunidad de ganar más competencias.
7. TEEN MALE: Me gusta cantar. Soy cantante en la iglesia de mi comunidad.
   TEEN FEMALE: Entonces, este club es para ti. Nosotros damos conciertos y nos divertimos mucho.
8. TEEN FEMALE: Me gusta mucho bailar. Quiero ser una bailarina profesional.
   TEEN MALE: ¿Qué tipo de baile te gusta?
   TEEN FEMALE: Yo prefiero el baile clásico, pero muchos en el club prefieren el baile moderno.

Track 08: Audio Act. 6, Writing, Audio & Video Workbook, p. 18

What do Lorena and her friends do after school? Listen to the conversations they are having at lunch and place the number of each conversation in the grid under the corresponding pictures. You will hear each conversation twice.

1. TEEN FEMALE 1: Después de las clases hay un partido de básquetbol. Todos los animadores tienen que estar en el gimnasio temprano.
2. TEEN MALE 1: Yo quiero ir al partido también, pero tengo que trabajar en el restaurante esta noche. ¡Qué asco!
3. TEEN FEMALE 2: Después de las clases hoy, tenemos una reunión del club de español. Como yo soy la presidente, tengo que asistir. ¿Cuántos de Uds. van? Es una reunión importante.
4. TEEN MALE 2: Voy a hablar con mi amiga de Venezuela en un salón de chat a las cuatro y media. Ella es muy inteligente. Le interesa todo de los Estados Unidos.
5. TEEN MALE 3: Tengo una competencia muy importante esta noche. Quiero ganar mi cinturón negro en artes marciales.
6. TEEN MALE 4: Regreso a mi casa después de clases. Quiero sacar mi cámara para la reunión del club de fotografía.
7. TEEN FEMALE 3: Ensayo con la banda esta tarde. Vamos a grabar tres canciones hoy y quiero practicar un poco más.
8. TEEN FEMALE 4: Hago gimnasia con el equipo a las cuatro. Practicamos cada día para la competencia de este fin de semana. ¡Vamos a ganar!

Track 09: Audio Act. 7, Writing, Audio & Video Workbook, p. 19

Although they are best friends, Ana and Elisa are very competitive with each other. Listen as each girl tries to convince the other that her boyfriend is as wonderful as the other girl's boyfriend! Write the letter of the picture that corresponds to each part of the conversation. You will hear each part of the conversation twice.

1. TEEN FEMALE 1: Voy al ensayo de la banda de mi novio, Marco. Él toca la guitarra muy bien.
   TEEN FEMALE 2: Mi novio, Andrés, toca la guitarra tan bien como tu novio. Hace cinco años que toca con su banda.
2. TEEN FEMALE 1: Mi novio es muy deportista. Él levanta cien kilos de pesas en el gimnasio.
   TEEN FEMALE 2: ¿Ah, sí? Mi novio levanta tantos kilos como él. Andrés practica muchos deportes.
3. TEEN FEMALE 1: Yo tengo el novio perfecto. Él me da muchas flores. Es muy romántico.
   TEEN FEMALE 2: Mi novio me da tantas flores como tu novio. Es tan romántico como él.
4. TEEN FEMALE 1: Mi novio es muy inteligente. Él saca muy buenas notas en los exámenes.
   TEEN FEMALE 2: Mi novio es tan inteligente como Marco. Andrés saca tan buenas notas como Marco.
5. TEEN FEMALE 1: Mi novio participa en muchas actividades extracurriculares... la orquesta, el coro y el club de fotografía.

TEEN FEMALE 2: Andrés participa en tantas actividades como él. Es miembro de un club atlético, del equipo de ajedrez y de la banda.

Track 10: Audio Act. 8, Writing, Audio & Video Workbook, p. 19

Javier's Mom does not know all of her son's friends by name, but she is familiar with what each one knows how to do well. Listen as she asks Javier about each of them. Match Javier's answers to the pictures below and write the name of his friend next to the picture. You will hear each conversation twice.

1. **MAMÁ:** ¿Quién es el chico que sabe sacar fotos para el periódico de la escuela? Él es muy talentoso, ¿no?
   JAVIER: Ah, sí. Se llama Marco. Es buen amigo.
2. **MAMÁ:** ¿Y la chica tan bonita que sabe cantar bien? ¿La conoces?
   JAVIER: Sí, mamá. Tú la conoces también. Su madre es tu amiga. Ella se llama Elena.
3. **MAMÁ:** ¿Quién es la animadora de pelo rubio? Es preciosa, ¿no?
   JAVIER: No hay nadie tan bonita como ella. Se llama Linda. No conozco muy bien a Linda.
4. **MAMÁ:** ¿Y la amiga de Linda? Creo que ella sabe tocar la guitarra.
   JAVIER: Se llama Flor. Mis amigos y yo la conocemos bien. Ella toca la guitarra tan bien como una guitarrista profesional.
5. **MAMÁ:** ¿Cómo se llama su amigo que sabe jugar a los bolos? Tu padre y tu tío lo conocen, pero no recuerdo su nombre.
   JAVIER: ¿Ramón? Sí, él sabe jugar a los bolos tan bien como papá.

Track 11: Audio Act. 9, Writing, Audio & Video Workbook, p. 20

We all know the expression "practice makes perfect." Listen as high school seniors are interviewed by a Hispanic radio station about the scholarships they received for their outstanding achievements in their extracurricular activities. Complete each sentence by writing the amount of time each of them has been involved with his or her particular interest. You will hear each interview twice.

1. **RADIO DJ:** Hola. ¿Vas a la universidad en septiembre?
   TEEN MALE 1: Sí. Tengo una beca para estudiar piano.
   RADIO DJ: ¿Cuánto tiempo hace que tocas el piano?
   TEEN MALE 1: Hace diez años que toco el piano. Mi mamá me da lecciones.
2. **RADIO DJ:** Buenos días. ¿Vas a escribir para el periódico de la universidad, ¿no?
   FEMALE TEEN 1: Sí. Hace dos años que escribo aquí en mi colegio. Algún día quiero trabajar para un periódico de Nueva York.

3. **RADIO DJ:** Hola. Eres una buena atleta, ¿no?
   FEMALE TEEN 2: Creo que sí. Hace ocho años que hago gimnasia. Quiero participar en los Juegos Olímpicos en el futuro.
4. **RADIO DJ:** Buenos días. ¿Vas a asistir a una universidad aquí, o lejos?
   FEMALE TEEN 3: Quiero vivir en casa con mi familia durante el primer año. Voy a asistir a una universidad local para estudiar música.
   RADIO DJ: ¿Cuánto tiempo hace que cantas?
   FEMALE TEEN 3: Mi mamá dice que hace quince años que canto. Pienso que tiene razón.
5. **RADIO DJ:** ¿Y tú? ¿Cuánto tiempo hace que participas en artes marciales en la escuela?
   MALE TEEN 2: Hace seis meses que participo, pero mi padre sabe enseñarme todo lo que necesito saber. ¡Él tiene cinturón negro!
6. **RADIO DJ:** Hola. Tú eres muy talentoso con la computadora, ¿no?
   MALE TEEN 3: Sí, muchos dicen que sí. Gano bastante dinero con mis páginas Web durante el verano. Hace cuatro años que las creo para otras personas.
7. **RADIO DJ:** Buenos días. Te interesa mucho la música clásica, ¿no?
   FEMALE TEEN 4: Sí. Quiero tocar el violín en una orquesta famosa.
   RADIO DJ: Eres muy ambiciosa. ¿Cuánto tiempo hace que tocas el violín?
   FEMALE TEEN 4: Hace siete años que toco el violín. Me encanta.

Track 12: *Repaso del capítulo*, Student Book, p. 68

Vocabulario y gramática
Escucha las palabras y expresiones que has aprendido en este capítulo.

See Student Book page 68 for vocabulary list.

Track 13: *Preparación para el examen*, Student Book, p. 69

Escuchar
Practice task
Listen as several teenagers describe what they do after school. See if you can understand: a) what they like to do; b) why they like to do it; c) how long they have been participating in that particular activity.

TEEN MALE: No conozco a muchas personas en la escuela. Soy un nuevo estudiante aquí y soy bastante tímido. Por eso, después de las clases regreso a mi casa. Me gustar visitar salones de chat en la Red. También me gusta cantar. Hace cinco años que canto con mi hermana en una banda musical.

TEEN FEMALE: ¿Te gusta cantar? ¡A mi también! ¿Quieres ir conmigo a la práctica del coro esta tarde? Hace dos años que canto en el coro. Es muy divertido.

Video Script

A primera vista: *Después de las clases*

PEDRO: Hola. ¿Qué tal?

PEDRO: Siéntense.

ANGÉLICA: Hola. Muy bien. Otro año escolar. Me encanta el primer día de clases. Hola, Lisa.

LISA: Hola, Angélica. Esteban, ¿cómo estás?

ESTEBAN: Un poco cansado. Es que no dormí bien anoche.

LISA: Lo siento.

LISA: ¿En qué actividades extracurriculares van a participar este año?

ESTEBAN: Soy miembro del Club de Computadoras. Miren. Aprendemos a navegar en la Red y a crear una nueva página Web…

LISA: ¿Cuánto tiempo hace que eres miembro?

ESTEBAN: Hace dos años. ¿Alguien quiere venir a la reunión esta tarde?

LISA: No sé…

ANGÉLICA: No.

PEDRO: Hoy no. Tengo que trabajar.

ESTEBAN: ¿Y tú, Lisa? ¿Qué haces después de las clases?

LISA: Soy miembro de la banda y la orquesta. Pero tengo que practicar más. Quiero tocar mejor el saxofón.

ANGÉLICA: ¿Y vas a cantar en el coro, también? Tienes una voz muy bonita.

LISA: Sí. Me gusta la música. Y tú, ¿por qué no cantas en el coro? Vamos a ensayar hoy. ¿Quieres venir?

ANGÉLICA: No sé. No canto tan bien como tú.

ESTEBAN: ¡No! Por favor…

ANGÉLICA: No. Tienes razón. Prefiero los deportes. Voy a ser miembro del equipo de natación en el invierno. Y en la primavera, voy a jugar al fútbol.

PEDRO: Y en el otoño, ¿otro deporte?

ANGÉLICA: Tú sabes que soy animadora. No tengo más tiempo. Tengo que estudiar un poco.

LISA: ¿Y tú, Pedro?

PEDRO: No participo en ninguna actividad de la escuela. Prefiero trabajar.

ANGÉLICA: ¿Por qué?

PEDRO: Me gusta ganar dinero.

ANGÉLICA: Ah.

ESTEBAN: Pero, aparte, Pedro tiene otro talento.

LISA: ¿De veras? ¿Qué es?

PEDRO: Pues, como lecciones de artes marciales en un club atlético. Me gusta mucho el karate.

ANGÉLICA: ¿Lo practicas mucho?

PEDRO: Participo en algunas competiciones.

LISA: ¿Ganas a veces?

ESTEBAN: Más que "a veces."

LISA: ¿Qué dices?

ESTEBAN: Pedro tiene cinturón negro. ¿Me permites…?

PEDRO: Está bien.

ESTEBAN: Mira. El cinturón negro.

ANGÉLICA: Pedro. Sí que eres muy talentoso. Felicidades.

PEDRO: Gracias.

LISA: De acuerdo. ¡Qué misterioso eres! ¿Tienes más secretos?

ANGÉLICA: Pues, vamos a clase. ¡Hasta luego!

TODOS: Adiós.

GramActiva Videos
Saber and *conocer*

HOST: I know the capital of Honduras. I know the name of the teddy bear you had as a child. And I know how many ants an anteater could eat if an anteater could eat ants. Which it can. I also know that in Spanish, there are two verbs that mean "to know."

HOST: These verbs are *saber* and *conocer*. Just as *ser* and *estar* both mean "to be," *saber* and *conocer* both mean "to know." And like *ser* and *estar*, each verb has specific situations that you use them in. Professor?

PROF. PEQUEÑO: Hola, soy profesor Pequeño, World's Smartest Baby. Use *saber* to say you know a fact or to say what you know how to do.
Sé todo.
Mi hermana sabe dar un discurso.

HOST: Use *conocer* to say you know or are familiar with a person, thing, or place. If you are saying you know a person, don't forget to use the personal *a*.

V.O.: *Conocen a mi amigo Raúl.*

ALIEN V.O.: *Conozco al presidente de los Estados Unidos.*

GUITAR HOST: *Saber* and *conocer* are irregular in their *yo* forms, but regular in all other forms. Here's the conjugation for *saber*.

V.O.: *Saber*
Sé. Sabes. Sabe. Sabemos. Sabéis. Saben.

GUITAR HOST: Now for the conjugation of *conocer*.

V.O.: *Conozco. Conoces. Conoce. Conocemos. Conocéis. Conocen.*

PERSON 1: Isabel, ¿de dónde eres?

PERSON 2: Soy de San Antonio.

PERSON 1: Conozco San Antonio. Mi hermano vive allí.

PERSON 2: Interesante. ¿Sabes inglés?

PERSON 1: No, no sé inglés. Mi hermano sabe inglés pero yo no.

Quiz

V.O.: All right! It's time for a quiz. *¿Saber o conocer?* Fill in the blank with the correct form of *saber* or *conocer*.
Yo _____ hacer gimnasia.
Yo sé hacer gimnasia.
María y Julie _____ al fotógrafo.
María y Julie conocen al fotógrafo.
¿_____ Ana la respuesta?
¿Sabe Ana la respuesta?

Making comparisons

BOY: I'm faster than you are.

GIRL: I agree you're faster, that is until you fall down.

BOY: Hey! In English we make comparisons every day without even thinking about it. The same thing goes for Spanish. So, let's get to learning about comparisons.

V.O.: You've already learned basic comparisons. *Más que,* "more than." And *menos que,* "less than."

V.O.: *Para mí, la biología es más difícil que la geometría.*

V.O.: *Creo que nadar es menos popular que correr.*

V.O.: Some commonly used comparisons are: *mayor que,* "older than;" *menor que,* "younger than;" *mejor que,* "better than;" and *peor que,* "worse than."
Ella es mayor que nosotros.
Somos menores que Ud.
Soy mejor que ustedes.

HOST: Now, if we're comparing two things that are the same, we can do it with: *tan + adjective + como.* Here's how to use it in a sentence.

V.O.: *Levantar pesas es tan divertido como correr.*

V.O.: Just insert the adjective in between *tan* and *como.* For instance, if Pedro is as hardworking as Susana, we'd say, *Pedro es tan trabajador como Susana.*

HOST: We use *tanto + noun + como* when making comparisons of equality with nouns. But don't forget that *tanto* agrees in gender and number with the noun that follows.

V.O.: For example, if we are saying, "Fish cost as much money as dogs," we would say, *Los peces cuestan tanto dinero como los perros.*
Now lets say, "She has as many dogs as Ana." *Tiene tantos perros como Ana.*

HOST: OK, guys, now it's time to show me what you've learned with a quiz.

Quiz

V.O.: Complete the sentences with *tan, tanto, tanta, tantos,* or *tantas.*
Pedro es _____ amable como Juan.
If you said *tan,* you're correct!
Alberto trabaja _____ rápidamente como ellos.
Tan. Kudos.
Imelda tiene _____ zapatos como ustedes.
That's right, it's *tantos.*
And last but not least:
Tú tienes _____ tarea como Eugenio.
Tanta. You got it.

Realidades 2

Capítulo 1B

Nombre

Fecha

Communicative Pair Activity **1B-1**

Estudiante **A**

Imagine that you are a student from the school newspaper who wants to know what Clara does for extracurricular activities every day of the week. Ask your partner the following questions. Record his or her answers in the spaces provided. Example: *Los lunes Clara toma lecciones de ballet.*

1. ¿Qué hace Clara los martes? _____

2. ¿Qué hace Clara los jueves por la tarde? _____

3. ¿Qué practica Clara los miércoles? _____

4. ¿Qué lecciones toma Clara los sábados? _____

5. ¿Qué hacen Clara y su amiga Camila los viernes? _____

Now imagine that your partner is the student writing about what extracurricular activities Pedro participates in during the week. Answer his or her questions based on the cues given. Example: *Pedro practica artes marciales los domingos.*

los lunes

los martes

los jueves

los sábados

los viernes

Realidades 2

Capítulo 1B

Nombre _____

Fecha _____

Communicative Pair Activity **1B-1**

Estudiante **B**

Imagine that your partner is the student writing about what extracurricular activities Clara participates in during the week. Answer his or her questions based on the cues given. Example: *Clara ensaya canciones los domingos.*

los martes   **los miércoles**   **los jueves**

los sábados   **los viernes**

Now imagine that you are a student from the school newspaper who wants to know what Pedro does for extracurricular activities every day of the week. Ask your partner the following questions. Record his or her answers in the spaces provided. Example: *Los miércoles Pedro va al club atlético.*

1. ¿Qué lecciones toma Pedro los martes? _____

2. ¿Qué practica Pedro los jueves? _____

3. ¿Qué hace Pedro los lunes? _____

4. ¿Qué hace Pedro los sábados? _____

5. ¿Qué hace Pedro los viernes por la tarde? _____

Realidades 2

Capítulo 1B

Nombre _____

Fecha _____

Communicative Pair Activity **1B-2**

Estudiante **A**

Your partner is very active in extracurricular activities. Interview him or her about how long it has been since he or she last did each activity below. Example: *¿Cuánto tiempo hace que participas en el coro?* Record your answers on the lines provided.

1. ¿Cuánto tiempo hace que tocas en la banda?

   _____

2. ¿Cuánto tiempo hace que visitas los salones de chat?

   _____

3. ¿Cuánto tiempo hace que juegas ajedrez?

   _____

4. ¿Cuánto tiempo hace que eres fotógrafo(a)?

   _____

5. ¿Cuánto tiempo hace que levantas pesas en el club atlético?

   _____

6. ¿Cuánto tiempo hace que tomas lecciones de baile?

   _____

Imagine that you are also very active in sports. Answer your partner's questions based on the information below. Write the answer under its corresponding illustration. Example: *Hace tres meses que participo en el coro.*

dos años

seis años

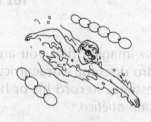
mucho tiempo

algunos meses

un año

cuatro años

Realidades 2

Capítulo 1B

Nombre

Fecha

Communicative Pair Activity **1B-2**

Estudiante **B**

Imagine that you are a student who is very active in extracurricular activities. Answer your partner's questions based on the information below. Write the answer under its corresponding illustration. Example: *Hace tres años que participo en el coro.*

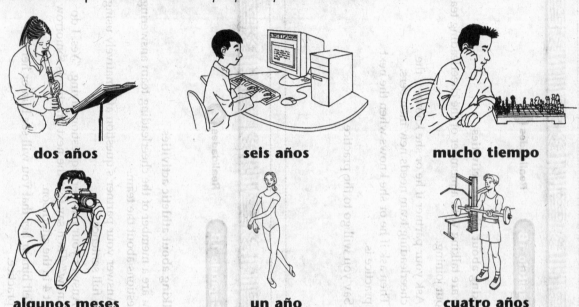

dos años   **seis años**   **mucho tiempo**

algunos meses   **un año**   **cuatro años**

Your partner is also very active in sports. Interview him or her about how long it has been since he or she last did each activity below. Example: *¿Cuánto tiempo hace que bailas?* Record your answers on the lines provided.

1. ¿Cuánto tiempo hace que juegas a los bolos?

_____

2. ¿Cuánto tiempo hace que practicas la gimnasia?

_____

3. ¿Cuánto tiempo hace que practicas la natación?

_____

4. ¿Cuánto tiempo hace que juegas al hockey?

_____

5. ¿Cuánto tiempo hace que practicas artes marciales?

_____

6. ¿Cuánto tiempo hace que levantas pesas en el club atlético?

_____

Talk!

Realidades 2

Capítulo 1B

Situation Cards

2A

Realidades 2

Capítulo 1B

Talking about athletic activities

You are talking with a member of the cheerleading team about joining.

— Ask your partner if he or she knows if the cheerleading team needs new members.

— Then ask if he or she knows when the next practice is.

— Say you will go to the practice.

© Pearson Education, Inc. All rights reserved.

2B

Realidades 2

Capítulo 1B

Talking about athletic activities

You are a member of the cheerleading team answering questions about the team.

— Answer your partner's question affirmatively using a full sentence.

— Answer your partner's question saying, "Yes. I do know." Then say that the next practice is tomorrow at 4 in the afternoon.

— Tell him or her that you will see him or her at practice.

© Pearson Education, Inc. All rights reserved.

1A

Realidades 2

Capítulo 1B

Talking about extracurricular activities and comparing people and things

You are talking with a music teacher in your school.

— Ask the music teacher if he or she knows if he can have more students in the student chorus.

— Answer his or her question saying that you've been singing for three years.

— Answer the music teacher's question saying that you play the piano. Ask if you can participate in both activities.

© Pearson Education, Inc. All rights reserved.

1B

Realidades 2

Capítulo 1B

Talking about extracurricular activities and comparing people and things

You are a music teacher talking with a student in your school.

— Respond to the student that you can have more students in the student chorus.

— Ask him or her how long has he or she been a singer.

— Ask him or her if he or she plays the piano.

— Answer the student's question affirmatively saying he or she can participate in both activities.

© Pearson Education, Inc. All rights reserved.

74 Capítulo 1B — Situation Cards

No lo sé.

No lo conozco.

Vocabulary Clip Art

Vocabulary Clip Art

Vocabulary Clip Art

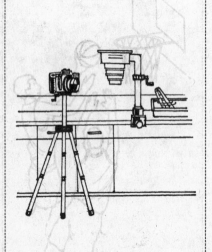

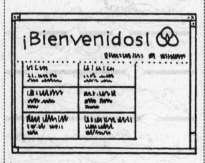

Vocabulary Clip Art

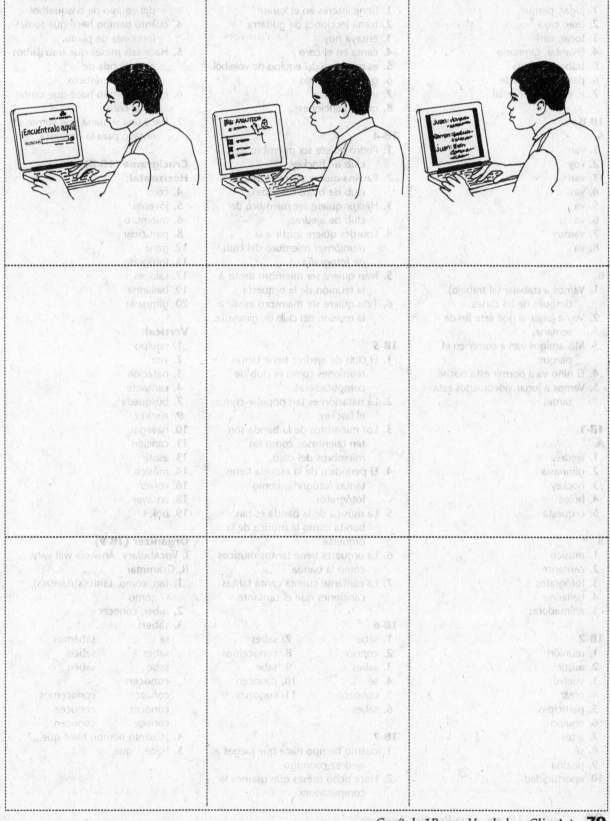

Core Practice Answers

1B–A
1. jugar, parque
2. usar, casa
3. tocar, café
4. levantar, gimnasio
5. trabajar, iglesia
6. pasar, restaurante
7. ir, centro comercial

1B-B
A.
1. van
2. voy
3. van
4. vas
5. va
6. va
7. vamos
8. va

B.
1. Vamos a trabajar (al trabajo) después de las clases.
2. Voy a jugar al golf este fin de semana.
3. Mis amigos van a correr en el parque.
4. El niño va a dormir esta noche.
5. Vamos a jugar videojuegos esta tarde.

1B-1
A.
1. ajedrez
2. gimnasia
3. hockey
4. bolos
5. orquesta

B.
1. músico
2. cantante
3. fotógrafos
4. bailarina
5. animadoras

1B-2
1. reunión
2. asistir
3. vuelvo
4. crear
5. participas
6. equipo
7. artes
8. sé
9. piscina
10. oportunidad

1B-3
1. tiene interés en el karate
2. toma lecciones de guitarra
3. ensaya hoy
4. canta en el coro
5. es miembro del equipo de vóleibol
6. gana un premio
7. vuelve a casa
8. graba canciones

1B-4
1. Pedro quiere ser miembro del club de hockey.
2. Paulina quiere ser miembro del club de bolos (boliche).
3. Héctor quiere ser miembro del club de ajedrez.
4. Lourdes quiere asistir a la reuniónser miembro del club de fotografía.
5. Iván quiere ser miembro asistir a la reunión de la orquesta.
6. Tina quiere ser miembro asistir a la reunión del club de gimnasia.

1B-5
1. El club de ajedrez tiene tantas reuniones como el club de computadoras.
2. La natación es tan popular como el hockey.
3. Los miembros de la banda son tan talentosos como los miembros del coro.
4. El periódico de la escuela tiene tantas fotógrafas como fotógrafos.
5. La música de la banda es tan bonita como la música de la orquesta.
6. La orquesta tiene tantos músicos como la banda.
7. La cantante cuenta canta tantas canciones que el cantante.

1B-6
1. sabe	7. sabes
2. conoce	8. conocemos
3. sabes	9. sabe
4. sé	10. conocen
5. conozco	11. conozco
6. sabes	

1B-7
1. cuánto tiempo hace que juegas al ajedrez conmigo
2. Hace ocho meses que usamos la computadora.

3. Hace un año que soy miembro del equipo de básquetbol.
4. cuánto tiempo hace que tomas lecciones de piano.
5. Hace seis meses que trabajamos en la tienda de electrodomésticos.
6. cuánto tiempo hace que cantas en el coro
7. Hace una semana que vamos al ensayo para la orquesta.

Crucigrama (1B-8)
Horizontal:
4. coro
5. jóvenes
6. miembro
8. participar
12. gana
15. fotógrafo
17. salones
19. bailarina
20. gimnasia

Vertical:
1. equipo
2. voz
3. natación
4. cantante
7. búsqueda
9. ajedrez
10. navegar
11. canción
13. asistir
14. músico
16. volver
18. ensayar
19. bolos

Organizer (1B-9)
I. Vocabulary Answers will vary.
II. Grammar
1. tan, como; tanto(s)/tanta(s), como
2. saber, conocer
3. saber:

sé	sabemos
sabes	sabéis
sabe	saben

conocer:

conozco	conocemos
conoces	conocéis
conoce	conocen

4. ¿Cuánto tiempo hace que...?
5. Hace... que...

The verb *ir* (p. 43)

• The verb **ir** is used to say where someone goes or is going.
  Voy a casa. *I'm going home.*
  Vamos al café. *We're going to the café.*
• Look at the forms of **ir** below:

yo	voy	nosotros/nosotras	vamos
tú	vas	vosotros/vosotras	vais
usted/él/ella	va	ustedes/ellos/ellas	van

A. Circle the correct form of the verb **ir** in each sentence. Follow the model.

Modelo Amalia (voy /**va**/ vamos) al gimnasio.

1. ¡Nosotros (van / **vamos**) al parque!
2. ¿A qué hora (**vas** / voy) tú a la biblioteca?
3. Mis padres (**van** / vas) a la piscina.
4. Yo (**voy** / van) al trabajo.
5. ¿Cuándo (voy / **va**) la familia al restaurante mexicano?

• To tell what someone is going to do, use **ir + a +** infinitive.
  Voy a ver una película. *I'm going to see a movie.*
  Vamos a estudiar esta tarde. *We are going to study this afternoon.*

B. Write the correct form of **ir + a** to tell what these people are going to do. Follow the model.

Modelo Jorge ___va___ *a* salir.

1. Ellas ___van___ *a* estudiar.
2. Yo ___voy___ *a* leer.
3. Marta ___va___ *a* nadar.
4. Tulio y Ana ___van___ *a* comer en un restaurante.
5. Chucho y yo ___vamos___ *a* comer.

realidades.com
• Web Code: jdd-0111

Write the Spanish vocabulary word or phrase below each picture. Be sure to include the article for each noun.

la cantante	el cantante	la banda
la orquesta	el músico	la música
grabar	la voz	la bailarina

Capítulo 1B ■ Guided Practice Answers **81**

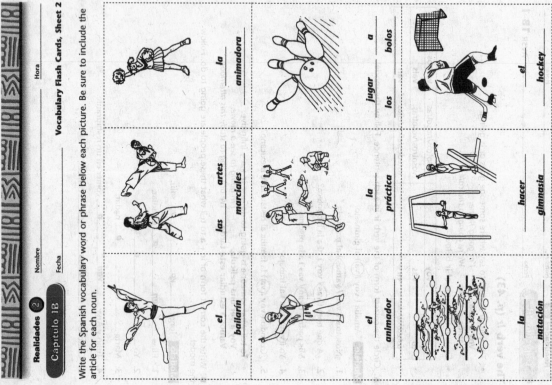

Realidades 2

Capítulo 1B

Nombre _____ Hora _____

Fecha _____ Vocabulary Flash Cards, Sheet 3

Write the Spanish vocabulary word or phrase below each picture. Be sure to include the article for each noun.

el fotógrafo

los jóvenes

la fotografía

crear una página Web

estar en línea

el ajedrez

la fotografía

hacer una búsqueda

visitar salones de chat

36 Guided Practice Activities — Vocabulary Flash Cards 1B

Realidades 2

Capítulo 1B

Nombre _____ Hora _____

Fecha _____ Vocabulary Flash Cards, Sheet 2

Write the Spanish vocabulary word or phrase below each picture. Be sure to include the article for each noun.

la animadora

jugar a los bolos

el hockey

las artes marciales

la práctica

hacer gimnasia

el bailarín

el animador

la natación

Guided Practice Activities — Vocabulary Flash Cards 1B **35**

Copy the word or phrase in the space provided. Be sure to include the article for each noun.

la canción	las actividades extracurriculares	navegar en la Red
la ___ canción	las ___ actividades extracurriculares	navegar ___ la ___ Red en
el club	el club atlético	el equipo
el ___ club	el ___ club atlético	el ___ equipo
ser miembro	el pasatiempo	la reunión
ser ___ miembro	el ___ pasatiempo	la ___ reunión

Copy the word or phrase in the space provided. Be sure to include the article for each noun.

el coro	ensayar	el ensayo
el ___ coro	___ ensayar	el ___ ensayo
asistir a	ganar	participar (en)
asistir ___ a	___ ganar	participar ___ (en)
tomar lecciones	volver	entre
tomar ___ lecciones	___ volver	___ entre

These blank cards can be used to write and practice other Spanish vocabulary for the chapter.

Copy the word or phrase in the space provided. Be sure to include the article for each noun.

el interés	la oportunidad	¿Cuánto tiempo hace que...?
el _____ interés	la _____ oportunidad	¿Cuánto _____ tiempo _____ hace _____ que...?

saber	conocer	el miembro
saber	conocer	el _____ miembro

Hace + time + que...	tantos, tantas + noun + como	tan + adj. + como
Hace + _____ time + _____ que...	tantos _____, tantas + _____ noun + _____ como	tan + _____ adj. + _____ como

Tear out this page. Write the Spanish words on the lines. Fold the paper along the dotted line to see the correct answers so you can check your work.

musician	*el músico, la música*
orchestra	*la orquesta*
team	*el equipo*
swimming	*la natación*
chess	*el ajedrez*
photography	*la fotografía*
to do a search	*hacer una búsqueda*
to be a member	*ser miembro*
to win, to earn	*ganar*
pastime	*el pasatiempo*
to participate (in)	*participar (en)*
meeting	*la reunión*
to return	*volver*
to attend	*asistir a*

- Fold In ↓

Tear out this page. Write the English words on the lines. Fold the paper along the dotted line to see the correct answers so you can check your work.

el músico, la música	*musician*
la orquesta	*orchestra*
el equipo	*team*
la natación	*swimming*
el ajedrez	*chess*
la fotografía	*photography*
hacer una búsqueda	*to do a search*
ser miembro	*to be a member*
ganar	*to win, to earn*
el pasatiempo	*pastime*
participar (en)	*to participate (in)*
la reunión	*meeting*
volver	*to return*
asistir a	*to attend*

- Fold In ↓

Realidades 2

Nombre _____ Hora _____

Capítulo 1B Fecha _____ **Vocabulary Check, Sheet 4**

Tear out this page. Write the Spanish words on the lines. Fold the paper along the dotted line to see the correct answers so you can check your work.

hockey	*el hockey*
to bowl	*jugar a los bolos*
to do gymnastics	*hacer gimnasia*
martial arts	*las artes marciales*
cheerleader	*el animador, la animadora*
practice	*la práctica*
young people	*los jóvenes*
club	*el club*
band	*la banda*
dancer	*el bailarín, la bailarina*
chorus, choir	*el coro*
to rehearse	*ensayar*
to take lessons	*tomar lecciones*
among, between	*entre*
interest	*el interés*

Fold In ↓

To hear a complete list of the vocabulary for this chapter, go to www.realidades.com and type in the Web Code jdd-0199. Then click on **Repaso del capítulo.**

Realidades 2

Nombre _____ Hora _____

Capítulo 1B Fecha _____ **Vocabulary Check, Sheet 3**

Tear out this page. Write the English words on the lines. Fold the paper along the dotted line to see the correct answers so you can check your work.

el hockey	*hockey*
jugar a los bolos	*to bowl*
hacer gimnasia	*to do gymnastics*
las artes marciales	*martial arts*
el animador, la animadora	*cheerleader*
la práctica	*practice*
los jóvenes	*young people*
el club	*club*
la banda	*band*
el bailarín, la bailarina	*dancer*
el coro	*chorus, choir*
ensayar	*to rehearse*
tomar lecciones	*to take lessons*
entre	*among, between*
el interés	*interest*

Fold In ↓

Realidades 2 — Capítulo 1B

Nombre _____ Hora _____

Fecha _____ **Guided Practice Activities 1B-1**

Making comparisons (p. 53)

- To say that people or things are equal to each other, use **tan** + adjective + **como**.
  El hockey es tan popular como la natación.
  Hockey is as popular as swimming.

- To say that people or things are not equal, use the negative verb form.
  El hockey no es tan popular como la natación.
  Hockey is not as popular as swimming.

A. Fill in the blank with **tan**, **como**, or **es** to correctly complete the sentences. Follow the model.

Modelo   El hockey es tan popular **como** la fotografía.

1. La banda es **tan** popular como la orquesta.

2. Jugar a los bolos no es tan popular **como** el ajedrez.

3. Hacer gimnasia **es** tan popular como las artes marciales.

4. Las animadoras no son **tan** populares como los miembros del equipo.

5. El bailarín no es tan popular **como** el cantante.

B. Each person thinks the activities below are equal. Complete their thoughts by filling in the correct form of **ser**, the comparative expression **tan...como**, and the adjective in parentheses. Follow the model.

Modelo   Yo creo que cantar **es** tan **divertido como** (divertido) bailar.

1. Creo que el ajedrez **es** tan **interesante como** (interesante) jugar a los bolos.

2. Yo creo que las dos actividades **son** tan **aburridas como** (aburridas) la fotografía.

3. Para mí el hockey **es** tan **emocionante como** (emocionante) bailar.

4. ¡Ay! Para mí, las actividades **son** tan **difíciles como** (difíciles) las clases de la escuela.

Realidades 2 — Capítulo 1B

Nombre _____ Hora _____

Fecha _____ **Guided Practice Activities 1B-2**

Making comparisons (continued)

- Use **tanto, -a** + noun + **como** to say "as much as":
  tanto interés como, *as much interest as*

- Use **tantos, -as** + noun + **como** to say "as many as":
  tantos jóvenes como, *as many young people as*

- Note that **tanto** also agrees in gender and number with the item that is being compared.
  Elena no hace tantas actividades extracurriculares como Juan.
  Elena doesn't do as many extracurricular activities as Juan.

C. Look at the following sentences and decide if the underlined word is masculine or feminine, singular or plural. Then, circle the correct form of **tanto** in parentheses. Follow the model.

Modelo   Yo asisto a ((tantas)/ tanta) reuniones como Elena.

1. Yo tengo (tantos /(tantas)) prácticas como mi hermano.

2. Juan toma ((tantas)/ tanta) lecciones de artes marciales como Carlos.

3. Elena tiene (tantas /(tantos)) pasatiempos como Angélica.

4. Camilo tiene ((tanto)/ tantos) interés en el hockey como Juan.

5. Hay ((tantas)/ tantos) bailarinas como bailarines.

D. Write the correct form of **tanto** (tanta/tantos/tantas) in the following phrases. Remember that **tanto** agrees in gender and number with the noun. Follow the model.

Modelo   Hay **tantos** chicos como chicas en el coro.

1. Hay **tantas** personas mayores como personas menores.

2. En la escuela hay **tantos** equipos de deportes como clubes.

3. Hay **tantos** profesores simpáticos como antipáticos.

4. Hago **tanto** trabajo como Javier.

5. La clase crea **tantas** páginas Web como los técnicos.

6. El hombre rico tiene **tantos** cuadros como un museo.

The verbs *saber* and *conocer* (p. 56)

• These are the present tense forms of **saber** and **conocer**.

yo	sé	nosotros/ nosotras	sabemos
tú	sabes	vosotros/ vosotras	sabéis
usted/ él/ella	sabe	ustedes/ ellos/ellas	saben

yo	conozco	nosotros/ nosotras	conocemos
tú	conoces	vosotros/ vosotras	conocéis
usted/ él/ella	conoce	ustedes/ ellos/ellas	conocen

A. Circle the correct form of the verb **saber** or **conocer**.

1. Mi amiga (**sabe**/ sabes) mucho del hockey.

2. Yo no (conoces /**conozco**) al cantante nuevo.

3. ¿Tú (**conoces** / conozco) a Juan?

4. ¿(Sabemos /**Saben**) ustedes cuándo son las reuniones del club?

5. Mi madre y yo (**conocemos**/ conocen) a un músico.

6. ¿(**Sabes** / Sabemos) tú mi número de teléfono?

• **Saber** means to know information and facts.

¿**Sabes** si tenemos una reunión mañana? *Do you know if we have a meeting tomorrow?*

• **Conocer** means to know a person or to be familiar with a place or thing. Use the *a personal* with **conocer** to say you know a person:

¿**Conocen** Uds. la música de Gloria Estefan? *Do you know/Are you familiar with the music of Gloria Estefan?*

¿**Conoces** a María? *Do you know María?*

B. Look at the following sentences. Decide if you would use the form of **conocer** or **saber** in parentheses. Circle your choice. Follow the model.

Modelo Julián ——— la orquesta de San Francisco. a.(conoce) b. sabe

1. ¿ ——— tú el equipo profesional de fútbol en tu ciudad? a. Sabes b.(Conoces)

2. La abuela ——— navegar en la Red. a.(sabe) b. conoce

3. Nosotros ——— la ciudad de Boston. a. sabemos b.(conocemos)

4. ¿ ——— Uds. que el equipo ganó el partido? a.(Saben) b. Conocen

5. Mis amigos y yo ——— jugar a los bolos. a. conocemos b.(sabemos)

The verbs *saber* and *conocer* (continued)

• Use the verb **saber** + *infinitive of another verb* to say that you know how to do something:

Sabemos hacer gimnasia. *We know how to do gymnastics.*

C. Look at the pictures below. Complete the answers with the verb form of **saber** and the infinitive of another verb. Follow the model.

Modelo Kiko y Roberto **saben** *patinar*.

1. Andrés ___*sabe*___ ___*jugar*___ a los bolos.

2.  Sara y Rebeca ___*saben*___ ___*hacer*___ gimnasia.

3. Yo ___*sé*___ ___*tocar*___ la guitarra.

4. ¿Tú no ___*sabes*___ ___*grabar*___ un disco?

D. Read the following sentences and decide whether **saber** or **conocer** should be used. Write an **S** for **saber** and a **C** for **conocer** in the first space. Then, write the form of the verb you chose to complete the sentence. The first one is done for you.

1. ___S___ Yo ___*sé*___ jugar a los bolos.

2. ___C___ Ellos no ___*conocen*___ al profesor de música.

3. ___S___ Él no ___*sabe*___ visitar salones de chat.

4. ___S___ Mis amigos y yo ___*sabemos*___ hacer una búsqueda en la Red.

5. ___C___ Nosotros no ___*conocemos*___ el club de ajedrez.

Left Page

Hace + time expressions (p. 58)

• When you want to ask how long something has been going on, you use **¿Cuánto tiempo + hace que + present-tense verb?** For example,

¿Cuánto tiempo hace que eres miembro del coro?
How long have you been a member of the choir?

A. Look at the sentences using **¿Cuánto tiempo + hace que...?** and write in the word that is missing from the sentence. Follow the model.

Modelo   ¿Cuánto tiempo hace _____**que**_____ ustedes ensayan con el club de música?

1. ¿Cuánto _____**tiempo**_____ hace que tú no asistes a las reuniones del club?

2. ¿Cuánto tiempo _____**hace**_____ que Juana toma lecciones de fotografía?

3. ¿Cuánto _____**tiempo**_____ hace que tus padres no vuelven a casa?

4. ¿_____**Cuánto**_____ tiempo hace que nosotros no hacemos gimnasia?

5. ¿Cuánto tiempo hace _____**que**_____ Paco no toca el saxofón?

• When you want to tell how long something has been going on, you use **hace + period of time + que + present-tense verb.** For example,

Hace cuatro meses que soy miembro del club atlético.
I have been a member of the athletic team for four months.

B. Complete the following answers using the present tense of the verb in parentheses. Follow the model.

Modelo   Hace tres días que nosotros _____**ensayamos**_____ (ensayar) con el club de música.

1. Hace un mes que ustedes no _____**vuelven**_____ (volver) al club atlético.

2. Hace dos años que Juana _____**toma**_____ (tomar) lecciones de fotografía.

3. Hace ocho semanas que tú no _____**asistes**_____ (asistir) a las reuniones del club.

4. Hace cinco años que Elena y yo no _____**bailamos**_____ (bailar).

5. Hace diez meses que Tomás no _____**va**_____ (ir) a Cancún.

Right Page

Hace + time expressions (continued)

C. Read the following questions and answer with the information provided in parentheses and the present tense of the verb. Follow the model.

Modelo   ¿Cuánto tiempo hace que tú participas en la natación? (dos meses)
Hace _____**dos**_____ _____**meses**_____ que yo _____**participo**_____ en la natación.

1. ¿Cuánto tiempo hace que Carlos juega en el equipo? (un año)
Hace _____**un**_____ _____**año**_____ que Carlos _____**juega**_____ en el equipo.

2. ¿Cuánto tiempo hace que ustedes navegan en la Red? (cinco semanas)
Hace _____**cinco**_____ _____**semanas**_____ que nosotros _____**navegamos**_____ en la Red.

3. ¿Cuánto tiempo hace que tú grabas música? (cuatro horas)
Hace _____**cuatro**_____ _____**horas**_____ que yo _____**grabo**_____ música.

4. ¿Cuánto tiempo hace que tu hermana visita salones de chat? (diez días)
Hace _____**diez**_____ _____**días**_____ que mi hermana _____**visita**_____ salones de chat.

5. ¿Cuánto tiempo hace que tú y Mariana trabajan en el café? (seis meses)
Hace _____**seis**_____ _____**meses**_____ que nosotras _____**trabajamos**_____ en el café.

6. ¿Cuánto tiempo hace que Jorge y Ana hablan por teléfono? (cuarenta minutos)
Hace _____**cuarenta**_____ _____**minutos**_____ que ellos _____**hablan**_____ por teléfono.

Left Panel (1B-5)

Lectura: ¡A bailar! (pp. 62-63)

A. The reading in your textbook is about a dance school. Here you will find information about the many dance classes at this school. What kind of information do you expect to find about each class? Some information has already been provided.

1. Tango: _____the cost of each class_____ **Answers will vary.**

2. Merengue: _____

3. Flamenco: _____

4. Swing: _____

B. Read the following schedule from the reading in your textbook. Then, answer the questions that follow.

Cursos	Día y hora
Tango	lunes 17.30h a 18.30h
Merengue	martes 17.00h a 18.00h

1. What course does the school teach on Tuesdays? _____**Merengue**_____

2. At what time does the tango course begin? _____**17.30**_____

C. Read the following class descriptions from the schedule in the reading. Then, look at the sentences that follow and write **L** (for **Lectura**) if the sentence tells about something you read. Write **N** (for **No**) if the sentence tells something you didn't read.

Swing
Baila toda la noche con tu pareja este baile muy popular de los Estados Unidos.

Tango
Ven a aprender este baile romántico de Argentina que se hizo famoso por las composiciones musicales de Gardel y de Piazzolla.

1. El tango es el baile tradicional de Argentina. __**L**__

2. El swing es un baile popular en los Estados Unidos. __**L**__

3. El tango es un baile romántico de Andalucía. __**N**__

4. El swing se baila con una pareja. __**L**__

realidades.com
• Web Code jdf-0117

Right Panel (1B-6)

Presentación escrita (p. 65) *Answers will vary.*

Task: Your school offers many extracurricular activities. Your teacher wants you to write about the activities you like and why you like them.

❶ **Prewrite.** Look at the following activities and circle the ones that you like to do.

jugar al béisbol	usar una computadora	jugar al ajedrez
sacar fotos	jugar a los bolos	tocar la guitarra
leer libros	hacer gimnasia	cantar en el coro

❷ **Draft.** Complete the sentences below using some of your answers from **part 1**. Tell why you like those activities, and how long you have been doing them.

1. Me llamo _____ y tengo _____ años.

2. Me gustaría _____ y _____

3. Me gustan estas actividades porque _____

4. Hace _____ que _____

❸ **Revise.** Use the completed sentences from **part 2** to help you write a paragraph. Then, read and check your paragraph by asking the following questions:

- Does my paragraph list two activities?
- Does my paragraph describe the activities?
- Does my paragraph explain why I like these activities?

❹ **Evaluation.** Your teacher may give you a rubric for how the paragraph will be graded. You will probably be graded on:

- how much information you provide about yourself
- use of vocabulary
- accuracy and use of the writing process

VIDEO

Antes de ver el video

Actividad 1

What extracurricular activities are there in your high school? When does each activity take place? Name at least five activities in your school and their schedules. Follow the model.

Actividades extracurriculares	El horario
club de español	De las tres y media a las cuatro y media de la tarde, todos los lunes
Answers will vary.	

¿Comprendes?

Actividad 2

Put the following scenes in the order in which they occur in the video. Write **1** under the first scene and **7** under the last scene.

_1_   _2_

_3_   _4_   _5_

_6_   _7_

VIDEO

Actividad 3

Read the following descriptions of the students in the video. Then, write the name of the student being described in the space provided.

1. Es miembro del club de computadoras. _Esteban_

2. Trabaja después de las clases. _Pedro_

3. Le encanta el primer día de clases. _Angélica_

4. Es miembro del coro y de la orquesta. _Lisa_

5. Es deportista. _Angélica_

6. Es talentosa. _Lisa_

7. Tiene computadora portátil. _Esteban_

8. Según Lisa es misterioso. _Pedro_

9. Toma lecciones de artes marciales en un club atlético. _Pedro_

10. Quiere ser miembro del equipo de natación en el invierno. _Angélica_

Y, ¿qué más?

Actividad 4

Look again at the six extracurricular activities from **Actividad 1**. Survey your class to find out how many students participate in each activity. Then, record your findings in the table below. The first one is done for you.

Actividades extracurriculares	¿Cuántos estudiantes?
club de español	Hay seis muchachos en el club de español.
Answers will vary.	

Realidades 2

Capítulo 1B

Nombre _____

Hora _____

Fecha _____

AUDIO

Actividad 7

Although they are best friends, Ana and Elisa are very competitive with each other. Listen as each girl tries to convince the other that her boyfriend (**novio**) is as wonderful as the other girl's boyfriend! Write the letter of the picture that corresponds to each part of the conversation. You will hear each part of the conversation twice.

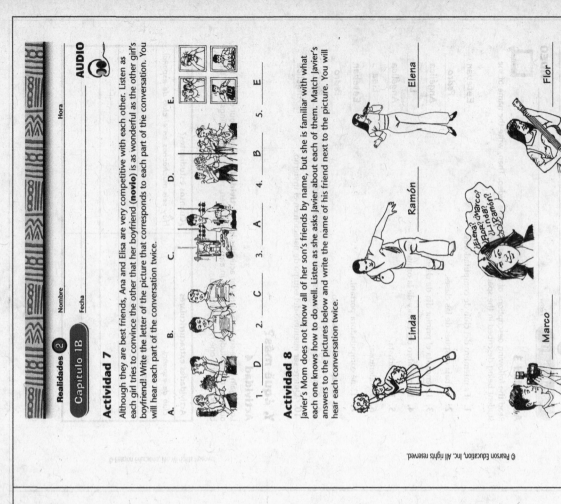

A.   B.   C.   D.   E.

1. __D__   2. __C__   3. __A__   4. __B__   5. __E__

Actividad 8

Javier's Mom does not know all of her son's friends by name, but she is familiar with what each one knows how to do well. Listen as she asks Javier about each of them. Match Javier's answers to the pictures below and write the name of his friend next to the picture. You will hear each conversation twice.

Linda _____   Ramón _____   Elena _____

Marco _____   Flor _____

Realidades 2

Capítulo 1B

Nombre _____

Hora _____

Fecha _____

AUDIO

Actividad 5

As part of freshman orientation, students can go to the **Feria de clubes** to find the perfect club or activity for them. Write the number of the conversation next to the name of the corresponding club or activity that is being discussed by the two people. You will hear each conversation twice.

El club de ajedrez	3	El club de arte	1
El club de artes marciales	6	El coro	7
El club de baile	8	El club de fotografía	5
La orquesta	2	El club de computadoras	4

Actividad 6

What do Lorena and her friends do after school? Listen to the conversations they are having at lunch and place the number of each conversation in the grid under the corresponding picture. You will hear each conversation twice.

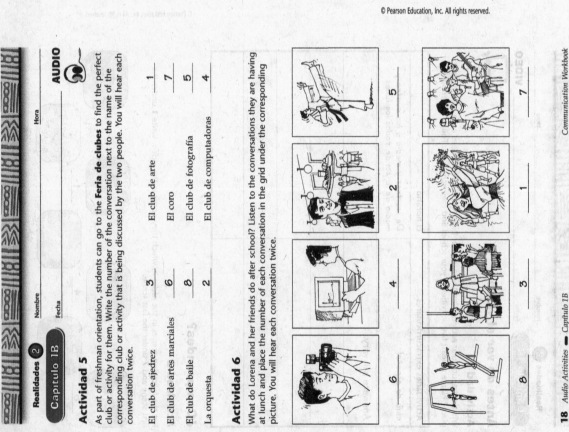

6   4   3   8

5   2   1   7

Actividad 9

We all know the expression "practice makes perfect." Listen as high school seniors are interviewed by a Hispanic radio station about the scholarships (**becas**) they received for their outstanding achievements in their extracurricular activities. Complete each sentence by writing the amount of time each of them has been involved with his or her particular interest. You will hear each interview twice.

1. Hace _____ **diez años** _____ que toma lecciones de piano.

2. Hace _____ **dos años** _____ que escribe para el periódico de la escuela.

3. Hace _____ **ocho años** _____ que hace gimnasia.

4. Hace _____ **quince años** _____ que canta en el coro.

5. Hace _____ **seis meses** _____ que participa en las artes marciales.

6. Hace _____ **cuatro años** _____ que crea páginas Web.

7. Hace _____ **siete años** _____ que toca el violín en la orquesta.

Actividad 10

It's time to submit biographies for the school yearbook. Answer the questions below based on the pictures, writing a complete sentence in response to each question.

1. ¿De qué club es miembro Rosa?

   Es miembro del club de fotografía.

   ¿A qué ensayo necesita asistir esta tarde?

   Necesita asistir al ensayo de la orquesta.

2. ¿A qué juegan Marcos y Jorge?

   Marcos y Jorge juegan al ajedrez.

   ¿En qué deporte participa Jorge también? ¿Y Marcos?

   Jorge participa en el fútbol. Marcos participa en las artes marciales.

3. ¿Qué deporte le gusta a Mariela?

   A Mariela le gusta la natación.

   ¿Qué más le gusta hacer?

   También le gusta cantar.

4. ¿Y tú? ¿En qué deportes o clubes participas?

   Answers will vary.

   ¿Qué te gusta hacer?

   Answers will vary.

Actividad 12

Imagine that you are preparing questions for a Spanish-language game show. You are given topics and must produce two logical and grammatically correct questions about each topic: one using the present tense of the verb **saber** and one using the present tense of the verb **conocer**. Use the model to help you write your questions.

Modelo   el alfabeto
¿ _Sabes las letras del alfabeto en español_ ?
¿ _Conoces el alfabeto español_ ?

1. Madrid   ¿ Answers will vary. _____ ?
   ¿ _____ ?

2. el ajedrez   ¿ _____ ?
   ¿ _____ ?

3. la natación   ¿ _____ ?
   ¿ _____ ?

4. el libro *Don Quijote de la Mancha*   ¿ _____ ?
   ¿ _____ ?

5. la música latina   ¿ _____ ?
   ¿ _____ ?

6. la fotografía   ¿ _____ ?
   ¿ _____ ?

7. las reglas de tu escuela   ¿ _____ ?
   ¿ _____ ?

Actividad 11

You are comparing all of the after-school clubs that you are thinking about joining. Look at their fliers below and write sentences comparing the clubs to each other. The first one has been done for you.

CLUB DE ESPAÑOL	**CLUB DE FOTOGRAFÍA**	**CLUB DE AJEDREZ**
Hay: –27 miembros –20 reuniones al año –más de 8 actividades al año	*Hay:* –16 miembros –14 reuniones al año –8 actividades cada año	*Hay:* –16 miembros –20 reuniones al año –8 actividades cada año
Es: –un club educativo –un club para todos	*Es:* –un club recreativo –un club para todos	*Es:* –un club recreativo –sólo para personas inteligentes
Cuesta: –12 dólares al año	*Cuesta:* –20 dólares al año	*Cuesta:* –12 dólares al año

Answers are in no particular order.

1. _El club de ajedrez es tan popular como el club de fotografía._

2. El club de español cuesta tanto dinero como el club de ajedrez.

3. El club de ajedrez es tan recreativo como el club de fotografía.

4. El club de español es para tantas personas como el club de fotografía.

5. El club de español tiene tantas reuniones como el club de ajedrez.

6. El club de fotografía tiene tantas actividades como el club de ajedrez.

7. El club de fotografía tiene tantos miembros como el club de ajedrez.

Reading Skills
214 2. B
215 2. C

Integrated Performance
Assessment
216
Answers will vary.

Practice Test: ¿Por qué está tan
nervioso?
218

1. B
2. H
3. A
4. C
5. Las respuestas variarán pero
deben incluir: son simpáticos y
sociables; son deportistas y les
gusta participar en toda clase de
actividades.
6. Las respuestas variarán pero
pueden incluir:
• ir a la reunión para nuevos
estudiantes.
• poner todo lo que necesito en
mi mochila.
• preparar mi almuerzo o llevar
dinero para comprarlo.
• decidir qué ropa voy a llevar.
• salir de casa temprano.
• llegar al autobús a tiempo.
• aprender de memoria el
horario de todas mis clases.
• prestar atención a lo que dicen
mis profesores.
• ir rápidamente de una clase a
otra.
• saber abrir mi armario.
• llevar el carnet de identidad.
• llevar los materiales a las clases.
• respetar a los demás.

Realidades ②

Capítulo 1B

Nombre _____ Hora _____

Fecha _____

WRITING

Actividad 13

A. Imagine that you are preparing to interview the busiest student in your school, Alfonso, to find out how long he has been participating in all of his activities. Below is a list of things he does during the week. Write the six questions you are going to ask him. Follow the model.

soy miembro del club de ajedrez   participo en la natación

hago gimnasia   tomo lecciones de artes marciales

ensayo con la orquesta   juego a los bolos

asisto a las reuniones del club de fotografía

Modelo   ¿Cuánto tiempo hace que juegas a los bolos?

1. ¿ _____ Answers will vary. _____

2. ¿ _____ ?

3. ¿ _____ ?

4. ¿ _____ ?

5. ¿ _____ ?

6. ¿ _____ ?

B. Now, write a paragraph about at least three activities you participate in and say how long you have been doing each of them. Supply at least two additional details about each activity. Follow the model.

Modelo   Hace tres años que juego a los bolos. Juego con mi papá los sábados y siempre gano.

Answers will vary.

_____

_____

_____

_____

_____

_____

Test Preparation Answers

Reading Skills
p. 214   2. **B**
p. 215   2. **C**

**Integrated Performance
    Assessment**
p. 216
Answers will vary.

**Practice Test: ¿Por qué está tan
    nervioso?**
p. 218

1. B
2. H
3. A
4. G
5. Las respuestas variarán pero
   deben incluir: son simpáticos y
   sociables; son deportistas y les
   gusta participar en toda clase de
   actividades.
6. Las respuestas variarán pero
   pueden incluir:
   • ir a la reunión para nuevos
     estudiantes
   • poner todo lo que necesito en
     mi mochila
   • preparar mi almuerzo o llevar
     dinero para comprarlo
   • decidir qué ropa voy a llevar
   • salir de casa temprano
   • llegar al autobús a tiempo
   • aprender de memoria el
     horario de todas mis clases
   • prestar atención a lo que dicen
     mis profesores
   • ir rápidamente de una clase a
     otra
   • saber abrir mi armario
   • llevar el carnet de identidad
   • llevar los materiales a las clases
   • respetar a los demás

Realidades 2

Tema 2

Table of Contents

Tema 2: Un evento especial
Capítulo 2A: ¿Cómo te preparas?

Capítulo 2B: ¿Qué ropa compraste?

Realidades 2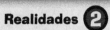

Tema 2

Theme Project

Un evento especial
Revista de moda

Overview:

You will create a spread from a fashion magazine featuring photos of people in fashionable clothing. You will write sentences using the preterite about what each person in the photo did to get ready, what clothing they bought, and where they went in their new outfits. Then you will present your magazine spread to the class.

Resources:

Electronic or print photos, image editing and page layout software and/or construction paper, markers, magazines, glue or tape, scissors

Sequence:

STEP 1. Review instructions with your teacher.

STEP 2. Submit a rough sketch of your fashion spread. Work with a partner and present your drafts to each other.

STEP 3. Create layouts, leaving room for photos and descriptions.

STEP 4. Submit a draft of the layout.

STEP 5. Present your fashion spread to the class, explaining each part and describing selected pictures.

Assessment:

Your teacher provide you with a rubric to assess this project.

Theme 2 Project: Revista de moda

Project Assessment Rubric

RUBRIC	Score 1	Score 3	Score 5
Evidence of Planning	No written draft or sketch provided.	Draft was written and layout created, but not corrected.	Evidence of corrected draft and layout.
Use of Illustrations	No photos/visuals included.	Very few photos/visuals included.	Several photos/visuals included.
Presentation	Contains details that develop ideas about clothing.	Describes at least three photos, including clothing, destination, and preparations.	Describes three or more photos, including clothing, destination, and preparations.

21st Century Skills Rubric: Develop Media Literacy

RUBRIC	Score 1	Score 3	Score 5
Reviews and references magazines (print or online)	Reviews and references up to two magazines	Reviews and references three or four magazines	Reviews and references at least five magazines
Creates list of ideas from research	Creates a list of three or fewer ideas	Creates a list of four to six ideas	Creates a list of seven or more ideas
Explains reasons for including ideas on list	Provides explanation for some of the ideas	Provides explanation for most of the ideas	Provides explanation for all of the ideas

School-to-Home Connection

Dear Parent or Guardian,

The theme of our current unit is *Un evento especial* (A special event). This chapter is called *¿Cómo te preparas?* (How do you get ready?).

Upon completion of this chapter students will be able to:
- describe getting ready for a special event
- talk about daily routines, people, and things
- express possession
- understand cultural perspectives on clothing

Students will also explore:
- consonants that change their sound

Our textbook, *Realidades,* helps with the development of reading, writing, and speaking skills through the use of strategies, process speaking, and process writing. In this chapter, students will:
- read about the *Teatro Colón* and its programs
- speak about special events in your community

To reinforce and enhance learning, students can access a wide range of online resources on **realidades.com**, the personalized learning management system that accompanies the print and online Student Edition. Resources include the eText, textbook and workbook activities, audio files, videos, animations, songs, self-study tools, interactive maps, voice recording (RealTalk!), assessments, and other digital resources. Many learning tools can be accessed through the student Home Page on **realidades.com**. Other activities, specifically those that require grading, are assigned by the teacher and linked on the student Home Page within the calendar or the Assignments tab.

You will find specifications and guidelines for accessing **realidades.com** on home computers and mobile devices on MyPearsonTraining.com under the SuccessNet Plus tab.

For: Tips to Parents
Visit: www.realidades.com
Web Code: jce-0010

Check it out! At the end of the chapter, have your child use the new vocabulary from this chapter to explain his or her daily routine when getting ready in the morning.

Sincerely,

Videocultura Script

La piñata

Spanish version:

En México y en algunos países de América Central y América de Sur, las fiestas de cumpleaños tienen una piñata.

La piñata se hace de barro y papel maché. Tienen la forma de un animal, o un objeto, como este balón de fútbol que vemos aquí. Las piñatas llevan dulces, caramelos y pequeños juguetes por dentro.

En la fiesta, la piñata se cuelga, y los niños le pegan con un palo hasta romperla, para que los caramelos caigan al suelo.

Se cree que Marco Polo trajo la piñata de China a Italia en los años 1200. Muchos años después las piñatas fueron traídas a las Américas por los españoles.

La tradición de romper la piñata se ha extendido por muchos países de Latinoamérica, y le agregan mucha diversión a cualquier fiesta.

English version:

In Mexico and some places in Latin America, the piñata is part of celebrating special occasions such as a birthday.

Piñatas come in a variety of shapes and colors. The traditional shape is a six-pointed star. Today families choose from piñatas that look like animals, clowns, numbers, soccer balls, and TV characters.

A piñata is made by building a papier-maché form around a clay container. The form is decorated with brightly colored tissue and crepe paper.

When completed, the piñata is filled with candy or small toys.

At the party, the piñata is hung from the ceiling or a tree. The children are blindfolded and try to hit the piñata with a stick with hopes of breaking it open. When it cracks and the goodies fall to the ground, all the children scramble to get their share.

It is generally believed that the piñata originated in China and was brought to Europe by Marco Polo in the late 1200s. Piñatas were brought to the Americas by the Spanish several centuries later.

In addition to their colorful decoration, piñatas add an exciting element to parties and celebrations!

Input Script

Presentation

Input Vocabulary: Before class, hang a sheet or place some kind of screen in the classroom and place a nice suit, a washbowl, bottle of water, mouthwash, comb, hairbrush, toothpaste, and toothbrush behind it. Come to class dressed very casually, perhaps wearing sweatpants and a T-shirt. Have your hair somewhat untidy and act as if you just woke up. Take out a calendar or a day planner and announce to the class in a shocked voice: *¡Uy! ¡Se me olvidó que hoy es el día de mi evaluación con el Señor (la Señora) _____* (the name of your school principal)!

Distribute copies of the Vocabulary Clip Art and have students cut them into individual pieces. Tell them to hold the images up as they hear you describe the actions and objects. Place the transparency showing Antonio's grooming activities on the screen. Point to the images as you explain that you woke up late and didn't have time to take a shower or a bath or any of the other grooming activities shown in the transparency.

Then, in a panic, carry out the following activities while explaining what you are doing: Rush behind the screen and put on the suit jacket. Step out from behind the screen while brushing or combing your hair. Bring out the washbowl, mouthwash, toothpaste, and toothbrush. Act as though you were brushing your teeth and using mouthwash. When you have finished, place the transparency showing the girls discussing preparations for a date on the screen. Present the transparency in a very formal manner, as though you were already being watched by the principal. Look at your watch nervously from time to time, and even go to the door and look down the hall for the principal. Finally, pick up the calendar and announce that you were wrong: Your evaluation is for next week! Or, if possible, arrange for your principal to actually pay you a visit during this lesson!

Input Monologue 1 and Dialogue 2: Have the boys and girls form two separate groups. Give them time to choose a student to act out the actions shown in the images while the rest of the group reads Rafael's monologue or the dialogue between the two girls. As the boys present the monologue, have the girls hold up the Clip Art images of the objects and actions. Have the boys hold up the Clip Art images when the girls present the dialogue.

After they have presented the monologue and dialogue, reinforce the expression *pedir prestados* by asking students if you can borrow different items. Make some of the items ones they would be likely to lend (their textbook) and ones that they would not be likely to lend (their toothbrush). Have them respond with *¡Por supuesto!* or *¡Lo siento, pero no!*

Comprehension Check

- Describe getting ready for three different special events. Have students arrange the Clip Art images of grooming activities on their desks in the order that you mention them.

- Place props to represent the different grooming activities on a table at the front of the classroom. Name an activity and have a volunteer hold up the correct prop for that activity.

Audio Script

Audio DVD, Capítulo 2A

Track 01: *A primera vista, ¿Cómo te preparas?*, Student Book, p. 74

Vocabulario y gramática en contexto

Lee en tu libro mientras escuchas la narración.

TEEN MALE: ¡Hola! Me llamo Antonio. ¿Qué hago yo antes de ir a un evento especial? Siempre me despierto temprano y me levanto de la cama. Primero me ducho lentamente—generalmente estoy en la ducha unos veinte minutos. Después de ducharme, me afeito… y me cepillo los dientes. Luego me seco el pelo con el secador y me arreglo el pelo con el peine. Después me pongo el desodorante y el agua de colonia y me visto.

Vas a escuchar cada palabra o frase dos veces. Después de la primera vez hay una pausa para que puedas pronunciar la palabra o frase. Luego vas a escuchar de nuevo la palabra o frase.

despertarse	afeitarse
la ducha	cepillarse los dientes
ducharse	arreglarse el pelo
la toalla	secarse
el desodorante	el secador
el agua de colonia	ponerse
el cepillo	vestirse
el peine	

Más vocabulario

Vas a escuchar cada palabra o frase dos veces. Después de la primera vez hay una pausa para que puedas pronunciar la palabra o frase. Luego vas a escuchar de nuevo la palabra o frase.

la audición	el concurso
la boda	por ejemplo

Track 02: *A primera vista*, Student Book, p. 75

Vocabulario y gramática en contexto

Lee en tu libro mientras escuchas el diálogo.

TEEN FEMALE 1: Tengo una cita con Rafael. ¡Vamos a un baile elegante!

TEEN FEMALE 2: Debes estar muy entusiasmada. ¿Qué vas a hacer para prepararte?

TEEN FEMALE 1: Primero, me baño… Luego me pinto las uñas. No puedo cortarme el pelo. Por eso quiero ir al salón de belleza.

TEEN FEMALE 2: ¿Puedo pedirte prestados tus aretes?

TEEN FEMALE 1: ¿De oro o de plata?

TEEN FEMALE 2: Depende… prefiero los aretes de plata.

NARRATOR: Después del baile…

TEEN FEMALE 1: Ahora tengo mucho sueño. Voy a lavarme la cara y acostarme. ¡Hasta mañana!

Vas a escuchar cada palabra o frase dos veces. Después de la primera vez hay una pausa para que puedas pronunciar la palabra o frase. Luego vas a escuchar de nuevo la palabra o frase.

pintarse las uñas	las joyas
cortarse el pelo	de oro
bañarse	de plata
el cinturón	lavarse la cara

Track 03: *A primera vista*, Act. 1, Student Book, p. 75

¿Qué haces por la mañana?

Vas a escuchar siete frases que describen qué hace alguien por la mañana. Representa cada una de estas acciones sin hablar. Vas a escuchar las frases dos veces.

1. Me levanto a las ocho.
2. Primero, me afeito.
3. Después me ducho.
4. Me pongo desodorante.
5. Me cepillo los dientes.
6. Me arreglo el pelo.
7. Me visto.

Track 04: *A primera vista*, Act. 2, Student Book, p. 75

¿Lógica o no?

Vas a escuchar siete frases. Algunas son lógicas y otras no. Señala con el pulgar hacia arriba si la frase es lógica y con el pulgar hacia abajo si no es lógica. Vas a escuchar las frases dos veces.

1. Me levanto antes de despertarme.
2. Me pongo los aretes en los pies.
3. Me seco el pelo con el secador.
4. Me lavo con el peine.
5. Me visto después de bañarme.
6. Me cepillo los dientes todos los días.
7. Me pongo el desodorante antes de bañarme.

Track 05: *A primera vista*, Videohistoria, Student Book, pp. 76–77

¿Más maquillaje?

¿Qué emergencia tiene Gloria? ¿Cómo se arreglan Raúl y Tomás? Lee la historia para saber.

Lee en tu libro mientras escuchas la *Videohistoria*.

See Student Book pages 76–77 for script.

Track 06: Audio Act. 5, Writing, Audio & Video Workbook, p. 28

Listen as a very frustrated mother tries to get her two teenage children, Luis y Catrina, out of the house on time to get to school. Each one gives her excuse after excuse. Look at the pictures below and match the number of the excuse you hear to each drawing. Write the number of the excuse on the line under the picture. You will hear each conversation twice.

1. **MADRE:** ¿Luis, qué haces? Son las siete ya.
   LUIS: Un minuto. Me arreglo el pelo. Ya voy.

2. **MADRE:** ¿Catrina, qué haces tú? ¿Catrina?
   CATRINA: Me ducho, mamá.
3. **MADRE:** Luis, son las siete y cinco. Tienes que salir para la escuela.
   LUIS: Me visto. ¿Sabes dónde está mi camiseta?
4. **MADRE:** ¡Catrina, vas a llegar tarde a tu cita con tu profesor en la escuela! ¿Qué haces?
   CATRINA: Me seco el pelo, mamá. ¡Un momento más!
5. **MADRE:** ¡Luis, tienes que afeitarte y no tienes mucho tiempo!
   LUIS: Muy bien, mamá. Me afeito en un momento.
6. **MADRE:** ¿Quieres un café con leche con tu desayuno?
   CATRINA: No, gracias mamá. No tengo tiempo y acabo de cepillarme los dientes.

Track 07: Audio Act. 6, Writing, Audio & Video Workbook, p. 28

Listen to people talking about an upcoming event in their lives. Based on the conversations, decide what event each person is getting ready for. Place a check mark in one box in each person's row. You will hear each set of statements twice.

TEEN MALE 1: Hola. Soy yo, Chucho. Sí, sí. Estoy un poco nervioso. Como tú sabes, no la conozco bien. Es una amiga de mi prima. Vamos a una película de acción. ¿Cómo? Ah, sí. Tienes razón. Una película romántica es mejor. Bueno. Solamente tengo una media hora para hacer muchas cosas: ducharme, peinarme y vestirme… ¿Cómo? Llevo jeans y una camisa blanca. Adiós.

TEEN FEMALE 1: Hola… habla Gloria. Sí, estoy muy entusiasmada. ¡Mañana mi hermana va a la iglesia para el día más romántico de su vida! ¿Yo? Me visto con un vestido muy elegante y me pongo una colonia muy especial. Voy a pedir prestados los aretes de mi mamá.

TEEN MALE 2: Hola. Soy Gabriel. ¡Claro, me encanta el básquetbol! Yo estoy en el equipo de la escuela. Soy el capitán. ¿Cómo? Mi equipo favorito son los Lakers. Voy a verlos mañana a las dos. Tenemos unos boletos muy buenos. ¡Estoy muy contento porque es el equipo número uno ahora!

TEEN MALE 3: ¡Hola! Soy yo, Roberto. Muy bien, gracias. Oye, ¿quieres ir a la fiesta de mi amigo Pedro? Sí, Pedro tiene una banda de música muy buena. ¿Verdad? ¡Qué bueno que puedes ir a la fiesta conmigo! Eres la chica más bonita de la escuela y bailas muy bien. ¡Muy bien, hasta luego!

TEEN FEMALE 2: Hola. Soy yo, Dana. ¿Cómo estás? ¿Yo?, muy bien. ¿Sabes? Mi profesora de español dice que soy la mejor estudiante. Por eso voy a participar en la competencia de español mañana. Sí, hacen preguntas muy difíciles. Por eso tengo que estudiar mucho.

TEEN FEMALE 3: ¿Qué tal? Soy yo, Marisol. ¡Ay, María! Estoy muy nerviosa. Tengo una cita en el teatro mañana. Sí, es el mejor teatro en la ciudad. Quiero ser Julieta en la obra de teatro. Sí, hay muchas chicas que quieren ser Julieta también. ¿Y sabes? ¡Carlos quiere ser Romeo!

Track 08: Audio Act. 7, Writing, Audio & Video Workbook, p. 29

Listen as a young model and her photographer describe a typical weekend photo shoot to a magazine reporter. They will mention specific activities that they do at particular times during the day. Write the time of day that the reporter and the model say that they do each thing. Be careful! Not all of the squares will be filled for both people. You will hear this dialogue twice.

REPORTERO: Hola. Me llamo Miguel. Escribo la sección para jóvenes del periódico. ¿Cómo están?

MODELO: Muy bien.

FOTÓGRAFO: Hola, Miguel.

REPORTERO: Muchos jóvenes piensan que la vida de las modelos y de los fotógrafos es muy glamorosa. ¿Es la verdad? ¿Qué hacen Uds. para prepararse para un día de trabajo?

MODELO: Glamorosa, no. Díficil, sí. Me levanto a las cinco y media de la mañana porque hay mucho que hacer antes de salir de mi casa. Me ducho a las cinco y cuarenta y cinco. ¡Tengo que usar cada minuto! Me cepillo los dientes a las seis. No puedo ni leer el periódico ni mirar la tele.

REPORTERO: ¡Susi, su día empieza MUY temprano!

FOTÓGRAFO: Yo no me despierto hasta las siete y media. No tengo que ser guapo para ser fotógrafo. Me ducho a las siete y cuarenta y cinco. Luego me afeito y me cepillo los dientes a las ocho.

REPORTERO: ¿Se visten con ropa cómoda para el trabajo?

MODELO: Sí, nos vestimos en jeans y camiseta. Normalmente me pongo el maquillaje a las seis y cuarto y me arreglo el pelo. Después como un poco de cereal. Luego me visto en mis jeans favoritos a las seis y media. Nunca me pinto las uñas.

REPORTERO: ¿Y Ud., Miguel?

FOTÓGRAFO: No me pinto las uñas tampoco, pero me pongo agua de colonia a las ocho y diez. Después de ducharme y lavarme el pelo, me arreglo el pelo muy rápidamente a las ocho y cuarto.

REPORTERO: ¿Cuándo se acuestan?

MODELO: Antes de acostarme, me baño con un poco de colonia en el agua a las nueve y cuarenta y cinco. Me acuesto a las diez y media.

FOTÓGRAFO: Me acuesto a las doce. No necesito dormir mucho.

REPORTERO: Muchas gracias por hablar conmigo.

You are going to hear this dialogue again.

Track 09: Audio Act. 8, Writing, Audio & Video Workbook, p. 30

Parents are sometimes surprised to learn from teachers that their children act differently at school than they do at home. Listen to mothers, who are volunteering in the school today, as they talk to their children's teachers. How do the mothers view their children? According to the teachers, how are they acting today in class? Fill in the chart below with adjectives as you listen. You will hear each dialogue twice.

1. **ADULT FEMALE 1:** Buenos días, Señora Ortiz. Soy la madre de Ana. ¿Cómo está mi princesa hoy?
   ADULT FEMALE 2: Ella está muy aburrida en mi clase hoy.
   ADULT FEMALE 1: ¿Aburrida? ¿Ana? No es posible. Ella es muy estudiosa y una estudiante muy seria.
2. **ADULT FEMALE 3:** Buenas tardes, Señor Lenis. Soy la madre de Javier. ¿Cómo está él en su clase hoy?
   ADULT MALE 1: Mucho gusto en conocerla, señora. Javier está muy impaciente hoy.
   ADULT FEMALE 3: ¡No puede ser Javier! Él es muy reservado.
3. **ADULT FEMALE 4:** Hola, Señor Torres. Soy la madre de Laura. ¿Cómo está mi ángel hoy?
   ADULT MALE 2: Laura está muy cansada hoy.
   ADULT FEMALE 4: No, Laura nunca está cansada. Ella es muy trabajadora.
4. **ADULT FEMALE 5:** Buenos días, Señora Martínez. Soy la madre de Mateo. ¿Cómo está mi niño hoy?
   ADULT FEMALE 6: Su niño está un poco enojado.
   ADULT FEMALE 5: ¿Cómo? No es posible. Mateo es muy tranquilo.
5. **ADULT FEMALE 7:** Buenas noches, Profesora Redondo. Soy la madre de Linda. ¿Cómo está ella en su clase hoy?
   ADULT FEMALE 8: ¡Ay, ella está muy atrevida hoy! Habla mucho y no presta atención.
   ADULT FEMALE 7: No, Profesora Redondo. Ella es una niña muy reservada.
6. **ADULT FEMALE 8:** Hola, Profesor Cruz. Soy la madre de Joaquín. ¿Cómo está mi hijo hoy?
   ADULT MALE 3: Joaquín está muy desordenado hoy.
   ADULT FEMALE 8: ¡Imposible! Joaquín es más ordenado que yo.

Track 10: *Manos a la obra*, Act. 23, Student Book, p. 88

Escucha y escribe

Hoy muchos clientes están en el salón de belleza. Escucha y escribe lo que dice Felipe mientras organiza el salón. Vas a escuchar las frases dos veces.

1. El secador blanco es de Matilda; este negro no es de ella.
2. El cepillo rojo es mío; el azul es tuyo.
3. No encuentro mi gel. ¿Me pueden prestar el gel de Uds.?
4. Felipe y Carmen, estas toallas están sucias. ¿Son suyas?
5. Tenemos que comprar peines nuevos. Los nuestros están viejos.

Track 11: Audio Act. 9, Writing, Audio & Video Workbook, p. 30

Listen as Claudia's father tries to sort out all of the items left at their home after his daughter's friend Laura spent the night. As you listen to the conversation, sort out which items belong to Claudia and which belong to Laura. Under each picture, write the first initial of the person the item belongs to. You will hear this conversation twice.

1. **PADRE:** Claudia, ¿de quién es la toalla amarilla? ¡Está en el sofá de la sala! ¿Es tuya? ¿Es de Laura?
   CLAUDIA: No es mía. Es suya.
2. **PADRE:** ¿Y esta agua de colonia? ¿De quién es?
   CLAUDIA: Es mía.
3. **PADRE:** ¿De quién es el cepillo que está en la cocina? Está muy sucio.
   CLAUDIA: Es suyo.
4. **PADRE:** ¡Estoy cansado de este desorden! ¿Estas joyas de oro? ¿Son de quién?
   CLAUDIA: Son suyas. Son muy bonitas, ¿no?
5. **PADRE:** ¿Y el desodorante en mi baño? ¿Es tuyo o de ella?
   CLAUDIA: Es mío. Es mi desodorante favorito. ¡No es para hombres, papá!
6. **PADRE:** Éste no es mi cinturón. Claudia, ¿de quién es el cinturón?
   CLAUDIA: No es mío. Es demasiado pequeño para mí.
7. **PADRE:** ¿De quién es el secador pequeño? ¿Es tuyo?
   CLAUDIA: Laura lo pide prestado, pero es mío.
8. **PADRE:** ¡Que niñas más desordenadas! Bueno, ¿de quién es este peine?
   CLAUDIA: Papá, es mío también.

Track 12: *Pronunciación, Consonantes que cambian de sonido*, Student Book, p. 89

In Spanish, when the letter *c* combines with *a, o,* or *u* ("strong" vowels), it makes the sound of the letter *k*. Listen and say these words:

You will hear each word twice. After the word is pronounced the first time, there will be a pause so you can pronounce it. Then you will hear the word a second time.

expli**c**a	¿**C**ómo?
bus**c**o	¿**C**uándo?
cuchillo	

When *c* combines with *e* or *i* ("weak" vowels), it makes the sound of the letter *s*. Listen and say these words:

You will hear each word twice. After the word is pronounced the first time, there will be a pause so you can pronounce it. Then you will hear the word a second time.

cepillo	cono**ce**s
ciencias	**ce**ntro de re**ci**claje

Practice saying these sentences:

Para mi cita con Carmen, voy a ponerme una corbata y un cinturón.

A Celia le gusta comer cacahuates cuando va al cine.

In Spanish, the letter *g* combined with *a, o,* or *u* ("strong" vowels) makes a hard *g* sound. Listen and say these words:

You will hear each word twice. After the word is pronounced the first time, there will be a pause so you can pronounce it. Then you will hear the word a second time.

ganga	al**g**odón
lue**g**o	yo**g**ur
al**g**ún	

In words with the letters *e* or *i* ("weak" vowels), you need to add a *u* after the *g* to keep the hard *g* sound. Listen to and say these words:

You will hear each word twice. After the word is pronounced the first time, there will be a pause so you can pronounce it. Then you will hear the word a second time.

espa**gue**tis	**gui**sante
pa**gué**	hambur**gue**sa

Practice saying these sentences:

Gasté mucho dinero en las gangas y pagué con cheque.
Compré un regalo para Guillermo: unos guantes de algodón.

Can you figure out the meaning of the following *refranes*?

Lo barato es caro cuando no es necesario.
Peseta guardada, dos veces ganada.

Track 13: *Repaso del capítulo*, Student Book, p. 96

Vocabulario y gramática
Escucha las palabras y expresiones que has aprendido en este capítulo.

See Student Book page 96 for vocabulary list.

Track 14: *Preparación para el examen*, Student Book, p. 97

Escuchar
Practice task
Everyone does things a little differently on the weekend. Most people sleep later, dress more casually, and do things they don't have time to do during the week. As you listen to each person, decide whether you think they are talking about the weekend or a weekday. Be prepared to explain why you made your choice.

TEEN FEMALE 1: Generalmente, me despierto muy lentamente a las diez o diez y media. Me visto en mi ropa favorita, una sudadera vieja con mis jeans cómodos, y no me pongo maquillaje. Es mi día favorito.

MALE TEEN 1: Me levanto muy temprano. Me ducho, me cepillo los dientes y me visto. Pongo los libros en mi mochila y voy a la escuela.

TEEN FEMALE 2: Hago la tarea y me acuesto temprano.

MALE TEEN 2: Voy al cine a las 7:00 de la noche y después voy a una fiesta. Me acuesto tarde.

Realidades 2

Capítulo 2A

Video Script

A primera vista: ¿Más maquillaje?

RAÚL: No dan nada interesante hoy.

TOMÁS: ¿Por qué no vamos a tomar un refresco?

GLORIA: Es para mí. Aló. Oh no. ¿Estás segura? ¿Qué podemos hacer? Tengo una idea… Sí, está bien. Hasta luego.

GLORIA: ¿Les gustaría participar en una obra de teatro?

RAÚL: ¿En qué? No.

GLORIA: No, no, de verdad. Es una emergencia. Alguien está enfermo y necesitamos a dos personas rápidamente, esta noche.

TOMÁS: ¿Qué tenemos que hacer?

GLORIA: No mucho. Les va a gustar. Va a ser muy fácil… y muy divertido.

RAÚL: No sé. ¿No vamos a tomar un refresco?

TOMÁS: Pero, ¿por qué no? Puede ser interesante.

GLORIA: ¡Fantástico! Tomás, te va a gustar.

TOMÁS: Sí, creo que sí.

RAÚL: Vamos a ver…

TOMÁS: ¿Cómo me preparo? ¿Tengo que ducharme? ¿Arreglarme el pelo?

GLORIA: No, tranquilo, Tomás. Te ves bien. Pero, tú, Raúl… antes de ir, tienes que…

RAÚL: Muy bien, hermana. Voy a prepararme. Me ducho, me lavo la cara, me cepillo los dientes, me pongo el desodorante, me visto…

TOMÁS: Bravo, bravo.

GLORIA: ¡Raúl, basta! Tienen treinta minutos.

[más tarde]

RAÚL: ¿Por qué tiene que ponerme tanto maquillaje?

TOMÁS: Y… ¿es necesario pintarme los labios?

RAÚL: ¿Tanto gel? Qué horrible.

MAKE-UP ARTIST: Y ahora necesito un cepillo y una toalla.

RAÚL: Esto es increíble. Y fue idea tuya.

TOMÁS: Tranquilo, Raúl. Es una obra de teatro, y no va a durar mucho.

RAÚL: Pues, generalmente estas obras duran dos horas. ¡Dos horas con este maquillaje!

TOMÁS: Tienes razón. Esto no es muy cómodo. Pero, te ves muy bien. Es más bonito que el mío.

RAÚL: No. Me gusta más el tuyo. Y mira estos zapatos. ¡Son horribles!

TOMÁS: Pues, son mejores que los míos… y más cómodos.

RAÚL: Esto va a ser un desastre. Es la última vez…

GramActiva Videos
Reflexive verbs

HOST: It's time we talked about reflexive verbs. What's a reflexive verb, you ask? Well it's when you say that people do something to or for themselves. Watch and learn.

HOST: I brush the dog's hair. I brush my hair. Brushing my own hair is reflexive. I brush the dog's teeth. I brush my—Mmm. Minty fresh. So as I was saying, brushing my own teeth is reflexive. Because I do the action to myself. Reflexive verbs have two parts: a reflexive pronoun and a verb form. In English, reflexive pronouns include *myself, herself*, etc. In Spanish, the reflexive pronouns are *me, te, se, nos, os,* and *se*.

HOST V.O.: Teach me about drying my hair. Pleeease?

V.O.: OK. Let's conjugate the reflexive verb *secarse* which means "to dry oneself."
Me seco. Te secas. Se seca. Nos secamos. Os secáis. Se secan.

V.O.: So, if we're saying the dog dries his hair, we'd say, *El perro se seca el pelo.*
Remember that in Spanish when referring to body parts, you use the articles (*el, la, un*, etc.), instead of possesives (*mi, tu, su*, etc.), as in *el pelo.*

V.O.: *Me cepillo los dientes por la mañana.*

V.O.: *Se afeita todos los días.*

DOG V.O.: *Me ducho.*

HOST: You can place the pronoun before the verb or attach it at the end. So we can say, *Me voy a vestir* or *Voy a vestirme.*

HOST: Now that we're all dressed, let's test your knowledge.

Quiz

V.O.: Fill in blank with the correct reflexive pronoun and verb.

(levantarse) Nosotros _____ temprano los lunes.
Nosotros nos levantamos temprano los lunes.

(ducharse) _____ después de desayunar.
Yo me ducho después de desayunar.

(levantarse) Ay, tú no puedes _____ tan temprano.
Ay, tú no puedes levantarte tan temprano.

Ser vs. estar

REAR-VIEW GUY: There's something back there. It's been so long since we passed it I forget what it is.

STORY MAN: This is the story of *Ser* vs. *estar*, "A Tale of Two Infinitives." Once upon a time, there were two verbs that lived in the Spanish language and both meant "to be."

STORY MAN V.O.: No one could tell them apart. Then, one day, even though they both meant "to be," they decided to mean different things. *Estar* decided to mean "to be something that tends to change," and *ser* decided to mean "to be something that generally stays the same." And they both lived happily ever after.

HOST: You know that both *ser* and *estar* mean "to be." You have seen, however that their uses are different. Before we get into that, let's review the verbs themselves.

HERO: To infinitives and beyond!

V.O.: *Estar* is an irregular verb, because the *yo* form ends in *-oy*, instead of *-o*. Let's see how it's conjugated.
Estoy. Estás. Está. Estamos. Estáis. Están.

V.O.: Here's *ser*.
Soy. Eres. Es. Somos. Sois. Son.

V.O.: Let's look at how to use *estar*. *Estar:* things that tend to change, like how a person or thing is or feels at the moment and where a person or thing is.
Está desordenada.
Estoy cansado.
Estamos ocupados.
Los gatos están debajo de los libros.
El perro está en la sala.

V.O.: *Ser:* things that are unlikely to change or that describe permanent characteristics of people.
Ser is used with nationality: *Soy de Honduras.*
Permanent characteristics: *Eres mi hermana.*
Possesive: *La luz es mía.*
Profession: *Somos profesores.*
Or what something is made of: *Son de plástico.*

Quiz

V.O.: Fill in the blanks with the proper form of *ser* or *estar*.
Mi hermana _____ muy cansada.
Mi hermana está muy cansada.
Este anillo _____ mío.
Este anillo es mío.
Yo _____ en mi casa.
Yo estoy en mi casa.

Realidades 2

Capítulo 2A

Nombre _____

Fecha _____

Communicative Pair Activity **2A-1**

Estudiantes **A y B**

What is your morning routine like? Choose five activities from your morning routine from the list below and write them down on the lines *JUEGO UNO*. For example: *Me despierto a las siete.* Take turns with a partner asking questions to try to be the first to discover the other person's five activities. Record your partner's answers by writing *Sí* or *No* on the blank space corresponding to each game next to the listed items. Answer your partner's questions in complete sentences. Use the expressions listed under *PALABRAS ÚTILES* in your answers. For *JUEGO DOS*, choose five activities that you never do in the morning or that you only do sometimes.

1   2

_____ _____ bañarse

_____ _____ afeitarse

_____ _____ arreglarse el pelo

_____ _____ cepillarse los dientes

_____ _____ despertarse

_____ _____ ducharse

_____ _____ levantarse

_____ _____ lavarse la cara

_____ _____ pintarse las uñas

_____ _____ ponerse

_____ _____ secarse

_____ _____ vestirse

_____ _____ escuchar la radio

_____ _____ leer el periódico

_____ _____ cortarse el pelo

JUEGO UNO

_____

_____

_____

_____

_____

JUEGO DOS

_____

_____

_____

PALABRAS ÚTILES:

. . . a las . . .

Primero . . .

Luego . . .

. . . después de . . .

. . . antes de . . .

Talk!

Realidades 2

Capítulo 2A

Nombre _____

Communicative Pair Activity **2A-2**

Fecha _____

Estudiante **A**

Your partner will play the role of your brother or sister. Imagine that you and your sibling are sorting out everything in the bathroom that everyone in your family shares. Ask your partner to whom each item belongs. Make a mark in the appropriate column.

	de Elena	de papá	de mamá	míos
1. ¿Es tuya esta agua de colonia?	_____	_____	_____	_____
2. ¿De quién es el cepillo?	_____	_____	_____	_____
3. ¿Es de papá ese gel?	_____	_____	_____	_____
4. ¿Son de mamá esas joyas?	_____	_____	_____	_____
5. ¿De quién es ese peine?	_____	_____	_____	_____
6. ¿Es tuya esta toalla?	_____	_____	_____	_____
7. ¿De quién es este secador?	_____	_____	_____	_____
8. ¿Son míos esos cinturones?	_____	_____	_____	_____

You will play the role of your partner's co-worker at a beauty salon. You are helping your partner sort out each item in the salon that four co-workers share. Use the following information to answer his or her questions. Follow this model:

—¿De quién es ese peine?

—Ese peine es tuyo.

de Paco   **tuyos**   **de Isabel**   **míos**

Realidades ❷

Capítulo 2A

Nombre _____

Fecha _____

You will play the role of your partner's brother or sister. You are helping your partner sort out each item in the bathroom that everyone in the family shares. Use the following information to answer his or her questions. Follow this model:

—¿De quién es ese peine?

—Ese peine es tuyo.

míos	de papá	de mamá	tuyos

You will play the role of your partner's co-worker at a beauty salon. You are helping your partner sort out each item in the salon that four co-workers share. Ask your partner to whom each item belongs. Make a mark in the appropriate column.

	de Paco	tuyos	de Isabel	míos
1. ¿Es tuya esta colonia?				
2. ¿De quién es el cepillo?				
3. ¿Es de Paco ese gel?				
4. ¿Son de Isabel esas joyas?				
5. ¿De quién es ese peine?				
6. ¿Es tuya esta toalla?				
7. ¿De quién es este secador?				
8. ¿Son míos esos cinturones?				

Talk!

Realidades 2

Capítulo 2A

Situation Cards

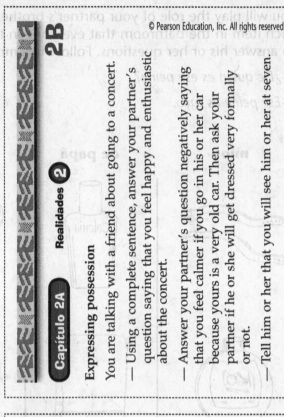

2A

Realidades 2

Capítulo 2A

Expressing possession

You are talking with a friend about going to a concert.

— Ask your partner how he or she feels about the concert you will go to.

— Then ask if he or she prefers to take his or her car.

— Answer your partner's question negatively saying that it is not a special event. Then say you will see him or her at seven.

2B

Realidades 2

Capítulo 2A

Expressing possession

You are talking with a friend about going to a concert.

— Using a complete sentence, answer your partner's question saying that you feel happy and enthusiastic about the concert.

— Answer your partner's question negatively saying that you feel calmer if you go in his or her car because yours is a very old car. Then ask your partner if he or she will get dressed very formally or not.

— Tell him or her that you will see him or her at seven.

1A

Realidades 2

Capítulo 2A

Talking about your daily routine

You are talking with a friend about your daily routine.

— Ask if he or she takes a shower after getting up in the morning or before going to bed at night.

— Answer his or her question.

— Answer that in the morning you brush your teeth, wash your face and get dressed. Then ask him or her about his or her routine in the morning.

1B

Realidades 2

Capítulo 2A

Talking about your daily routine

You are talking with a friend about your daily routine.

— Respond to the student. Ask him or her when he or she takes a shower and how long it takes him or her.

— Then, ask him or her about his or her routine in the morning.

— Answer that you wake up very early and read the paper, then you get dressed and brush your teeth.

GramActiva

¿Cómo te preparas?

¿Por la mañana o por la noche?, p. 79

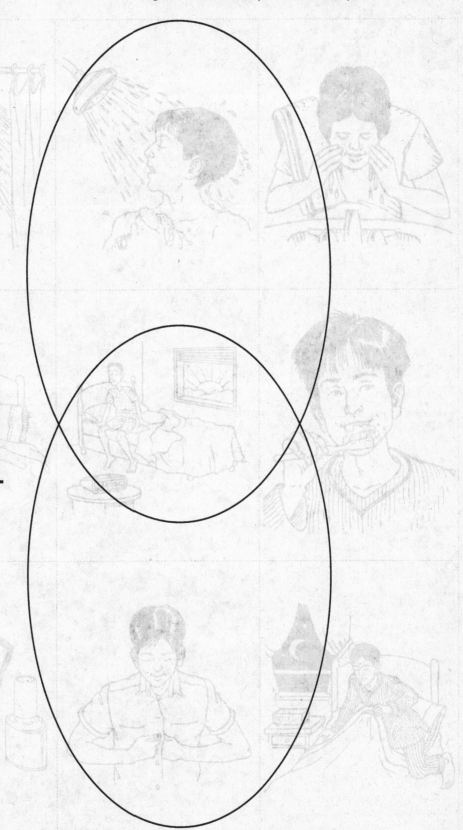

por la noche

por la mañana
y
por la noche

por la mañana

Vocabulary Clip Art

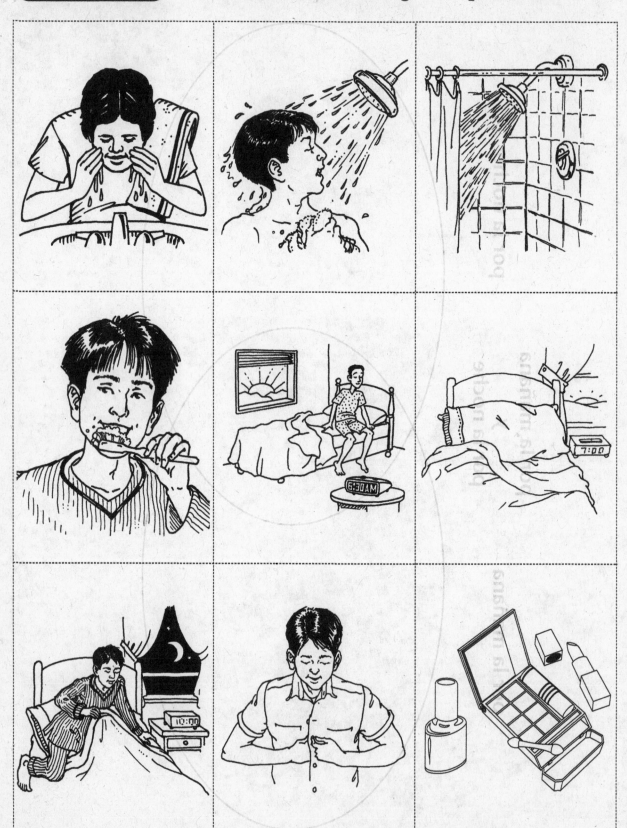

Vocabulary Clip Art

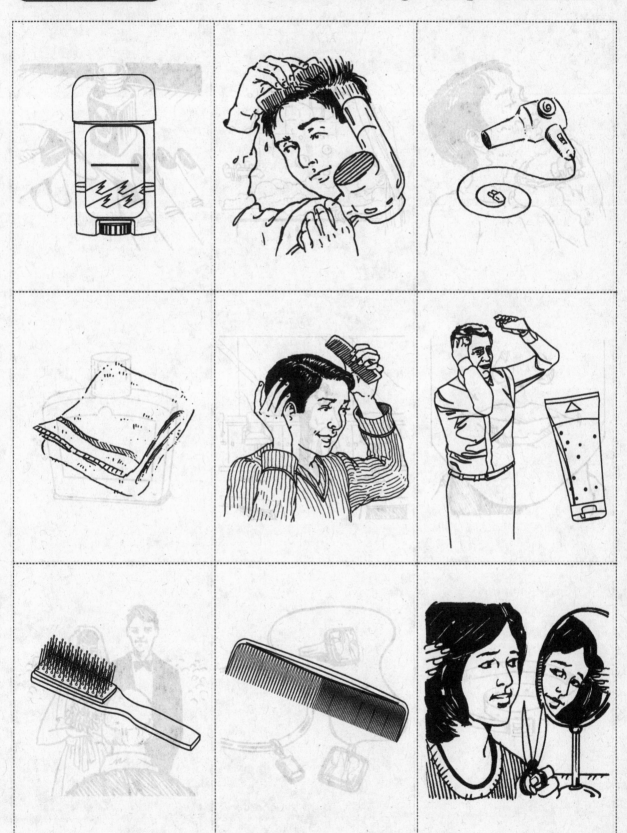

Vocabulary Clip Art

Vocabulary Clip Art

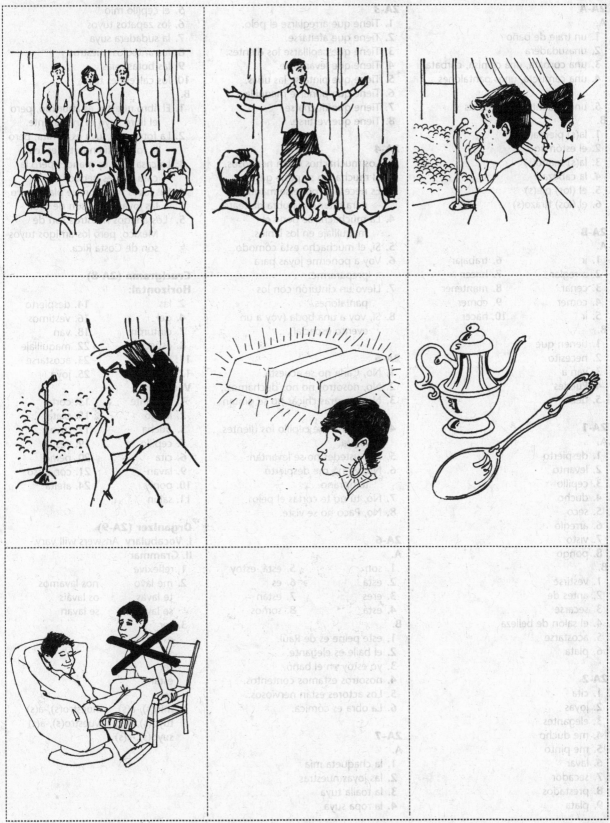

Core Practice Answers

2A-A

A.
1. un traje de baño
2. unasudadera
3. una corbata, una camisa, corbata
4. una camiseta, unos pantalones cortos
5. unos guantes, unas botas

B.
1. la(s) pierna(s)
2. el estómago
3. la(s) mano(s)
4. la cabeza
5. el (los) pie(s)
6. el (los) brazo(s)

2A-B

A.
1. ir
2. arreglar
3. cenar
4. comer
5. ir
6. trabajar
7. hacer
8. mantener
9. comer
10. hacer

B.
1. tienen que
2. necesito
3. van a
4. Puedes
5. debo

2A-1

A.
1. despierto
2. levanto
3. cepillo
4. ducho
5. seco
6. arreglo
7. visto
8. pongo

B.
1. vestirse
2. antes de
3. secarse
4. el salón de belleza
5. acostarse
6. plata

2A-2
1. cita
2. joyas
3. elegantes
4. me ducho
5. me pinto
6. lavar
7. secador
8. prestados
9. plata

2A-3
1. Tiene que arreglarse el pelo.
2. Tiene que afeitarse.
3. Tiene que cepillarse los dientes.
4. Tiene que levantarse.
5. Tiene que pintarse las uñas.
6. Tiene que ponerse maquillaje.
7. Tiene que ducharse.
8. Tiene que vestirse.

2A-4
1. Los muchachos están nerviosos.
2. El muchacho se pone gel.
3. Es necesario ponerse maquillaje para estar en la obra de teatro.
4. La muchacha se pone el maquillaje en los labios.
5. Sí, el muchacho está cómodo.
6. Voy a ponerme joyas para prepararme.
7. Llevo un cinturón con los pantalones.
8. Sí, voy a una boda (voy a un evento especial).

2A-5
1. No, Carla no se acuesta.
2. No, nosotros no nos duchamos.
3. No, las otras chicas no se pintan las uñas.
4. No, yo no me cepillo los dientes ahora.
5. No, ustedes no se levantan.
6. No, yo no me despierto temprano.
7. No, tú no te cortas el pelo.
8. No, Paco no se viste.

2A-6

A.
1. son
2. está
3. eres
4. está
5. está, estoy
6. es
7. están
8. somos

B.
1. este peine es de Raúl.
2. el baile es elegante.
3. yo estoy en el baño.
4. nosotros estamos contentos.
5. Los actores están nerviosos.
6. La obra es cómica.

2A–7

A.
1. la chaqueta mía
2. las joyas nuestras
3. la toalla tuya
4. la ropa suya

5. el cepillo mío
6. los zapatos tuyos
7. la sudadera suya
8. los anteojos nuestros
9. las botas mías
10. los calcetines tuyos

B.
1. El libro nuestro es aburrido, pero el libro suyo es interesante.
2. La fotografía tuya es bonita, pero la fotografía nuestra es fea.
3. La casa tuya es grande, pero la casa mía es pequeña.
4. Las joyas mías son de plata, pero las joyas suyas son de oro.
5. Los amigos nuestros son de México, pero los amigos tuyos son de Costa Rica.

Crucigrama (2A-8)

Horizontal:
2. las
4. gel
7. cinturón
8. especial
11. secador
12. boda
14. despierto
16. vestimos
18. van
22. maquillaje
23. acostarse
25. joya

Vertical:
1. elegante
2. luego
3. ducha
5. cepillo
6. cita
9. lavan
10. pones
11. salón
13. corto
15. plata
17. tuyas
19. ves
20. peine
21. concurso
24. afeita

Organizer (2A-9)

I. Vocabulary Answers will vary.

II. Grammar
1. reflexive
2. me lavo / nos lavamos
   te lavas / os laváis
   se lava / se lavan
3. ser
   estar
   ser
   ser
   estar
   ser
4. mío(s),-a(s) / nuestro(s),-a(s)
   tuyo(s),-a(s) / vuestro(s),-a(s)
   suyo(s),-a(s)

Realidades 2

Capítulo 2A

Nombre

Hora

Fecha

AVSR 2A-1

Verbs and expressions that use the infinitive (p. 71)

• Many verbs are often followed by the infinitive. Some of the most common verbs of this type are:

me gusta/gustaría	I like/would like	querer (e → ie)	to want
me encanta	I love	pensar (e → ie)	to plan to
poder (o → ue)	to be able to	necesitar	to need
preferir (e → ie)	to prefer	tener que	to have to
deber	ought to, should	ir a	to be going to

A. The sentences below each contain two verbs. Circle the conjugated verb in each sentence and underline the verb in the infinitive. Follow the model.

Modelo   Sara (necesita) salir temprano.

1. Rafael y Jorge (van) a trabajar por la noche.

2. Yo (prefiero) jugar al fútbol.

3. Tú (debes) poner la mesa.

4. Oscar (piensa) hacer una búsqueda en la Red.

5. Nosotros (queremos) estar de vacaciones.

6. El camarero (puede) servir ocho bebidas a la vez (at the same time).

B. Write in the missing word or phrase for each sentence using the cues given in English. Follow the model.

Modelo   Me **encanta** bailar la rumba.
(I love)

1. **Prefiero** jugar a los bolos.
(I prefer)

2. **Tengo** **que** sacar buenas notas en la escuela.
(I have to)

3. Me **gusta** cantar en el coro.
(I like)

4. **Quiero** ir de compras.
(I want)

5. **Debo** decir la verdad.
(I should)

A ver si recuerdas — 2A-1   **53**

Realidades 2

Capítulo 2A

Nombre

Hora

Fecha

AVSR 2A-2

Verbs and expressions that use the infinitive (continued)

• The verb acabar + de + infinitive is used to say what someone just finished doing. *Alicia acaba de volver.* *Alicia has just come back.*

C. Tell what the people just finished doing by writing forms of acabar + de + infinitive in the blanks. Use the pictures to help you. The first one is done for you.

1. María **acaba** **de** **leer** una revista.

2. Javier **acaba** **de** **esquiar**

3. Yo **acaba** **de** **tocar** la guitarra.

4. Los Rodríguez **acaban** **de** **navegar** en la Red.

D. Use the sentence parts to create a complete sentence. Follow the model.

Modelo   Yo / tener que / estudiar / esta noche
Yo tengo que estudiar esta noche.

1. Tú / acabar de / almorzar
Tú acabas de almorzar.

2. Me gustaría / pasar tiempo con mis amigos / mañana
Me gustaría pasar tiempo con mis amigos mañana.

3. Alejandro / pensar / visitar a sus primos / durante las vacaciones
Alejandro piensa visitar a sus primos durante las vacaciones.

4. Los buenos estudiantes / deber / practicar el español
Los buenos estudiantes deben practicar el español.

5. Nosotros / no poder / hacer mucho ruido / en la biblioteca
Nosotros no podemos hacer mucho ruido en la biblioteca.

54   A ver si recuerdas — 2A-2

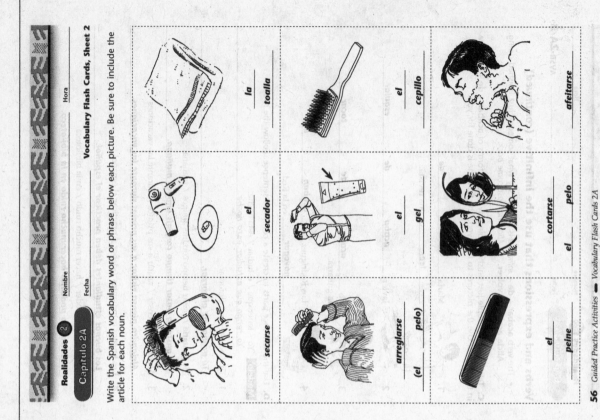

Nombre _____ Hora _____

Fecha _____ **Vocabulary Flash Cards, Sheet 2**

Write the Spanish vocabulary word or phrase below each picture. Be sure to include the article for each noun.

la
_____
toalla

el
_____
secador

_____
secarse

el
_____
cepillo

el
_____
gel

(el pelo)
_____
arreglarse

_____
afeitarse

cortarse
_____
el   pelo

el
_____
peine

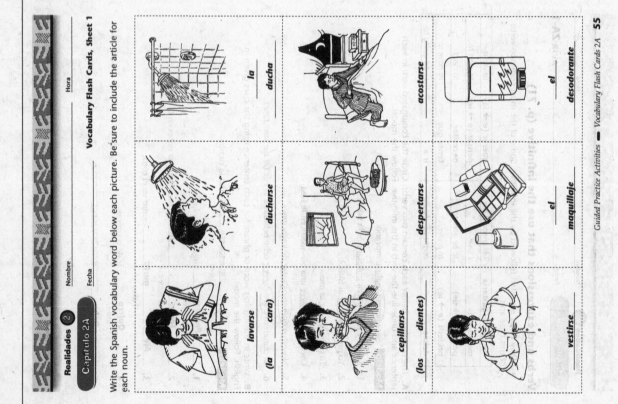

Nombre _____ Hora _____

Fecha _____ **Vocabulary Flash Cards, Sheet 1**

Write the Spanish vocabulary word below each picture. Be sure to include the article for each noun.

la
_____
ducha

_____
ducharse

(la   cara)
_____
lavarse

_____
acostarse

_____
despertarse

(los   dientes)
_____
cepillarse

el
_____
desodorante

el
_____
maquillaje

_____
vestirse

Realidades 2

Capítulo 2A

Nombre

Fecha

Hora

Vocabulary Flash Cards, Sheet 4

Write the Spanish vocabulary word below each picture. If there is a word or phrase, copy it in the space provided. Be sure to include the article for each noun.

de	de	un _____ evento
plata	oro	especial

el	pedir prestado,	
pelo	prestada (a)	cómodo
el	pedir _____ prestado ,	
pelo	prestada _____ (a)	levantarse

nervioso,	entusiasmado,	
nerviosa	entusiasmada	
nervioso ,	entusiasmado ,	levantarse
nerviosa	entusiasmada	

Realidades 2

Capítulo 2A

Nombre

Fecha

Hora

Vocabulary Flash Cards, Sheet 3

Write the Spanish vocabulary word or phrase below each picture. Be sure to include the article for each noun.

los	pintarse	el
labios	(las _____ uñas)	bañarse

el	el	el
cinturón	agua	salón
	de colonia	de belleza

el	la	las
concurso	boda	joyas

Copy the word or phrase in the space provided. Be sure to include the article for each noun. These blank cards can be used to write and practice other Spanish vocabulary for the chapter.

luego	por ejemplo	rápidamente
luego	_por_ _ejemplo_	_rápidamente_
te ves (bien)	ser	estar
_te_ _ves_ _(bien)_	_ser_	_estar_

Copy the word or phrase in the space provided. Be sure to include the article for each noun.

tranquilo, tranquila	las uñas	la cita
tranquilo, _tranquila_	_las_ _uñas_	_la_ _cita_
ponerse	prepararse	antes de
ponerse	_prepararse_	_antes_ _de_
depende	elegante	lentamente
depende	_elegante_	_lentamente_

Sheet 2

Tear out this page. Write the Spanish words on the lines. Fold the paper along the dotted line to see the correct answers so you can check your work.

- Fold In ↓

to go to bed	*acostarse*
to shave	*afeitarse*
to fix (one's hair)	*arreglarse (el pelo)*
to take a bath	*bañarse*
to brush (one's teeth)	*cepillarse (los dientes)*
to cut one's hair	*cortarse el pelo*
to wake up	*despertarse*
to take a shower	*ducharse*
to get up	*levantarse*
to wash (one's face)	*lavarse (la cara)*
to paint, to polish (one's nails)	*pintarse (las uñas)*
to put on	*ponerse*
to get ready	*prepararse*
to dry	*secarse*

Sheet 1

Tear out this page. Write the English words on the lines. Fold the paper along the dotted line to see the correct answers so you can check your work.

- Fold In ↓

acostarse	*to go to bed*
afeitarse	*to shave*
arreglarse (el pelo)	*to fix (one's hair)*
bañarse	*to take a bath*
cepillarse (los dientes)	*to brush (one's teeth)*
cortarse el pelo	*to cut one's hair*
despertarse	*to wake up*
ducharse	*to take a shower*
levantarse	*to get up*
lavarse (la cara)	*to wash (one's face)*
pintarse (las uñas)	*to paint, to polish (one's nails)*
ponerse	*to put on*
prepararse	*to get ready*
secarse	*to dry*

Tear out this page. Write the Spanish words on the lines. Fold the paper along the dotted line to see the correct answers so you can check your work.

- Fold In ↓

cologne	*el agua de colonia*
brush	*el cepillo*
belt	*el cinturón*
deodorant	*el desodorante*
shower	*la ducha*
gel	*el gel*
(gold, silver) jewelry	*las joyas (de oro, de plata)*
make-up	*el maquillaje*
comb	*el peine*
hair	*el pelo*
beauty salon	*el salón de belleza*
blow dryer	*el secador*
towel	*la toalla*
nails	*las uñas*

To hear a complete list of the vocabulary for this chapter, go to www.realidades.com and type in the Web Code jdd-0289. Then click on **Repaso del capítulo.**

Tear out this page. Write the English words on the lines. Fold the paper along the dotted line to see the correct answers so you can check your work.

- Fold In ↓

el agua de colonia	*cologne*
el cepillo	*brush*
el cinturón	*belt*
el desodorante	*deodorant*
la ducha	*shower*
el gel	*gel*
las joyas (de oro, de plata)	*(gold, silver) jewelry*
el maquillaje	*make-up*
el peine	*comb*
el pelo	*hair*
el salón de belleza	*beauty salon*
el secador	*blow dryer*
la toalla	*towel*
las uñas	*nails*

Reflexive verbs (p. 80)

- You use reflexive verbs to say that people do something to or for themselves. All reflexive verbs in the infinitive form end with **-se**. For example, **secarse el pelo** means "to dry one's hair."

- The reflexive pronouns are **me**, **te**, **se**, **os**, and **nos**. Here is the present-tense form of the reflexive verb **secarse**:

yo	me seco	nosotros/nosotras	nos secamos
tú	te secas	vosotros/vosotras	os secáis
usted/él/ella	se seca	ustedes/ellos/ellas	se secan

A. Look at the underlined word(s) and circle the correct reflexive pronoun for each sentence.

1. <u>Ellos</u> (nos / **se**) lavan el pelo.

2. <u>Tú</u> (**te**/ se) pintas las uñas.

3. <u>Javier y yo</u> (**nos**/ se) preparamos.

4. <u>Roberto</u> (nos /**se**) viste.

5. <u>Yo</u> (**me**/ se) baño.

6. <u>Lola y Rita</u> (**se**/ nos) arreglan.

7. <u>Maya</u> (te /**se**) acuesta tarde.

8. <u>Tú</u> (**te**/ me) secas el pelo.

B. Write the correct reflexive pronoun and form of the verb in parentheses to complete each sentence. Follow the model.

Modelo (despertarse) Yo siempre _me_ _despierto_ a las 6:30.

1. (ducharse) Nosotras **_nos_** **_duchamos_** a las 7:00 de la mañana.

2. (arreglarse) Yo **_me_** **_arreglo_** el pelo a las 7:30 de la mañana.

3. (cepillarse) Tú **_te_** **_cepillas_** los dientes todos los días.

4. (acostarse) Sandra **_se_** **_acuesta_** temprano durante la semana.

5. (secarse) Uds. **_se_** **_secan_** después de ducharse.

Reflexive verbs (continued)

- Some verbs can be used in reflexive and non-reflexive forms.

  Me lavo el pelo todos los días. *I wash my hair every day.*
  Lavo el coche. *I wash the car.*

C. Read these sentences. First, circle the whole verb (for example, **lavo** or **me despierto**). Then, write if it is reflexive **[R]** or non-reflexive **[N]**. Follow the model.

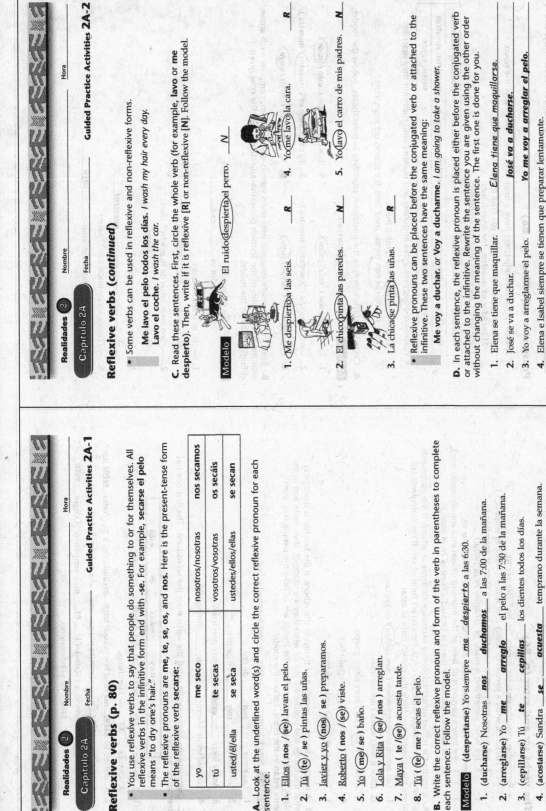

Modelo El ruido (despierta) el perro. _**N**_

1. (Me despierto) a las seis. _**R**_

2. El chico (pinta) las paredes. _**N**_

3. La chica (se pinta) las uñas. _**R**_

4. Yo (me lavo) la cara. _**R**_

5. Yo (lavo) el carro de mis padres. _**N**_

- Reflexive pronouns can be placed before the conjugated verb or attached to the infinitive. These two sentences have the same meaning:

  Me voy a duchar. or **Voy a ducharme.** *I am going to take a shower.*

D. In each sentence, the reflexive pronoun is placed either before the conjugated verb or attached to the infinitive. Rewrite the sentence you are given using the other order without changing the meaning of the sentence. The first one is done for you.

1. Elena se tiene que maquillar. _Elena tiene que maquillarse._

2. José se va a duchar. _**José va a ducharse.**_

3. Yo voy a arreglarme el pelo. _**Yo me voy a arreglar el pelo.**_

4. Elena e Isabel siempre se tienen que preparar lentamente.
   **Ellas siempre tienen que prepararse lentamente.**

5. Tú acabas de vestirte. _**Tú te acabas de vestir.**_

Possessive adjectives (p. 88)

- Spanish possessive adjectives have a long form that comes after the noun:

  ¿Tienes un peine mío? *Do you have a comb of mine?*
  El secador es nuestro. *The dryer is ours.*

- These forms are often used for emphasis:

mío/mía	míos/mías	nuestro/nuestra	nuestros/nuestras
tuyo/tuya	tuyos/tuyas	vuestro/vuestra	vuestros/vuestras
suyo/suya	suyos/suyas	suyo/suya	suyos/suyas

- Possessive adjectives agree in gender and number with the noun they describe:

  El peine es mío. *The comb is mine.*
  Sara, las tijeras son tuyas, ¿no? *Sara, the scissors are yours, right?*

A. Circle the correct form of the possessive adjectives in parentheses. Follow the model.

Modelo El jabón es (suyo / suyos).

1. Los peines son (mía /(míos)).
2. Las toallas son ((nuestras)/ nuestro).
3. El cinturón es (tuyas /(tuyo)).
4. Los cepillos son (mío /(míos)).
5. El maquillaje es ((nuestro)/ nuestra).
6. La corbata es (suyo /(suya)).

B. Read the conversations about who owns various objects. Then, complete each answer with the correct form of the Spanish possessive adjective, using the cues given in English. Follow the model.

Modelo —¿Es tu secador? *(mine)*
        —Sí, el secador es ___mío___.

1. —¿Es tu toalla? *(mine)*
   —Sí, la toalla es ___mía___

2. —¿Son estas joyas de tu madre? *(hers)*
   —Sí, las joyas son ___suyas___

3. —¿Son nuestros cepillos? *(ours)*
   —No, los cepillos no son ___nuestros___

4. —¿Tienes un cinturón mío? *(yours)*
   —No, no tengo ningún cinturón ___tuyo___

realidades.com
• Web Code: jdd-0206

The verbs *ser* and *estar* (p. 86)

- Remember that the verb **ser** means "to be." Use **ser** to:
  1. describe what a person or thing is or is like *(María es simpática.)*
  2. tell where someone or someting is from *(Soy de Argentina.)*
  3. tell what something is made of *(El anillo es de plata.)*

- Remember that the verb **estar** also means "to be." Use **estar** to:
  1. tell how a person is or feels at the moment *(Elena está entusiasmada hoy.)*
  2. tell where a person or thing is located *(Yo estoy en el baño.)*

A. A student is telling others about the exchange students at school. If the statements tell where the students are from, circle the correct form of **ser**. If the statements tell where the students are, circle the correct form of **estar**.

1. Los estudiantes japoneses (son /(están)) en la clase.
2. Ellos ((son)/ están) interesantes.
3. Arnaldo ((es)/ está) muy alto y guapo.
4. Arnaldo (es /(está)) preocupado hoy.
5. Tatiana (es /(está)) en la cafetería.

B. A teacher describes people and things in the school. If the teacher is describing what the things and people are like or what they are made of, then write **son** in the blank. If the teacher describes how the things are or how the people feel, then write **están** in the blank. Follow the model.

Modelo Sara y Jenny ___están___ entusiasmadas hoy.

1. Las joyas ___son___ de oro.
2. Los anillos ___son___ elegantes.
3. Ana y Jorge ___están___ muy nerviosos.
4. Los padres de Mateo ___son___ inteligentes.

C. Complete the conversation using the verbs from the word bank. The first one has been done for you.

soy	estoy	estás	es	está

1. CARMEN: Yo ___soy___ de México. ¿De dónde ___es___ él?
   ELENA: Él ___es___ de Honduras.

2. CARMEN: Yo ___estoy___ nerviosa hoy porque tengo una audición. Y tú, ¿cómo ___estás___ hoy?
   ELENA: Yo ___estoy___ muy contenta porque tengo una cita con Rafael.

3. CARMEN: ¿Sí? Yo conozco a Rafael. Él ___es___ muy simpático. ¿Dónde ___está___ él?
   ELENA: Rafael ___está___ en el laboratorio.

realidades.com
• Web Code: jdd-0205

Realidades ②

Capítulo 2A

Nombre

Fecha

Hora

Guided Practice Activities 2A-6

Presentación oral (p. 93) *Answers will vary.*

Task: Pretend you are an exchange student in Mexico. Your host family wants to know how you celebrate special events in the United States. Bring in a photo from home or from a magazine that shows a special event.

A. Look at your photo and use it to answer the following questions.

1. What is the special event? _____

2. What clothing are people wearing? _____

3. How do you think the people feel? _____

B. Look again at your photo and your answers from **part A**. Imagine you are going to attend the special event in the photo. How do you get ready? How do you feel before, during, and after the special event? Complete the sentences below in Spanish using your chapter vocabulary.

Me gusta prepararme antes de un evento especial. Primero, yo **1.** _____

Después, yo **2.** _____ Antes de salir, yo **3.** _____

Antes de un evento especial yo estoy **4.** _____ En un evento especial,

me gusta estar **5.** _____ Después de un evento, yo estoy

6. _____

C. Write your answers in complete sentences from **part B** on index cards. Make sure you describe the event, how you prepare for the event, and how you feel before, during, and after the event.

D. Then, practice giving an oral presentation using your completed index cards and your photo. Go through your presentation several times. Try to:

• provide as much information as you can about each point
• use complete sentences
• speak clearly

Realidades ②

Capítulo 2A

Nombre

Fecha

Hora

Guided Practice Activities 2A-5

Lectura: El Teatro Colón: Entre bambalinas (pp. 90–91)

A. The reading in your textbook is about a theater in Argentina called **El Teatro Colón.** Look at the word below that describes how you feel before giving a performance in such a theater. Then, write four more descriptive words in English.

nervous, *Answers will vary.*

B. How do you think the author of the reading feels about singing and acting in a theater? Look at the following reading selection and underline the words that describe how the author feels. *Answers will vary.*

Pasar una noche en el Teatro Colón de Buenos Aires siempre es un evento especial y hoy es muy especial para mí. Vamos a presentar la ópera "La traviata" y voy a cantar en el coro por primera vez. ¡Estoy <u>muy nervioso</u>! ... "La traviata" fue la ópera que se presentó en la inauguración del teatro el 27 de abril de 1857. Por eso estamos <u>muy</u> entusiasmados.

C. Now, read the following advertisement about student auditions from your textbook reading. Then, use the information to decide if the following students are qualified to audition. Circle **Sí** if they are qualified or **No** if they are not qualified.

AUDICIONES

Si quieres ser música, cantante o bailarín, tienes talento, eres joven y vives en Buenos Aires, tienes la oportunidad de hacer tus sueños realidad.

_____ para jóvenes de 15 a 25 años de edad.

1. José Luis es músico y tiene mucho talento. Él tiene 15 años.
   (**Sí**)/ No)

2. A Isabel no le gusta bailar ni cantar. Le interesa la tecnología y el arte. Ella tiene 18 años.
   (**Sí**)/ No)

3. Elena quiere ser bailarina. Ella tiene 13 años.
   (Sí /(**No**))

4. Enrique toca la guitarra. Él tiene 30 años y vive en Los Ángeles. Tiene 25 años.
   (Sí /(**No**))

5. A Juan le gusta cantar. También sabe tocar el piano. Tiene 25 años.
   (**Sí**)/ No)

realidades.com
• Web Code: jdd-0207

Nombre _____ Hora _____

Fecha _____

VIDEO

Antes de ver el video

Actividad 1

What do you do every morning? In the table below, write at least five activities you do each day. One has been done for you.

Por la mañana...	
Me despierto.	
Answers will vary.	

¿Comprendes?

Actividad 2

Decide whether each statement about the video is **cierto** or **falso.** If a statement is false, rewrite it to make it true.

1. Raúl y Tomás están muy interesados en el programa de televisión.

   Falso, no dan nada interesante en la televisión hoy.

2. Gloria recibe una llamada de teléfono.

   Cierto.

3. Raúl y Tomás quieren participar en una obra de teatro.

   Falso, Raúl no quiere participar.

4. Hay una emergencia en el teatro y Gloria necesita la ayuda de tres personas mañana.

   Falso, Gloria necesita la ayuda de dos personas esta noche.

Nombre _____ Hora _____

Fecha _____

VIDEO

6. Según Raúl la obra va a ser _____ un desastre _____ .

Y, ¿qué más?

Actividad 4

Write four complete sentences to tell about your morning routine. Use the phrases in the bank. Follow the model.

me acuesto	me ducho
me afeito	me lavo
me baño	me levanto
me cepillo	

Modelo *Cada día, me levanto a las 7 de la mañana.*

Answers will vary.

Nombre _____ Hora _____

Fecha _____

VIDEO

5. Tomás piensa que la experiencia puede ser interesante.

Cierto.

6. Tomás se ve mal.

Falso, Tomás se ve bien.

7. Raúl tiene que lavarse la cara, cepillarse los dientes, ponerse desodorante y vestirse.

Cierto.

8. Los muchachos tienen cincuenta minutos para prepararse.

Falso, tienen treinta minutos.

Actividad 3

Write the appropriate word or words in the spaces provided.

1. Raúl no se quiere poner tanto _____ maquillaje _____ .

2. Tomás pregunta: ¿Es necesario _____ pintarme _____ los labios?

3. La señora de maquillaje pide _____ un cepillo _____ y _____ una toalla _____ .

4. Esto fue idea de _____ Tomás _____ .

5. Tomás le dice a Raúl que la ropa de payaso (*clown*) no es muy _____ cómoda _____ .

Realidades 2

Capítulo 2A

Nombre _____

Fecha _____

Hora _____

AUDIO

Actividad 5

Listen as a very frustrated mother tries to get her two teenage children, Luis and Catrina, out of the house on time to get to school. Each one gives her excuse after excuse. Look at the pictures below and match the number of the excuse you hear to each drawing. Write the number of the excuse on the line under the picture. You will hear each conversation twice.

_____ 2   _____ 1   _____ 6

_____ 5   _____ 3   _____ 4

Actividad 6

Listen to people talking about an upcoming event in their lives. Based on the conversations, decide what event each person is getting ready for. Place a check mark in one box in each person's row. You will hear each set of statements twice.

	Una cita para ir al cine	Un partido	Un concurso	Una audición	Una boda	Una fiesta
Chucho	✓					
Gloria					✓	
Gabriel		✓				
Roberto						✓
Dana			✓			
Marisol				✓		

Communication Workbook

Realidades 2

Capítulo 2A

Nombre _____

Fecha _____

Hora _____

AUDIO

Actividad 7

Listen as a young model and her photographer describe a typical weekend photo shoot to a magazine reporter. They will mention specific activities that they do at particular times during the day. Write the time of day that the reporter and the model say that they do each thing. Be careful! Not all of the squares will be filled for both people. You will hear this dialogue twice.

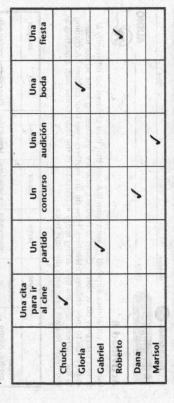

	La modelo	El fotógrafo
	6:00 A.M.	
	5:30 A.M.	7:30 A.M.
	5:45 A.M.	7:45 A.M.
	6:00 A.M.	8:00 A.M.
	6:15 A.M.	
		8:00 A.M.
	6:15 A.M.	8:15 A.M.
		8:10 A.M.
	6:30 A.M.	
	10:30 P.M.	12:00 A.M.
	9:45 P.M.	

Communication Workbook

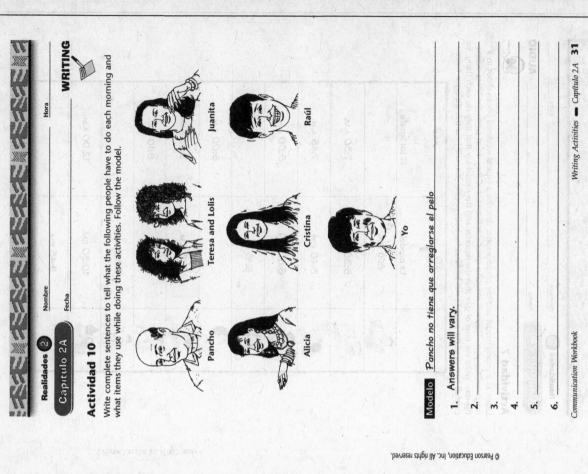

Nombre _____ Hora _____

Capítulo 2A

Fecha _____

WRITING

Actividad 10

Write complete sentences to tell what the following people have to do each morning and what items they use while doing these activities. Follow the model.

Pancho   Teresa and Lolis   Juanita

Alicia   Cristina   Raúl

Yo

| Modelo | *Pancho no tiene que arreglarse el pelo* |

1. Answers will vary. _____

2. _____

3. _____

4. _____

5. _____

6. _____

Communication Workbook   Writing Activities — Capítulo 2A   **31**

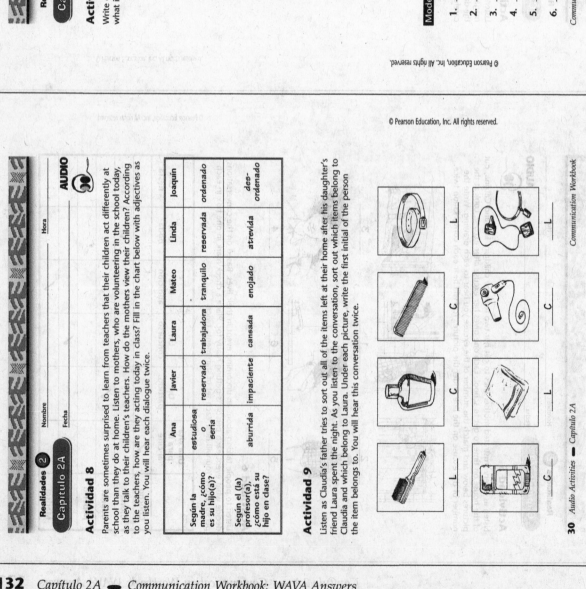

Nombre _____ Hora _____

Capítulo 2A

Fecha _____

AUDIO

Actividad 8

Parents are sometimes surprised to learn from teachers that their children act differently at school than they do at home. Listen to mothers, who are volunteering in the school today, as they talk to their children's teachers. How do the mothers view their children? According to the teachers, how are they acting today in class? Fill in the chart below with adjectives as you listen. You will hear each dialogue twice.

	Ana	Javier	Laura	Mateo	Linda	Joaquín
Según la madre, ¿cómo es su hijo(a)?	estudiosa o seria	reservado	trabajadora	tranquilo	reservada	ordenado
Según el (la) profesor(a), ¿cómo está su hijo en clase?	aburrida	impaciente	cansada	enojado	atrevida	des-ordenado

Actividad 9

Listen as Claudia's father tries to sort out all of the items left at their home after his daughter's friend Laura spent the night. As you listen to the conversation, sort out which items belong to Claudia and which belong to Laura. Under each picture, write the first initial of the person the item belongs to. You will hear this conversation twice.

L   C   C   L

C   L   C   C

30 Audio Activities — Capítulo 2A   Communication Workbook

Actividad 12

The people below are on vacation. First, complete the questions about them and their trips by circling the correct verbs. Then, answer the questions in complete sentences.

1. ¿Dónde (es, está) Lola?
   Está en la playa.

2. ¿De dónde (es está)?
   Es de Ohio.

3. ¿Cómo (es, está) ella hoy? ¿Contenta?
   Está preocupada/nerviosa.

4. ¿Cómo (es) está) ella? ¿Baja?
   Es alta.

5. ¿Qué (es, está) haciendo en este momento?
   Está corriendo.

6. ¿Dónde (son, están) los señores Obregón?
   Están en las montañas.

7. ¿De dónde (son están)?
   Son de España.

8. ¿Cómo (son están)? ¿Perezosos?
   Son activos/atrevidos/deportistas.

9. ¿Cómo (son, están) hoy? ¿Tristes?
   Están contentos.

10. ¿Qué (son, están) haciendo en este momento?
    Están esquiando en las montañas.

Communication Workbook   Writing Activities — Capítulo 2A   **33**

Actividad 11

Esteban is never able to get to school on time. Describe what he does each morning, using the pictures to guide you. ¡OJO! Some of the verbs are reflexive, while others are not. The first one has been done for you.

Primero, Esteban se levanta. Luego, se ducha. Se viste, se cepilla los dientes,

se peina (se arregla el pelo), come el desayuno y sale para la escuela. Llega

tarde.

_____

_____

32 Writing Activities — Capítulo 2A   Communication Workbook

Capítulo 2A ▬ Communication Workbook: WAVA Answers **133**

Nombre _____ Hora _____

Fecha _____

WRITING

Actividad 13

A. Think of the items you and your family members use every day. Which things are yours, which are theirs, and which are common to everyone in the family? Make a list of three items in each column.

Mine	My family members'	Ours
Answers will vary.		

B. Now, write a descriptive paragraph about what you and your family members do with each of these items. Follow the model.

Modelo   *Yo me arreglo el pelo todos los días con el gel mío.*

Answers will vary.

Test Preparation Answers

Reading Skills
p. 220   2. **A**
p. 221   2. **C**

**Integrated Performance
    Assessment**
p. 222

Answers will vary.

Capítulo 2B

School-to-Home Connection

Dear Parent or Guardian,

The theme of our current unit is *Un evento especial* (A special event). This chapter is called *¿Qué ropa compraste?* (What clothes did you buy?).

Upon completion of this chapter students will be able to:

- describe clothing and fashion
- talk about going shopping
- describe events in the past
- point out specific objects
- avoid repetition when comparing similar things
- understand cultural perspectives about parties

Students will also explore:

- the Arabic origin of words in Spanish

Our textbook, *Realidades,* helps with the development of reading, writing, and speaking skills through the use of strategies, process speaking, and process writing. In this chapter, students will:

- read about the history of jeans and some Spanish variations of the name for bluejeans
- write an e-mail about a shopping trip

To reinforce and enhance learning, students can access a wide range of online resources on **realidades.com**, the personalized learning management system that accompanies the print and online Student Edition. Resources include the eText, textbook and workbook activities, audio files, videos, animations, songs, self-study tools, interactive maps, voice recording (RealTalk!), assessments, and other digital resources. Many learning tools can be accessed through the student Home Page on **realidades.com**. Other activities, specifically those that require grading, are assigned by the teacher and linked on the student Home Page within the calendar or the Assignments tab.

You will find specifications and guidelines for accessing **realidades.com** on home computers and mobile devices on MyPearsonTraining.com under the SuccessNet Plus tab.

realidades.com

For: Tips to Parents
Visit: www.realidades.com
Web Code: jce-0010

Check it out! At the end of the chapter, have your child select five items of clothing from his or her closet and tell you the fabric they're made of. Then have him or her explain how those items fit.

Sincerely,

Videocultura Script

La piñata

Spanish version:

En México y en algunos países de América Central y América de Sur, las fiestas de cumpleaños tienen una piñata.

La piñata se hace de barro y papel maché. Tienen la forma de un animal, o un objeto, como este balón de fútbol que vemos aquí. Las piñatas llevan dulces, caramelos y pequeños juguetes por dentro.

En la fiesta, la piñata se cuelga, y los niños le pegan con un palo hasta romperla, para que los caramelos caigan al suelo.

Se cree que Marco Polo trajo la piñata de China a Italia en los años 1200. Muchos años después las piñatas fueron traídas a las Américas por los españoles.

La tradición de romper la piñata se ha extendido por muchos países de Latinoamérica, y le agregan mucha diversión a cualquier fiesta.

English version:

In Mexico and some places in Latin America, the piñata is part of celebrating special occasions such as a birthday.

Piñatas come in a variety of shapes and colors. The traditional shape is a six-pointed star. Today families choose from piñatas that look like animals, clowns, numbers, soccer balls, and TV characters.

A piñata is made by building a papier-maché form around a clay container. The form is decorated with brightly colored tissue and crepe paper.

When completed, the piñata is filled with candy or small toys.

At the party, the piñata is hung from the ceiling or a tree. The children are blindfolded and try to hit the piñata with a stick with hopes of breaking it open. When it cracks and the goodies fall to the ground, all the children scramble to get their share.

It is generally believed that the piñata originated in China and was brought to Europe by Marco Polo in the late 1200s. Piñatas were brought to the Americas by the Spanish several centuries later.

In addition to their colorful decoration, piñatas add an exciting element to parties and celebrations!

Input Script

Presentation

Input Vocabulary: Set up a clothing rack similar to the one shown in *A primera vista*, as well as signs showing sales of 70 percent and 50 percent off certain items and signs showing the *salida* and *entrada*. Distribute copies of the Vocabulary Clip Art. Play the role of a shopkeeper videotaping a commercial for his or her clothing store. Say: *¡Si le encanta ir de compras cuando hay una liquidación, tiene que venir a Ropa Loca este fin de semana! ¡Descuentos hasta del 70 por ciento! ¡Con precios tan bajos, va a encontrar una ganga fenomenal! Aquellas blusas: ¡50 por ciento! ¡Aquellos bolsos: ¡70 por ciento! ¡Tenemos todas las buenas marcas y nuestros estilos están de última moda. ¿Le gustan los colores vivos? ¿Oscuros? ¿Pasteles? ¡Tenemos todos los colores! Pero… tiene que pagar en efectivo. ¡No aceptamos ni las tarjetas de crédito, ni los cheques personales!* Have students hold up the Clip Art images of the *A primera vista* vocabulary words you use in your commercial.

Input Dialogue: Perform the first part of the dialogue with a volunteer. Then ask individual students questions to check for comprehension, such as: *¿Te gusta ir de compras cuando hay una liquidación? ¿En este momento, hay una liquidación grande en una tienda que te gusta? ¿Están de moda las blusas de colores?*

Perform the second part of the dialogue with a different volunteer. Use the clothing from the vocabulary presentation to convey the meanings of *buena marca, talla mediana*, and *el estilo*.

Perform the final part of the dialogue with a new volunteer. Act out paying for a blouse with a second volunteer acting as the cashier. Then hold up other clothing items from the rack, tell how much the item costs and have students tell you if it is *un precio alto* or *un precio bajo*.

Then have pairs of students practice one of the sections of the dialogue. Have volunteers act out their section in your store, with you playing the role of shopkeeper.

Comprehension Check

- Give groups of students fashion magazines. Call out different colors (*azul oscuro, verde claro*…) and have them race to the first to find that color. Then call out clothing items in specific colors and have students see if they can find that item in the color you specify in their magazine.

- Bring an ad for a clothing store and make statements about it to the class using *A primera vista* terms. For each statement, have students make a pile of the Clip Art images for the terms you used to describe the ad.

Audio DVD, Capítulo 2B

Track 01: *A primera vista, ¿Qué ropa compraste?*, **Student Book, p. 102**

Vocabulario y gramática en contexto

Vas a escuchar cada palabra o frase dos veces. Después de la primera vez hay una pausa para que puedas pronunciar la palabra o frase. Luego vas a escuchar de nuevo la palabra o frase.

la entrada	los colores pastel
la salida	azul oscuro
los colores vivos	azul claro

Lee en tu libro mientras escuchas el diálogo.

Teen Female 1: Mira, Lupita. Aquellas blusas tienen un descuento del cincuenta por ciento. ¡Me encanta ir de compras cuando hay una liquidación!

Teen Female 2: ¡Es una ganga! Pero no me gustan los colores tan vivos.

Teen Female 1: ¡No importa! Están de moda. Con precios tan bajos, voy a probarme dos o tres.

Teen Female 2: Y mira aquellos bolsos en la mesa. El letrero anuncia un descuento del setenta por ciento. ¡Vamos!

Track 02: *A primera vista*, **Student Book, p. 103**

Vocabulario y gramática en contexto

Vas a escuchar cada palabra o frase dos veces. Después de la primera vez hay una pausa para que puedas pronunciar la palabra o frase. Luego vas a escuchar de nuevo la palabra o frase.

Más vocabulario

el cheque de viajero
el cupón de regalo
la lana
el número
la seda
la caja
la cajera

Lee en tu libro mientras escuchas el diálogo.

Teen Female 1: Es una buena marca. Y encontré mi talla, mediana.

Teen Female 2: En realidad, no necesito estos bolsos. Pero me gusta el estilo y no cuestan mucho.

Teen Female 1: Tienes razón. Y pueden ser regalos para tus amigas. Vamos a la caja para pagar.

Teen Female 2: ¿Por qué siempre pagas en efectivo?

Teen Female 1: Porque no me gusta usar ni mi tarjeta de crédito ni un cheque personal.

Teen Female 2: Yo estoy contenta. No gasté mucho. Con esta liquidación los precios no están muy altos. Compré esta blusa pero, ¿no piensas que es un poco exagerada? ¿Qué te parece?

Teen Female 1: Me parece muy bien. Y pagaste muy poco por todas las blusas.

Track 03: *A primera vista*, **Act. 1, Student Book, p. 103**

¿Dónde está?

Imagina que estás en la tienda de las páginas 102 y 103. Mira los dibujos y escucha las siguientes frases. Señala lo que escuchas. Vas a escuchar las frases dos veces.

1. Yo te espero en la entrada. ¿Está bien?
2. ¿Puedo pagar con mi tarjeta de crédito?
3. ¿Dónde están los bolsos?
4. ¡Mira! Liquidación del cincuenta por ciento.
5. Voy a pagar en la caja.
6. Prefiero la blusa de color azul claro.
7. Perdón, señora. ¿Dónde está la salida?

Track 04: *A primera vista*, **Act. 2, Student Book, p. 103**

¿Cierto o falso?

Escucha las siguientes frases que describen a Lupita y su amiga. Si la frase es cierta, señala con el pulgar hacia arriba y si la frase es falsa, señala con el pulgar hacia abajo. Vas a escuchar las frases dos veces.

1. Las camisas en la tienda tienen un descuento del veinticinco por ciento.
2. A Lupita le gustan los colores vivos.
3. Según la amiga de Lupita, los colores vivos están de moda.
4. Los bolsos en la tienda no cuestan mucho.
5. Las chicas no quieren comprar bolsos.
6. Las chicas nunca pagan con dinero en efectivo.
7. Los precios en la tienda son muy bajos.

Track 05: *A primera vista, Videohistoria*, **Student Book, pp. 104–105**

Buscando una ganga

¿Qué pasó cuando Gloria fue de compras con Raúl y Tomás?

Lee en tu libro mientras escuchas la *Videohistoria*.

See Student Book pages 104–105 for script.

Track 06: *Manos a la obra*, **Act. 4, Student Book, p. 106**

¿Quién es?

Escucha los comentarios sobre la ropa y la moda. Escribe las frases que oyes. Vas a escuchar las frases dos veces.

1. Siempre escojo ropa de la misma marca.
2. La ropa floja me parece mucho más cómoda.
3. En realidad, el estilo de la ropa no me importa nada.
4. No me importan los precios altos si la ropa está de moda.
5. Me gustan mucho los colores vivos.

Track 07: Audio Act. 5, Writing, Audio & Video Workbook, p. 38

Listen to a group of friends as they shop in the popular Madrid department store El Corte Inglés. As you listen, figure out which of the factors below is most important to

each of them when deciding what to buy. Some may have more than one answer. Put an X in the appropriate column or columns for each girl. You will hear this conversation twice.

1. **ALICIA:** Me gustan aquellas faldas cortas. Están muy de moda. En mi telenovela favorita, todas las chicas las llevan. Son muy populares. A Alejandro le encantan también. Quiero probarme la blanca. Me gusta mucho. ¿Qué piensas, Marta?

2. **MARTA:** ¡Qué bueno, Alicia! El letrero anuncia una liquidación. Busco una chaqueta negra para mis vacaciones de esquiar. Mira aquella chaqueta cerca de la caja. Es de un color bastante vivo, pero no me importa mucho. ¡Es una ganga fantástica! ¿Verdad, Carmen?

3. **CARMEN:** ¡Madre mía! Los precios son muy bajos. Los pantalones en aquel estante son de marcas muy buenas. Me gusta mucho este pantalón azul oscuro. ¡Es de mi marca favorita, y al precio tan bajo! Mira, Luz.

4. **LUZ:** Sí. Y aquellos zapatos son muy bonitos también. Tienen un descuento del cincuenta por ciento. ¿Tiene estos zapatos en el número cuarenta y dos? ¡Muchas gracias! Voy a probarme los zapatos. Me quedan muy bien. ¿Qué te parecen, Lorena? ¡Fantástico!

5. **LORENA:** ¡Qué marcas tan buenas hay en esta tienda de descuentos! Tienen todas mis marcas favoritas. Voy a probarme dos pantalones, una falda y dos blusas. Todo tiene un estilo muy bonito. Voy a pagar con dinero en efectivo porque no tengo mi tarjeta de crédito.

Track 08: Audio Act. 6, Writing, Audio & Video Workbook, p. 38

Some people enjoy shopping, while others find it frustrating. Listen to several conversations as people look for particular items in a department store. Match the conversations to the pictures by writing the number of the conversation it represents under each picture. You will hear each conversation twice.

1. **ADULT FEMALE 1:** ¿Cuál vestido te gusta más, Mauricio? ¿Este vestido oscuro de seda, o aquél de color pastel?
   ADULT MALE 1: No me importa. Escoge uno, por favor. Ir de compras me aburre mucho.

2. **ADULT FEMALE 1:** ¡Ay! Estos jeans son demasiados flojos. Los prefiero un poco apretados. ¿Qué te parecen?
   ADULT FEMALE 2: A mí me gusta la ropa floja. Pero a ti, no. ¿Por qué no los pruebas en una talla más pequeña?

3. **ADULT FEMALE 1:** ¡Decisiones, decisiones! No sé que escoger. Las dos blusas tienen un estilo muy bonito y son de marcas muy buenas. ¡Qué ganga! En realidad necesito sólo una. ¡Qué difícil!
   ADULT FEMALE 2: Sí, es muy difícil escoger.

4. **ADULT MALE 2:** Necesito un suéter nuevo. Los precios no están altos. Vamos a ver… Encontré un suéter de mi talla. Mi talla es mediana.
   ADULT MALE 3: Bueno. ¡Vamos!

5. **ADULT FEMALE 1:** ¡Ah! Me gustan mucho las chaquetas de cuero. Aquella chaqueta es la más bonita, pero el precio está muy alto. No tengo tanto dinero.
   ADULT FEMALE 2: ¿Por qué no usas tu tarjeta de crédito?

6. **ADULT FEMALE 1:** El total es doscientos veinticinco dólares. ¿Va a pagar en efectivo, con cheque personal o con tarjeta de crédito?
   ADULT MALE 2: Con cheque personal. No tengo ni dinero en efectivo ni tarjeta de crédito.

Track 09: Audio Act. 7, Writing, Audio & Video Workbook, p. 39

Listen to the following teenagers describe to a radio announcer the most daring thing they have ever done. As the radio interviewer asks each one: *¿Cuál es la cosa más atrevida que hiciste?* look at the pictures below. Write the number of each response under the corresponding picture. You will hear each response twice.

1. **TEEN MALE 1:** ¿La cosa más atrevida que hice? Pues… la semana pasada pinté un letrero para vender el coche nuevo de mi amigo David. Es un coche bastante caro y el letrero anunciaba un precio de sólo trescientos dólares. Muchas personas lo llamaron para comprarlo. ¡Fue muy cómico… para mí!

2. **TEEN FEMALE 1:** El fin de semana pasado, mi prima Elena y yo llamamos a la Pizzería Alberto a la medianoche y compramos veinte pizzas para nuestra profesora de español. Ellos nos prometieron entregarlas en menos de treinta minutos. Qué malo, ¿no? No pagamos en efectivo. Mi hermana mayor tiene más de diez tarjetas de crédito. Yo usé una de ellas para comprarlas.

3. **TEEN FEMALE 2:** El mes pasado le escribí una carta muy romántica a Pedro. ¡Pedro es tan guapo! Hace tres semanas encontró mi carta en su escritorio. Cuando la encontró, me escribió para invitarme a la fiesta de Alma. Anoche llevé un traje muy bonito a la fiesta. A Pedro le gustó mucho el traje. ¡Me dio un beso! ¡Qué atrevido!

4. **TEEN MALE 2:** Anoche decoré los árboles de la casa de Juan con papel de colores muy vivos. Los árboles verdes son muy aburridos. Necesitan más color. El papá de Juan está muy enojado. Él es muy aburrido porque no le gustó mi decoración. Realmente, toda la gente pensó que los árboles estaban muy bonitos.

5. **TEEN FEMALE 3:** Lo más atrevido… ¡Ya sé! El año pasado me vestí como mi maestra de inglés. Llevé una blusa y una falda larga con flores muy grandes. A ella le gustan las flores del jardín. ¡Que divertido! Todos los estudiantes se divirtieron mucho.

6. **TEEN FEMALE 4:** La semana pasada escribí el número de teléfono de Alejandro en mi cuaderno. Alejandro es un chico muy romántico. Mi amiga Rosa está muy triste porque no tiene novio. Alejandro es perfecto para Rosa. Anoche Rosa le habló por teléfono. Ahora son novios.

Track 10: *Manos a la obra,* **Act. 20, Student Book, p. 114**

Escucha y escribe

En una hoja de papel escribe los números del 1 al 8. Escucha y escribe las frases. Luego indica si el objeto de la frase está al lado de, cerca de o lejos de la persona que habla. Vas a escuchar las frases dos veces.

1. Me gustan esos zapatos verdes.
2. Aquella corbata es horrible.
3. Estas botas rojas son de cuero.
4. No me gusta aquel traje azul oscuro.
5. Esta blusa es de colores vivos.
6. Aquellos guantes negros son grandes.
7. Podemos salir por esta salida.
8. Aquel cajero puede ayudarnos.

Track 11: Audio Act. 8, Writing, Audio & Video Workbook, p. 40

This semester, Eleanor is hosting an exchange student from Ecuador named Marta. Listen as they talk about different items in a department store. Based on each description, place an X in the box labeled "A" or "B" to indicate which one accurately represents what is said in each conversation. You will hear each conversation twice.

1. **ELEANOR:** Esta chaqueta de cuero negro es muy bonita. ¿Qué te parece?
   MARTA: No está mal, pero prefiero aquella chaqueta blanca. Está hecha de lana. Es más práctica y menos cara.
   ELEANOR: No soy una chica práctica. Me importa mucho estar de moda. Esta chaqueta es más elegante, con mucho estilo.
2. **ELEANOR:** Quiero gastar mi cupón de regalo hoy. Es un regalo de mi tía Lorena. ¿Qué te parecen estos bolsos? Sólo cuestan treinta dólares.
   MARTA: ¿Por cuánto es tu cupón de regalo?
   ELEANOR: Es por cien dólares.
   SALESCLERK: ¿Qué te parecen estos bolsos de aquí? Son de cuero y muy de moda. No se pueden encontrar bolsos de cuero por menos de ciento cincuenta dólares, pero aquí sólo cuestan cien dólares.
   ELEANOR: Qué ganga, ¿no?
3. **ELEANOR:** Esos zapatos azules pastel están muy de moda. El precio no está muy alto. ¿Tiene esos zapatos en número cuarenta?
   SALESCLERK: ¡Sí, un momento!
   MARTA: Aquellos zapatos de colores vivos son más bonitos. Tienen un estilo muy popular entre las chicas de la escuela.
   SALESCLERK: Aquí tiene los zapatos azules pastel.
   ELEANOR: ¡No, no! Quiero aquellos de colores vivos.
4. **ELEANOR:** Estos pantalones oscuros están en liquidación. Tienen un setenta y cinco por ciento de descuento. Son de mi marca favorita y están hechos de algodón. ¿Te gustan?

MARTA: No me gusta el algodón. Aquellos pantalones blancos que están cerca de la entrada son más bonitos. Están hechos de tela sintética.
   ELEANOR: Muy bien, pero voy a comprar estos pantalones porque me gustan más.

Track 12: Audio Act. 9, Writing, Audio & Video Workbook, p. 41

Listen as Mariana shops for several gifts for her friends, as well as a few things for herself. In each department she is able to narrow her choices down to two, and then finally makes her selection. In the spaces below, check off all the items that she decides to buy. You will hear each conversation twice.

1. **MARIANA:** Es difícil escoger. No sé si me gusta más este suéter de sólo un color o el blanco y negro. Me gustan los dos.
   CLERK: ¿Quiere probarse uno? El blanco y negro es de talla mediana. El de sólo un color es de talla grande.
   MARIANA: El de la talla mediana va a estar apretado. Mejor el suéter de sólo un color.
2. **MARIANA:** Necesito comprar un bolso para Teresa. Esta tienda tiene una ganga en bolsos. Ella necesita un bolso grande, pero los bolsos pequeños son más bonitos. ¡Ay, no sé!
   CLERK: Los pequeños son muy populares. Están muy de moda. Los grandes son de colores muy feos.
   MARIANA: Sí, el pequeño es mejor. Ella tiene muchos bolsos grandes.
3. **MARIANA:** Hace mucho sol. Voy a comprar una gorra. Aquella gorra es de cuero y ésta es de algodón. Las dos son muy bonitas. ¿Cuál compro?
   CLERK: La de cuero es de una marca muy famosa. La de algodón es un poco exagerada. ¿Te importa el precio? El precio de la de cuero es un poco alto.
   MARIANA: Me parece que la de cuero es mejor.
4. **MARIANA:** No tengo jeans para la fiesta de Pepe. Quiero unos jeans de moda. Pero no sé si quiero comprar jeans apretados o flojos. ¿Qué te parece?
   CLERK: Las jóvenes como tú prefieren los apretados. No muchas chicas llevan los flojos.
   MARIANA: Sí, es mejor. Compro los apretados.
5. **MARIANA:** Es el cumpleaños de Julia. Ella quiere unos aretes nuevos. Todos los aretes en esta tienda son muy bonitos. Me gustan estos aretes pequeños, pero aquellos aretes grandes están en liquidación. ¿Cuáles compro?
   CLERK: Los pequeños son de oro blanco. Los grandes son de plata.
   MARIANA: A Julia le gusta mucho el oro. Voy a comprar los pequeños.

Track 13: *Repaso del capítulo,* **Student Book, p. 124**

Vocabulario y gramática

Escucha las palabras y expresiones que has aprendido en este capítulo.

See Student Book page 124 for vocabulary list.

Track 14: *Preparación para el examen,* **Student Book,**

Escuchar

Practice task

Listen as Marta explains why she bought her outfit. Was it because: a) it was a bargain; b) it was a good brand name; c) it fit well; or d) it was very "in style."

TEEN FEMALE: Pasé mucho tiempo buscando algo perfecto para llevar al concierto. Encontré un suéter de una buena marca, pero cuando me lo probé, no me quedó bien. En realidad, no me importa mucho la marca. Después de muchas horas, compré uno de otra marca porque me quedó perfectamente.

Video Script

A primera vista: *Buscando una ganga*

GLORIA: ¡Mira aquel letrero!

TOMÁS: A ver… ¿Qué anuncia?

GLORIA: ¡Una liquidación fabulosa! ¿Qué les parece? ¿Entramos a ver qué tienen?

RAÚL: Bueno, no me importa, pero yo creo que los precios son muy altos.

GLORIA: No, no es verdad. Yo compré esta blusa allí hace unos días. ¡Una ganga!

TOMÁS: Es muy bonita. Me gustan los colores vivos.

GLORIA: Gracias.

RAÚL: Podemos entrar pero, ¿por cuánto tiempo?

GLORIA: Ay, Raúl. No mucho.

RAÚL: Y tampoco tengo dinero para gastar.

GLORIA: No importa. Yo tengo dinero.

TOMÁS: ¿Hay un mercado cerca de aquí?

GLORIA: Sí, pero es para turistas…

TOMÁS: Bueno, soy un turista… más o menos… Me gustaría ir al mercado.

GLORIA: Está bien.

RAÚL: Siempre tienen buenas gangas allí.

GLORIA: Vamos.

GLORIA: ¡Mira aquellas blusas! ¡Qué estilo tan bonito tienen… ¡Y los colores son tan vivos!

RAÚL: Gloria, por favor, ¿otra blusa?

GLORIA: A ver, mediana, grande, extra-grande, pequeña… Aquí está mi talla.
Me queda un poco floja. Pero me gusta así…

TOMÁS: ¿De qué está hecha?

GLORIA: Está hecha… de algodón. ¿Les gusta?

TOMÁS: Sí, es bonita.

GLORIA: ¿Raúl? ¿Qué te parece?

RAÚL: No me parece mal. ¿Cuál es el precio?

GLORIA: ¿El precio? A ver… 9,400 colones. ¿Cuál escojo? ¿Ésta, o aquélla de un sólo color?

RAÚL: No nos importa…

GLORIA: ¿Les gustan las blusas de color oscuro? ¿O las de color claro?

RAÚL: Pues…

GLORIA: ¿O aquéllas de colores vivos?

RAÚL: ¡Gloria, la verdad es que no nos importa nada! ¡Compra algo y termina ya!

GLORIA: ¡Ay, tú! ¡Qué impaciente eres! ¿Por qué no van a mirar otras cosas mientras yo me pruebo las blusas?

RAÚL: Vamos, Tomás. Regresamos en unos quince minutos.

RAÚL: Mira. Aquellas chaquetas de cuero.

TOMÁS: Sí. Están de moda.

RAÚL: Voy a probarme una.

TOMÁS: Pero no tienes dinero.

RAÚL: Ssssh. Sí tengo dinero.

GLORIA: Quiero comprarme esta blusa.

DEPENDIENTA: Muy bien, señorita. ¿Cómo va a pagar?

GLORIA: En efectivo. Aquí está.

DEPENDIENTA: Muchas gracias. Adiós.

GLORIA: Gracias. Hasta luego.

GramActiva Videos
Demonstrative adjectives

HOST: In English, the words *this, these, that,* and *those* have a fancy name. They're called demonstrative adjectives. You can think of them as "pointing adjectives" because they point out nouns. *This* shirt. *That* ball. *Those* brains!

HOST: You've already learned the Spanish demonstrative adjectives: *este, esta, estos, estas. Ese, esa, esos,* and *esas.* But there are more Spanish demonstrative adjectives. More, more, MORE! Ha ha ha ha! Ha ha ha ha! Actually, there are just a few more that you have to know.

HOST: First, let's review *este, esta, estos,* and *estas.*

V.O.: *Este* and *esta* mean "this." The plural forms, *estos* and *estas,* mean "these." These adjectives are used for objects that are close to you.
Este libro.
Esta camisa clara.
Estos zapatos grandes.
Estas gangas.

V.O.: *Ese* and *esa* mean "that." The plural forms, *esos* and *esas,* mean "those." These adjectives are used for objects that are close to someone else.
Ese libro.
Esa camisa clara.
Esos zapatos grandes.
Esas gangas.

HOST 1: Now it's time for the new adjectives: *aquel* and *aquella,* and their plurals, *aquellos* and *aquellas.*

HOST 2: Like *ese* and *esa, aquel* and *aquella* also mean "that," but they are used to point out someone or something that is far from both you and the person you are talking with. Something that's way over there.

HOST 1 V.O.: So, *aquel cajero* means "that cashier, over there."

HOST 2: If you're with a friend and the object is far away from you both, use *aquel* and *aquella.*

HOST 1: Check it out.

V.O.: *Aquel* and *aquella* mean "that."
Aquel cajero.
Aquella salida.
The plural forms, *aquellos* and *aquellas,* mean "those."
Aquellos dependientes.
Aquellas joyas.

HOST: Think you got that? Check your knowledge with this quiz.

Quiz

V.O.: Which demonstrative adjective is appropriate for the situation?

1. The object is far from you and your friend. *Esta, esa,* or *aquella*?
2. The object is closer to the person you are talking to. *Esta, esa,* or *aquella*?
3. The object is close to you. *Esta, esa,* or *aquella*?

1. *aquella*
2. *esa*
3. *esta*

Regular preterite verbs

HOST 1: The preterite tense is used to talk about actions completed in the past.

HOST 2: Like if you said, "The chicken jumped over the moon." The chicken completed the action in the past, so if you said this sentence in Spanish, you would use the preterite tense.

HOST 1: What happened to the cow?

HOST 2: She got replaced.

HOST 1: Where is she now?

HOST 2: Last I heard, jumping over foothills.

V.O.: Coming up over the horizon are the preterite forms for regular *-ar, -er,* and *-ir* verbs.

HOST: Let's cover *-ar* verbs first. Let's start with *comprar,* "to buy."

V.O.: *Compré. Compraste. Compró. Compramos. Comprasteis. Compraron.*

V.O.: *Compré el collar.*

V.O.: *Compraron unas gorras.*

HOST: Here's an *-er* verb. *Aprender* means "to learn." I didn't learn how to con-ga. Which you probably know-ow.

V.O.: *Aprendí. Aprendiste. Aprendió. Aprendimos. Aprendisteis. Aprendieron.*

V.O.: Here's an *-ir* verb, *escribir.*
Escribí. Escribiste. Escribió. Escribimos. Escribisteis. Escribieron.

V.O.: *Aprendí a cocinar espaguetis.*
Escribí un cuento para la clase de español.

HOST: Did you get all that? Here's your chance to find out.

Quiz

V.O.: Fill in the blank with the correct preterite form of the verb.

(escuchar) Ana _____ un programa musical ayer.
Ana escuchó un programa musical ayer.

(aprender) Javier _____ a esquiar.
Javier aprendió a esquiar.

(escribir) Ellas _____ el problema en el papel.
Ellas escribieron el problema en el papel.

Realidades 2

Capítulo 2B

Nombre _____

Fecha _____

Communicative Pair Activity **2B-1**

Estudiante **A**

Imagine that you and your friend are shopping. You are asking questions about items your partner bought, comparing items he or she wants to buy, and asking questions about your friend's preferences and opinions on what to buy. Ask your partner the following questions and then write his or her answers in the spaces provided. Pay close attention to the articles (un, una, unos, unas, el, la, los, las). Follow this example:

—¿Cuáles prefieres, los zapatos blancos o los negros?

—Prefiero los negros.

1. ¿Cuál prefieres, la chaqueta de lana o la de cuero?_____

2. ¿Compraste unos calcetines blancos o unos negros? _____

3. ¿Compraste las joyas baratas o las caras? _____

4. ¿Cuál prefieres, la camisa grande o la mediana? _____

5. ¿Cuáles prefieres, los pantalones flojos o los apretados?

_____

6. ¿Cuál prefieres, el suéter de tela sintética o el de algodón?

_____

Imagine that you and your friend are shopping. Your friend is asking questions about items you bought, and comparing and asking questions about your preferences and opinions on what to buy. Answer your partner's questions according to the cues below and then write your answers in the spaces provided. Pay close attention to the articles (un, una, unos, unas, el, la, los, las). Follow this example:

—¿Cuáles prefieres, los zapatos blancos o los negros?

—Prefiero los negros.

1. (claro)   2. (de seda)   3. (de algodón)

_____   _____   _____

4. (blanca)   5. (mediana)   6. (flojos)

_____   _____   _____

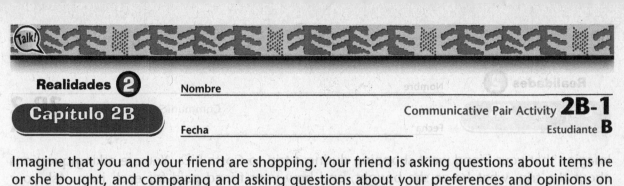

Realidades 2

Capítulo 2B

Nombre _____

Fecha _____

Communicative Pair Activity **2B-1**

Estudiante **B**

Imagine that you and your friend are shopping. Your friend is asking questions about items he or she bought, and comparing and asking questions about your preferences and opinions on what to buy. Answer your partner's questions according to the cues below and then write your answers in the spaces provided. Pay close attention to the articles *(un, una, unos, unas, el, la, los, las)*. Example:

—*¿Cuáles prefieres, los zapatos blancos o los negros?*

—*Prefiero los negros.*

1. (de cuero)

2. (blancos)

3. (caras)

4. (grande)

5. (apretados)

6. (de algodón)

_____ _____ _____

Imagine that you and your friend are shopping. You are asking questions about items your partner bought, comparing items he or she wants to buy, and asking questions about your friend's preferences and opinions on what to buy. Ask your partner the following questions and then write his or her answers in the space provided. Pay close attention to the articles *(un, unos, una, unas, el, los, la, las)*. Example:

—*¿Cuáles prefieres, los zapatos blancos o los negros?*

—*Prefiero los negros.*

1. ¿Cuál prefieres, el suéter claro o el oscuro?_____

2. ¿Compraste una camisa de algodón o una de seda?_____

3.   ¿Compraste los pantalones cortos de algodón o los de tela sintética?

_____

4. ¿Compraste la sudadera blanca o la negra?_____

5. ¿Cuál prefieres, la camiseta grande o la mediana?_____

6. ¿Cuáles prefieres, los jeans flojos o los apretados?_____

Realidades 2

Capítulo 2B

Nombre _____

Fecha _____

Communicative Pair Activity **2B-2**

Estudiante **A**

Imagine that your friend went shopping during a trip to Costa Rica. You are asking questions about the trip, what he or she bought, and how your friend paid for each item. Ask your partner the following questions. Write the answers in the spaces provided. Example: *Compré los zapatos con una tarjeta de crédito.*

1. ¿Cuánto pagaste por esa camisa? _____

2. ¿Cómo pagaste por esos zapatos? _____

3. ¿Qué usaste para pagar esas joyas? _____

4. ¿Cómo pagaste en el restaurante? _____

5. ¿Qué usaste para pagar por la corbata? _____

6. ¿Cómo pagaste por el hotel? _____

Imagine that you went shopping during a trip to Costa Rica. You are talking about the trip, what you bought, and how you paid for each item. Answer each question with the cues given below. Use each verb in parentheses in the past tense to answer each question. Then write your answers in the space provided next to each verb. Follow this model:

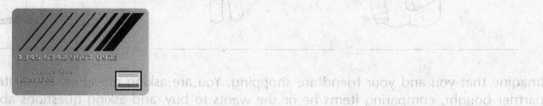

(comprar)—*Compré los zapatos con una tarjeta de crédito.*

1. (pagar)_____ 2. (pagar) _____ 3. (usar) _____

_____ _____ _____

4. (pagar)_____ 5. (usar) _____ 6. (usar) _____

_____ _____ _____

Talk!

Realidades ②

Capítulo 2B

Nombre _____

Fecha _____

Communicative Pair Activity **2B-2**

Estudiante **B**

Imagine that you went shopping during a trip to Costa Rica. You are talking about the trip, what you bought, and how you paid for each item. Answer each question with the cues given below. Use each verb in parentheses in the past tense to answer each question. Then write your answers in the space provided next to each verb. Follow this model:

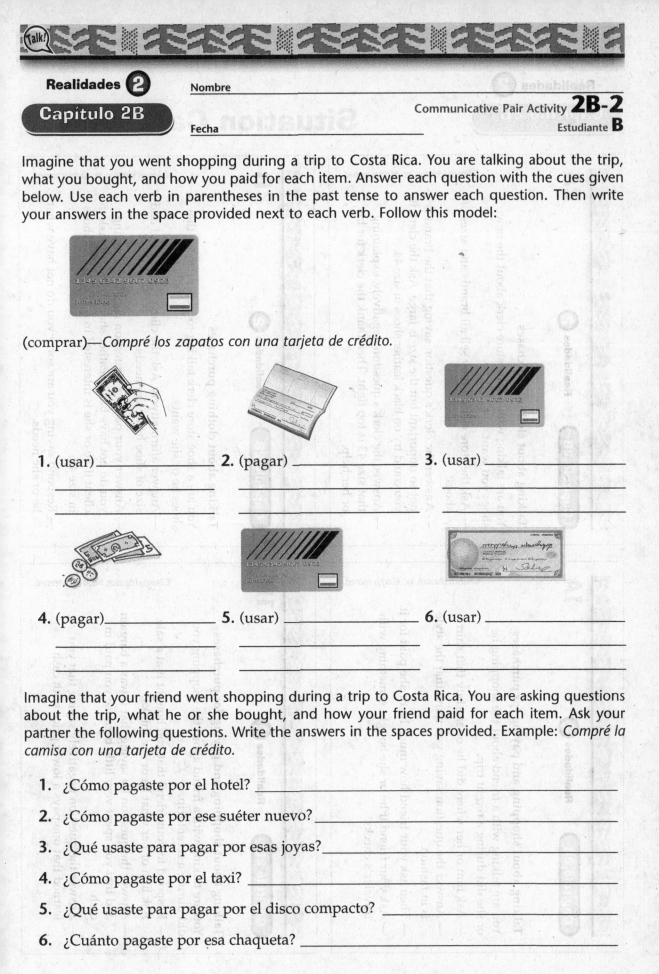

(comprar)—*Compré los zapatos con una tarjeta de crédito.*

1. (usar)_____
_____
_____

2. (pagar)_____
_____
_____

3. (usar)_____
_____
_____

4. (pagar)_____
_____
_____

5. (usar)_____
_____
_____

6. (usar)_____
_____
_____

Imagine that your friend went shopping during a trip to Costa Rica. You are asking questions about the trip, what he or she bought, and how your friend paid for each item. Ask your partner the following questions. Write the answers in the spaces provided. Example: *Compré la camisa con una tarjeta de crédito.*

1. ¿Cómo pagaste por el hotel? _____

2. ¿Cómo pagaste por ese suéter nuevo? _____

3. ¿Qué usaste para pagar por esas joyas?_____

4. ¿Cómo pagaste por el taxi? _____

5. ¿Qué usaste para pagar por el disco compacto? _____

6. ¿Cuánto pagaste por esa chaqueta? _____

Situation Cards

2A

Realidades 2

Capítulo 2B

Talking about clothing purchases

You are talking with a shoe store clerk about the new shoes you want.

— Ask the store clerk if they sell all brands and sizes of shoes.

— Answer the clerk's question saying that the brand is not so important but that the size is large. Ask the clerk if you could try on black leather shoes in size 44.

— Answer the clerk's question negatively, explaining that size 43 is too tight. Then thank the clerk for his or her help.

2B

Realidades 2

Capítulo 2B

Talking about clothing purchases

You are a shoe store clerk talking to a client about the shoes he or she wants.

— Answer affirmatively. Ask the client what brand and size of shoe he or she needs.

— Answer your partner's question negatively saying you do not have black leather shoes that size. Ask the client if he or she is interested in black leather shoes in size 43.

— Respond saying you are sorry you do not have what he or she needs.

1A

Realidades 2

Capítulo 2B

Talking about shopping and paying for purchases

You are talking with a friend about the shopping he or she did during a recent trip.

— Ask him or her where did he or she buy that shirt.

— Answer the question saying you think that the style is in fashion.

— Then ask your friend how much he or she paid for it.

— Ask your friend if he or she bought something with traveler's checks.

1B

Realidades 2

Capítulo 2B

Talking about shopping and paying for purchases

You are talking with a friend about the shopping you did during a recent trip.

— Respond to your friend that you bought it at a sale. Ask him or her what he or she thinks.

— Answer the question by saying that it was a bargain and that you spent very little because you paid in cash.

— Answer the question negatively saying that you learned that one pays a lower price with cash.

GramActiva

¿Qué ropa compraste?

¿Qué compran y cómo pagan?, p. 107

¿Quién?	¿Qué?	¿Cómo?

Vocabulary Clip Art

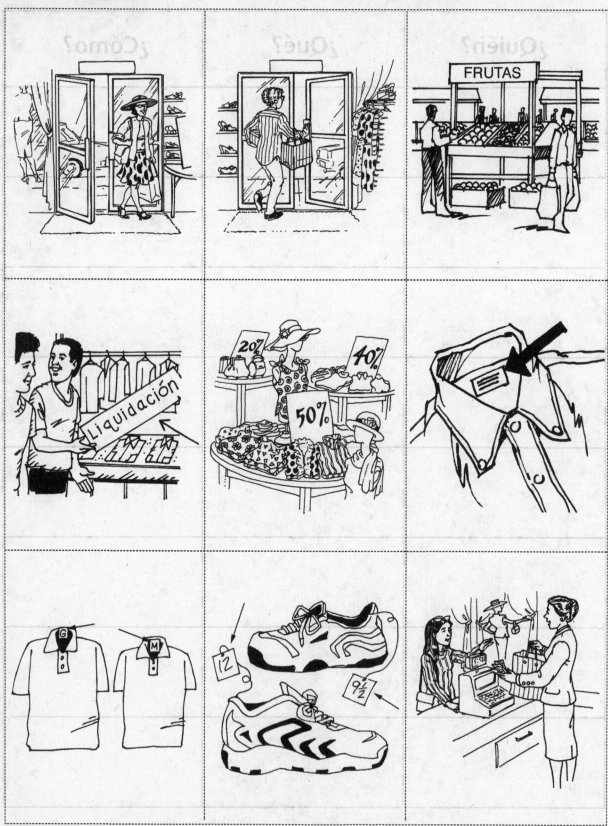

Vocabulary Clip Art

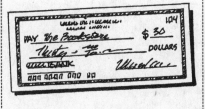

Capítulo 2B

Vocabulary Clip Art

Core Practice Answers

2B-A
1. tienda de descuentos
2. comprar
3. regalos
4. centro comercial
5. electrodomésticos
6. anteojos de sol
7. zapatería

2B-B
A.
1. marrón
2. negro
3. amarillas
4. verde
5. grises
6. blanca
B.
1. Roberto y Felipe compran diez collares.
2. Yo compro cincuenta discos compactos.
3. Tú compras tres carteras.
4. Uds. compran veinte videojuegos.
5. Nosotros compramos doce botellas de perfume.

2B-1
A.
1. caja
2. se prueba
3. cheque
4. talla
5. cupón de regalo
B.
1. estilos
2. gasté
3. tarjeta
4. cheque
5. efectivo

2B-2
A.
1. antónimo
2. sinónimo
3. antónimo
4. antónimo
5. sinónimo
B.
1. pruebo
2. parece
3. vivos
4. aquella
5. marcas
6. precios
7. exagerados
8. estilo

9. moda
10. mediana
11. letrero
12. ganga

2B-3
1. Está hecho de lana.
2. Me quedan apretados.
3. Voy a pagar con tarjeta de crédito.
4. Voy a pagar en la caja.
5. Voy al mercado para gastar mi dinero.
6. La talla mediana me queda mejor.
7. El letrero anuncia una liquidación.
8. Voy paraUso la salida.

2B-4
Wording of answers will vary.
1. Tatiana busca ropa para el invierno.
2. En realidad Tatiana no quiere una ganga. Mariana habla más de liquidaciones y de gangas.
3. A Tatiana le gusta la falda porque se ve bien con la blusa. No le importa la tela.
4. La ropa le queda bastante bien; la blusa está un poco floja y la fallada está un poco apretada.
5. Answers will vary.

2B-5
A.
1. Alicia y sus amigos llegaron
2. Tú viste
3. Ellos entraron
4. Alicia recibió
5. La tienda anunció
6. Jorge escogió
7. Marta y Felisa encontraron
8. Todos gastaron
B.
1. Llegué
2. navegué
3. Toqué
4. Almorcé
5. Busqué
6. Empecé

2B-6
A.
1. Aquellos cupones de regalo son suyos.
2. Aquella tarjeta de crédito es nuestra.
3. Aquellos cheques personales son tuyos.
4. Aquella bolsa es suya.

5. Aquella cartera es mía.
6. Aquellas joyas son suyas.
B.
1. esta camisa
2. aquellos pantalones
3. ese traje
4. esos zapatos

2B-7
1. Compramos el de tela.
2. Encontré una azul.
3. Se probó unos de color oscuro.
4. Escogí uno caro.
5. Vimos unos nuevos.
6. Busqué una negra.
7. Escribimos unas cortas.
8. Me gustó más el de Laura.

Crucigrama (2B-8)
Horizontal:
1. importa
3. marca
8. dinero
9. letrero
10. estilos
13. realidad
17. entradas

19. mercado
21. escoger
23. anuncian
27. liquidación
28. encuentro
29. aquellos

Vertical:
2. talla
4. cuero
5. vivos
6. alto
7. prueba
11. gastamos
12. venta
14. algodón

15. descuento
16. claro
18. apretado
20. mediano
22. cajero
24. cupones
25. número
26. ganga

Organizer (2B-9)
I. Vocabulary Answers will vary.
II. Grammar
1. **mirar:**

miré	miramos
miraste	mirasteis
miró	miraron

comer:

comí	comimos
comiste	comisteis
comió	comieron

escribir:

escribí	escribimos
escribiste	escribisteis
escribió	escribieron

2.
Row 1: aquél (aquello) / aquellos
Row 2: aquella / aquellas
3. adjective

Write the Spanish vocabulary word below each picture. Be sure to include the article for each noun.

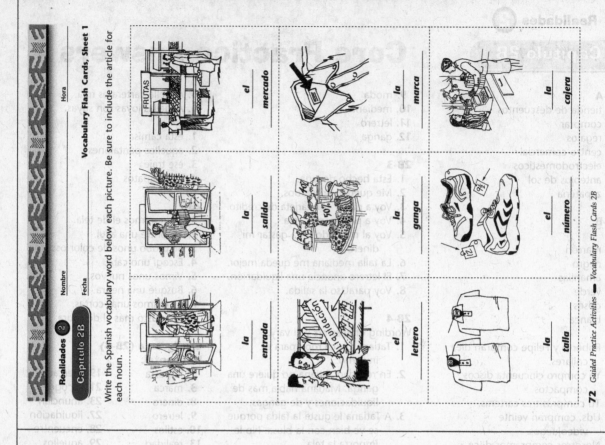

el mercado   la salida   la entrada

la marca   la ganga   el letrero

la cajera   el número   la talla

Cardinal numbers (p. 99)

- Cardinal numbers are used for counting and for telling quantities of things.
- Remember that **uno** and **cientos** change to agree in gender with the nouns that follow them.

treinta y un perros   thirty-one dogs
seiscientas personas   six hundred people

A. Match the series of numbers on the left with the numerals on the right.

1. _c_ mil ochocientos setenta y tres   a. 2104
2. _d_ cinco mil quinientos   b. 1707
3. _b_ mil setecientos siete   c. 1873
4. _f_ mil cuatrocientos noventa y dos   d. 5500
5. _a_ dos mil ciento cuatro   e. 1928
6. _e_ mil novecientos veintiocho   f. 1492

B. Write the numbers indicated numerically. Follow the model.

Modelo   ciento cuarenta y seis   146

1. trescientos treinta y tres   333
2. mil ochenta y cinco   1,085
3. dos mil novecientos   2,900
4. quinientos setenta y seis   576
5. ciento cuarenta y cuatro mil   144,000
6. doscientos noventa y ocho   298
7. cincuenta mil veinticinco   50,025
8. nueve mil seiscientos treinta   9,630

realidades.com
• Web Code: jkd-0211

Copy the word or phrase in the space provided. Be sure to include the article for each noun.

me/te importa(n)	tan + adjective	la liquidación
me/te ___ importa(n) ___	tan ___ + adjective ___	la ___ liquidación ___
oscuro, oscura	de sólo un color	claro, clara
oscuro ___ , oscura ___	de ___ sólo ___ un ___ color ___	claro ___ , clara ___
Está hecho, hecha de...	¿De qué está hecho, hecha?	pastel
Está ___ hecho ___ , hecha ___ de...	¿De ___ qué ___ está ___ hecho ___ , hecha? ___	pastel ___

Write the Spanish vocabulary word below each picture. If there is a word or phrase, copy it in the space provided. Be sure to include the article for each noun.

el ___ cajero ___	la ___ caja ___	la ___ tarjeta ___ de ___ crédito ___
el ___ cheque ___ (personal) ___	en ___ efectivo ___	el ___ cupón ___ de ___ regalo ___
flojo, floja	apretado, apretada	vivo, viva
flojo ___ , floja ___	apretado ___ , apretada ___	vivo ___ , viva ___

Copy the word or phrase in the space provided. Be sure to include the article for each noun.

escoger	estar de moda	el estilo
escoger	estar __ de __ moda	el __ estilo

exagerado, exagerada	mediano, mediana	probarse
exagerado , exagerada	mediano , mediana	probarse

anunciar	encontrar	en realidad
anunciar	encontrar	en __ realidad

Copy the word or phrase in the space provided. Be sure to include the article for each noun.

algodón	cuero	lana
algodón	cuero	lana

seda	tela sintética	alto, alta
seda	tela sintética	alto , alta

bajo, baja	gastar	el precio
bajo , baja	gastar	el __ precio

Sheet 7

These blank cards can be used to write and practice other Spanish vocabulary for the chapter.

Sheet 6

Copy the word or phrase in the space provided. Be sure to include the article for each noun. These blank cards can be used to write and practice other Spanish vocabulary for the chapter.

inmediatamente

____inmediatamente____

me parece que

me ____ parece

____ que

¿Qué te parece?

¿Qué ____ te

____ parece?

recientemente

____recientemente____

el cheque de viajero

el ____ cheque

de ____ viajero

Nombre _____ Hora _____

Fecha _____ **Vocabulary Check, Sheet 1**

Tear out this page. Write the English words on the lines. Fold the paper along the dotted line to see the correct answers so you can check your work.

la entrada	*entrance*
la ganga	*bargain*
el letrero	*sign*
la liquidación	*sale*
el mercado	*market*
la salida	*exit*
el cajero, la cajera	*cashier*
el cheque (personal)	*(personal) check*
el cheque de viajero	*traveler's check*
el cupón de regalo	*gift certificate*
en efectivo	*cash*
el precio	*price*
la marca	*brand*
la talla	*size*

Fold In ↓

Nombre _____ Hora _____

Fecha _____ **Vocabulary Check, Sheet 2**

Tear out this page. Write the Spanish words on the lines. Fold the paper along the dotted line to see the correct answers so you can check your work.

entrance	*la entrada*
bargain	*la ganga*
sign	*el letrero*
sale	*la liquidación*
market	*el mercado*
exit	*la salida*
cashier	*el cajero, la cajera*
(personal) check	*el cheque (personal)*
traveler's check	*el cheque de viajero*
gift certificate	*el cupón de regalo*
cash	*en efectivo*
price	*el precio*
brand	*la marca*
size	*la talla*

Fold In ↓

Tear out this page. Write the Spanish words on the lines. Fold the paper along the dotted line to see the correct answers so you can check your work.

cotton	*algodón*
leather	*cuero*
wool	*lana*
silk	*seda*
synthetic fabric	*tela sintética*
tight	*apretado, apretada*
loose	*flojo, floja*
medium	*mediano, mediana*
to be in fashion	*estar de moda*
to find	*encontrar*
to announce	*anunciar*
to choose	*escoger*
to try on	*probarse*
to buy	*comprar*

- Fold In ↓

To hear a complete list of the vocabulary for this chapter, go to www.realidades.com and type in the Web Code jdd-0299. Then click on Repaso del capítulo.

Tear out this page. Write the English words on the lines. Fold the paper along the dotted line to see the correct answers so you can check your work.

algodón	*cotton*
cuero	*leather*
lana	*wool*
seda	*silk*
tela sintética	*synthetic fabric*
apretado, apretada	*tight*
flojo, floja	*loose*
mediano, mediana	*medium*
estar de moda	*to be in fashion*
encontrar	*to find*
anunciar	*to announce*
escoger	*to choose*
probarse	*to try on*
comprar	*to buy*

- Fold In ↓

Preterite of regular verbs (continued)

- Note that **-ar** and **-er** verbs that have a stem change in the present tense do not have a stem change in the preterite.

Present tense: Siempre **encuentro** gangas en el mercado.
I always find bargains at the market.
Preterite tense: Ayer no **encontraste** gangas en el mercado.
Yesterday you didn't find bargains at the market.

C. Complete the following paragraph by filling in each blank with the correct preterite form of the verb in parentheses. The first one is done for you.

La semana pasada yo __fui__ (ir) al centro comercial, pero yo no __encontré__ (encontrar) una camiseta de mi talla porque soy grande. Mi mamá también buscó la camiseta ayer pero __costó__ (costar) mucho dinero. Recientemente, me __probé__ (probar) una camiseta apretada y no me gustó. Esta mañana nosotros __nos despertamos__ (despertarse) temprano para ir de compras. ¡Qué bien, porque yo __volví__ (volver) a la tienda y compré mi camiseta!

- Verbs that end in **-car, -gar,** and **-zar** have a spelling change in the **yo** form of the preterite.
- Other preterite forms of these verbs are regular.

buscar	c → qu	yo busqué	él/ella buscó	ellos/ellas buscaron
pagar	g → gu	yo pagué	él/ella pagó	ellos/ellas pagaron
almorzar	z → c	yo almorcé	él/ella almorzó	ellos/ellas almorzaron

D. Read the following conversation. Circle the verb in each question. Then, write the appropriate form of that same verb in the blank. The first one has been done for you.

1. JUAN: ¿(Buscaste) una camisa nueva?
EMILIO: Sí, yo __busqué__ una camisa nueva. Tere __buscó__ zapatos.

2. JUAN: ¿(Pagaste) la camisa en efectivo?
EMILIO: Sí, yo __pagué__ en efectivo. Miguel __pagó__ con tarjeta de crédito.

3. JUAN: ¿(Almorzaste) con Elena en el restaurante?
EMILIO: Sí, yo __almorcé__ con Elena. Nosotros __almorzamos__ a las dos.

4. JUAN: ¿(Llegaste) temprano a la tienda?
EMILIO: Sí, yo __llegué__ a las nueve. Emilia y Víctor __llegaron__ tarde.

realidades.com
• Web Code: jdd-0214

Preterite of regular verbs (p. 110)

- Use the preterite tense to talk about actions that were completed in the past. To form the preterite tense of a regular verb, add the preterite endings to the stem of the verb.
- Here are the preterite forms for the verbs **mirar** (to look), **aprender** (to learn), and **escribir** (to write):

yo	miré / aprendí / escribí	I looked / I learned / I wrote
tú	miraste / aprendiste / escribiste	you looked / you learned / you wrote
usted/él/ella	miró / aprendió / escribió	you/he/she looked / you/he/she learned / you/he/she wrote
nosotros/nosotras	miramos / aprendimos / escribimos	we looked / we learned / we wrote
vosotros/vosotras	mirasteis / aprendisteis / escribisteis	you looked / you learned / you wrote
ustedes/ellos/ellas	miraron / aprendieron / escribieron	you/they looked / you/they learned / you/they wrote

A. Read the sentences below. If they tell what happens regularly in the present (using the present tense), write a 1. If they tell what happened in the past (using the preterite tense), write a 2. Follow the model.

Modelo Yo aprendí a leer. **2**

1. Tú miraste el letrero. **2**
2. Mi papá escribió un cheque. **2**
3. Las chicas estudian mucho en la clase. **1**
4. Uds. escriben el libro. **1**
5. Yo miré la tele anoche. **2**

B. Write the appropriate ending to complete each verb stem. Follow the model.

Modelo (comer) Nosotros com**imos** en la cafetería.

1. (aprender) Uds. aprend**ieron** a leer en la escuela.
2. (escribir) Yo no escrib**í** la carta.
3. (aprender) Carlos y yo aprend**imos** el inglés.
4. (mirar) Rafael no mir**ó** el precio de la camisa.
5. (enviar) Mis abuelos me envi**aron** una carta.
6. (comer) Tú com**iste** con Antonio anoche, ¿verdad?
7. (preparar) Mi padre prepar**ó** la comida.

realidades.com
• Web Code: jdd-0214

Nombre _____

Fecha _____ Hora _____

Guided Practice Activities 2B-3

Demonstrative adjectives (p. 114)

• Demonstrative adjectives show how close something is to the speaker. Here's a chart that compares the demonstrative adjectives:

Singular		Plural	
este/esta	this	estos/estas	these
ese/esa	that	esos/esas	those
aquel/aquella	that (over there)	aquellos/aquellas	those (over there)

A. Write the equivalent word(s) in English for each underlined demonstrative adjective. Follow the model.

Modelo Me gustan aquellas camisas blancas. *English:* **those (over there)**

1. Yo prefiero estas camisas rojas. *English:* **these**
2. A mí me gusta esta gorra roja. *English:* **this**
3. Yo quiero comprar esos zapatos. *English:* **those**
4. A mi madre le gusta aquella blusa elegante. *English:* **that (over there)**
5. Ella compró ese bolso cuando fue a París. *English:* **that**

B. Circle the correct demonstrative adjective in parentheses to complete the dialogue. Remember adjectives must agree in gender and number with the noun they describe.

LUPE: Mamá, ¡mira (**este**/ esta) suéter de lana! Es perfecto para papá.

MADRE: Sí, pero él prefiere (**esos**/ esas) pantalones azules allí. Son más prácticos.

LUPE: ¡Oh! Quiero comprar (aquellos /**aquella**) faldas bonitas cerca de la ventana.

MADRE: Me gustan, pero (este /**esta**) falda es tu número, el dos.

LUPE: Pero no va bien con (**ese** /esa) camisa que me gusta, la roja.

MADRE: Entonces, prueba las dos.

LUPE: Bien. Gracias, mamá.

Guided Practice Activities — 2B-3   85

Nombre _____

Fecha _____ Hora _____

Guided Practice Activities 2B-3a

Demonstrative adjectives (*continued*)

C. Look at the pictures of clothing below. Then, answer the question by writing in the correct demonstrative adjective for each article of clothing. The smallest article of clothing is the farthest away. Follow the model.

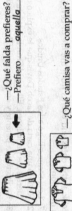

Modelo —¿Qué falda prefieres?
—Prefiero **aquella** falda.

1. —¿Qué camisa vas a comprar?
—Voy a comprar **esta** camisa.

2. —¿Qué pantalones te gustan?
—Me gustan **aquellos** pantalones.

3. —¿Qué traje prefieres?
—Prefiero **esa** traje.

4. —¿Qué zapatos piensas comprar?
—Pienso comprar **esos** zapatos.

D. Write the correct demonstrative adjectives based on the English cues you are given.

1. (*this*) Debes leer **este** libro. Es muy interesante.
2. (*those over there*) ¿Quiénes son **aquellas** señoritas?
3. (*that*) ¿Leíste **esa** novela antes?
4. (*these*) ¿De quiénes son **estos** cheques de viajero?
5. (*this*) No me gusta **este** lápiz. Prefiero uno azul.

86 Guided Practice Activities — 2B-3a

Capítulo 2B ⚊ *Guided Practice Answers* **163**

Lectura: Los jeans (pp. 118–119)

A. The reading in your textbook is about the history of jeans. Before you read the selection, think about and answer the following questions. **Answers will vary.**

1. Do you like to wear jeans? Why? _____

2. Why are jeans popular with many students? _____

B. The second section from your textbook reading is about one of the inventors of jeans. Read the selection and answer the questions. Use the *Hints* below to help you answer the questions.

Un poco de historia

Levi Strauss, un joven alemán, llegó a los Estados Unidos con su familia en 1847 a la edad de 18 años. Después de trabajar algunos años con su familia, Strauss viajó a California para abrir una tienda de ropa y accesorios. Esta tienda se convirtió en un negocio próspero durante los siguientes 20 años, y Strauss se hizo rico.

1. What type of store did Levi Strauss open in California? *Hint:* Look for the words *una tienda de*.
   Answers will vary.

2. What happened over the next 20 years? *Hint:* Look for the words *próspero* and *rico*.
   Answers will vary.

C. Now, look at the dates and events from the life of Levi Strauss and answer the following questions.

1847: Levi Strauss llegó a los Estados Unidos.
1872: Recibió una carta de Jacob Davis que le explicó un proceso para hacer más fuertes los pantalones. Ellos pidieron la patente de este proceso.
1873: Recibieron la patente y empezaron a fabricar *waist overalls*.

1. When did Levi Strauss arrive in the United States?
   a. 1873 (b.) 1847

2. Before Levi Strauss and Jacob Davis began to make waist overalls, they needed a
   (a.) patent. b. letter.

3. When Strauss and Davis received the patent, they began to
   (a.) make waist overalls. b. explain the process.

Using adjectives as nouns (p. 116)

- When you compare two similar things, you can avoid repetition by dropping the noun and using the *article* + the *adjective* for the second thing.

  ¿Cuál prefieres, el vestido apretado o el flojo? *Which do you prefer, the tight dress or the loose one?*

  Prefiero el flojo. *I prefer the loose one.*

A. Read the questions below. Circle the noun in each question. Then, answer the questions using the appropriate article and adjective as a noun.

Modelo —¿Pagaste el (precio) alto o el bajo?
       —Pagué el **bajo**

1. —¿Compraste la (blusa) clara o la oscura?
   —Compré **la** **clara**

2. —¿Probaste los (zapatos) caros o los baratos?
   —Probé **los** **baratos**

3. —¿Encontraste el (vestido) grande o el mediano?
   —Encontré **el** **mediano**

4. —¿Te gustan los (jeans) apretados o los flojos?
   —Me gustan **los** **apretados**

B. Read the sentences below. Complete the second sentence in each pair using an article and the opposite adjective as a noun. Choose from the word bank. Follow the model.

antipáticos	blanca	claro	floja	largas	pequeñas

Modelo A Juan le encanta la ropa negra. No le encanta **la** **blanca**

1. Nosotros preferimos las tiendas grandes. No preferimos **las** **pequeñas**

2. A ellas les gustan los cajeros simpáticos. No les gustan **los** **antipáticos**

3. Yo no me pruebo la ropa apretada. Me pruebo **la** **floja**

4. Emily no prefiere las faldas cortas. Prefiere **las** **largas**

5. No compraste el traje oscuro. Compraste **el** **claro**

Nombre _____ Hora _____

Fecha _____ **Guided Practice Activities 2B-6**

Presentación escrita (p. 121) *Answers will vary.*

Task: You received $200 for your birthday and have just purchased some articles of clothing. Write an e-mail to your friend describing your shopping trip.

A. Before you write the e-mail, it would be helpful to organize the information about your purchases. Fill in the table below. The first line is done for you.

¿Qué compraste?	¿Dónde...?	¿Cuánto pagaste?
camiseta	*en el centro comercial*	*$20*
1. _____	_____	_____
2. _____	_____	_____
3. _____	_____	_____

B. Answer the following questions about your shopping trip. You can look back at your answers in **part A** to help you.

1. ¿Qué compraste?

   Yo _____

2. ¿Dónde compraste la ropa?

   Yo _____

3. ¿Cuánto pagaste?

   Yo _____

4. ¿Por qué compraste esta ropa?

   Yo _____

C. Use the answers to the questions in **parts A** and **B** to write an e-mail to your friend below. You may use the following model.

¡Hola _____! Yo recibí _____ en mi cumpleaños. Yo compré ropa

*en el _____ Compré _____ Pagué _____ Yo pagué

Luego, compré _____ Pagué _____ por _____

ropa? Adiós, _____ está de moda y me gusta mucho. ¿Qué te parece mi

D. Check your e-mail for spelling, forms of the preterite, and agreement. Then, send it to your teacher or a classmate.

Guided Practice Activities — 2B-6 **89**

Antes de ver el video

Actividad 1

Write seven sentences to tell about what kind of clothes you like to wear. Use the words in the box to help you.

la ganga	la liquidación	el mercado	algodón	de cuero
está hecho(a) de	claro(a)	oscuro(a)	vivo(a)	apretado(a)
flojo(a)	mediano(a)	la talla	el dinero	el regalo
el precio	los pantalones	la blusa	la falda	la chaqueta
tela sintética				

1. Answers will vary. _____

2. _____

3. _____

4. _____

5. _____

6. _____

7. _____

¿Comprendes?

Actividad 2

Circle the correct response below.

1. Gloria ve un letrero que
   a. anuncia una liquidación fabulosa.
   b. informa al público de una tienda nueva.
   c. tiene el horario de la tienda favorita de Gloria.

2. A Raúl y a Tomás no les gusta
   a. ir al mercado.
   b. ir de compras.
   c. tomar refrescos.

3.
Gloria compró una blusa que era
a. de talla extra-grande.
b. muy fea.
c. **una ganga.**

4.
Tomás quiere ir
a. a casa.
b. al centro comercial.
c. **al mercado.**

5.
Gloria exclama: "Aquellas blusas tienen
a. **un estilo muy bonito".**
b. unos colores aburridos".
c. muchas tallas, pero ninguna me sirve".

6.
A Gloria le gusta la blusa
a. **un poco floja.**
b. bien apretada.
c. de cuero.

7.
La blusa está hecha de
a. lana.
b. **algodón.**
c. seda.

8. Gloria dice que
a. **Raúl es muy impaciente.**
b. Raúl es su hermano favorito.
c. Raúl no se viste de moda.

9. Raúl
a. **tiene dinero para gastar, aunque le dijo a Gloria que no tenía nada.**
b. no tiene nada de dinero.
c. le pide prestado dinero a Gloria.

10.
Gloria paga por su blusa
a. con cheque.
b. **en efectivo.**
c. con tarjeta de crédito.

Communication Workbook

Actividad 3

Match each character with three things he or she said in the video. Write the number of the statement next to the corresponding name.

El personaje   **Lo que dice**

Gloria 1   5   7   1. ¡Una liquidación fabulosa! ¿Qué les parece?

2. Bueno, no me importa, pero creo que los precios son muy altos.

3. ¿Hay un mercado cerca de aquí?

4. ... por favor, ¿otra blusa?

Tomás 3   6   9   5. Me queda un poco floja. Pero me gusta así...

6. ¿De qué está hecha?

7. ¿El precio? A ver... 9,400 colones.

8. Mira. Aquellas chaquetas de cuero.

Raúl 2   4   8   9. Pero no tienes dinero.

Y, ¿qué más?

Actividad 4

Do you like to shop? Write a short paragraph telling why or why not.

Modelo *A mí no me gusta mucho ir de compras. A mi hermana, sin embargo, le encanta comprar de todo. Por eso no me gusta salir con ella. Pero cuando quiero comprar discos compactos, vamos al centro comercial. Yo voy a las tiendas de discos y ella va a las de ropa. Ella gasta todo su dinero y yo no gasto mucho. Lo mejor de todo es que al final puedo comprarme un helado.*

Answers will vary.

Communication Workbook

Realidades 2

Capítulo 2B

Nombre _____

Hora _____

Fecha _____

AUDIO

Actividad 7

Listen to the following teenagers describe to a radio announcer the most daring thing they have ever done. As the radio interviewer asks each one "**¿Cuál es la cosa más atrevida que hiciste?**", look at the pictures below. Write the number of each response under the corresponding picture. You will hear each response twice.

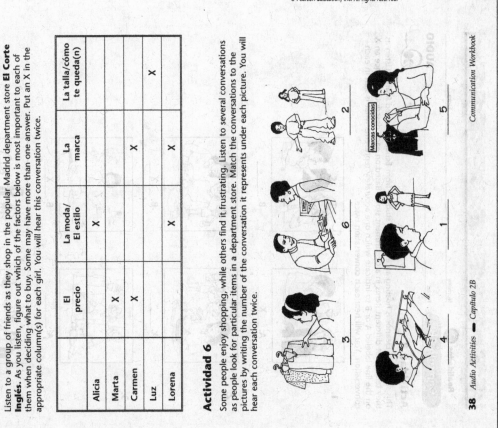

_____ 4

_____ 3

_____ 1

_____ 2

_____ 6

_____ 5

Realidades 2

Capítulo 2B

Nombre _____

Hora _____

Fecha _____

AUDIO

Actividad 5

Listen to a group of friends as they shop in the popular Madrid department store **El Corte Inglés**. As you listen, figure out which of the factors below is most important to each of them when deciding what to buy. Some may have more than one answer. Put an X in the appropriate column(s) for each girl. You will hear this conversation twice.

	El precio	La moda/ El estilo	La marca	La talla/cómo te queda(n)
Alicia		X		
Marta	X			
Carmen	X		X	
Luz				X
Lorena		X	X	

Actividad 6

Some people enjoy shopping, while others find it frustrating. Listen to several conversations as people look for particular items in a department store. Match the conversations to the pictures by writing the number of the conversation it represents under each picture. You will hear each conversation twice.

_____ 3

_____ 6   1

_____ 2

Marcas conocidas

_____ 4

_____ 5

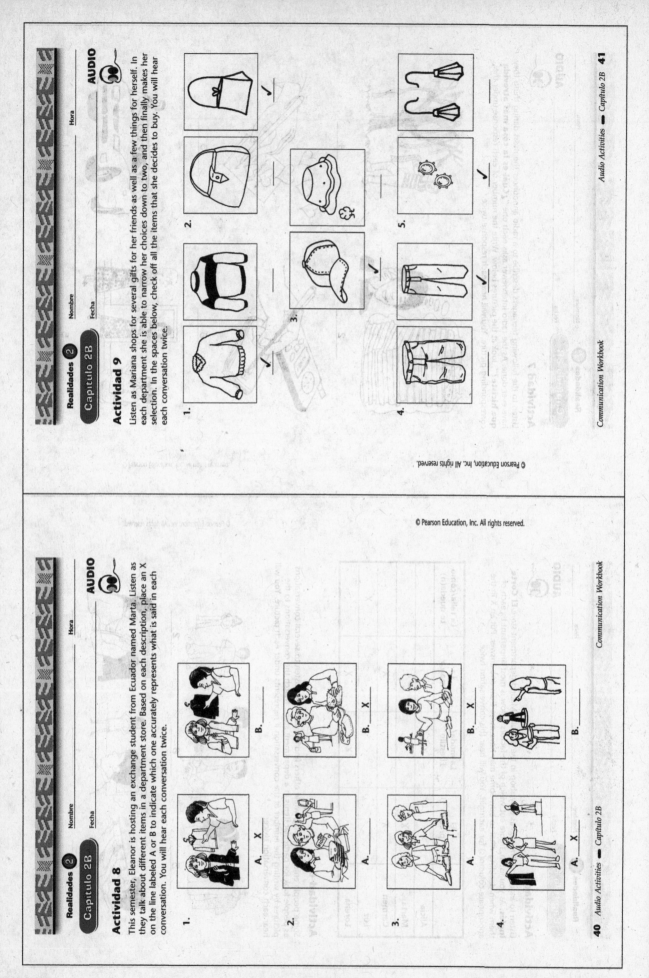

Actividad 9

Listen as Mariana shops for several gifts for her friends as well as a few things for herself. In each department she is able to narrow her choices down to two, and then finally makes her selection. In the spaces below, check off all the items that she decides to buy. You will hear each conversation twice.

1.

2.

3.

4.

5.

Actividad 8

This semester, Eleanor is hosting an exchange student from Ecuador named Marta. Listen as they talk about different items in a department store. Based on each description, place an X on the line labeled A or B to indicate which one accurately represents what is said in each conversation. You will hear each conversation twice.

1. A. __X__   B. ____

2. A. ____   B. __X__

3. A. ____   B. __X__

4. A. __X__   B. ____

WRITING

Actividad 11

Write complete sentences to tell what the following people did yesterday. Use the correct preterite form of the verbs suggested by the pictures. Follow the model and be creative.

Modelo Marisa _escribió una carta a su abuela en Uruguay_

Answers will vary. Possible answers below.

1. Yo _pagué diez dólares por unos pantalones cortos_

2. Nosotras _vimos una liquidación en el letrero_

3. Tú _te probaste una camisa en la tienda de ropa_

4. Ellos _se arreglaron, se peinaron y se secaron el pelo porque salieron anoche._

5. Mi mamá y yo _comimos en un restaurante_

6. La tienda _anunció una liquidación_

7. Los estudiantes _prestaron atención en la clase_

Communication Workbook

WRITING

Actividad 10

There is a sale at your local department store this weekend and you've run into many of your friends there, shopping for bargains. Complete the mini-conversations below.

Modelo
—¡Aquellos zapatos cuestan sólo veinte dólares!
—¿Cómo sabes que son tan baratos?
—_El letrero anuncia la liquidación_

1. —¿De qué color es el suéter que tienes en la mano?
—_Es de color (azul) oscuro_
—¿Y cuesta sólo nueve dólares?
—Sí, _es una ganga_

2. —Señor, me gustaría ver aquellos zapatos.
—Claro, señorita. ¿ _Cuál es su número_ ?
—Siete y medio.

3. —¿Ud. paga con cheque personal?
—No, _uso mi tarjeta de crédito_

4. —Ramón, tengo unas camisas en colores pastel para ti.
—Gracias, papá, pero _prefiero los colores vivos_

Communication Workbook

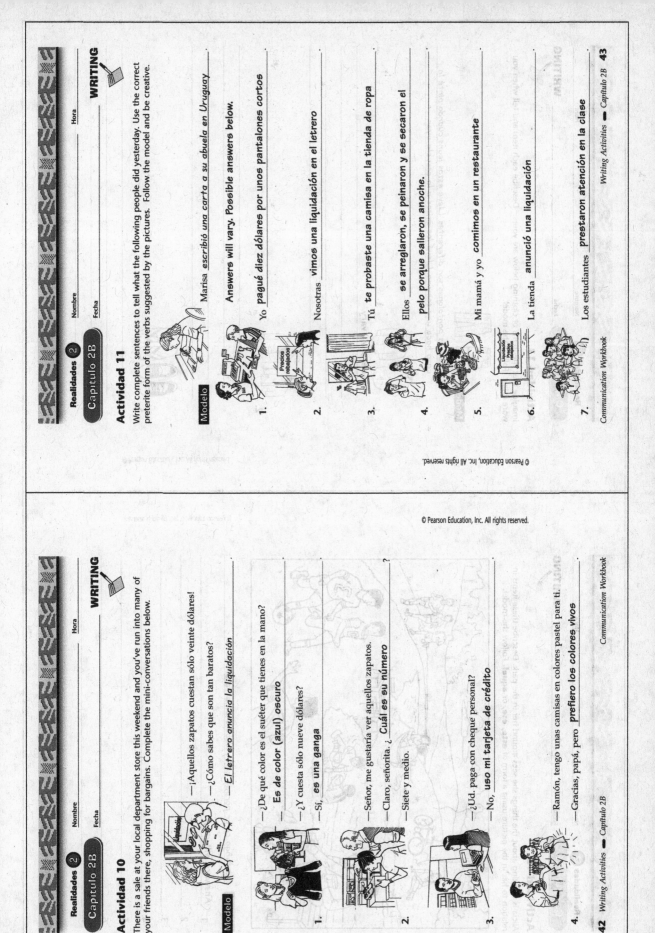

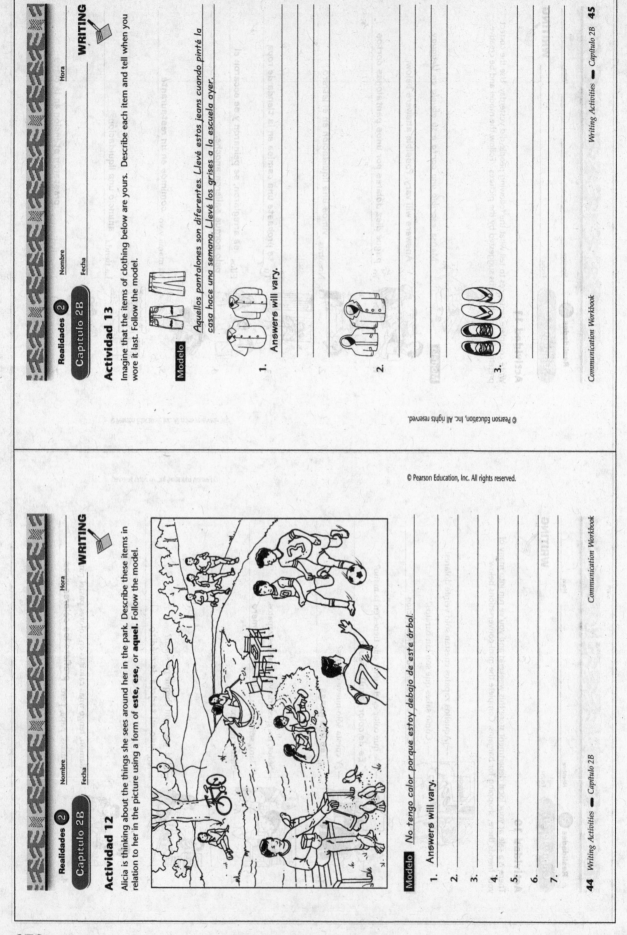

Actividad 13

Actividad 13

Imagine that the items of clothing below are yours. Describe each item and tell when you wore it last. Follow the model.

Modelo *Aquellos pantalones son diferentes. Llevé estos jeans cuando pinté la casa hace una semana. Llevé los grises a la escuela ayer.*

1. Answers will vary.

2. _____

3. _____

Actividad 12

Alicia is thinking about the things she sees around her in the park. Describe these items in relation to her in the picture using a form of **este**, **ese**, or **aquel**. Follow the model.

Modelo *No tengo calor porque estoy debajo de este árbol.*

1. Answers will vary.

2. _____

3. _____

4. _____

5. _____

6. _____

7. _____

Test Preparation Answers

Reading Skills
p. 223   2. **D**
p. 224   2. **B**

**Integrated Performance
  Assessment**
p. 226
Answers will vary.

**Practice Test: ¿Qué está de
  moda?**
p. 227

1. C
2. G
3. A
4. H
5. Las respuestas variarán, pero asegúrese de que los estudiantes den razones que apoyen su respuesta.
6. Answers will vary but may include: The black, unisex clothing of the beatniks was a reaction to the conservative, very clearly differentiated fashions for men and women in the fifties. The simplicity of the beatniks' clothes indicated that they were interested in more serious matters than fashion. Miniskirts were a turning away from the traditional clothes and roles for women and expressed women's growing sense of independence. The dresses worn by hippie girls indicate their rejection of progress, since both the Indian and the granny dresses evoke simpler places and times.

Table of Contents

Theme Project

Tú y tu comunidad
Lugares en mi comunidad

Overview:

You will write a paragraph giving directions from school to various areas around town and explaining what one can do/buy at specific locations. You will be assigned a specific place (*la farmacia, el dentista,* etc.). You can decorate your paper with pictures or drawings, or create a map to accompany your writing.

Resources:

Electronic or print photos, page layout/word processing software and/or construction paper, markers, photos, glue or tape, scissors

Sequence:

STEP 1. Review instructions with your teacher.

STEP 2. Submit a rough sketch of your page of directions. Work with a partner and present your drafts to each other.

STEP 3. Create layouts, leaving room for photos and descriptions.

STEP 4. Submit a draft of your paragraph.

STEP 5. Present your directions to the class, explaining each page and describing selected pictures.

Assessment:

Your teacher will provide you with a rubric to assess this project.

Theme 3 Project: Lugares en mi comunidad

Project Assessment Rubric

RUBRIC	Score 1	Score 3	Score 5
Evidence of Planning	No written draft or sketch provided.	Draft was written and layout created, but not corrected.	Evidence of corrected draft and layout.
Use of Illustrations	No photos/visuals included.	Very few photos/visuals included.	Several photos/visuals included.
Presentation	Contains details that develop ideas about the community.	Gives partially complete directions.	Gives complete directions.

21st Century Skills Rubric: Encourage Collaboration

RUBRIC	Score 1	Score 3	Score 5
Roles and responsibilities	Does not assign or describe roles and responsibilities for group members	Assigns roles but does not detail responsibilities for group members	Assigns roles and clarifies responsibilities for group members
Listens to others in group	Is always talking; never allows others to speak	Listens but sometimes talks too much	Listens and speaks a fair amount
Contribution to group work	Always relies on others to do the work	Usually does the assigned work but at times needs reminding	Always does the assigned work without needing reminding

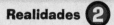

Realidades ②

Capítulo 3A ‎ **School-to-Home Connection**

Dear Parent or Guardian,

The theme of our current unit is *Tú y tu comunidad* (You and your community). This chapter is called *¿Qué hiciste ayer?* (What did you do yesterday?).

Upon completion of this chapter students will be able to:

- talk about things he or she did and where he or she did them
- explain why he or she couldn't do certain things
- describe things the student bought and where he or she bought them
- understand cultural perspectives on shopping

Students will also explore:

- correct stress in pronouncing words and sentences, and the use of accent marks in Spanish

Our textbook, *Realidades,* helps with the development of reading, writing, and speaking skills through the use of strategies, process speaking, and process writing. In this chapter, students will:

- read about the Sister Cities International program
- speak about what they do to prepare for a trip

To reinforce and enhance learning, students can access a wide range of online resources on **realidades.com**, the personalized learning management system that accompanies the print and online Student Edition. Resources include the eText, textbook and workbook activities, audio files, videos, animations, songs, self-study tools, interactive maps, voice recording (RealTalk!), assessments, and other digital resources. Many learning tools can be accessed through the student Home Page on **realidades.com**. Other activities, specifically those that require grading, are assigned by the teacher and linked on the student Home Page within the calendar or the Assignments tab.

You will find specifications and guidelines for accessing **realidades.com** on home computers and mobile devices on MyPearsonTraining.com under the SuccessNet Plus tab.

realidades.com ✔

For: Tips to Parents
Visit: www.realidades.com
Web Code: jce-0010

Check it out! At the end of the chapter, have your child use the new vocabulary from this chapter to point out seven items he or she would take on a trip. Then have him or her tell you where one would buy those items if they were forgotten.

Sincerely,

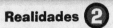
Videocultura Script

Comunidades latinas

Spanish version:

Nueva York, la ciudad más poblada de los Estados Unidos, es un centro de gran diversidad cultural. En esta ciudad se hablan más de 100 lenguas. Después del inglés, el español es la lengua más hablada con más de dos millones de latinos que viven en la ciudad y sus alrededores.

Muchos inmigrantes hispanos llegaron a Nueva York en los años 50 y se asentaron en ciertos barrios de acuerdo a su nacionalidad: los puertorriqueños en Spanish Harlem, los dominicanos en Washington Heights y los colombianos en Queens.

En estos barrios, las tiendas y los restaurantes se establecieron y prosperaron con gran fuerza. Ofrecieron comidas, productos y servicios que los inmigrantes debieron dejar atrás en sus países de origen. De esta manera, estos barrios lograron desarrollar un sentido de pertenencia y comunidad. Hoy día, estos negocios continúan satisfaciendo las necesidades de los clientes de habla hispana en Nueva York.

Aunque las comunidades latinas siguen distribuidas en estos barrios, hoy día los latinos viven y trabajan por todas partes de la ciudad de Nueva York.

Cada día, los latinos se integran más a la cultura neoyorquina. La comunidad latina se abre y comparte su cultura con todos los habitantes de la Gran Manzana.

English version:

New York City, the most populous city in the United States, is a great center of cultural diversity, with well over 100 languages spoken. After English, Spanish is the second most popular language, with over two million Latinos living in and around New York City.

Many Hispanics began arriving in New York City in the 1950s. Immigrants from different Spanish-speaking countries tended to settle in certain neighborhoods, depending on their nationality.

Puerto Ricans settled in Spanish Harlem, which is also known as El Barrio, and the Lower East Side. Many Dominicans moved into Washington Heights, and new arrivals from Colombia settled in Queens.

Within these neighborhoods, businesses and restaurants were established and thrived. They offered the foods, products, and services that were left behind in their native countries. In addition, these neighborhoods fostered a sense of culture and community. Today they continue to cater to the needs of their Spanish-speaking clientele.

Although neighborhoods such as El Barrio are still important cultural centers, Spanish speakers now live and work in boroughs and neighborhoods located throughout the city.

In New York and in towns and cities across the United States, immigrants from Spanish-speaking countries adapt to living in a new community while preserving traditions of their home countries. This rich exchange of culture contributes to the "melting pot" that is the United States.

Input Script

Presentation

Input Vocabulary: Rush into the classroom with a suitcase. Announce that you are going on vacation after school today, but you have many things to do before you can leave. Place the overhead transparency on the screen. Distribute copies of the Vocabulary Clip Art for *el correo, el supermercado, la farmacia, la tienda de equipo deportivo, la biblioteca, el consultorio,* and *el banco,* and have students cut them into individual images. Point to the places on the transparency, tell what time each place opens and closes and what you have to do there (*A ver, la tienda de equipo deportivo se abre a las nueve de la mañana. Quiero comprar una raqueta de tenis y unas pelotas antes de ir de vacaciones.*). With an erasable marker, write the time each place opens and closes beside the places on the transparency. Then have students help you decide in which order you should visit the places, based on when they open and close. Write a "to do" list on the chalkboard or on a transparency. Students will arrange the Clip Art images of the places on their desks in the order you plan to do your errands.

Input Dialogue: Perform the dialogue with a volunteer. Have him or her answer with the opening and closing times you wrote for the post office in the vocabulary presentation activity. Then repeat with other students, substituting other places and activities on the transparency for *el correo.*

Input Monologue: Before class, write the monologue on p. 131 on a piece of stationary and put it in an envelope. Present the monologue by telling students that you received a letter from your niece who is living in Spain. Open the letter and read the monologue. Make comments and ask questions about each section of the monologue to reinforce and check comprehension: *¡Ella tiene mucha paciencia para cuidar a los niños por cinco horas! ¿Les gustan los zoológicos? Ella fue a pie al zoológico. Debe estar bastante cerca de su casa.*

Comprehension Check

- Write the place names on sheets of paper and tape the names to the back rests of chairs. Place the chairs in a circle with the seats facing out. You will say: *Tengo que, tengo que, tengo que…* as the students walk around the chairs. When you finish the sentence with an errand, students will try to be the one to sit in the chair with the correct place name to earn a point. After several rounds, the student with the most points wins.

- Distribute copies of the Vocabulary Clip Art for the places in *A primera vista.* Tell students the opening and closing times of each place. Have them write the times by the correct images. Then make statements that employees of each place would make: *Trabajo de las ocho de la mañana hasta las siete de la noche. Vendemos pasta dental y champú.* Have students tell you where each person works.

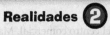

Audio Script

Audio DVD, Capítulo 3A

Track 01: *A primera vista, ¿Qué hiciste ayer?*, Student Book, p. 130

Vocabulario y gramática en contexto
Vas a escuchar cada palabra o frase dos veces. Después de la primera vez hay una pausa para que puedas pronunciar la palabra o frase. Luego vas a escuchar de nuevo la palabra o frase.

el champú	echar una carta
el jabón	el buzón
el cepillo de dientes	la raqueta de tenis
la pasta dental	los patines
el centro	la pelota
la farmacia	el palo de golf
el supermercado	el sello
la tienda de equipo deportivo	la tarjeta
el correo	la carta

Lee en tu libro mientras escuchas el diálogo.

TEEN FEMALE: ¿A qué hora se abre el correo en el centro? Quiero comprar unos sellos y enviar una carta.
TEEN MALE: Se abre a las nueve de la mañana y se cierra a las ocho de la noche.

Track 02: *A primera vista*, Act. 1, Student Book, p. 130

¿Lógica o no lógica?
Escucha las frases y señala con el pulgar hacia arriba si la frase es lógica y con el pulgar hacia abajo si no es lógica. Vas a escuchar las frases dos veces.

1. Puedo comprar jabón en el banco.
2. Es posible comprar sellos en el correo.
3. Busco un buzón para echar una carta.
4. Para sacar un libro, debes ir al consultorio.
5. Para comprar un palo de golf, debes ir a la tienda de equipo deportivo.
6. Para cobrar un cheque, debes ir al banco.
7. Para comprar cereal, debes ir al supermercado.
8. Para ver al dentista, debes ir a la farmacia.

Track 03: *A primera vista*, Student Book, p. 131

Vocabulario y gramática en contexto
Vas a escuchar cada palabra o frase dos veces. Después de la primera vez hay una pausa para que puedas pronunciar la palabra o frase. Luego vas a escuchar de nuevo la palabra o frase.

el consultorio	el banco
el dentista	sacar un libro
la dentista	devolver un libro
el médico	cobrar un cheque
la médica	cuidar a los niños

Lee en tu libro mientras escuchas la narración.

TEEN FEMALE: Ayer cuidé a Carlota y a Paco por cinco horas. Fuimos a pie al zoológico.

Nos quedamos allí hasta la una. Fue muy divertido. Luego regresamos a casa. Sus padres me pagaron por cuidarlos. Me gusta cuidar niños porque puedo ganar dinero. Es importante tener mi propio dinero.

Track 04: *A primera vista*, Act. 2, Student Book, p. 131

¿Cómo van?
Escribe en una hoja de papel los números del 1 al 4. Escucha los diálogos y escribe la letra de la respuesta apropiada. Vas a escuchar los diálogos dos veces.

1. **TEEN MALE 1:** Necesito comprar un cepillo de dientes y champú.
   TEEN MALE 2: ¿Por qué no entramos en esa farmacia?
2. **TEEN FEMALE 1:** ¿Qué tienes que hacer esta tarde?
   TEEN FEMALE 2: Primero voy al banco y después al consultorio de la doctora Sánchez.
3. **TEEN MALE 1:** Tengo que enviar una carta, pero no tengo sellos.
   TEEN MALE 2: Vamos al correo para comprarlos. Allí puedes enviarla.
4. **TEEN FEMALE 1:** Vamos a la biblioteca para devolver los libros.
   TEEN FEMALE 2: Pero no tenemos el coche. Hay que caminar.

Track 05: *A primera vista, Videohistoria*, Student Book, pp. 132–133

¿Qué hiciste esta mañana?
Lee en tu libro mientras escuchas la *Videohistoria*.

See Student Book pages 132–133 for script.

Track 06: *Manos a la obra*, Act. 6, Student Book, p. 135

Escucha y escribe
Tu mamá necesita tu ayuda para hacer todos los quehaceres. Escucha lo que ella dice y escribe las seis frases. Vas a escuchar las frases dos veces.

1. Esta tarde necesitas quedarte en casa.
2. Necesito varias cosas de la farmacia, como jabón y champú.
3. Esta noche tienes que cuidar a tu hermanito.
4. Por favor, devuelve estos libros a la biblioteca.
5. ¿Me puedes echar esta carta en el buzón?
6. ¿Puedes ir en bicicleta al banco a cobrar un cheque?

Track 07: Audio Act. 5, Writing, Audio & Video Workbook, p. 49

Miguel is calling his friends to make plans for the day, but no one is available. Listen as each friend tells Miguel what he or she is doing, then write his or her name in the space under the picture that best illustrates the activity. You will hear each conversation twice.

1. **Male Teen 1:** Grisel, ¿vamos al cine hoy?
   Female Teen 1: ¡Ay, no! Voy al supermercado hoy porque tengo que comprar todo para la fiesta de mis padres esta noche.
2. **Male Teen 1:** Pedro, ¿por qué no vienes conmigo al estadio?
   Male Teen 2: Porque tengo que cuidar a los niños de la señora Pacheco.
3. **Male Teen 1:** Rosi, ¿tienes planes para esta tarde?
   Female Teen 2: Sí, voy a una tienda de equipo deportivo. Tengo que comprar una raqueta nueva para la temporada.
4. **Male Teen 1:** David, ¿me puedes llevar al gimnasio ahora mismo?
   Male Teen 3: No, mi coche tiene poca gasolina. Tengo que llenar el tanque primero.
5. **Male Teen 1:** Priscila, ¿vienes conmigo al trabajo hoy?
   Female Teen 3: No, tengo muchos quehaceres en casa. Y luego tengo que enviar una carta a España antes de que se cierre el correo.
6. **Male Teen 1:** Paco, ¿puedes venir a mi casa para jugar videojuegos?
   Male Teen 4: No, voy a la biblioteca hoy. Quiero estudiar y también necesito sacar un libro.

Track 08: Audio Act. 6, Writing, Audio & Video Workbook, p. 50

Felipe has been trying to catch up with his friend Moisés all day. As he asks people where they saw Moisés last, write the time and place each person mentions on the line beneath the appropriate picture. After you have heard everyone's answers, number the pictures chronologically, with 1 being the first place Moisés went and 8 being the last place Moisés went. You will hear each conversation twice.

1. **Male Teen 1:** Carmen, ¿viste a Moisés? Necesito hablar con él.
   Female Teen 1: Sí. Vi a Moisés esta mañana muy temprano en el correo, con una carta para echar a los Estados Unidos. A las nueve de la mañana, más o menos.
   Male Teen 1: Muchas gracias. Voy al correo.
2. **Male Teen 1:** Hola, Jesús. Busco a Moisés. Son las siete de la tarde ya, y necesito hablar con él.
   Male Teen 2: Hace unos minutos vi a Moisés en la estación de servicio. Probablemente está allí todavía. Él tuvo un problema con su coche.
3. **Male Teen 1:** Hola, María. No puedo encontrar a mi amigo en ningún lugar. ¿Viste a Moisés?
   Female Teen 2: Sí. No sé exactamente la hora, más o menos a las dos, pero vi a Moisés y a su hermana en el consultorio del médico. Ella me pareció bastante enferma.
   Male Teen 1: Gracias, María.
4. **Male Teen 1:** Buenas tardes, Paco. No encuentro a Moisés en ningún lugar. Lo estoy buscando.
   Male Teen 3: Hola, Felipe. Moisés… Hace un momento que vi a Moisés. Compró unos zapatos deportivos en la tienda de equipo deportivo del centro comercial. Más o menos a las diez de la mañana.
5. **Male Teen 1:** ¡Ay, Isabel! No encuentro a Moisés. ¿Sabes dónde está?
   Female Teen 3: Vi a Moisés en el banco a las cuatro y media de la tarde. Cobró un cheque bastante grande. Necesitaba dinero en efectivo para pagar por sus palos de golf.
6. **Male Teen 1:** Hola, Federico. Busco y busco a Moisés pero no lo encuentro en ningún lugar.
   Male Teen 4: Yo vi a Moisés hace un momento, como a las ocho de la noche. Compró algunas verduras y mucha carne en el supermercado de don Alejandro. Él tiene una cena especial con su familia esta noche.
7. **Male Teen 1:** Lourdes, es mediodía y no puedo encontrar a Moisés. ¿Lo viste?
   Female Teen 4: Sí, vi a Moisés hace poco. Fue a pie a la biblioteca. Sacó unos libros para su informe de la clase de historia.
8. **Male Teen 1:** Hola, Antonio. Busco a Moisés. Necesito hablar con él.
   Male Teen 5: Vi a Moisés en la farmacia como a las tres de la tarde. Moisés necesitaba un cepillo de dientes nuevo y pasta dental.

Track 09: Audio Act. 7, Writing, Audio & Video Workbook, p. 50

Listen as you hear several people describe a moment when they saw someone who they thought was good-looking. After each statement, complete the sentence below with the correct location of the encounter. You will hear each statement twice.

1. **Adult Female 1:** ¡Cuando lo vi entre las manzanas, las uvas y las naranjas, mi corazón empezó a sentir como una explosión! ¡Qué guapo! Él compró jabón, champú, leche y mantequilla. ¡Yo no compré nada! Solo lo miré por cinco minutos sin decir nada.
2. **Adult Male 1:** Ayer saqué dinero para mis vacaciones. En el momento que ella llegó, la vi… con sus ojos profundos y oscuros. Ella cobró un cheque y salió, y yo me quedé en silencio. ¡Ay! ¡Y no sé su nombre!
3. **Teen Female:** ¿Cómo puedo describir el momento que los vi por primera vez? Fui a comprar una raqueta de tenis en mi tienda favorita. De repente, la puerta se abrió y dos jóvenes guapísimos entraron. Casi no pude hablar.
4. **Teen Male:** ¡Ay, que muchachas tan bonitas! Las vi cuando compraron unos sellos para enviar un paquete muy grande. Hablé con ellas por un momento. Se llaman Andrea y Alejandra. Las voy a llamar luego.
5. **Adult Male 2:** Sentí una explosión en mi cabeza. ¡Qué horrible! No hay aspirinas en mi casa. Tomé el autobús al centro y cuando pagué por las aspirinas la vi en la caja. ¡Un ángel! No pude decir nada, solo la miré por cinco minutos.

Track 10: Audio Act. 8, Writing, Audio & Video Workbook, p. 51

When Eric went to Mexico for the summer, he brought his high school yearbook with him so that his host family could see what his school was like. Listen as his host parents look through his yearbook and reminisce about their own high school days. They will ask each other if they remember (*¿recuerdas?*) certain events from their past. Match their memories with the corresponding pictures.

1. **ADULT MALE:** Ay, ¿recuerdas ese año en que asistimos a la universidad?
   ADULT FEMALE: Sí, Javier. Recuerdo bien aquella noche cuando fuimos al parque con nuestro picnic a medianoche.
2. **ADULT FEMALE:** Hace veinte años. ¿Pero recuerdas cuando fuimos a la casa de tu abuela para la fiesta de quinceañera de tu hermana?
   ADULT MALE: Sí, mi amor. Fue una celebración muy importante para ella.
3. **ADULT FEMALE:** ¿Recuerdas cuando trabajé en el laboratorio del doctor Martínez? El doctor Martínez era un profesor excelente.
   ADULT MALE: Si, recuerdo cuando el experimento te explotó en la cara. Fue un desastre.
4. **ADULT MALE:** Mira, ellos fueron los mejores amigos de Eric. ¿Recuerdas cuando Andrés y Juan, mis mejores amigos, fueron a mi fiesta de cumpleaños?
   ADULT FEMALE: Sí, fue una fiesta fantástica.
5. **ADULT FEMALE:** ¿Recuerdas cuando fuimos novios en la escuela?
   ADULT MALE: Sí, como ayer. Fue un tiempo muy romántico. Fuimos los novios más populares de la escuela.

Track 11: *Manos a la obra*, Act. 21, Student Book, p. 143

Una raqueta de tenis nueva
Santiago acaba de comprar una raqueta de tenis. Primero lee las preguntas. Después escucha la descripción dos veces y escribe respuestas a las preguntas.

El verano pasado trabajé mucho para ganar dinero. Mis abuelos también me dieron dinero para comprar una raqueta de tenis nueva. La semana pasada fui a la tienda de equipo deportivo con mi amigo, Héctor. Fue una experiencia divertida para mí. Héctor y yo tuvimos que mirar varias raquetas de diferentes colores y precios. No pude decidir qué raqueta comprar. Estuvimos en la tienda hasta que cerraron sus puertas. Luego escogí la raqueta que tengo. Me encanta mi raqueta.

Vas a escuchar esta descripción otra vez.

Track 12: Audio Act. 9, Writing, Audio & Video Workbook, p. 51

Sometimes there just aren't enough hours in the day! Listen as each person tells a friend what he or she had to do yesterday but just wasn't able to. As you listen to each conversation, fill in the grid below with short phrases. You will hear each conversation twice.

1. **TEEN MALE 1:** Tuve que estudiar para mi examen de español, pero no pude porque estuve en mi trabajo anoche hasta las once.
2. **TEEN FEMALE 1:** Ayer mi madre y yo tuvimos que ir de compras para comprar un regalo para mi primo. Pero ella fue sola porque yo estuve en el consultorio por dos horas.
3. **TEEN FEMALE 2:** Tuve que cobrar un cheque en el banco porque necesitaba dinero en efectivo. Mi hermano cobró el cheque porque estuve en el supermercado hasta las cinco y treinta de la tarde.
4. **TEEN MALE 2:** Ayer por la noche tuvimos que ir a la biblioteca para sacar un libro de español, pero no pudimos porque estuvimos en la fiesta de Juan.
5. **TEEN FEMALE 3:** Ellos tuvieron que comprar aspirinas en la farmacia de don Pepe, pero no pudieron porque estuvieron estudiando toda la noche.

Track 13: *Pronunciación*, The written accent, Student Book, p. 144

You already know the standard rules for stress and accent in Spanish.
- When words end in a **vowel, n,** or **s**, the stress is on the next-to-last syllable.
- When words end in a **consonant** (except, **n** or **s**), the stress is on the last syllable.
- Words that do not follow these patterns must have a written accent (called *acento ortográfico* or *tilde*). The accent indicates that you should place the stress on this syllable as you pronounce the word. Listen to and say these examples:

You will hear each word twice. After the word is pronounced the first time, there will be a pause so you can pronounce it. Then you will hear the word a second time.

champú	cómodo
película	jabón
demás	fútbol
olvidó	médico
patín	adiós
césped	lápiz

¡Compruébalo! Here are some new words that all require accent marks. Copy the words and, as you hear them pronounced, write the accent mark over the correct vowel.

antropologo	util
lucho	ejercito
cajon	tipico
nilon	fosforo
carcel	lider

Listen to and say the following *refrán:*
Del árbol caído, todos hacen leña.

Track 14: *Repaso del capítulo*, Student Book, p. 152

Vocabulario y gramática
Escucha las palabras y expresiones que has aprendido en este capítulo.

See Student Book page 152 for vocabulary list.

Track 15: *Preparación para el examen,* **Student Book, p. 153**

Escuchar

Practice task

As sponsor for the school's summer trip to Mexico, the Spanish teacher has heard many excuses about why students don't return to the bus in time to depart for the next stop. Listen to the excuses to determine where the students went and why they were late.

1. **TEEN MALE 1:** Lo siento, señora. Fui al banco a las cuatro y media para cobrar mi cheque. El banco se cierra a las cinco y tuve que ir enseguida.
2. **TEEN FEMALE 1:** ¡Caramba, señora! Se me olvidó regresar. Fui a la tienda de equipo deportivo y compré una pelota.
3. **TEEN MALE 2:** Lo siento, señora. Fui a la farmacia para comprar un nuevo cepillo de dientes, pero la tienda no se abre hasta las dos y tuve que esperar.
4. **TEEN FEMALE 2:** ¡Hola, señora! Fui al correo para comprar sellos. Tuve que mandar una tarjeta a mi mamá.

Video Script

A primera vista: *¿Qué hiciste esta mañana?*

TERESA: Hola, Claudia, ¿cómo estás?

CLAUDIA: Bien, Teresa. ¿Y tú? Oye, tenemos que darnos prisa. Manolo y Ramón nos esperan a las dos, ¿verdad?

TERESA: Sí, sí. ¿Sabes qué vamos a hacer?

CLAUDIA: Creo que vamos a ver una película de ciencia ficción. Será interesante.

TERESA: Tengo que comprar varias cosas aquí. ¿Entramos?

CLAUDIA: Pero, ¿por qué no fuiste ayer?

TERESA: No pude. Tuve que ir a la biblioteca a devolver un libro.

CLAUDIA: Está bien. Pero, de prisa. No tenemos demasiado tiempo.

TERESA: A ver, el champú… ¿Éste o ése? No sé…

CLAUDIA: Teresa…, ¿qué importa? Los dos son buenos. Vamos.

TERESA: Ah, sí, la pasta dental. ¿Qué más, qué más?

CLAUDIA: Nada más. ¡Vámonos ya!

TERESA: Ya voy, ya voy. Aquí tiene.

CLERK: Muchas gracias. Que le vaya bien.

TERESA: Gracias.

CLAUDIA: Vamos, vamos. Ramón y Manolo ya deben de estar allí.

TERESA: Ay, casi se me olvida. Tengo que enviar esta carta. Pero necesito comprar sellos…

CLAUDIA: Teresa, vamos a llegar tarde. ¿Por qué no lo hiciste esta mañana?

TERESA: Lo siento. Se me olvidó. ¿Sabes a qué hora cierra el correo?

CLAUDIA: Pues, lo cierran a las cinco. Pero la película empieza a las dos y media, ¿recuerdas?

TERESA: Tranquila, Claudia. Todavía es temprano.

CLAUDIA: Vamos.

TERESA: Ahora regreso.

RAMÓN: ¿Sí?

CLAUDIA: Bueno, Ramón. Aquí Claudia.

RAMÓN: Hola, Claudia, ¿qué tal?

CLAUDIA: Muy bien. Tuvimos que ir a varios sitios, pero ya casi llegamos. Y Uds., ¿qué hicieron esta mañana?

RAMÓN: Pues, primero fuimos a una tienda de deportes.

MANOLO: Señor, por favor, ¿cuánto cuestan estos patines?

CLERK: Cuatrocientos pesos.

MANOLO: No. Son un poco caros.

RAMÓN: Mira, del Cruz Azul.

RAMÓN's V.O.: Y me compré una camiseta del Cruz Azul.

CLAUDIA: ¡Genial! ¿Y qué hicieron después?

RAMÓN's V.O.: Después, fuimos a la estación de servicio.

MANOLO: Buenos días, señor.

MAN: Buenos días.

MANOLO: ¿Puede llenar el tanque, por favor?

MAN: Sí. ¡Cómo no!

TERESA: ¡Ay, se me olvidó!

CLAUDIA: Espera, Ramón. ¿Ahora qué, Teresa?

TERESA: Mañana es el cumpleaños de mi abuela. Tengo que comprarle algo.

CLAUDIA: ¿Ahora? Pero ya es la una y media. Bueno, estamos cerca del Bazar San Ángel. ¿Por qué no vamos allí? No está lejos.

TERESA: Buena idea.

CLAUDIA: Ramón…

RAMÓN: ¿Sí?

CLAUDIA: Vamos al Bazar San Ángel. Tenemos que comprar un regalo. ¿Por qué no nos vemos allí?

RAMÓN: Está bien. Nos vemos allí.

CLAUDIA: Claro. Adiós.

GramActiva Videos
Irregular preterite: *ir, ser, hacer, tener, estar, poder*

OLD COWBOY: Oh, hi there. I was just sitting here thinking about the good ol' days of Spanish grammar. Like when we learned about the preterite tense. I remember it like it was yesterday.

HOST 1: In English, when you say something like, "I filled my car with gas," you are using the preterite tense.

HOST 2: The preterite tense is used to talk about actions completed in the past.

HOST: But things are never completely regular in the land of language. Like English, many often-used Spanish verbs are irregular in the preterite. *Ir,* "to go," is one of these verbs. Here's how you conjugate it.

V.O.: *Fui. Fuiste. Fue. Fuimos. Fuisteis. Fueron.*

V.O.: *Fui al teatro.*
¿Fuiste al museo?
Fue al zoológico.
Anoche fuimos al cine.
Fuisteis a la zapatería.
Fueron a la farmacia.

COWBOY: Yep those were fine times. Heh, *yo fui…* OH! *(excited)* speaking of *yo fui,* didja know that in the preterite, the forms of *ser* are the same as the forms of *ir?* Here, let me show you.

V.O.: The preterite forms of *ser,* "to be," are:
Fui. Fuiste. Fue. Fuimos. Fuisteis. Fueron.

COWBOY: Oh, you might notice that these irregular preterite forms do not have any accents. Don't know why that is. Some things just happen.

COWBOY: To remember the conjugations of *fui* and *fue,* just remember the *yo* form has an "I" every day. The *usted, él, ella* form ends in an *-e,* and that turns out to be *fue,* don't you see?

HOST: Now that we've learned about *ir* and *ser,* let's take a look at a preterite you already know and a few new ones.

V.O.: Remember how to conjugate *hacer* in the preterite?
Hice. Hiciste. Hizo. Hicimos. Hicisteis. Hicieron.

HOST: Well if you know how to conjugate *hacer,* the preterite forms of *tener, estar,* and *poder* follow a similar conjugation pattern. Let's start with *tener,* "to have."

V.O.: *Tuve. Tuviste. Tuvo. Tuvimos. Tuvisteis. Tuvieron.*

COWBOY: You got that? Good. Take a look at *estar*, "to be."

V.O.: *Estuve. Estuviste. Estuvo. Estuvimos. Estuvisteis. Estuvieron.*

COWBOY: And one more, *poder*, "to be able."

V.O.: *Pude. Pudiste. Pudo. Pudimos. Pudisteis. Pudieron.*

HOST: Now, I know that's a lot to learn, but let's take a little quiz anyway.

Quiz

V.O.: Complete the sentences with the correct preterite form.
(ir) ¿Adónde _____ ustedes el verano pasado?
¿Adónde fueron ustedes el verano pasado?
(poder) Tú _____ entrar.
Tú pudiste entrar.
(tener) Nosotros _____ un cupón de regalo.
Nosotros tuvimos un cupón de regalo.

Direct object pronouns: *me, te, nos, os*

FORTUNE TELLER: Ahh, welcome. Tell me, do you want to know about your past, or future? Wait! Don't tell me. I'm getting a very strong feeling you want to know about your past. A-ha! You want to remember direct object pronouns. Well, ask and you shall receive.

V.O.: Direct object pronouns replace the person or noun that receives the action. Let's review the direct object pronouns you already know—*lo, la, los, las.*

V.O.: Let's see a couple of examples.
Leí el libro.
Lo leí.
Compraste las pelotas de tenis.
Las compré.

COWBOY: Are we talking about a disagreement?

HOST: As always, the pronoun you use, must agree in gender and number with the noun it replaces.

FORTUNE TELLER: Now let's see what your present has to offer.

HOST: Waa, ha, ha. I am your present! Waaa! Ahem! Just kidding. But I am here to teach you about some more direct object pronouns.

V.O.: A couple more singular direct object pronouns are *me*, which means "me," and *te* which means "you," but in a familiar way. The other plural direct object pronoun are *nos*, which means "us," and *os* which means the plural of "you" familiar.

V.O.: Let's see some examples.
Ana te invitó a una fiesta.
Mi padre me llevó al partido.
Mis tíos nos visitan en el verano.

FORTUNE TELLER: Now we must remember that the direct object pronouns usually come right before the conjugated verb. Like in the sentence *No te veo*. But! When an infinitive follows a verb, the direct object pronoun can be placed before the first verb or attached to the infinitive! Ohhhh! *No te puedo ver* or *No puedo verte.*

V.O.: Would you like one more example? Here we go.
Lo necesito comprar.
Necesito comprarlo.

FORTUNE TELLER: I see a quiz in your future.

Quiz

V.O.: Fill in the blank with the correct direct object pronoun.
(us) _____ escucha bien.
Nos escucha bien.
(you, singular) _____ llevan al parque.
Te llevan al parque.
(me) _____ visitó un amigo.
Me visitó un amigo.

Videomisterio: *En busca de la verdad*, Episodio 1

LINDA: Hola. Yo soy Linda, Linda Toledo. Vivo en San Antonio, Texas, y estudio en una escuela bilingüe. Estoy en el último año de secundaria. Quiero presentarles a mi familia. Éste es mi papá, Enrique, mi hermano Paco; a Paco le encanta jugar al fútbol. Y mi mamá, Carmen. Mi mamá es profesora en la escuela donde yo estudio. Pero bueno, esta historia empezó un día cuando mi mamá fue a ver al director de la escuela. Quería establecer un programa de intercambio con una escuela en Guanajuato, México.

DIRECTOR: Hay una escuela en Guanajuato muy interesada en un intercambio.

CARMEN: Perfecto.

DIRECTOR: ¿Quieres ir allí para hablar con ellos?

CARMEN: Me gustaría mucho ir. Pero, ¿no quiere acompañarme Ud.?

DIRECTOR: Imposible. Tengo demasiadas cosas que hacer.

CARMEN: Lástima. Mire, ¿qué le parece si me acompaña mi hija, Linda? Le gusta viajar.

DIRECTOR: ¿Y la escuela? ¿Cuántos días de clases va a perder?

CARMEN: Sólo dos o tres. El próximo jueves y viernes no hay clases, así que podemos usarlos para el viaje. Yo necesito estar en Guanajuato sólo una semana.

LINDA'S V.O.: Esa noche, mi mamá, mi papá, mi hermano y yo nos reunimos y hablamos sobre el viaje. Yo estaba muy contenta. Por fin, ¡mi primer viaje a México! Al día siguiente mi mamá y yo fuimos a una agencia de viajes para comprar los boletos de avión.

CARMEN: ¿Sr. Balzar?

BALZAR: Sí. ¿En qué puedo servirles?

CARMEN: Soy Carmen Toledo, y mi hija Linda.

BALZAR: Ah, claro, siéntense, por favor. El director Ruiz me habló de sus planes. Van a Guanajuato, ¿no?

CARMEN: Así es; necesitamos dos boletos de ida y vuelta. Para el jueves de la próxima semana, si es posible.

BALZAR: Vamos a ver… Lo más fácil es ir en avión a León, y de allí tomar un taxi hasta Guanajuato. ¿Está bien?

CARMEN: Muy bien.

BALZAR: Hay un vuelo que sale a las diez de la mañana y otro, a las seis de la tarde.

CARMEN: El de las diez, ¿no?

LINDA: Sí, mamá. Así llegamos un poco más temprano.

CARMEN: Bien, para nosotras dos, mi hija y yo.

BALZAR: Y, ¿cuándo quieren regresar?

CARMEN: Una semana después.

BALZAR: Bueno, no va a ser problema… A ver, hay un vuelo que llega aquí a las cuatro de la tarde. Va a ser 355 dólares por cada boleto.

CARMEN: Me parece bien. Aquí está mi tarjeta.

BALZAR: Carmen y Linda Toledo, ¿verdad?

LINDA: Sí.

BALZAR: Gracias. ¿Y ya tienen reservaciones de hotel en Guanajuato?

CARMEN: Todavía no. ¿Nos puede recomendar algo?

BALZAR: Umm… la verdad, no conozco los hoteles de Guanajuato. Pero puedo llamar a una colega allí. Un momento.

BALZAR: Hola, Berta. Habla Ramón Balzar, de San Antonio.

BERTA: Hola, Ramón, ¿qué tal?

BALZAR: Bien, gracias. Tengo aquí a dos clientas que buscan un hotel en Guanajuato por una semana. Llegan el próximo jueves. ¿Puedes ayudarnos?

BERTA: Creo que sí… ¿Por qué no vienen ellas aquí a "Ultramar" cuando lleguen? Voy a reservarles un buen hotel.

BALZAR: Muy bien. Gracias. Adiós.

BALZAR: Bueno, la agencia Ultramar va a reservarles el hotel. Deben pasar por allí cuando lleguen a Guanajuato. Es una excelente agencia. Aquí está el número y la dirección. Y aquí tienen su itinerario. Tienen boletos electrónicos; pueden escoger los asientos en el aeropuerto.

LINDA's V.O.: Cuando salimos de la agencia de viajes, pasamos por el hospital donde estuvo mi abuelo.

LINDA: Mira, mamá. El hospital en el que murió el abuelo.

LINDA: ¿Cómo estás, abuelito?

ABUELO: Bien, bien… Quiero dictarte algunas cosas. Escribe, hija. Yo llegué a este país durante la guerra mundial… la segunda, claro. Lo recuerdo como si fuera ayer. El país necesitaba soldados y yo entré en el ejército. Salí de allí como ciudadano norteamericano y me quedé a vivir aquí… Pero nunca olvidé a México, mi país de nacimiento, y siempre recuerdo a mi querida familia mexicana.

LINDA: Pero, ¿qué familia, abuelo?

ABUELO: Eso te lo explico otro día. Estoy cansado y tengo que dormir. Deja el papel, querida, y continuamos otro día.

LINDA: Hasta luego, abuelito.

LINDA: ¿Mi querida familia mexicana? ¿Qué quería decir eso? Mi abuelo murió antes de explicarlo. Era muy extraño…

Talk!

Realidades 2

Capítulo 3A

Nombre _____

Fecha _____

Communicative Pair Activity **3A-1**

Estudiante **A**

Imagine that you are asking your friend about what he or she did yesterday. Ask your partner the following questions. Write the answers in the spaces provided. Example: *Primero fui al....*

1. ¿Adónde fuiste primero ayer? _____

2. ¿Adónde fuiste después? _____

3. Luego, ¿qué hiciste? _____

4. Y entonces, ¿adónde fuiste? _____

5. ¿Adónde fuiste más tarde? _____

6. Y finalmente, ¿qué hiciste? _____

Imagine that you are telling your friend about what you did yesterday. Tell your partner about your day following the cues below. Example: *Primero fui al mercado al aire libre.*

1. Primero/ir

2. Después/estar

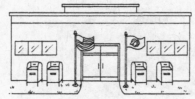

3. Luego/ir

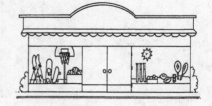

4. Entonces/tener que ir

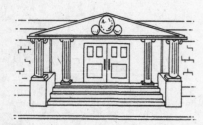

5. Más tarde/poder ir

6. Finalmente/regresar

Realidades 2

Capítulo 3A

Nombre _____

Fecha _____

Communicative Pair Activity **3A-1**

Estudiante **B**

Imagine that you are telling your friend about what you did yesterday. Tell your partner about your day following the cues below. Example: *Primero fui al...*.

1. Primero/ir

2. Después/tener que ir

3. Luego/llegar

4. Entonces/pasar por

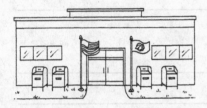

5. Más tarde/estar

6. Finalmente/ir

Imagine that you are asking your friend about what he or she did yesterday. Ask your partner the following questions. Write the answers in the spaces provided. Example: *Primero fui al mercado al aire libre.*

1. ¿Adónde fuiste primero ayer? _____

2. ¿Adónde fuiste después? _____

3. Luego, ¿qué hiciste? _____

4. ¿Y entonces, ¿adónde fuiste? _____

5. ¿Adónde fuiste más tarde? _____

6. Y finalmente, ¿qué hiciste? _____

Realidades 2

Capítulo 3A

Nombre

Communicative Pair Activity **3A-2**

Fecha

Estudiantes **A y B**

Write your answers to the following questions on line A. Then ask your partner the same questions and write the answers on line B.

1. ¿Qué compraste la última vez que estuviste en una farmacia?

   A. _____

   B. _____

2. ¿Adónde fuiste después?

   A. _____

   B. _____

3. ¿Qué compraste la última vez que estuviste en una tienda de equipo deportivo?

   A. _____

   B. _____

4. ¿Cuándo fue la última vez que estuviste en el correo?

   A. _____

   B. _____

5. ¿Qué hiciste en el correo?

   A. _____

   B. _____

6. ¿Cuándo fue la última vez que tuviste que escribir una carta?

   A. _____

   B. _____

7. ¿Cuándo fue la última vez que estuviste en el consultorio del dentista?

   A. _____

   B. _____

Situation Cards

2A

Realidades **2**

Capítulo 3A

Talking about errands and places in the community

You are talking with a clerk at the post office.

— Ask the clerk if they sell stamps to send a post card.

— Answer the clerk's question saying that you need various stamps. Ask the clerk if you can use the same stamps to mail a letter.

— Respond to the clerk's question affirmatively, saying that you want to buy a stamp to send one card. Then thank the clerk for his or her help.

2B

Realidades **2**

Capítulo 3A

Talking about errands and places in the community

You are a clerk at the post office talking to a customer.

— Answer affirmatively saying, "Of course!" Ask the customer how many stamps he or she wants.

— Answer your partner's question negatively saying that letters cost a little more. Then ask if he or she wants to buy some stamps now.

— Answer, "Of course! You are welcome."

1A

Realidades **2**

Capítulo 3A

Talking about errands and using useful expressions

You are talking with a friend about the errands he or she did yesterday.

— Ask him or her where he or she bought shampoo and toothpaste.

— Respond to his or her answer with surprise and ask if he or she had to go back right away.

— Tell your friend you plan to go to the pharmacy soon.

1B

Realidades **2**

Capítulo 3A

Talking about errands and using useful expressions

You are talking with a friend about the errands you did yesterday.

— Respond to your friend that you bought them at the pharmacy, but that you forgot to buy a toothbrush.

— Answer the question negatively by saying you did not have the time to go back right away.

— Tell your friend you will go with him or her when he or she goes to the pharmacy.

Situation Cards

GramActiva

¿Qué hiciste ayer?

Muchas cosas que hacer, p. 134

Lugares	Tengo que . . .

Vocabulary Clip Art

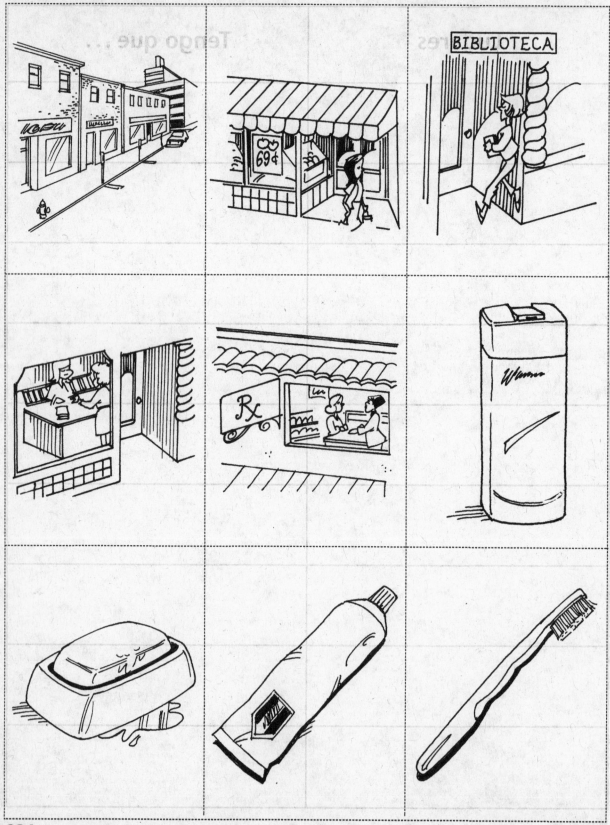

Vocabulary Clip Art

Vocabulary Clip Art

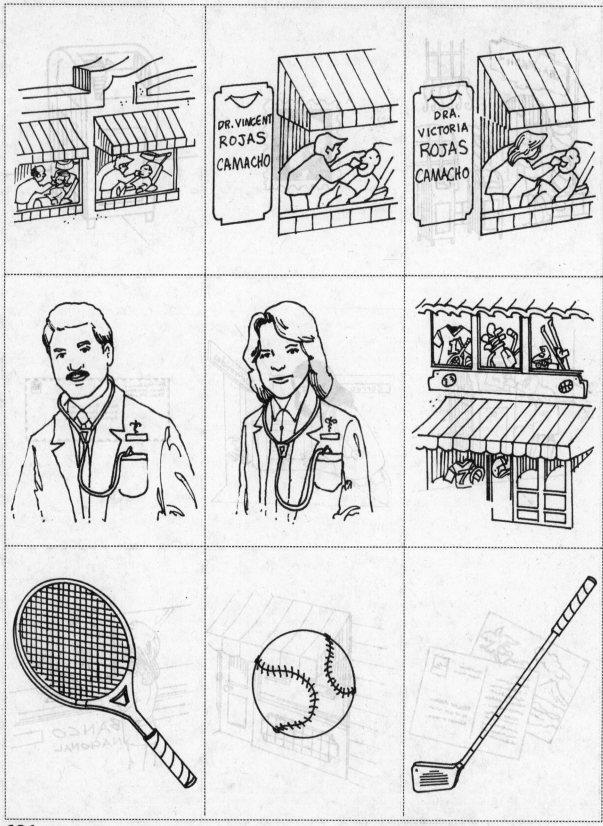

Vocabulary Clip Art

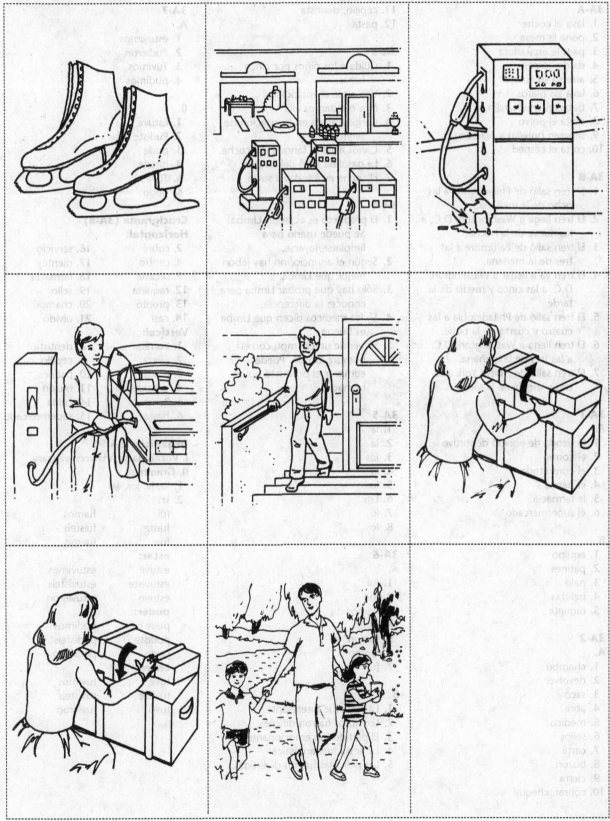

Core Practice Answers

3A-A
1. lava el coche
2. pone la mesa
3. pasa la aspiradora
4. da de comer
5. arregla su cuarto
6. lava los platos
7. trabajan en el jardín
8. quita el polvo
9. separan botellas y plástico
10. corta el césped

3A-B
1. El tren salió de Philadelphia a las ocho de la mañana.
2. El tren llega a Washington, D.C. a las nueve de la noche.
3. El tren salió de Baltimore a las tres de la mañana.
4. El tren va a llegar a Washington, D.C. a las cinco y media de la tarde.
5. El tren salió de Philadelphia a las cuatro y cuarto de la tarde.
6. El tren llega a Washington, D.C. a las tres de la mañana.
7. El tren salió de Nueva York a las tres y media de la tarde.

3A-1
A.
1. la tienda de equipo deportivo
2. el correo
3. el consultorio
4. el banco
5. la farmacia
6. el supermercado

B.
1. equipo
2. patines
3. palo
4. pelotas
5. raqueta

3A-2
A.
1. champú
2. devolver
3. sacó
4. abre
5. médico
6. sellos
7. carta
8. buzón
9. cierra
10. cobrar, cheque

11. cepillo, dentista
12. pasta

3A-3
1. Cuida a los niños por cinco horas.
2. Van a pie al zoológico.
3. Nos quedamos allí.
4. Carlos trabaja en la estación de servicio.
5. Carlos llena el tanque del coche.
6. La gasolina salió del tanque.
7. El coche está todavía sucio.

3A-4
1. El producto es el jabón **Limba**. Se puede usarlo para limpiarse/lavarse.
2. Según el anuncio, no hay jabón mejor que Limba.
3. Sólo hay que probar Limba para conocer la diferencia.
4. Sí, los médicos dicen que Limba es bueno.
5. Se vende un champú con el nombre **Limba**. Puedes comprar el producto en las farmacias.

3A-5
1. la
2. la
3. los
4. la
5. lo
6. Los
7. lo
8. los

3A-6
A.
1. fui
2. fue
3. fuimos
4. fuiste
5. fueron
6. fueron
7. fue

B.
1. La clase fue interesante.
2. Los libros fueron difíciles.
3. El partido fue emocionante.
4. La fiesta fue fantástica.
5. Las películas fueron divertidas.

3A-7
A.
1. estuvimos
2. Pudieron
3. Tuvimos
4. pudimos

B.
1. Estuve
2. Pudiste
3. pude
4. hiciste
5. Tuve
6. pudo

Crucigrama (3A-8)
Horizontal:

2. cobré	16. servicio
4. centro	17. dientes
9. sacaste	18. farmacia
12. raqueta	19. sello
13. pronto	20. champú
14. casi	21. olvidó

Vertical:

1. correo	7. dentista
2. cierra	8. cepillo
3. enviar	10. patines
4. consultorio	11. buzón
5. llenar	14. cuida
6. hasta	15. supermercado

Organizer (3A-9)
I. Vocabulary Answers will vary.
II. Grammar
1. lo, la, los, las
2. **ir:**

fui	fuimos
fuiste	fuisteis
fue	fueron

estar:

estuve	estuvimos
estuviste	estuvisteis
estuvo	estuvieron

poder:

pude	pudimos
pudiste	pudisteis
pudo	pudieron

tener:

tuve	tuvimos
tuviste	tuvisteis
tuvo	tuvieron

Realidades ②

Capítulo 3A

Nombre _____

Fecha _____

Hora _____

AVSR **3A-1**

Telling time

- Remember that to tell time, you use **es** or **son** + numbers and time expressions.
Some common time-telling expressions are:

y	Son las cinco y veinte.	*It's twenty after five (5:20).*
cuarto	Son las dos y **cuarto**.	*It's quarter after two (2:15).*
media	Es la una y **media**.	*It's one thirty (1:30).*
menos	Son las doce **menos** cuarto.	*It's quarter of twelve (11:45).*

A. Fill in the blanks with the words necessary to complete the times shown in the drawings. The first one is done for you.

1. [3:05] Son ___las___ tres ___y___ cinco.

2. [5:15] Son las cinco ___y___ ___**cuarto**___.

3. [4:10] Son ___**las**___ cuatro ___**y**___ diez.

4. [8:52] Son las ___**nueve**___ ___**menos**___ ocho.

5. [6:30] Son ___**las**___ seis y ___**media**___.

- Use *a* in order to tell at what time you do something or something takes place. Use *de* to tell what part of the day it is.

¿A qué hora es la clase de español?	*At what time is Spanish class?*
A las nueve y media de la mañana.	*At nine thirty in the morning (AM).*
A la una de la tarde.	*At one o'clock in the afternoon (PM).*

B. Look at the television listings below and answer the questions that follow.

6:30 AM	Las noticias	12:00 PM	Plaza Sésamo	6:55 PM	Concierto
7:15 AM	El tiempo	1:30 PM	Telenovelas		

Modelo ¿A qué hora es Plaza Sésamo? *A las doce de la tarde.*

1. ¿A qué hora es el concierto? *A las siete menos cinco de la noche.*

2. ¿A qué hora son las noticias? *A las seis y media de la mañana.*

3. ¿A qué hora son las telenovelas? *A la una y media de la tarde.*

4. ¿A qué hora es el tiempo? *A las siete y cuarto de la mañana.*

90 *A ver si recuerdas* ← 3A-1

Capítulo 3A   Fecha _____   **Vocabulary Flash Cards, Sheet 2**

Write the Spanish vocabulary word or phrase below each picture. Be sure to include the article for each noun.

echar   una _____ carta

el _____ buzón

el _____ sello

la _____ tarjeta

la _____ carta

el _____ correo

el _____ dentista

el _____ consultorio

el _____ banco

Capítulo 3A   Fecha _____   **Vocabulary Flash Cards, Sheet 1**

Write the Spanish vocabulary word or phrase below each picture. Be sure to include the article for each noun.

devolver   (un _____ libro)

el _____ supermercado

el _____ centro

el _____ jabón

el _____ champú

la _____ farmacia

enviar

el _____ cepillo de _____ dientes

la _____ pasta dental

Write the Spanish vocabulary word below each picture. If there is a word or phrase, copy it in the space provided. Be sure to include the article for each picture.

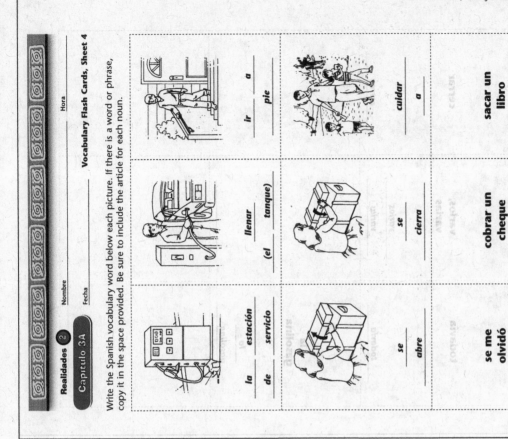

la _____ estación _____
de _____ servicio _____

(el) _____ tanque) _____
llenar _____

ir _____ a _____
a _____ pie _____

se _____
abre _____

se _____
cierra _____

cuidar _____
a _____

se me _____
olvidó _____

cobrar un _____
cheque _____

sacar un _____
libro _____

se _____ me _____
olvidó _____

cobrar _____ un _____
cheque _____

sacar _____ un _____
libro _____

Write the Spanish vocabulary word or phrase below each picture. Be sure to include the article for each noun.

la _____
dentista _____

el _____
médico _____

la _____
médica _____

el _____ equipo _____
deportivo _____

la _____ raqueta _____
de _____ tenis _____

la _____
pelota _____

el _____ palo _____
de _____ golf _____

los _____
patines _____

las _____ estaciones _____
de _____ servicio _____

Sheet 6

Copy the word or phrase in the space provided. Be sure to include the article for each noun. These blank cards can be used to write and practice other Spanish vocabulary for the chapter.

cerrar	varios, varias	todavía
cerrar	_varios varias_	_todavía_
		la gasolina
		la gasolina

Sheet 5

Copy the word or phrase in the space provided. Be sure to include the article for each noun.

¡Cómo no!	por	quedarse
¡Cómo no!	_por_	_quedarse_
casi	hasta	Hasta pronto.
casi	_hasta_	_Hasta pronto._
caramba	en seguida	pronto
caramba	_en seguida_	_pronto_

Sheet 2 (top panel)

Tear out this page. Write the Spanish words on the lines. Fold the paper along the dotted line to see the correct answers so you can check your work.

- Fold In ↓

pharmacy	*la farmacia*
supermarket	*el supermercado*
bank	*el banco*
downtown	*el centro*
service station	*la estación de servicio*
to send	*enviar*
stamp	*el sello*
card	*la tarjeta*
mailbox	*el buzón*
still	*todavía*
to close	*cerrar*
to take care of	*cuidar a*
to return (a book)	*devolver (un libro)*
See you soon.	*Hasta pronto.*
to go on foot	*ir a pie*

Sheet 1 (bottom panel)

Tear out this page. Write the English words on the lines. Fold the paper along the dotted line to see the correct answers so you can check your work.

- Fold In ↓

la farmacia	*pharmacy*
el supermercado	*supermarket*
el banco	*bank*
el centro	*downtown*
la estación de servicio	*service station*
enviar	*to send*
el sello	*stamp*
la tarjeta	*card*
el buzón	*mailbox*
todavía	*still*
cerrar	*to close*
cuidar a	*to take care of*
devolver (un libro)	*to return (a book)*
Hasta pronto.	*See you soon.*
ir a pie	*to go on foot*

Tear out this page. Write the Spanish words on the lines. Fold the paper along the dotted line to see the correct answers so you can check your work.

letter	*la carta*
to mail a letter	*echar una carta*
post office	*el correo*
sports equipment	*el equipo deportivo*
golf club	*el palo de golf*
skates	*los patines*
ball	*la pelota*
tennis racket	*la raqueta de tenis*
toothbrush	*el cepillo de dientes*
shampoo	*el champú*
soap	*el jabón*
toothpaste	*la pasta dental*
good gracious	*caramba*
almost	*casi*

- Fold In ↓

To hear a complete list of the vocabulary for this chapter, go to www.realidades.com and type in the Web Code jdd-0389. Then click on **Repaso del capítulo.**

Tear out this page. Write the English words on the lines. Fold the paper along the dotted line to see the correct answers so you can check your work.

la carta	*letter*
echar una carta	*to mail a letter*
el correo	*post office*
el equipo deportivo	*sports equipment*
el palo de golf	*golf club*
los patines	*skates*
la pelota	*ball*
la raqueta de tenis	*tennis racket*
el cepillo de dientes	*toothbrush*
el champú	*shampoo*
el jabón	*soap*
la pasta dental	*toothpaste*
caramba	*good gracious*
casi	*almost*

- Fold In ↓

Direct object pronouns (p. 138)

- A direct object tells who or what receives the action of the verb. Direct objects may represent people or things.
- To avoid repeating a direct object noun, you can replace it with a direct object pronoun.

¿Martín echó la carta ayer? (Carta is the direct object noun.)
No, la echó hoy. (La is the direct object pronoun. It replaces the word carta.)

- Here are the direct object pronouns you have already used:

Singular	Plural
lo it, him, you (masculine formal)	los them, you (masculine formal)
la it, her, you (feminine formal)	las them, you (feminine formal)

A. Circle the direct object noun in each sentence. Then, write the direct object pronoun that replaces the circled words. Follow the model.

Modelo Margarita cobró el cheque __lo__ ayer.

1. Paquito pasó la aspiradora ayer. __la__
2. Juanucho buscó los patines. __los__
3. Tú llenaste el tanque del coche. __lo__
4. Yo envié las tarjetas a la tía. __las__
5. Uds. sacaron los libros de la biblioteca. __los__
6. Ella cerró la estación de servicio. __la__

B. Look at the sentences from exercise A. Replace the direct object noun you circled with the pronoun that corresponds to it. Follow the model.

Modelo Margarita __lo__ cobró.

1. Paquito __la__ pasó ayer.
2. Juanucho __los__ buscó.
3. Tú __lo__ llenaste.
4. Yo __las__ envié a la tía.
5. Uds. __los__ sacaron de la biblioteca.
6. Ella __la__ cerró.

Direct object pronouns (continued)

C. Circle the direct object noun in each question. Then, answer each question by using a direct object pronoun in your answer. Use the verbs given. Follow the model.

Modelo ¿El cobró el cheque el martes pasado?
Sí, __lo__ __cobró__ el martes pasado.

1. ¿Ella pasó la aspiradora ayer? Sí, __la__ __pasó__ ayer.
2. ¿Ellos arreglaron el cuarto esta semana? No, no __lo__ __arreglaron__ esta semana.
3. ¿Quién echó la carta en el buzón? Anita __la__ __echó__ en el buzón.
4. ¿Quién envió las tarjetas de cumpleaños? Billy __las__ __envió__.
5. ¿Ellas sacaron los libros de la biblioteca? Sí, __los__ __sacaron__ de la biblioteca.
6. ¿Jenny y Miguel cerraron la estación de servicio? No, no __la__ __cerraron__.
7. ¿El lavó los platos anoche? Sí, __los__ __lavó__ anoche.

- The direct object pronoun is placed before conjugated verbs. When an infinitive is present, the pronoun may come before the conjugated verb or attached to the infinitive.

Lo tengo que hacer. or Tengo que hacerlo.

D. Rewrite the following sentences to show a second possibility for where the direct object pronouns can be placed. Follow the model.

Modelo ¿La raqueta? La voy a comprar mañana. Voy **a comprarla mañana** .

1. ¿Las cartas? Las vamos a echar hoy. **Vamos a echarlas hoy**
2. ¿El palo de golf? Lo tengo que comprar. **Tengo que comprarlo**
3. ¿Los patines? Los vas a usar esta tarde. **Vas a usarlos esta tarde**
4. ¿La mesa? La voy a poner hoy. **Voy a ponerla hoy**
5. ¿Los periódicos? Los voy a separar esta noche. **Voy a separarlos esta noche**
6. ¿El dentista? Lo tengo que visitar hoy. **Tengo que visitarlo hoy**

Right page (3A-3)

Irregular preterite verbs: *ir, ser* (*continued*)

B. Write the correct form of the verb within parentheses. Follow the model.

Modelo   Rafael y Hernando no _fueron_ (ir) al consultorio ayer.

1. Anoche yo _fui_ (ir) al centro.
2. Luego, Marcela y yo _fuimos_ (ir) a cobrar un cheque.
3. La noche _fue_ (ser) divertida.
4. Y tú ¿adónde _fuiste_ (ir)?
5. La tarde _fue_ (ser) aburrida.
6. Ellos _fueron_ (ir) a un concierto en el parque.
7. El plato principal _fue_ (ser) bistec y papas.
8. Nosotras _fuimos_ (ir) a la playa.

Irregular preterite verbs: *hacer, tener, estar, poder* (p. 142)

• The preterite of the irregular verbs *hacer* (*to do*) and *tener* (*to have*) follow a similar pattern.

yo	hice / tuve	nosotros/nosotras	hicimos / tuvimos
tú	hiciste / tuviste	vosotros/vosotras	hicisteis / tuvisteis
usted/él/ella	hizo / tuvo	ustedes/ellos/ellas	hicieron / tuvieron

A. Complete the dialogue by circling the correct form of the verb within parentheses. The first one is done for you.

1. LAURA: ¿Qué (hicieron / **hizo**) tú y tu familia ayer?
   DANIEL: Nosotros (**tuvimos** / tuvieron) que ir al centro.
2. LAURA: ¿Qué (**hizo** / hice) tu papá?
   DANIEL: Él (tuve / **tuvo**) que enviar una carta.
3. LAURA: ¿Qué (hiciste / **hizo**) tu mamá?
   DANIEL: Ella (**tuvo** / tuve) que devolver un libro.
4. DANIEL: Y tú Laura, ¿qué (hizo / **hiciste**) en la noche?
   LAURA: Yo (**tuve** / tuviste) que cuidar a mi hermanito.

Left page (3A-2)

Irregular preterite verbs: *ir, ser* (p. 140)

• The preterite forms of *ser* (*to be*) and *ir* (*to go*) are the same.

yo	fui	nosotros/nosotras	fuimos
tú	fuiste	vosotros/vosotras	fuisteis
usted/él/ella	fue	ustedes/ellos/ellas	fueron

• Usually the context of the verb is what makes the meaning clear:
   Mi doctora fue la Dra. Serrano. *My doctor was Dr. Serrano.*
   El año pasado fue muy difícil. *Last year was very difficult.*
   Yo fui a la farmacia. *I went to the pharmacy.*

(If you see the preposition "a" following one of these verb forms, the verb is **ir** and the meaning is *"went"*.)

A. Circle the correct conjugated verb in parentheses.

¡Hola Margarita!
Ayer (fuimos / **fue**) un día muy interesante. Primero, mi
familia y yo (**fuimos** / fue) al parque zoológico. Mis padres
(**fueron** / fue) a ver los monos y mis hermanos y yo
(fueron / **fuimos**) a comer un helado. ¡(Fuimos / **Fue**)
delicioso! A las cinco todos nosotros (fueron / **fuimos**)
a comer en un restaurante argentino. La comida (fui / **fue**)
fantástica y yo (fuiste / **fui**) a la casa muy contenta.
¿Y tú? ¿Adónde (fue / **fuiste**) ayer?

Un abrazo
–Victoria

Lectura: La unidad en la comunidad internacional (pp. 146–147)

A. The reading in your textbook is about **Ciudades Hermanas Internacional** or the Sister Cities program. As you look at the reading, you will notice several headings. Headings are a way of organizing ideas in a reading. Look at the headings below from the reading to help you complete the following activity.

> *Ciudades Hermanas Internacional*
> *¡Quiero tener una ciudad hermana!*
> *Intercambio económico*
> *Intercambio cultural*
> *Intercambio educativo*

Now, write **L** (for **Lectura**) next to the sentence below if it is something you might find in the reading. Write **N** (for **No**) next to the sentence if it is something you might not find in the reading.

1. The Sister Cities International program is for sports teams. __**N**__

2. The mission of the Sister Cities International program is exchange and cooperation. __**L**__

3. The sister cities can have educational, economic, and cultural exchanges. __**L**__

4. How to have a sister city. __**L**__

5. Sister cities cannot be from different countries. __**N**__

B. Read the following excerpt from the reading in your textbook. Then, determine the important ideas of the excerpt and place a ✓ next to them.

> *¡Quiero tener una ciudad hermana!*
> *Cualquier (Any) ciudad en los Estados Unidos puede tener una ciudad hermana. Primero es necesario encontrar otra ciudad extranjera (foreign). Esta ciudad puede tener alguna relación con la ciudad original. Por ejemplo, ciudades que tienen el mismo nombre, como Toledo, Ohio y Toledo, España, pueden asociarse. También, las ciudades que celebran el mismo festival pueden formar relaciones de hermandad.*

1. It is difficult for people in the United States to find a sister city. ____

2. People in the United States can easily find a sister city. __✓__

3. Cities with the same names can become sister cities. __✓__

4. Cities that don't celebrate the same festivals can become sister cities. ____

realidades.com
• Web Code: jdd-0307

Irregular preterite verbs: hacer, tener, estar, poder (continued)

- Like the verbs **hacer** and **tener**, the verbs **estar** (to be) and **poder** (to be able) are also irregular in the preterite.
- Unlike regular preterite verbs, **hacer, tener, estar,** and **poder** do not have accent marks on their preterite forms.
- Here are the preterite forms of **estar** and **poder**:

yo	estuve	nosotros/nosotras	estuvimos
tú	estuviste	vosotros/vosotras	estuvisteis
usted/él/ella	estuvo	ustedes/ellos/ellas	estuvieron

yo	pude	nosotros/nosotras	pudimos
tú	pudiste	vosotros/vosotras	pudisteis
usted/él/ella	pudo	ustedes/ellos/ellas	pudieron

B. Write the missing endings of the preterite forms of **estar** and **poder** in the sentences below.

1. Ayer yo estuv_**e**_ en el parque por una hora.

2. Mi amigo Pablo no pud_**o**_ venir.

3. Pablo y su papá estuv_**ieron**_ en la oficina del doctor.

4. Después, Pablo no pud_**o**_ ir a la escuela.

5. Él estuv_**o**_ enfermo por tres días.

6. Tú estuv_**iste**_ enfermo también, ¿no?

C. Complete the sentences below with the correct preterite form of the verb in parentheses. Follow the model.

Modelo   Yo __hice__ (hacer) mucha tarea anoche.

1. El fin de semana pasado, yo __estuve__ (estar) en casa.

2. Mi hermano Tito __tuvo__ (tener) que hacer una tarjeta para nuestro tío, Julio.

3. Tito casi no __pudo__ (poder) terminarla a tiempo.

4. Después, echó la tarjeta al buzón y por la noche, nosotros __hicimos__ (hacer) la cena.

5. ¿Dónde __estuvieron__ (estar) Uds. el fin de semana?

realidades.com
• Web Code: jdd-0306

Realidades 2

Nombre _____ Hora _____

Capítulo 3A

Fecha _____ **Guided Practice Activities 3A-6**

Presentación oral (p. 149) *Answers will vary.*

Task: Pretend you need to prepare for a trip to Mérida, Mexico. You will visit some Mayan ruins and the beach in Cancún. Remember that it will be very hot and humid.

A. Complete the following chart. In the **¿Lo necesitas?** column, write **Sí** if you need the item or **No** if you do not need the item. Then, place a ✓ in the right column, **¿Lo tienes?**, if you already have the item.

Ropa	¿Lo necesitas?	¿Lo tienes?
pantalones cortos		
camisetas		
abrigo		
traje de baño		
sombrero para el sol		
botas		
cepillo de dientes		

B. Review your answers in **part A**. List three items that you need but that you already have at home.

1. _____ 2. _____ 3. _____

C. Pretend you already went shopping for the items you did not have. In the left column, list those items you had to buy for your trip. In the right column, write down where you bought them. The first one is done for you.

Tuve que comprar...	¿Dónde?
pantalones cortos	el almacén

D. Use the information in **parts B** and **C** to talk about your trip preparation. Tell what you need and what you have or don't have. You may also bring in and show articles of clothing as props. You can use the following as a model.

▓ *Para mi viaje a México necesito camisetas, pero ya las tengo.*
   Tuve que comprar unos pantalones cortos en el almacén...

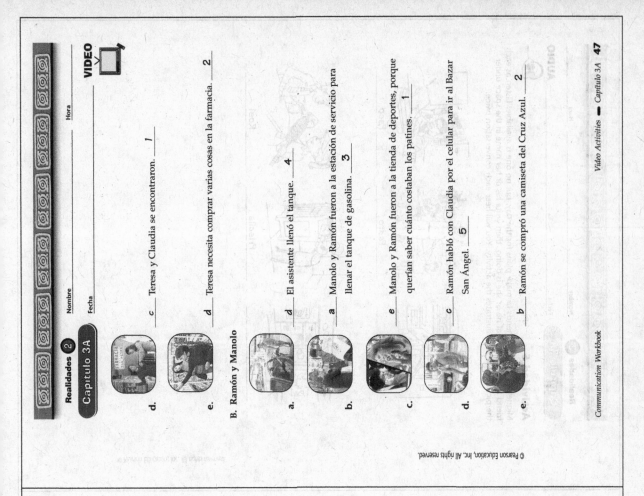

VIDEO

Antes de ver el video

Actividad 1

Following is a list of things that the characters from the video did during the day. In the second column, write the place where they probably went to do each thing. The first one has been done for you.

Cosas que hacer	Lugar
ir a ver una película	el cine
1. comprar champú y pasta dental	la farmacia o el supermercado
2. llenar el tanque de gasolina	la estación de servicio
3. enviar una carta	el correo
4. comprar unos patines	la tienda de equipo deportivo
5. comprar un regalo	el centro comercial o el mercado
6. comprar sellos	el correo

¿Comprendes?

Actividad 2

First, match each statement on the right with its corresponding picture, using the letters **a-e**. Then, number the scenes in each section in the order in which they occur in the video. Write **1** for the first scene and **5** for the last. One is done for you.

A. Teresa y Claudia

a.

b.

c.

___b___ Claudia habló con Ramón por el celular para ir al Bazar San Ángel. 5

___e___ Teresa escoge el champú que va a comprar. 3

___a___ Teresa fue al correo para comprar sellos. 4

___c___ Teresa y Claudia se encontraron. 1

___d___ Teresa necesita comprar varias cosas en la farmacia. 2

B. Ramón y Manolo

a.

b.

c.

d.

v.e.

___d___ El asistente llenó el tanque. 4

___a___ Manolo y Ramón fueron a la estación de servicio para llenar el tanque de gasolina. 3

___e___ Manolo y Ramón fueron a la tienda de deportes, porque querían saber cuánto costaban los patines. 1

___c___ Ramón habló con Claudia por el celular para ir al Bazar San Ángel. 5

___b___ Ramón se compró una camiseta del Cruz Azul. 2

Realidades 2

Capítulo 3A

Nombre _____

Hora _____

Fecha _____

VIDEO

Actividad 3

Circle the correct word that completes the following sentences.

1. Los cuatro amigos quieren ir al (cine/ correo) a ver una película (romántica / de ciencia ficción).

2. Teresa no compró el champú (ayer/ hoy), porque fue a (devolver/ comprar) un libro a la biblioteca.

3. (Claudia /Teresa) compra pasta dental en la farmacia.

4. El correo (abre /cierra) a las cinco.

5. A Teresa se le olvidó (llenar el tanque /enviar la carta) esta mañana.

6. Manolo (compra /no compra) los patines en la tienda de equipo deportivo.

7. Teresa olvidó (enviar /comprar) un regalo para el cumpleaños de su (abuela/ mamá).

8. Claudia y Teresa van a ver a Ramón y a Manolo en el (correo /Bazar San Ángel) porque (no está muy lejos/ está muy lejos) de allí.

Y, ¿qué más?

Actividad 4

Write four complete sentences that tell about things you and your friends do and places that you and your friends go to in your free time. Follow the model.

Modelo *Me gusta ir con mis amigos(as) a jugar a los bolos.*

Answers will vary.

_____

_____

_____

_____

Realidades 2

Capítulo 3A

Nombre _____

Hora _____

Fecha _____

AUDIO

Actividad 5

Miguel is calling his friends to make plans for the day, but no one is available. Listen as each friend tells Miguel what he or she is doing, then write his or her name in the space under the picture that best illustrates the activity. You will hear each conversation twice.

David _____

Pedro _____

Paco _____

Grisel _____

Priscila _____

Rosi _____

Actividad 8

When Eric went to Mexico for the summer, he brought his high school yearbook with him so that his host family could see what his school was like. Listen as his host parents look through his yearbook and reminisce about their own high school days. They will ask each other if they remember (**¿recuerdas?**) certain events from their past. Match their memories with the corresponding pictures. You will hear this conversation twice.

Actividad 9

Sometimes there just aren't enough hours in the day! Listen as each person tells a friend what he or she had to do yesterday but just wasn't able to. As you listen to each conversation, fill in the grid below with short phrases. You will hear each conversation twice.

	¿Qué tuvo que hacer la persona?	¿Por qué no pudo hacerlo?
1.	Tuvo que estudiar.	Estuvo en el trabajo. / Tuvo que trabajar.
2.	Tuvo que ir de compras.	Estuvo en el consultorio.
3.	Tuvo que cobrar un cheque.	Estuvo en el supermercado.
4.	Tuvieron que ir a la biblioteca.	Estuvieron en la fiesta de Juan.
5.	Tuvieron que comprar aspirinas.	Estuvieron estudiando.

Actividad 6

Felipe has been trying to catch up with his friend Moisés all day. As he asks people where they saw Moisés last, write the time and place each person mentions on the line beneath the appropriate picture. After you have heard everyone's answers, number the pictures chronologically, with **1** being the first place Moisés went and **8** being the last place Moisés went. You will hear each conversation twice.

A. 3:00 P.M. / farmacia   # 5
B. 4:30 P.M. / banco   # 6
C. 9:00 A.M. / correo   # 1
D. 8:00 P.M. / supermercado   # 8
E. 10:00 A.M. / tienda de equipo deportivo   # 2
F. 7:00 P.M. / estación de servicio   # 7
G. 12:00 P.M. / biblioteca   # 3
H. 2:00 P.M. / consultorio del médico   # 4

Actividad 7

Listen as you hear several people describe a moment when they saw someone who they thought was good-looking. After each statement, complete the sentence below with the correct location of the encounter. You will hear each statement twice.

1. Lo vio en <u>el supermercado</u> .
2. La vio en <u>el banco</u> .
3. Los vio en <u>la tienda de equipo deportivo</u> .
4. Las vio en <u>el correo</u> .
5. La vio en <u>la farmacia</u> .

Realidades 2

Capítulo 3A

Nombre _____

Fecha _____

Hora _____

WRITING

Actividad 10

Write complete sentences telling where these people have to go today in order to accomplish the tasks depicted in the drawings.

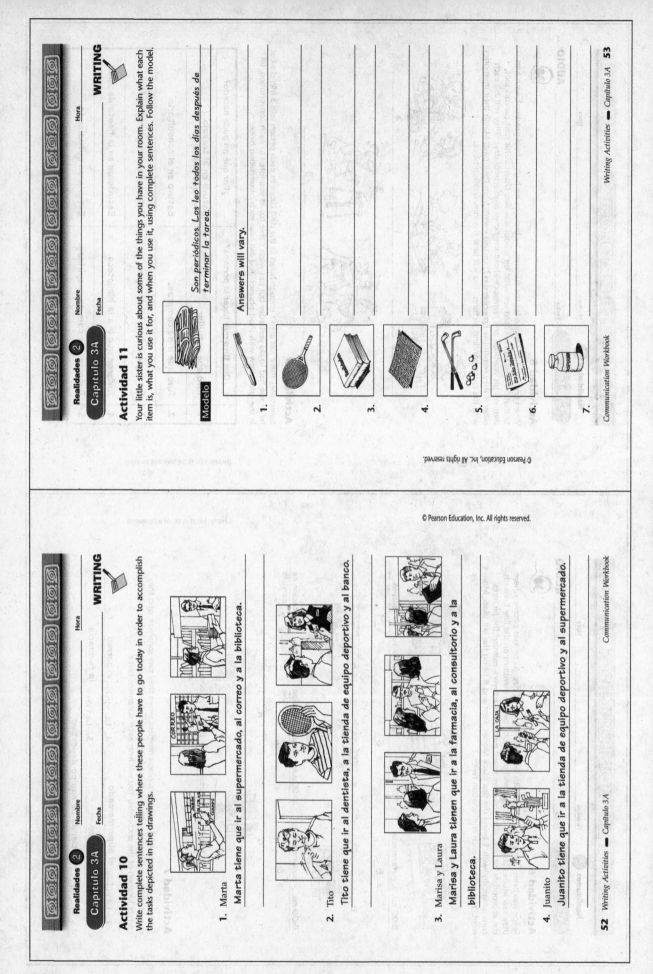

1. Marta

   Marta tiene que ir al supermercado, al correo y a la biblioteca.

2. Tito

   Tito tiene que ir al dentista, a la tienda de equipo deportivo y al banco.

3. Marisa y Laura

   Marisa y Laura tienen que ir a la farmacia, al consultorio y a la biblioteca.

4. Juanito

   Juanito tiene que ir a la tienda de equipo deportivo y al supermercado.

Realidades 2

Capítulo 3A

Nombre _____

Fecha _____

Hora _____

WRITING

Actividad 11

Your little sister is curious about some of the things you have in your room. Explain what each item is, what you use it for, and when you use it, using complete sentences. Follow the model.

Modelo

Son periódicos. Los leo todos los días después de terminar la tarea.

Answers will vary.

1.

2.

3.

4.

5.

6.

7.

Actividad 13

Your family just took a trip and you are going through your photos, reminiscing about the good and bad parts of the vacation. Write a caption for each picture below to describe what everyone did, where they went, what they were able to do there, etc.

Modelo

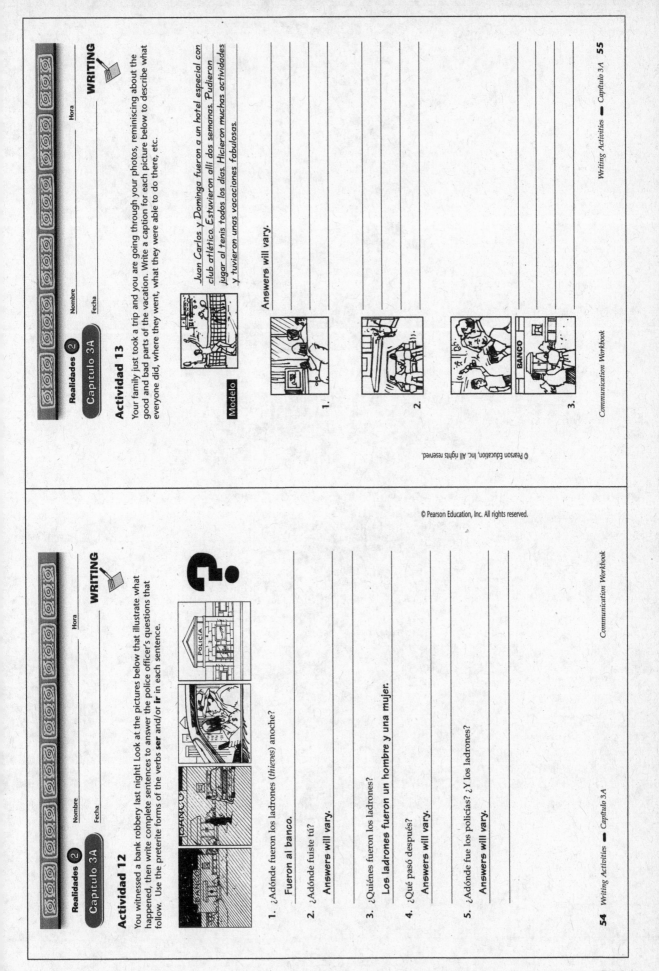

Juan Carlos y Dominga fueron a un hotel especial con club atlético. Estuvieron allí dos semanas. Pudieron jugar al tenis todos los días. Hicieron muchas actividades y tuvieron unas vacaciones fabulosas.

Answers will vary.

1. _____

2. _____

3. _____

Actividad 12

You witnessed a bank robbery last night! Look at the pictures below that illustrate what happened, then write complete sentences to answer the police officer's questions that follow. Use the preterite forms of the verbs **ser** and/or **ir** in each sentence.

1. ¿Adónde fueron los ladrones (*thieves*) anoche?

   Fueron al banco.

2. ¿Adónde fuiste tú?

   Answers will vary.

3. ¿Quiénes fueron los ladrones?

   Los ladrones fueron un hombre y una mujer.

4. ¿Qué pasó después?

   Answers will vary.

5. ¿Adónde fue los policías? ¿Y los ladrones?

   Answers will vary.

Test Preparation Answers

Reading Skills
p. 229   2. **A**
p. 230   2. **C**

Integrated Performance
   Assessment
p. 231
Answers will vary.

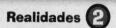
School-to-Home Connection

Dear Parent or Guardian,

The theme of our current unit is *Tú y tu comunidad* (You and your community).
This chapter is called *¿Cómo se va?* (How do I get there?).

Upon completion of this chapter students will be able to:

- give directions and explain how to get to places in a town or a city
- give a friend directions for a task
- discuss driving a car and good driving habits
- understand cultural perspectives about neighborhoods

Students will also explore:

- using gestures and body language as an important form of communication

Our textbook, *Realidades,* helps with the development of reading, writing, and speaking skills through the use of strategies, process speaking, and process writing. In this chapter, students will:

- read a driver's manual
- write about safe driving practices and special traffic signs

To reinforce and enhance learning, students can access a wide range of online resources on **realidades.com**, the personalized learning management system that accompanies the print and online Student Edition. Resources include the eText, textbook and workbook activities, audio files, videos, animations, songs, self-study tools, interactive maps, voice recording (RealTalk!), assessments, and other digital resources. Many learning tools can be accessed through the student Home Page on **realidades.com**. Other activities, specifically those that require grading, are assigned by the teacher and linked on the student Home Page within the calendar or the Assignments tab.

You will find specifications and guidelines for accessing **realidades.com** on home computers and mobile devices on MyPearsonTraining.com under the SuccessNet Plus tab.

Check it out! At the end of the chapter, have your child use the new vocabulary from this chapter to give you three pieces of driving advice. Then have him or her explain the advice to you in English.

Sincerely,

For: Tips to Parents
Visit: www.realidades.com
Web Code: jce-0010

Videocultura Script

Comunidades latinas

Spanish version:

Nueva York, la ciudad más poblada de los Estados Unidos, es un centro de gran diversidad cultural. En esta ciudad se hablan más de 100 lenguas. Después del inglés, el español es la lengua más hablada con más de dos millones de latinos que viven en la ciudad y sus alrededores.

Muchos inmigrantes hispanos llegaron a Nueva York en los años 50 y se asentaron en ciertos barrios de acuerdo a su nacionalidad: los puertorriqueños en Spanish Harlem, los dominicanos en Washington Heights y los colombianos en Queens.

En estos barrios, las tiendas y los restaurantes se establecieron y prosperaron con gran fuerza. Ofrecieron comidas, productos y servicios que los inmigrantes debieron dejar atrás en sus países de origen. De esta manera, estos barrios lograron desarrollar un sentido de pertenencia y comunidad. Hoy día, estos negocios continúan satisfaciendo las necesidades de los clientes de habla hispana en Nueva York.

Aunque las comunidades latinas siguen distribuidas en estos barrios, hoy día los latinos viven y trabajan por todas partes de la ciudad de Nueva York.

Cada día, los latinos se integran más a la cultura neoyorquina. La comunidad latina se abre y comparte su cultura con todos los habitantes de la Gran Manzana.

English version:

New York City, the most populous city in the United States, is a great center of cultural diversity, with well over 100 languages spoken. After English, Spanish is the second most popular language, with over two million Latinos living in and around New York City.

Many Hispanics began arriving in New York City in the 1950s. Immigrants from different Spanish-speaking countries tended to settle in certain neighborhoods, depending on their nationality.

Puerto Ricans settled in Spanish Harlem, which is also known as El Barrio, and the Lower East Side. Many Dominicans moved into Washington Heights, and new arrivals from Colombia settled in Queens.

Within these neighborhoods, businesses and restaurants were established and thrived. They offered the foods, products, and services that were left behind in their native countries. In addition, these neighborhoods fostered a sense of culture and community. Today they continue to cater to the needs of their Spanish-speaking clientele.

Although neighborhoods such as El Barrio are still important cultural centers, Spanish speakers now live and work in boroughs and neighborhoods located throughout the city.

In New York and in towns and cities across the United States, immigrants from Spanish-speaking countries adapt to living in a new community while preserving traditions of their home countries. This rich exchange of culture contributes to the "melting pot" that is the United States.

Input Script

Presentation

Input Vocabulary: Bring a toy car and a toy truck to class. Distribute copies of the Vocabulary Clip Art to students and have them cut them into individual images. Draw the city map shown in *A primera vista* on the chalkboard. Draw the map large enough to drive the toy vehicles down the avenues. Include a narrow bridge on your map, as shown on p. 159, and label all the streets, stores, vehicles, and people shown on the map. Then take students on a tour of the town by "driving" the car or truck along the avenues and describing the different features you drive by. Have students arrange their Clip Art images in the order in which you mention them.

Input Dialogue 1: Perform the dialogue. Play both parts and demonstrate meaning by driving the toy car or toy truck from the vocabulary presentation along the city map on the chalkboard. Then have students ask you: *¿Cómo se va al (a la) ____?* about other places on the map. Demonstrate with the car or truck as you describe how to get to the new places. Then repeat, but with a student "driving" the car according to your directions.

Input Dialogues 2 and 3: Describe to students a fictional accident involving a car, a big truck, and a narrow bridge. You were a passenger in the car and your friend Miguel was driving. Present Dialogues 2 and 3 as if they were the conversations you had with Miguel right before the accident. Use the toy car and toy truck to demonstrate what happened and where on the city map the accident occurred. Then check for comprehension by making statements that you or Miguel might have said before, during, or after the accident. Have students raise their right hand if the statement is something you would have said and their left hand if the statement is something Miguel would have said.

Comprehension Check

- Describe a fictional city map. Give the names of the streets and tell where different businesses and services are located. Have students draw the map based on your description. Tell students where they are (at the library, bank, etc.), then give them directions to another place on the map. Have them identify the destination.

- Distribute copies of the Vocabulary Clip Art and have students cut them into individual images. Write fill-in-the-blank sentences on the chalkboard with the vocabulary words from *A primera vista* missing from the sentences. Have students arrange their Clip Art images for the missing words on their desks in the order of the sentences on the chalkboard. Ask for volunteers to tape the correct images in the blanks and give the Spanish words for the images.

Audio Script

Audio DVD, Capítulo 3B

Track 01: *A primera vista, ¿Cómo se va…?*, **Student Book, p. 158**

Vocabulario y gramática en contexto
Lee en tu libro mientras escuchas el diálogo.

MALE TEEN: Hola, me llamo Miguel. Hoy estoy en el centro y necesito ir al Banco Nacional. Voy a preguntarle a este policía cómo se va al banco.

MIGUEL: Señor policía, ¿cómo se va al Banco Nacional?

POLICEMAN: Es muy fácil.

Cruza esta calle y sigue derecho hasta llegar a la señal de parada.

Allí, dobla a la izquierda.

Después de manejar por una cuadra, dobla a la derecha.

El banco queda a mano izquierda en medio de la Avenida Juárez.

Vas a escuchar cada palabra o frase dos veces. Después de la primera vez hay una pausa para que puedas pronunciar la palabra o frase. Luego vas a escuchar de nuevo la palabra o frase.

el camión	la plaza
la avenida	el policía
el semáforo	la esquina
la fuente	una cuadra

Track 02: *A primera vista,* **Student Book, p. 159**

Vocabulario y gramática en contexto
Vas a escuchar cada palabra o frase dos veces. Después de la primera vez hay una pausa para que puedas pronunciar la palabra o frase. Luego vas a escuchar de nuevo la palabra o frase.

el cruce de calles	estrecha
el tráfico	la carretera
la estatua	ancho
el peatón	ancha
la señal de parada	el permiso de manejar
el puente	poner una multa
estrecho	el conductor

Más vocabulario
hasta

Lee en tu libro mientras escuchas el diálogo.

ADULT MALE: Miguel, ten cuidado. Es un poco peligroso por aquí. La carretera es ancha pero vamos a pasar por un puente que es bastante estrecho.

MIGUEL: ¡Basta! Ya sé manejar.

ADULT MALE: ¡Hombre! Ve más despacio. La policía te va a poner una multa y a veces te quitan el permiso de manejar.

MIGUEL: Me estás poniendo nervioso. Déjame en paz por un momento.

Track 03: *A primera vista,* **Act. 1, Student Book, p. 159**

¿Qué es y dónde queda?
Escucha las descripciones y busca la palabra o expresión apropiada del vocabulario en el mapa en las páginas 158 y 159. Señala la palabra o expresión y dila en voz alta para indicar que la encontraste. Vas a escuchar las descripciones dos veces.

1. Es una persona que camina al lado de una calle.
2. Tiene los colores rojo, amarillo y verde. Es importante mirarlo.
3. Es la persona que maneja un coche.
4. Esta señal indica que es necesario parar el coche.
5. Es la intersección de dos calles.
6. Es similar a un monumento. Generalmente es una reproducción de una persona.
7. Es similar a un parque. Es un lugar en el centro de la ciudad.

Track 04: *A primera vista,* **Act. 2, Student Book, p. 159**

¿Dónde estoy ahora?
Escucha las direcciones y síguelas en el mapa de las páginas 158 y 159. Empieza cada vez en las palabras "Estás aquí." Indica adónde llegas y contesta con "Estoy delante de…" Vas a escuchar las direcciones dos veces.

1. Cruza la Calle Allende. Estás detrás del museo. Cruza la Avenida de la Constitución. ¿Dónde estás?
2. Cruza la Avenida de la Constitución. Estás delante del cine. Sigue derecho una cuadra. Cruza la Avenida Juárez. ¿Dónde estás?
3. Cruza la Avenida de la Constitución. Estás delante del cine. Sigue derecho hasta llegar a la esquina. Dobla a la derecha cruzando la Calle Allende. Sigue derecho una cuadra. Dobla a la izquierda cruzando la calle. ¿Dónde estás?
4. Cruza la Calle Allende. Estás detrás del museo. Sigue derecho hasta llegar a la señal de parada. Sigue derecho cruzando la calle. Dobla a la izquierda y cruza la calle otra vez. ¿Dónde estás?
5. Cruza la Avenida de la Constitución. Estás delante del cine. Sigue derecho hasta llegar a la Avenida Juárez. Cruza la calle y luego dobla a la derecha cruzando la calle otra vez. ¿Dónde estás?
6. Cruza la Calle Allende. Estás detrás del museo. Sigue derecho hasta llegar a la señal de parada. Cruza la calle y luego dobla a la izquierda, cruzando la Avenida de la Constitución. Sigue derecho una cuadra. ¿Dónde estás?

Track 05: *A primera vista, Videohistoria,* **Student Book, pp. 160–161**

¿Cómo llegamos a la plaza?
¿Cómo van los cuatro amigos al Bazar San Ángel? Lee la historia.

Lee en tu libro mientras escuchas la *Videohistoria*.

See Student Book pages 160–161 for script.

Track 06: *Manos a la obra,* **Act. 7, Student Book, p. 163**

Escucha y escribe

Tus parientes saben que estás aprendiendo a manejar y todos tienen consejos. Pero algunas de sus ideas no son muy lógicas. Escucha lo que dicen y escribe las frases. Después escribe *L* si es una idea lógica o *I* si es una idea ilógica. Vas a escuchar las frases dos veces.

1. Cuando manejas, deja tu permiso de manejar en la casa.
2. No debes tener mucha prisa cuando manejas.
3. A veces les quitan el permiso de manejar a los malos conductores.
4. Ten cuidado si manejas cerca de un camión grande.
5. Cuando el semáforo está en rojo, sigue derecho sin parar.
6. No es necesario prestar atención a las señales de tráfico.

Track 07: *Manos a la obra,* **Act. 9, Student Book, p. 164**

¿Cómo se va a...?

Estás de vacaciones con tu familia en el Viejo San Juan, Puerto Rico. Empiezas tu excursión hoy en el Parque de las Palomas. Ve la estrella en el mapa. Escucha las direcciones que te dan tres personas y síguelas en el mapa. Escribe el nombre de cada lugar adonde llegas. Vas a escuchar las direcciones dos veces.

ADULT FEMALE: Cuando sales del Parque de las Palomas, dobla a la izquierda y sigue la Calle del Cristo. Cruza la Calle Fortaleza y camina por una cuadra. Dobla a la derecha. Camina por una cuadra en la Calle de San Francisco. Pasa el cruce de calles. Está a mano derecha. ¿Dónde estás?

TEEN MALE: Después de visitar la Plaza de Armas, sigue la Calle de San Francisco hasta llegar a la Calle de la Cruz. En el cruce de calles, dobla a la derecha. Sigue derecho por dos cuadras. Dobla a la izquierda. Queda a mano izquierda, en medio de la cuadra. ¿Dónde estás?

TEEN FEMALE: Cuando sales de la Iglesia de Santa Ana, dobla a la derecha y toma la Calle Tetuán. Cruza la Calle de la Cruz y sigue derecho aproximadamente dos cuadras hasta llegar a la Calle del Cristo. Para aquí. Queda a la izquierda. ¿Dónde estás?

Track 08: Audio Act. 5, Writing, Audio & Video Workbook, p. 59

Listen as people in a hotel call the front desk for help. As you listen to each conversation, match each caller to the spot on the map below by writing the number of the conversation in the corresponding circle. You will hear each conversation twice.

1. **ADULT MALE 1:** Buenos días. Hotel Santiago. Dígame.
   ADULT MALE 2: Hola. Soy el señor Montero. Necesito comprar un periódico de Francia.
   ADULT MALE 1: Para comprar periódicos de otros países, doble a la izquierda del hotel y siga por la Calle San Juan. Cruce el semáforo. Hay una tienda a una cuadra más, en la esquina cerca de la señal de parada.

2. **ADULT MALE 1:** Buenos días. Hotel Santiago. Dígame.
   ADULT FEMALE 1: Soy la señora Martín. Tengo que enviar un documento muy importante a mi oficina. Tiene que llegar mañana. ¿Dónde queda el correo?
   ADULT MALE 1: No está muy lejos. Al salir del hotel, Ud. está en la Calle San Juan. Doble a la derecha y siga derecho hasta llegar al cruce de la Avenida San José. Doble a la izquierda y siga una cuadra hasta llegar a la Calle Santiago. El correo está en la esquina del cruce de la Calle Santiago y la Avenida San José.

3. **ADULT MALE 1:** Buenos días. Hotel Santiago. Dígame.
   ADULT MALE 2: Sí. Buenos días. Hoy quiero jugar al tenis con un amigo, pero no tengo mi raqueta de tenis aquí. ¿Puede decirme dónde puedo comprar una raqueta?
   ADULT MALE 1: Sí, señor. Hay una tienda de equipo deportivo muy cerca del hotel. Al salir del hotel, doble a la izquierda hasta la Avenida San Felipe. No cruce la calle, sino doble a la derecha. La tienda de equipo deportivo está al lado de la fuente. Y, ¡buena suerte en su partido de tenis!

4. **ADULT MALE 1:** Buenos días. Hotel Santiago. Dígame.
   ADULT FEMALE 2: Perdón, señor, tengo un terrible dolor de cabeza. ¿Estamos muy lejos de una farmacia? Necesito aspirina.
   ADULT MALE 1: La farmacia está al lado del hotel. Al salir del hotel, doble a la derecha. Espero que se sienta mejor muy pronto, señora.

5. **ADULT MALE 1:** Buenos días. Hotel Santiago. Dígame.
   ADULT MALE 3: Hola. ¿Me puede indicar dónde queda un supermercado? Me gustaría comprar unas manzanas o unos plátanos.
   ADULT MALE 1: Pues el supermercado no queda lejos de aquí. Al salir del hotel, doble a la izquierda y siga hasta la Avenida San Felipe. Cruce la avenida en el semáforo y doble a la derecha. El supermercado está enfrente de la estatua del soldado.

Track 09: Audio Act. 6, Writing, Audio & Video Workbook, p. 60

Parents always seem to worry about their children as soon as they step out the door! As you listen to the parent's last piece of advice as each young person leaves, determine whether the young person is walking, riding a bicycle, or driving a car to his or her destination. Use the grid below to mark your answers. You will hear each piece of advice twice.

1. **MADRE:** Ten cuidado cuando cruces la calle. Debes mirar para la derecha y para la izquierda antes de cruzar.
2. **PADRE:** Ten cuidado, hijo. Es un poco peligroso en la carretera con todos los camiones. Casi todo el mundo maneja muy rápidamente.
3. **MADRE:** Espera, hijo. Necesitas tu chaqueta. Hace mucho frío. Y recuerda... no puedes ir más de unas cuadras de la casa. Cuidado con los peatones cerca de la escuela.

4. **PADRE:** No debes manejar muy rápido porque hay mucho tráfico en la avenida. Puedes tener un accidente. Hay mucha gente loca que maneja y habla por sus teléfonos celulares en las carreteras.

5. **MADRE:** Pedrito, no hables con gente que no conozcas. Si una persona que no conoces te habla, busca un policía rápidamente.

6. **PADRE:** ¡Un momento, Benito! Recuerda ir a la estación de servicio antes de ir a la casa de Andrea. No tenemos nada de gasolina.

7. **MADRE:** Sí, sí. Sé que es más lento que manejar, pero puedes llegar a la biblioteca más rápido que si caminas. Ten cuidado con los coches porque van muy rápido.

Track 10: Audio Act. 7, Writing, Audio & Video Workbook, p. 60

Pilar is very ambitious today, but she can't get to where she wants to go without a little assistance. Follow her route by listening to the conversations she has with various people. Under each picture, write the name of the person who takes her there or *a pie* if she goes on foot. Then number the places in the order in which she visits them. You will hear each conversation twice.

1. **TEEN FEMALE 1:** ¡Hola, Carlos! ¿Qué haces?
   TEEN MALE: Nada, ¿por qué?
   TEEN FEMALE 1: ¿Puedes llevarme al correo ahora? Necesito comprarme unos sellos.
   TEEN MALE: Sí, ¿en dónde estás?
   TEEN FEMALE 1: En casa. Te espero en la esquina cerca de mi casa.

2. **TEEN FEMALE 1:** ¡Hola, Sara! Soy Pilar. ¿Me puedes llevar a tu casa?
   TEEN FEMALE 2: ¿Por qué no caminas? ¿No estás en casa?
   TEEN FEMALE 1: No, estoy en el banco. Carlos me dejó en el correo y caminé hasta aquí.
   TEEN FEMALE 2: Está bien. Hasta pronto.

3. **TEEN FEMALE 1:** ¡Hola, Ricardo! ¿Qué hacen Uds. ahora mismo?
   TEEN MALE 1: Vamos al estadio para ver un partido de fútbol. ¿Por qué?
   TEEN FEMALE 1: Sara y yo estamos en su casa sin coche y queremos ir a la ciudad. ¿Pueden llevarnos?
   TEEN MALE 1: ¿A qué parte quieren ir?
   TEEN FEMALE 1: No sabemos. ¿Pueden dejarnos en el metro?
   TEEN MALE 1: De acuerdo. Espérenos enfrente de la casa.

4. **TEEN FEMALE 1:** Hola, papá. ¿Puedes venir a recogerme?
   ADULT MALE: Pilar, ¿eres tú? No te entiendo bien. ¿En dónde estás?
   TEEN FEMALE 1: Estoy enfrente del museo. Sara y yo fuimos a la ciudad en el metro. Luego caminamos por un rato hasta llegar al museo. Nos perdimos en el museo y no nos encontramos hasta tres horas más tarde. Ahora estamos demasiado cansadas para caminar más.
   ADULT MALE: Está bien, hija. Voy por ti ahora mismo.

Track 11: Audio Act. 8, Writing, Audio & Video Workbook, p. 61

Listen as an elementary school teacher gives instructions to several of her students during a field trip to a local park. Match each command to a picture of one of the children. In the blanks below, write in the letter of the corresponding picture. You will hear each set of instructions twice.

1. Esteban, ven acá. Puedes jugar con el perro otro día.
2. Ana, ten cuidado. No debes cruzar el puente.
3. Marco, sé un buen chico y quita la gorra de la estatua.
4. Lisa, ve más despacio.
5. Gracias, María. Pon el refresco en la mesa.
6. Ana, ven acá y toma el balón.
7. Antonio, sal del autobús en este momento. Todos te esperan.
8. Carmen, ¡sé buena amiga y comparte los juguetes!
9. Carlos, dime dónde está el almuerzo de Susi.
10. José, hazme el favor de llevar la comida a la mesa.

Track 12: Audio Act. 9, Writing, Audio & Video Workbook, p. 62

The teacher in charge of after-school detention is going to be absent for a few days. Listen as she describes the students to the substitute teacher. Write the name of each student in the blank under the corresponding picture. You will hear each description twice.

ADULT FEMALE: Ésta es la clase. Todos son muy diferentes, pero en realidad son buenos. El joven que está sirviendo comida es uno de mis favoritos. Es muy travieso, pero simpático. Se llama Miguel.

ADULT FEMALE: El que lleva la chaqueta y está leyendo la revista de deportes es Carlos. Él es muy popular, pero no le interesan mucho los estudios.

ADULT FEMALE: Y aquí está Ryan. Como siempre, está trayéndome un mensaje con su excusa por llegar tarde. Los otros profesores siempre escriben excusas para él.

ADULT FEMALE: Aquella muchacha es Diana. Siempre está viniendo a clase con su carpeta de dibujos. Pasa toda la clase, todos los días, dibujando.

ADULT FEMALE: Juan siempre está aburrido en la escuela, pero le gusta ir a muchas fiestas en la plaza. Se acuesta a las tres de la mañana todas las noches. Es el que está durmiendo en el escritorio.

ADULT FEMALE: ¡Ay, Carmen! La más traviesa. Siempre está diciendo cosas malas para que todos puedan escuchar. Nunca me presta atención. Sólo busca atención.

ADULT FEMALE: Aquí está Ana. Ella no sabe hacer la tarea. Siempre está pidiendo ayuda a un amigo. Sus amigos son muy buenos.

ADULT FEMALE: Allá va Enrique. Él siempre está siguiendo a esa muchacha. Las muchachas dicen que es muy guapo, pero está loco por las muchachas bonitas, como ella.

Track 13: *Repaso del capítulo*, **Student Book, p. 180**

Vocabulario y gramática

Escucha las palabras y expresiones que has aprendido en este capítulo.

See Student Book page 180 for vocabulary list.

Track 14: *Preparación para el examen*, **Student Book, p. 181**

Escuchar

Practice task

Gabriel's father is teaching him to drive. Listen as he cautions Gabriel about what to do. a) Do you think they're driving on a highway or just around town? b) Give at least two reasons why you think so.

ADULT MALE: Ten cuidado, hijo. Estamos en una zona escolar. ¡Ay! ¡Espera! Hay peatones, hijo... ¡Más despacio, por favor! Mira el semáforo.

Video Script

A primera vista: ¿Cómo llegamos a la plaza?

RAMÓN: Está bien. Nos vemos allí.

CLAUDIA: Claro. Adiós, Ramón.

TERESA: ¿Y cómo llegamos al Bazar San Ángel?

CLAUDIA: Vamos a tomar el metro.

TERESA: Muy bien. Vamos.

MANOLO: Bueno, entonces, ¿adónde vamos?

RAMÓN: Al Bazar San Ángel. Claudia y Teresa nos esperan allí. Mira, Manolo, aquí hay un banco. ¿Tienes prisa?

MANOLO: No, no. Tenemos tiempo.

RAMÓN: Puedes parar un momento, por favor. Tengo que sacar dinero.

RAMÓN: Bueno, vamos a reunirnos ahora con Claudia y Teresa.

MANOLO: Sí. Pero antes, vamos a dejar el coche en casa. Mejor caminamos.

RAMÓN: ¿Podemos caminar hasta allí?

MANOLO: Claro. Queda aproximadamente a veinte minutos de mi casa.

RAMÓN: Vamos.

MANOLO: De acuerdo.

RAMÓN: ¿Y cómo es el mercado?

MANOLO: Hace mucho tiempo que no voy por ahí. Pero te va a gustar.

RAMÓN: ¿Estás seguro que sabes cómo llegar?

MANOLO: Sí, claro. Está a unas siete cuadras de aquí. Mira, seguimos hasta aquel semáforo. Doblamos a la derecha, caminamos cinco cuadras más, y ya casi estamos allí.

MANOLO: Aquí, a la derecha.

RAMÓN: Ahora, ¿adónde? ¿A la izquierda o a la derecha?

MANOLO: Espera… Esto es complicado. Creo que doblamos a la derecha. No, seguimos por aquí.

RAMÓN: ¿Estás seguro?

MANOLO: Sí, sí… Yo sé por dónde vamos. En la esquina tenemos que doblar.

RAMÓN: Manolo, ¿estás seguro que vamos bien? Creo que…

MANOLO: Claro, claro. Me estás poniendo nervioso. Yo sé por dónde vamos.

TERESA: ¿Cuánto cuesta?

VENDEDORA: Ochenta pesos.

TERESA: Es un muy buen precio. Me la llevo.

TERESA: Ya son las dos y cuarto. ¿Dónde andarán Ramón y Manolo?

CLAUDIA: Seguro que se perdieron…

CLAUDIA: Gracias.

TERESA: Gracias.

CLAUDIA: Vámonos.

RAMÓN: ¡Basta! Vamos a preguntar a alguien.

RAMÓN: Perdone, señor, ¿cómo se va al Bazar San Ángel?

MAN: Pues, la verdad, no sé.

RAMÓN: Gracias.

RAMÓN: ¿Me puede decir cómo se va al Bazar San Ángel?

WOMAN: Lo siento, pero, no sé.

MANOLO: ¿Ves?

RAMÓN: Perdone, ¿cómo se va al Bazar San Ángel?

MAN: ¿El Bazar San Ángel? Pues miren. En este cruce de calles van a doblar a la izquierda…

RAMÓN: Gracias. Vamos, rápido.

MANOLO: Oye, ¿podemos caminar un poco más despacio?

RAMÓN: Ya son las tres menos cuarto. Mira. Allí está el Bazar.

RAMÓN: Claudia, Teresa, aquí estamos…

MANOLO: ¡Claudia!

TERESA: Oye, ¿qué tal? Por fin, ¿dónde estaban?

CLAUDIA: ¿Por qué se tardaron tanto?

MANOLO: Culpa de él. Él, derecha…, izquierda…

GramActiva Videos

Irregular affirmative *tú* commands

BOY: You know Martha, we've been together a long time. And I feel really comfortable with you.

GIRL: Yes, Mark?

BOY: Martha, is it ok if I use an affirmative *tú* form with you?

GIRL: Oh, Mark! Yes, yes you can use the affirmative *tú* form with me!

HOST: Informal affirmative *tú* commands are used in informal situations, like talking to friends or family members. Folks you already know.

V.O.: It's easy. To give someone an affirmative *tú* command, just use the present tense form of the verb for *usted, él, ella*.

GIRL: *Marcos, ¡espera!*

HOST: Now here's a little something new for you. If you use a direct or indirect object pronoun with a command, you must attach the pronoun to the end of the command. As in: *Martín, espérame en la plaza, por favor.*

V.O.: Did you notice the accent mark? When a pronoun is added to a command of two or more syllables, a written accent mark is needed. The accent goes over the stressed vowel.

Here's another example.

Martín, tráeme el lápiz.

Gracias.

BOY: I should tell you something.

GIRL: Yes, Mark?

BOY: Some verbs have irregular affirmative *tú* commands. Five of these commands are formed from verbs whose *yo* form ends in *-go*, like *poner* and *tener*.

GIRL: Mark, don't say any more. I know.

BOY: You do?

GIRL: Yes, to form *tú* commands with these verbs, you take the *yo* form of the present tense and drop the *-go*.

BOY: You know exactly what I'm thinking!

V.O.: Let's take another look at *tú* commands using the *yo* form of the present tense.

The *yo* form of the verb *salir, salgo* becomes *¡Sal!*

Pongo becomes *¡Pon!*

Tengo becomes *¡Ten!*

Digo becomes *¡Di!*

Vengo becomes *¡Ven!*

Sal del coche.

Pon las manos aquí.

Ten cuidado.

Di la verdad.

Ven conmigo.

V.O.: You thought that was all! Close. Three very common verbs have an irregular command form: for *hacer* it's *haz, ser* is *sé*, and *ir* is *ve*.

¡Haz el letrero!

¡Sé sencillo!

¡Ve inmediatamente!

Quiz

V.O.: Now let's see what you've learned. Provide the affirmative *tú* command.

(esperar) María, _____ enfrente de tu casa.

María, espera enfrente de tu casa.

(parar) _____ en la esquina.

Para en la esquina.

(salir) ¡_____ más tarde!

¡Sal más tarde!

(tener) ¡_____ cuidado!

¡Ten cuidado!

Present progressive: Irregular forms

JOGGER: Hey there, I'm jogging, and reading, and learning. I'm also speaking in the present progressive, that is, I'm talking about an action that is going on right now. Let's see this again.

JOGGER: *Hola, estoy corriendo, leyendo y aprendiendo.*

HOST: To form the present progressive, use the present tense of *estar* + present participle of another verb. The present participle for *-ar* verbs is *-ando* and for *-er* and *-ir* verbs, it's *-iendo*.

V.O.: *¿Está usted manejando el coche?*

[Are you driving the car?]

V.O.: When you use an object pronoun with the present progressive, you can put it before the form of *estar*.

V.O.2: *Sí, lo estoy manejando.*

[Yes, I am driving it.]

V.O.: Or attach it to the end of the participle.

HOST: Notice that if a pronoun is attached to the end of the present participle, an accent mark is needed, as in *Sí, estoy manejándolo.* The accent goes over the stressed vowel.

EXCLAMATION MAN: But wait, there's more!

HOST: Now, some verbs have irregular present participle forms. To form the present participle of *-ir* stem-changing verbs, *e* changes to *i* as in *pedir* and *o* changes to *u* as in *dormir*.

V.O.: Let's take a look at some irregular present participle forms.

Diciendo. Repitiendo. Siguiendo. Sirviendo. Vistiendo.

EXCLAMATION MAN: OK! One last thing!

HOST: When the stem of an *-er* or *-ir* verb ends in a vowel the *i* changes to *y*. Let's see two examples: the verb *creer* becomes *creyendo* and *leer* becomes *leyendo*.

EXCLAMATION MAN: But wait, that's it. Well, except for this quiz.

Quiz

V.O.: Fill in the blank.

(doblar) Estoy _____ a la izquierda.

Estoy doblando a la izquierda.

(esperar) ¿Están Uds. _____ el autobús?

¿Están Uds. esperando el autobús?

(seguir) La policía está _____ al conductor.

La policía está siguiendo al conductor.

(leer) Estás _____ el cartel.

Estás leyendo el cartel.

Videomisterio: *En busca de la verdad*, Episodio 2

ROBERTO: Hola. Yo soy Roberto Toledo. Tengo 19 años y vivo en la ciudad de Guanajuato, en México. Guanajuato está al norte de la Ciudad de México y es una ciudad de mucha historia y cultura. Ésta es mi familia: mi papá Tomás. Él es médico. Todos dicen que es muy serio. Mi mamá Berta. Tiene una agencia de viajes, aquí en Guanajuato. Mi hermana Daniela. Ah, y Julio… mi mejor amigo. En esta ciudad siempre hay muchos turistas. El año pasado, dos turistas norteamericanas, de San Antonio, Texas, fueron a la agencia de viajes de mi mamá…

BERTA: Buenas tardes. ¿En qué puedo servirles?

CARMEN: Buenas tardes. Yo soy Carmen Toledo y mi hija, Linda. Venimos de San Antonio. El Sr. Balzar, de la agencia Fuera, habló por teléfono con Ud. la semana pasada, sobre una reservación de hotel para nosotras.

BERTA: Ah, sí, claro, bienvenidas a Guanajuato. Yo soy Berta Toledo, a sus órdenes.

CARMEN: Encantada.

LINDA: Mucho gusto.

BERTA: Todo está preparado. Tengo una reservación para Uds. en uno de nuestros mejores hoteles. Aquí, en el centro…

CARMEN: Perfecto. La escuela "Benito Juárez," ¿está muy lejos del hotel? Mañana tengo que ir allí.

BERTA: Para nada. Miren, está cerca. Mis hijos estudian allí.

BERTA: Un momento.

ROBERTO: Mamá, necesito usar el coche, ¿recuerdas?

BERTA: Sí… ah, perdona. Mi hijo Roberto y su amigo, Julio. Las señoras son de San Antonio. Van al hotel San Diego. ¿Por qué no las llevan al hotel?

ROBERTO: Un placer, no hay problema. Señora… Toledo, y señorita Toledo… Nosotros también somos Toledo.

LINDA: Cierto… ¿Es el apellido de todos aquí en Guanajuato?

BERTA: De todos, no, pero es un nombre bastante común.

JULIO: Pues yo no soy Toledo, sino Julio Lobero, a sus órdenes.

ROBERTO: Llevamos las maletas al coche.

JULIO: Bien. Ésta la tomo yo.

LINDA: Ésta es mía. Yo la puedo llevar.

JULIO: Permíteme.

CARMEN: Y bien, muchas gracias, Sra. Toledo.

BERTA: No, gracias a Ud. Ha sido un placer. Que les vaya bien.

DANIELA: Hola.

BERTA: Ah, Daniela. Mi hija, Daniela. Daniela, te presento a la Sra. Toledo y a su hija Linda. Son de San Antonio. Mañana van a visitar tu escuela. ¿Por qué no las acompañas?

DANIELA: Claro que sí.

ROBERTO: Pero mamá…

JULIO: Yo también puedo…

BERTA: Entonces, ya está. Ellas van al hotel San Diego. Si vas con ellas, pueden hablar de sus planes para mañana.

DANIELA: De acuerdo.

ROBERTO'S V.O.: Y así es como Julio y yo conocimos a Linda.

ROBERTO: Julio, ¿no vienes?

JULIO: Ahora recuerdo. Mañana tengo un partido de fútbol y ahora tengo que ir al gimnasio. Discúlpenme, pero no los puedo acompañar. Nos vemos, ¿eh?

ROBERTO: Julio es el mejor jugador del equipo. Es muy buen atleta.

ROBERTO'S V.O.: Al día siguiente mi hermana Daniela llevó a Linda y a su mamá a conocer nuestra escuela.

CARMEN: Yo me quedo aquí. Tengo que hablar con la directora.

LINDA: Bueno, mamá. Daniela va a mostrarme la escuela.

CARMEN: Perfecto, así puedes contarles a tus compañeros en San Antonio. Hasta más tarde.

DANIELA: Volveremos en una hora, Sra. Toledo.

LINDA: Uds. estudian inglés aquí, ¿verdad?

DANIELA: Sí, el idioma, pero también la cultura, la historia, todo.

LINDA: …Y en mi escuela en San Antonio estudiamos español, la historia y la cultura de México. Nuestras escuelas tienen mucho en común.

LINDA: Mira, allí está Julio.

JULIO: Hola.

LINDA: Hola.

DANIELA: Él juega muy bien.

LINDA: Y parece muy simpático.

ROBERTO: Sí, Julio, mi mejor amigo, es muy simpático y les gusta a todas las chicas.

Talk!

Realidades 2

Capítulo 3B

Nombre _____

Fecha _____

Communicative Pair Activity **3B-1**

Estudiante **A**

Imagine that you are a tourist asking for information at a tourist office in Madrid. Ask your partner the following questions. Your partner will use the map to give you directions. Write the answers in the spaces provided. Example: *Cruza a la derecha y sigue hasta la señal de parada.*

1. ¿Cómo se va al banco? _____

2. ¿Cómo se va al correo? _____

3. ¿Cómo se va a la heladería? _____

4. ¿Cómo se va al cine? _____

5. ¿Cómo se va al restaurante Don Pepe? _____

6. ¿Cómo se va a la Farmacia San Ángel? _____

Talk!
Realidades **2**

Capítulo 3B

Communicative Pair Activity **3B-1**
Estudiante **B**

Nombre _____

Fecha _____

Imagine that you are a tourist asking for information at a tourist office in Madrid. Ask your partner the following questions. Your partner will use the map to give you directions. Write the answers in the spaces provided. Example: *Cruza a la derecha y sigue hasta la señal de parada.*

1. ¿Cómo se va a la plaza? _____

2. ¿Cómo se va al museo? _____

3. ¿Cómo se va a la panaderia? _____

4. ¿Cómo se va a la tienda de la esquina? _____

5. ¿Cómo se va a la joyeria? _____

6. ¿Cómo se va al mercado Ramos? _____

Realidades 2

Nombre _____

Capítulo 3B

Fecha _____

Communicative Pair Activity **3B-2**

Estudiante **A**

In this activity, ask your partner the location of people and objects according to the picture below. If the response is incorrect, ask him or her to try again. Write out the correct answer in the spaces provided. Example: *La ciudad está debajo del avión.*

¿Dónde está?

Las preposiciones: a la derecha, a la izquierda, al lado de, cerca de, debajo de, delante de, detrás de, encima de, entre, lejos de

1. ¿Dónde está el taxi? _____

2. ¿Dónde está el tren? _____

3. ¿Dónde está el monumento (el obelisco)? _____

4. ¿Dónde está la mamá con el niño? _____

5. ¿Dónde está la bicicleta? _____

Now your partner will ask you some questions about the location of things in the picture above. Write the question on line A and then write your answer on line B.

Example:

    A. *¿Dónde está la ciudad?*

    B. *La ciudad está debajo del avión.*

1. **A.** _____

   B. _____

2. **A.** _____

   B. _____

3. **A.** _____

   B. _____

4. **A.** _____

   B. _____

5. **A.** _____

   B. _____

Realidades ②

Capítulo 3B

Nombre _____

Fecha _____

Communicative Pair Activity **3B-2**

Estudiante **B**

In this activity, your partner will ask you some questions about the location of things in the picture below. Write the question on line A and then write your answer on line B.

Example:

    A. *¿Dónde está la ciudad?*

    B. *La ciudad está debajo del avión.*

1. A. _____

    B. _____

2. A. _____

    B. _____

3. A. _____

    B. _____

4. A. _____

    B. _____

5. A. _____

    B. _____

Now ask your partner the location of people and objects according to the picture below. If the response is incorrect, ask him or her to try again. Write out the correct answer in the spaces provided. Example: *La ciudad está debajo del avión.*

¿Dónde está?

Las preposiciones: a la derecha, a la izquierda, al lado de, cerca de, debajo de, delante de, detrás de, encima de, entre, lejos de

1. ¿Dónde está el autobús? _____

2. ¿Dónde está el avión? _____

3. ¿Dónde está la glorieta? _____

4. ¿Dónde está el coche? _____

5. ¿Dónde está el metro? _____

Situation Cards

2A

Capítulo 3B   **Realidades** ②

Talking about driving, and giving and receiving advice

You are in a car giving directions to your friend, who is driving.

— Ask your friend to drive more slowly because he or she is making you nervous.

— Answer the driver's question affirmatively. Then tell him or her to turn right at the next intersection where there is a stop sign.

— Respond to your friend's question, saying that you believe the market is three blocks from there.

2B

Capítulo 3B   **Realidades** ②

Talking about driving, and giving and receiving advice

You are driving a car, and your friend is giving you directions.

— Answer affirmatively saying, "OK!" or "Agreed!" impatiently. Ask your friend if he or she knows the directions to the market.

— Ask him or her what to do after you turn right at the corner.

1A

Capítulo 3B   **Realidades** ②

Asking and giving directions

Imagine that you are a tourist and you are asking a police officer for directions.

— Call the officer's attention saying, "Police officer," and ask if he or she can tell you how to get to Plaza San José.

— Respond to the officer's question affirmatively, saying that you see the stoplight one block away. Ask if you should turn right or left at the corner.

— When the officer is finished giving directions, say, "OK" or "Agreed." Thank the officer for his or her help.

1B

Capítulo 3B   **Realidades** ②

Asking and giving directions

Imagine you are a police officer and a tourist is asking for directions.

— Respond to the tourist's request for directions affirmatively saying that it is not too far from the next corner. Then ask him or her if he or she can see the stoplight at the corner.

— Answer the question saying to turn left at the stoplight and continue going straight for two blocks until he or she sees a narrow street that is for pedestrians only. Then say that Plaza San José is located at the corner near the narrow street.

GramActiva

¿Cómo se va?

Y tú, ¿qué dices?, p. 165

Casi todos los días		
Sólo el fin de semana		
Tres o cuatro veces a la semana		
Casi nunca		
No tengo coche		

Vocabulary Clip Art

Vocabulary Clip Art

Vocabulary Clip Art

Vocabulary Clip Art

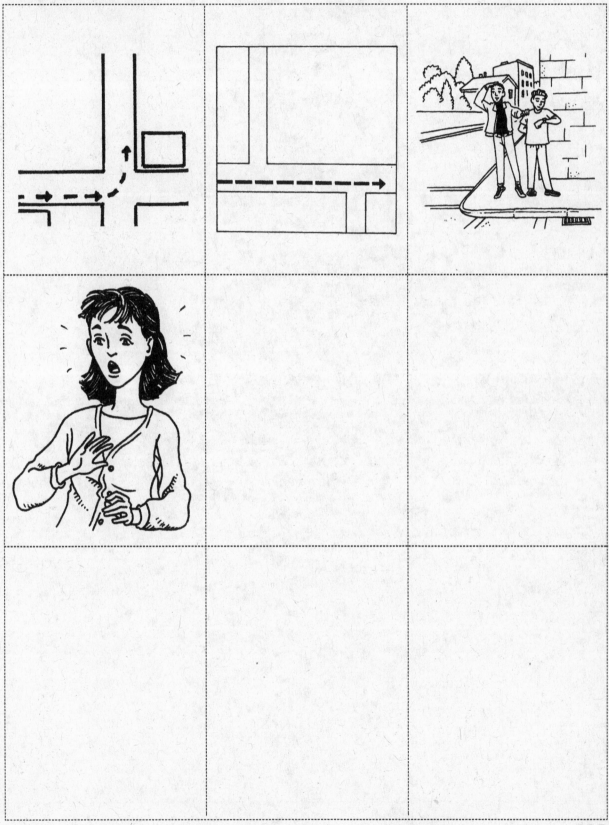

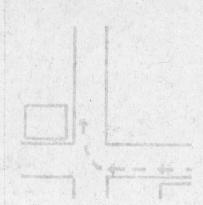

Core Practice Answers

3B-A
1. están debajo de
2. está a la izquierda de
3. está detrás de
4. está al lado
5. está entre
6. está encima de

3B-B
A.
1. avión
2. tren
3. autobús
4. un taxi
5. coche
6. barco

B.
1. No, salgo a las nueve.
2. No, traigo dulces.
3. No, digo que es peor.
4. No, vengo mañana.
5. No, tengo una bicicleta.

3B-1
1. camión
2. Maneja
3. Dobla, esquina
4. peligroso
5. plaza
6. Sigue
7. Cruza, carretera

3B-2
1. una multa
2. el cruce de calles
3. un puente
4. el semáforo
5. la señal de parada
6. la fuente
7. peatones
8. la esquina

3B-3
A.
1. Los peatones
2. El conductor
3. El metro
4. El policía
5. El tráfico
6. Despacio
7. Aproximadamente
8. Complicado

B.
1. el metro
2. doblar
3. parar
4. espera
5. el puente

3B-4
1. una multa
2. prisa
3. parar
4. seguro
5. aproximadamente
6. dejar
7. De acuerdo
8. complicado

3B-5
1. me
2. lo
3. Nos
4. te
5. nos
6. me
7. los
8. Me, te

3B-6
A.
1. Sé
2. Pon
3. Ven
4. Ve
5. Di
6. Haz
7. Sal
8. Ten

B.
1. Hazla.
2. Espéralos al lado de la estatua.
3. Déjalo en el garaje.
4. Dila.
5. Ponlo en la mesa.
6. Escúchalas.

3B-7
1. está diciendo
2. están siguiendo
3. estamos repitiendo
4. se están vistiendo (están vistiéndose)
5. están leyendo
6. está cruzando
7. estoy trayendo
8. me estás poniendo
9. está durmiendo
10. estamos pidiendo

Crucigrama (3B-8)
Horizontal:
2. fuente
5. puente
8. medio
9. cruce
11. basta
13. peligrosa
14. señal
15. complicado
18. esperamos
19. despacio
20. peatones
21. permiso
22. queda

Vertical:
1. multa
3. tráfico
4. semáforo
5. paz
6. estrecha
7. poniendo
10. cuadras
12. metro
15. conductora
16. prisa
17. carretera

Organizer (3B-9)
I. Vocabulary Answers will vary.
II. Grammar
1. lo, la, los, las; me, te, os, nos
2. col. 1.   col. 2.

col. 1.	col. 2.
di	sal
haz	sé
ve	ten
pon	ven

3. col. 1.   col. 2.

col. 1.	col. 2.
creyendo	repitiendo
diciendo	siguiendo
durmiendo	sirviendo
leyendo	trayendo
pidiendo	vistiendo

Nombre _____ Hora _____

Fecha _____ **AVSR 3B-1**

The verbs *salir*, *decir*, and *venir* (p. 155)

Salir, decir, and venir are three -ir verbs that have irregular yo forms in the present tense (salgo, digo, and vengo). Decir and venir follow stem-changing patterns e → i and e → ie.

	salgo	I left	nosotros/ nosotras	salimos	we left
yo	digo	I said, I told		decimos	we said, we told
	vengo	I came		venimos	we came
	sales	you left	vosotros/ vosotras	salís	you left
tú	dices	you said, you told		decís	you said, you told
	vienes	you came		venís	you came
	sale	you/he/she left	ustedes/ ellos/ellas	salen	you/they left
usted/ él/ella	dice	you/he/she said; told		dicen	you/they said; told
	viene	you/he/she came		vienen	you/they came

A. Circle the correct form of the verb in parentheses. Follow the model.

Modelo   Yo (**salgo** / sale) de la casa.

1. Nosotros (**decimos** / dicen) la verdad.

2. Las hermanas (vienes /(**vienen**)) tarde.

3. Yo (viene /(**vengo**)) a tiempo.

4. Mis padres (sales /(**salen**)) del trabajo a las cinco.

5. Tú (**dices** / digo) que sabes más que yo.

B. Write the correct verb form to complete each sentence.

1. Mi profesor ____ **dice** ____ (decir) que soy buen estudiante.

2. Yo ____ **salgo** ____ (salir) de casa muy temprano por la mañana.

3. Mis tíos ____ **vienen** ____ (venir) a mi casa esta noche.

4. Yo siempre ____ **digo** ____ (decir) la verdad.

5. Nosotros ____ **salimos** ____ (salir) de la escuela a las tres y media.

6. La profesora está enferma y no ____ **viene** ____ (venir) a clase hoy.

108 *A ver si recuerdas* ▬ 3B-1

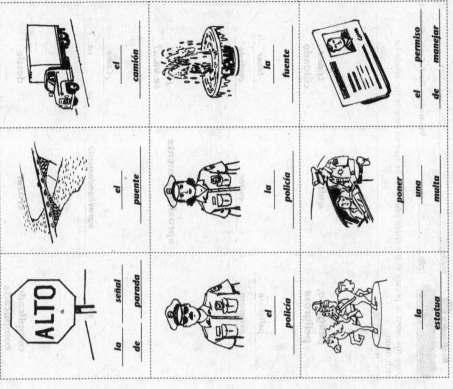

Realidades 2

Capítulo 3B

Nombre _____ Hora _____

Fecha _____ **Vocabulary Flash Cards, Sheet 2**

Write the Spanish vocabulary word or phrase below each picture. Be sure to include the article for each noun.

el _____
camión

la _____
fuente

el _____ permiso
de _____ manejar

el _____
puente

la _____
policía

poner
una _____
multa

la _____ señal
de _____ parada

el _____
policía

la _____
estatua

110 Guided Practice Activities ● Vocabulary Flash Cards 3B

Realidades 2

Capítulo 3B

Nombre _____ Hora _____

Fecha _____ **Vocabulary Flash Cards, Sheet 1**

Write the Spanish vocabulary word below each picture. Be sure to include the article for each noun.

el _____
semáforo

la _____
carretera

la _____
esquina

el _____
tráfico

el _____
peatón

estrecho ,
estrecha _____

la _____
plaza

el _____ cruce
de _____ calles

ancho ,
ancha _____

Guided Practice Activities ● Vocabulary Flash Cards 3B 109

Capítulo 3B ● Guided Practice Answers 239

Sheet 3 (left side)

Write the Spanish vocabulary word below each picture. If there is a word or phrase, copy it in the space provided. Be sure to include the article for each noun.

¡Basta!	Déjame en paz.	Me estás poniendo nervioso, nerviosa.
¡Basta!	_Déjame_ _en_ _paz._	_Me_ _estás_ _poniendo_ _nervioso_ _nerviosa._
derecho	dejar	estar seguro, segura
derecho	_dejar_	_estar_ _seguro_, _segura_
doblar	De acuerdo.	despacio
doblar	_De_ _acuerdo._	_despacio_

Sheet 4 (right side)

Copy the word or phrase in the space provided. Be sure to include the article for each noun.

tener cuidado	quitar	peligroso, peligrosa
tener _cuidado_	_quitar_	_peligroso_, _peligrosa_
¿Cómo se va...?	aproximadamente	ya
¿Cómo _se_ _va...?_	_aproximadamente_	_ya_
desde	cruzar	complicado, complicada
desde	_cruzar_	_complicado_, _complicada_

Copy the word or phrase in the space provided. Be sure to include the article for each noun. These blank cards can be used to write and practice other Spanish vocabulary for the chapter.

pasar	el conductor, la conductora	esperar
_____ pasar	el _____ conductor , la _____ conductora	_____ esperar

manejar	el metro	
_____ manejar	el _____ metro	

Copy the word or phrase in the space provided. Be sure to include the article for each noun.

hasta	por	quedar
_____ hasta	_____ por	_____ quedar

seguir	tener prisa	la avenida
_____ seguir	_____ tener prisa	la _____ avenida

la cuadra	en medio de	parar
la _____ cuadra	en _____ medio _____ de	_____ parar

Sheet 2

Realidades 2

Nombre _____ Hora _____

Capítulo 3B

Fecha _____ **Vocabulary Check, Sheet 2**

Tear out this page. Write the Spanish words on the lines. Fold the paper along the dotted line to see the correct answers so you can check your work.

- Fold In ↓

avenue	*la avenida*
truck	*el camión*
highway	*la carretera*
driver	*el conductor, la conductora*
traffic	*el tráfico*
intersection	*el cruce de calles*
block	*la cuadra*
corner	*la esquina*
statue	*la estatua*
fountain	*la fuente*
pedestrian	*el peatón*
driver's license	*el permiso de manejar*
plaza	*la plaza*
police officer	*el policía, la policía*
bridge	*el puente*

Sheet 1

Realidades 2

Nombre _____ Hora _____

Capítulo 3B

Fecha _____ **Vocabulary Check, Sheet 1**

Tear out this page. Write the English words on the lines. Fold the paper along the dotted line to see the correct answers so you can check your work.

- Fold In ↓

la avenida	*avenue*
el camión	*truck*
la carretera	*highway*
el conductor, la conductora	*driver*
el tráfico	*traffic*
el cruce de calles	*intersection*
la cuadra	*block*
la esquina	*corner*
la estatua	*statue*
la fuente	*fountain*
el peatón	*pedestrian*
el permiso de manejar	*driver's license*
la plaza	*plaza*
el policía, la policía	*police officer*
el puente	*bridge*

Tear out this page. Write the Spanish words on the lines. Fold the paper along the dotted line to see the correct answers so you can check your work.

- Fold In ↓

wide	*ancho, ancha*
Enough!	*¡Basta!*
OK. Agreed.	*De acuerdo.*
to leave, to let	*dejar*
Leave me alone.	*Déjame en paz.*
slowly	*despacio*
to wait	*esperar*
dangerous	*peligroso, peligrosa*
to be careful	*tener cuidado*
already	*ya*
to cross	*cruzar*
stop	*parar*
to pass, to go	*pasar*
to be located	*quedar*

To hear a complete list of the vocabulary for this chapter, go to www.realidades.com and type in the Web Code jdd-0399. Then click on **Repaso del capítulo.**

Tear out this page. Write the English words on the lines. Fold the paper along the dotted line to see the correct answers so you can check your work.

- Fold In ↓

ancho, ancha	*wide*
¡Basta!	*Enough!*
De acuerdo.	*OK. Agreed.*
dejar	*to leave, to let*
Déjame en paz.	*Leave me alone.*
despacio	*slowly*
esperar	*to wait*
peligroso, peligrosa	*dangerous*
tener cuidado	*to be careful*
ya	*already*
cruzar	*to cross*
parar	*stop*
pasar	*to pass, to go*
quedar	*to be located*

Direct object pronouns: *me, te, nos* (p. 166)

- Remember that you can replace a direct object noun with a direct object pronoun.
- The pronouns **lo, la, los,** and **las** can refer to people, places, or things. The pronouns **me, te, nos,** and **os** refer only to people, not to places or things.
- Here are all the direct object pronouns.

Singular		Plural	
me	me	**nos**	us
te	me *(familiar)*	**os**	you *(familiar)*
lo	it, him, you *(masculine formal)*	**los**	them, you *(masculine formal)*
la	it, her, you *(feminine formal)*	**las**	them, you *(feminine formal)*

- Remember that in Spanish the subject and the verb ending tell who does the action. The direct object pronoun indicates who receives the action:

  ¿Me escuchas, por favor?   *Can you listen to me please?*

A. Read the following sentences. In each sentence, circle the subject of the verb and underline the verb ending that matches the subject. Follow the model.

Modelo (Lola) me lleva a mí a la ciudad.

1. (Lola) me lleva a mí a la ciudad.
2. (Nuestros amigos) nos esperan allí.
3. (Yo) los busqué a Ricardo y a Enrique ayer.
4. (Tú) nos dices la verdad, pero tu hermano no.
5. (Elena) me ayuda a ir hasta la plaza.
6. (La banda) te sigue porque eres conductora.

B. Now, look again at the sentences from exercise A. This time, draw an arrow pointing to the direct object pronoun. Follow the model.

Modelo   Lucas te habló por teléfono anoche.

1. Lola me lleva a mí a la ciudad.
2. Nuestros amigos nos esperan allí.
3. Yo los busqué a Ricardo y a Enrique ayer.

Direct object pronouns (*continued*)

4. Tú nos dices la verdad, pero tu hermano no.
5. Elena me ayuda a ir hasta la plaza.
6. La banda te sigue porque eres conductora.

C. Read the questions below and circle the letter of the correct answer for each. Follow the model.

Modelo   Julio te ayuda a veces, ¿no?

  a. Sí, me ayuda mucho.   **b.** Sí, te ayuda mucho.

1. ¿Me esperas en la esquina cerca del museo?
   a. Sí, nos espera en la esquina.   (**b**) Sí, te espero allí.

2. El policía siempre nos deja pasar, ¿verdad?
   (**a**) No, a veces no nos deja pasar.   **b.** No, no nos dice la verdad.

3. ¿Te pongo nerviosa?
   (**a**) Sí, me pones nerviosa.   **b.** Sí, me pongo nervioso.

4. ¿El policía me va a dejar en paz?
   a. No, no me pones una multa.   (**b**) No, te va a poner una multa.

5. Señor policía, ¿me puede quitar la multa, por favor?
   a. Sí, me puede quitar la multa.   (**b**) Sí, le puedo quitar la multa.

Irregular affirmative *tú* commands (p. 168)

• Remember that to form an affirmative command in the **tú** form, use the **él/ella/Ud.** form of the verb.

Habla con la policía. *Talk to the police.*

A. Write the affirmative **tú** command of the regular verbs in parentheses. Follow the model.

Modelo (manejar) Patricia, ___**maneja**___ con cuidado, por favor.

1. (esperar) Tere, ___**espera**___ un minuto, por favor.

2. (escribir) Ramón, ___**escribe**___ tu nombre aquí, por favor.

3. (dejar) Esteban, ___**deja**___ el coche aquí, por favor.

4. (leer) Lisa, ___**lee**___ el párrafo, por favor.

5. (doblar) Raúl, ___**dobla**___ a la derecha aquí.

• Some verbs have irregular forms for the affirmative **tú** commands. To form the command, take the **yo** form of the present tense and drop the ending **-go**.

infinitive	yo form	command form	example
poner	pongo	pon	Pon la mesa.
tener	tengo	ten	¡Ten cuidado!
decir	digo	di	¡Di la verdad!
salir	salgo	sal	Sal de la casa.
venir	vengo	ven	Ven acá, por favor.

B. Complete the following sentences with the **tú** command of the verb in parentheses. Follow the model.

Modelo (Salir) ___**Sal**___ del coche sucio.

1. (Tener) ___**Ten**___ tu nuevo permiso de manejar.

2. ¡Miguel, (venir) ___**ven**___ rápido; el tren va a salir!

3. (Decir) ___**Di**___ tu nombre al policía.

4. (Poner) ___**Pon**___ el libro en la mesa.

5. (Salir) ___**Sal**___ a las doce para llegar a tiempo.

Irregular affirmative *tú* commands (*continued*)

• The verbs **hacer**, **ser**, and **ir** also have irregular **tú** commands:

hacer:	haz	ser:	sé	ir:	ve

C. Complete the following exchanges with the **tú** command of the verb in parentheses. Follow the model.

Modelo ELISA: ¿Cómo llego a la fiesta, Mamá?

MAMÁ: ¡(Ir) ___**Ve**___ en un coche!

1. CARLOS: No sé dónde queda la plaza. ¿Qué hago?

MAMÁ: ¡(Hacer) ___**Haz**___ una pregunta!

2. PATTY: ¿Qué debo hacer para no recibir multas de la policía?

RUTH: (Ser) ___**Sé**___ una buena conductora.

3. ALBERTO: ¿Cómo llego a la Avenida Juárez?

LOLA: ¡(Ir) ___**Ve**___ en el metro!

4. JUANJO: Tengo miedo de hablar con la policía sobre la multa que recibí.

RAÚL: (Ser) ___**Sé**___ cortés y todo va a estar bien.

• If you need to use an affirmative command with a direct object pronoun, the pronoun is attached to the end of the command. Remember to add a written accent over the stressed vowel if the command had two or more syllables.

Ponlo aquí. *Put it here.*

Búscame en el parque. *Look for me in the park.*

D. Read the sentences below. Complete the second sentence in each pair by writing the appropriate direct object pronoun in the space provided. Don't forget to add any necessary written accents.

Modelo Manda la carta. Mánda ___**la**___

1. Haz la pregunta. Haz ___**la**___

2. Pide las direcciones. Pide ___**las**___

3. Visita el Parque de las Palomas. Visita ___**lo**___

4. Pon el permiso de manejar en tu mochila. Pon ___**lo**___ en tu mochila.

5. Mira las señales cuando manejas. Mira ___**las**___

6. Invita a tu amigo y a mí a la fiesta. Invita ___**nos**___ a la fiesta.

Left page (123)

Realidades 2

Capítulo 3B

Nombre _____ Hora _____

Fecha _____ **Guided Practice Activities 3B-4**

Present progressive: irregular forms (p. 171)

• Remember that you form the present progressive by using **estar** + the present participle:

Estoy hablando con Lucía.   *I am talking to Lucía.*

A. Fill in the blanks using **estar** + the present participle of the verbs in parentheses. The first one is done for you.

1. (hablar) Mis padres **están** **hablando** con la policía.
2. (compartir) Juanita y Pepito **están** **compartiendo** la comida.
3. (quedar) Yo me **estoy** **quedando** en el hotel.
4. (poner) Tú me **estás** **poniendo** nerviosa.
5. (doblar) El coche **está** **doblando** en la esquina.

• Some verbs have irregular present participle forms. To form the present participle of -**ir** stem-changing verbs, the **e** in the stem of the infinitive changes to **i**, and then the **o** in the stem changes to **u**:

decir → **diciendo**	pedir → **pidiendo**	repetir → **repitiendo**
servir → **sirviendo**	seguir → **siguiendo**	dormir → **durmiendo**

B. Fill in the missing vowels to form the present participle of the verbs that have been started in each sentence below. Follow the model.

Modelo   La camarera está s_i_rv_i_ _e_ndo a las chicas primero.

1. El perro está d_u_rm_i_ _e_ndo en el piso.
2. Mi mamá me está s_i_gu_i_ _e_ndo en su coche.
3. La profesora está rep_i_t_i_ _e_ndo la tarea.

• To form the present participle of the following -**er** verbs, add -**yendo** instead of -**iendo**:

creer → **creyendo**	leer → **leyendo**	traer → **trayendo**

C. Write the present participle of each verb in parentheses to complete the sentence. The first one has been done for you.

1. Yo estoy **creyendo** en mi equipo. (creer)
2. Los estudiantes están **trayendo** sus tareas. (traer)
3. Nosotras estamos **leyendo** un libro. (leer)
4. Mario está **trayendo** la comida. (traer)

realidades.com
• Web Code: jdd-0316

Right page (124)

Realidades 2

Capítulo 3B

Nombre _____ Hora _____

Fecha _____ **Guided Practice Activities 3B-4a**

Present progressive: irregular forms (continued)

D. Change the underlined verb in the following sentences from the present tense to the present progressive tense. Follow the model.

Modelo   Adriana <u>dice</u> la verdad.   **está** **diciendo**

1. Tú <u>pides</u> ayuda.   **estás** **pidiendo**
2. Mi padre <u>lee</u> el periódico.   **está** **leyendo**
3. La profesora <u>repite</u> la pregunta.   **está** **repitiendo**
4. Ana y yo <u>traemos</u> las bebidas.   **estamos** **trayendo**
5. El camarero <u>sirve</u> la comida.   **está** **sirviendo**
6. Paulo y Javier <u>duermen</u> en clase.   **están** **durmiendo**
7. Los estudiantes <u>siguen</u> al profesor.   **están** **siguiendo**
8. Yo no te <u>creo</u>.   **estoy** **creyendo**

• When you use a direct object pronoun with a present progressive verb, the pronoun can either come before **estar** or attached to the present participle. It is necessary to add a written accent if the pronoun is attached to the present participle.

Lara lo está trayendo.   or   **Lara está trayéndolo.**

E. Rewrite the sentences adding the direct object pronoun to the end of the present progressive form. Remember to write an accent on the stressed **a** or **e**. Follow the model.

Modelo   Felipe nos está llevando.   *Felipe está llevándonos*

1. Nosotros lo estamos esperando.   **Nosotros estamos esperándolos**
2. Ella me está siguiendo.   **Ella está siguiéndome**
3. Tú las estás leyendo.   **Tú estás leyéndolas**
4. Sancho me está diciendo la verdad.   **Sancho está diciéndome la verdad**
5. El profesor nos está enseñando.   **El profesor está enseñándonos**

realidades.com
• Web Code: jdd-0316

© Pearson Education, Inc. All rights reserved.

Presentación escrita (p. 177)

Task: Pretend that you have received your first driver's license. Make a poster that reminds your classmates of safe driving practices and important traffic signs.

A. Look at the traffic signs below. Then, write the meaning of each sign in English in the middle column and in Spanish in the right column.

	English	Spanish
1. ALTO	*stop*	*parar*
2.	*no turns*	*no doblar*
3.	*pedestrian crossing*	*cruce de peatones*

B. From the following list, circle the word describing the meaning of each traffic light color.

rojo (seguir / (parar))
amarillo (parar /(manejar))
verde ((seguir)/ parar)

C. The following are two actions a driver should take to drive safely. Think about two other actions for safe driving which you have read about in the chapter. Then write them below.

1. manejar despacio por calles estrechas
2. tener cuidado cerca de las señales de tráfico
3. ___*Answers will vary.*___
4. _____

D. Read through your answers in **parts A, B,** and **C.** Decide which information to use to make a poster about safe driving practices. Be sure to include drawings or photos of traffic signs and some of the safe driving practices.

E. Share your poster with a partner who will check the following:
___ Does the poster present important and accurate information?
___ Is the visual representation clear and easy to understand?
___ Is there anything to add, change, or correct?

126 *Guided Practice Activities* — 3B-6

Lectura: Guía del buen conductor (pp. 174–175)

A. The reading in your textbook is about developing safe driving habits. You may not understand the meaning of some important words in the reading. Sometimes you can use context clues to guess the meaning of these unknown words. Read the following sentences and answer the questions.

Manejar bien requiere muchos años de práctica. Si puedes practicar todos los días después de obtener tu permiso de manejar de estudiante, es mejor porque así vas adquiriendo experiencia.

1. In the first sentence, what words tell you what **requiere** means?
___*años de práctica*___

2. What do you think **vas adquiriendo experiencia** means? How do you know? (Hint: Do any of these words look or sound like English?)
___*Answers will vary.*___

B. This excerpt is taken from the first section of your textbook reading. Read the excerpt and find the meaning of the underlined words below by using context clues. Circle the choice that that best describes the meaning of each word.

Guía del buen conductor
Un buen conductor siempre debe estar alerta para evitar accidentes. No es difícil: simplemente tienes que estar atento.

Conductores agresivos
Si el conductor es muy agresivo, puedes reportarlo con la policía.

1. alerta:
   a. (atento)
   b. aburrido

2. reportar:
   a. hacer una pregunta
   b. (informar)

C. Imagine that you are driving a car. You want to reassure your passenger that you have safe driving habits. Circle the word in parentheses that best completes each sentence.

1. Estoy ((manejando) / vistiendo) con atención.
2. La carretera es estrecha, por eso estoy (siguiendo /(poniendo)) mucha atención.
3. No estoy (diciendo /(leyendo)) en el coche.
4. No estoy (manejando /(durmiendo)).
5. Estoy ((siguiendo)/ durmiendo) las señales de tráfico.

Guided Practice Activities — 3B-5 **125**

Nombre _____ Hora _____

Fecha _____

VIDEO

Antes de ver el video

Actividad 1

How do you get to your Spanish classroom from the cafetería? Write the directions on the lines below.

Answers will vary.

_____

_____

_____

¿Comprendes?

Actividad 2

Who made each comment or asked each question below? Write the name of the corresponding character from the video in the space provided.

1. Vamos a tomar el metro. **Claudia**

2. Mira, aquí hay un banco... ¿Tienes prisa? **Ramón**

3. Hace mucho tiempo que no voy por allí. Pero te va a gustar. **Manolo**

4. ¿Estás seguro que sabes cómo llegar? **Ramón**

Nombre _____ Hora _____

Fecha _____

VIDEO

5. Espera... Esto es complicado. **Manolo**

6. Claro, claro. Me estás poniendo nervioso. Yo sé por dónde vamos. **Manolo**

7. Ya son las dos y cuarto. ¿Dónde estarán...? **Teresa**

8. ¡Basta! Vamos a preguntar a alguien. **Ramón**

9. Oye, ¿podemos caminar un poco más despacio? **Manolo**

10. Mira. Allí está el bazar. **Ramón**

VIDEO

Actividad 3

Manolo and Ramón want to meet up with Teresa and Claudia. Answer the questions below about the events that take place along the way.

1. ¿Cómo van Manolo y Ramón al Bazar San Ángel? ¿Y cómo llegan Claudia y Teresa allí?

   Manolo y Ramón van a pie al Bazar San Ángel. Claudia y Teresa van a

   usar el metro.

2. ¿Quién llega al bazar primero? ¿Qué hacen allí?

   Teresa y Claudia llegan primero. Van de compras en el bazar.

3. ¿A cuántas personas pregunta Ramón sobre cómo se va al Bazar San Ángel?

   Ramón pregunta a tres personas sobre cómo se va al Bazar San Ángel.

Y, ¿qué más?

Actividad 4

You want to tell your friend how to get to the local YMCA, since she wants to play basketball. Use the following expressions to write directions.

doblas a (la derecha / la izquierda)

sigues (la avenida *nombre* / la calle *nombre*)

hasta (el primero / el segundo / el próximo) semáforo

sigues derecho por (esa avenida / esa calle) aproximadamente (dos / tres / cinco) millas

sigues esa avenida por (seis / siete / ocho) cuadras, hasta que veas el gimnasio

Answers will vary.

_____

_____

_____

Estaciona el coche, y ¡a jugar al básquetbol!

Communication Workbook

Actividad 5

Listen as people in a hotel call the front desk for help. As you listen to each conversation, match each caller to the spot on the map below by writing the number of the conversation in the corresponding circle. You will hear each conversation twice.

Communication Workbook

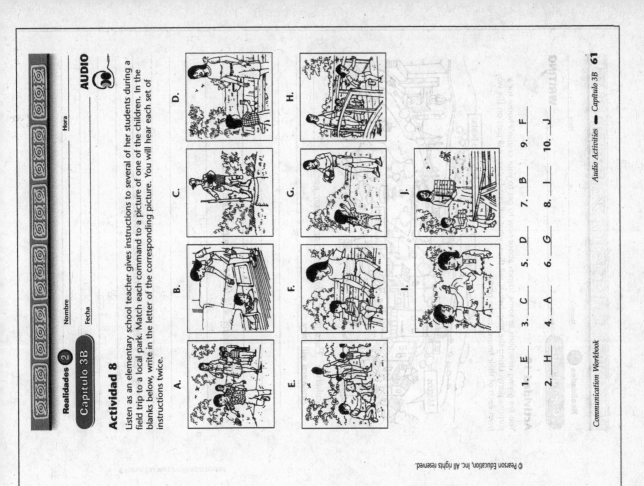

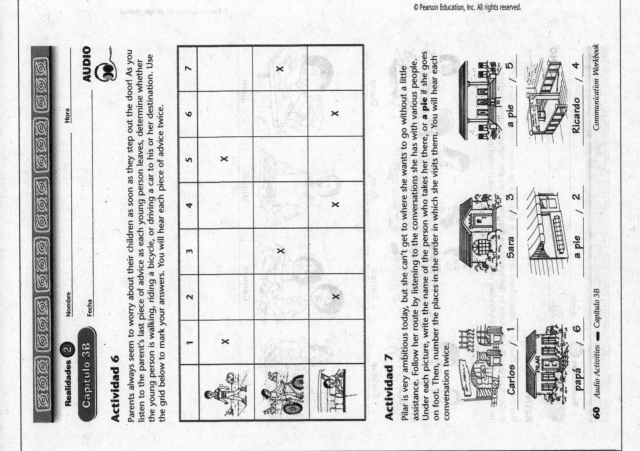

Actividad 10

You are giving directions to some friends about how to get to your cousin's house for a surprise party. Using the map below, tell them what landmarks they will pass on the way from each of their houses to the party.

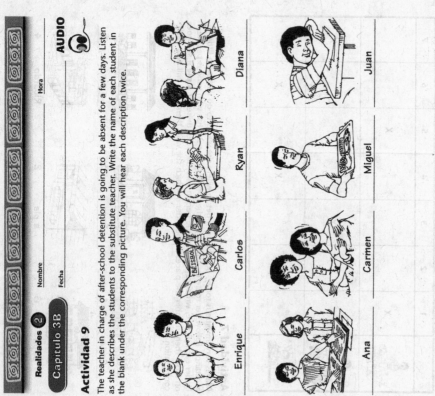

Julieta

Marcos

Guillermo

La fiesta

1. Guillermo *Para llegar a la fiesta, vas a pasar por...* Answers will vary.

_____

_____

2. Julieta *Para llegar a la fiesta, vas a pasar por...*

_____

_____

3. Marcos *Para llegar a la fiesta, vas a pasar por...*

_____

_____

Actividad 9

The teacher in charge of after-school detention is going to be absent for a few days. Listen as she describes the students to the substitute teacher. Write the name of each student in the blank under the corresponding picture. You will hear each description twice.

Enrique   Carlos   Ryan   Diana

Ana   Carmen   Miguel   Juan

Actividad 12

As part of the interview process to become a camp counselor, you are asked to describe to the head counselor what you would tell kids to do in certain situations. Look at each drawing and write two affirmative **tú** commands for each, based on the hints provided. Include at least one of the following verbs each time: **poner, tener, decir, salir, venir, descansar, jugar, quedarse, hacer, ir,** and **ser.**

Answers will vary. Possible answers:

1. ve una serpiente *(snake)*

   Ten cuidado.

   Sé tranquilo.

2. acaba de comer

   Sal del agua.

   Descansa antes de nadar.

3. no quiere participar

   Haz alguna actividad.

   Juega con otra gente.

4. está enferma

   Dile a un adulto.

   Quédate en la cama.

5. tiene frío

   Sal del agua.

   Ponte una toalla.

6. no quiere hacer sus quehaceres

   Haz los quehaceres.

   Lava los platos.

Actividad 11

Your friends rely on you for help with various things. Write out your responses to the questions your friends ask you. You may answer in the affirmative or negative. Follow the model.

Modelo —¿Quieres hablar conmigo sobre la fiesta?

—*No, te hablé anoche*

Answers will vary. Possible answers below.

1. —¿En dónde vas a esperar a María y a Elena?

   —*Las espero al lado del gimnasio*

2. —¿Vas a buscarme enfrente de la escuela?

   —*Sí, te busco allí*

3. —¿Necesito llamar a Alejandro para saber dónde es la fiesta?

   —*No, lo llamé anoche*

4. —¿Alejandro nos invitó a ti y a mí a la fiesta?

   —*Sí, nos invitó a la fiesta*

5. —¿Tengo que traer algo a la fiesta para ti?

   —*Sí, ¿me traes un pastel?*

6. —¿Necesitas ayuda con algo?

   —*Sí, ¿me puedes ayudar a preparar la comida?*

7. —¿Vienen tus tíos a la fiesta contigo?

   —*No, me visitaron la semana pasada*

8. —¿Hablaste con ellos anoche?

   —*Sí, les hablé a las nueve anoche*

9. —¿Quieres ver a alguien en la fiesta?

   —*Realmente no. Los vi a todos ayer*

10. —¿Conoces a la familia Rodríguez?

    —*Sí, la conozco*

Realidades ②

Nombre _____ Hora _____

Capítulo 3B

Fecha _____

WRITING

Actividad 13

You are keeping a journal of things that happen throughout the day. Look at each picture, and write a complete sentence to tell what time it is and what the people are doing at the moment. Follow the model.

Answers may vary.

Modelo Pablo

Son las dos y diez y Pablo está pidiéndole ayuda a la profesora

Mónica

Son las siete y cinco y Mónica está vistiéndose

1. Jorge

Es la una y cuarto y Jorge está sirviendo la comida

2. Yo

Son las once y media y yo estoy durmiendo

3. Nosotros

Son las diez y cuarto y nosotros estamos repitiendo palabras

4. Tú

Son las cinco menos cuarto y tú estás leyendo

5. La señora Vargas

Son las cinco y media y la señora Vargas está pidiendo comida

6.

© Pearson Education, Inc. All rights reserved.

66 Writing Activities — Capítulo 3B

Communication Workbook

254 Capítulo 3B — Communication Workbook: WAVA Answers

Test Preparation Answers

Reading Skills
p. 232   2. **B**
p. 233   2. **D**

Integrated Performance Assessment
p. 234
Answers will vary.

Practice Test: La Casa de los Azulejos
p. 236

1. C
2. F
3. C
4. G
5. C
6. Las respuestas variarán pero pueden incluir: Porque los padres trabajan mucho para tener dinero, y no les gusta gastarlo en cosas tontas. También porque muchas veces los hijos compran cosas que no les gustan a los padres o que los padres consideran demasiado caras.

Theme Project

Recuerdos del pasado
Un álbum de fotos

Overview:

You will create a photo album or memory book of past family holidays featuring photos of family members at different holiday celebrations and brief descriptions under each photo. Then present your book to the class, explaining each picture and holiday and describing selected family members.

Resources:

Digital or print photos, page layout/word processing software and/or construction paper, markers, photos, glue or tape, scissors

Sequence:

STEP 1. Review instructions with your teacher.

STEP 2. Submit a rough sketch of each page of your photo book. Work with a partner and present your drafts to each other.

STEP 3. Create layouts, leaving room for photos and descriptions.

STEP 4. Submit a draft of the photo captions.

STEP 5. Complete and present your book to the class. Explain each picture and holiday and describe selected family members.

Assessment:

Your teacher will provide you with a rubric to assess this project.

Theme 4 Project: Un álbum de fotos

Project Assessment Rubric

RUBRIC	Score 1	Score 3	Score 5
Evidence of Planning	No written draft or poster layout provided.	Draft was written and layout created, but not corrected.	Evidence of corrected draft and layout.
Use of Illustrations	No photos/visuals included.	Very few photos/visuals included.	Several photos/visuals included.
Presentation	Contains details that develop characters.	Describes at least three family celebrations.	Describes three or more family celebrations.

21st Century Skills Rubric: Foster Initiative and Self-Direction

RUBRIC	Score 1	Score 3	Score 5
Reflection	Does not study and discuss previous rubrics and projects	Studies and discusses up to two rubrics and projects	Studies and discusses three or more rubrics and projects
Recording of reflections on previous rubrics and projects	Does not create a list of comments or creates a list that contains four or fewer comments	Creates a list of up to five comments from reflection	Creates a list of six or more comments from reflection
Evidence of improvement	Project does not incorporate any ideas from list	Project incorporates up to two ideas from list	Project incorporates three or more ideas from list

School-to-Home Connection

Dear Parent or Guardian,

The theme of our current unit is *Recuerdos del pasado* (Memories). This chapter is called *Cuando éramos niños* (When we were children).

Upon completion of this chapter students will be able to:

- discuss childhood games and toys
- describe what he or she was like as a child
- talk about activities they used to do as a child
- discuss to whom or for whom something is done
- understand cultural perspectives on clothing

Students will also explore:

- the correct pronunciation of the consonants *r* and *rr*

Our textbook, *Realidades,* helps with the development of reading, writing, and speaking skills through the use of strategies, process speaking, and process writing. In this chapter, students will:

- read a fable from Mexico
- speak about what they were like when they were younger

To reinforce and enhance learning, students can access a wide range of online resources on **realidades.com**, the personalized learning management system that accompanies the print and online Student Edition. Resources include the eText, textbook and workbook activities, audio files, videos, animations, songs, self-study tools, interactive maps, voice recording (RealTalk!), assessments, and other digital resources. Many learning tools can be accessed through the student Home Page on **realidades.com**. Other activities, specifically those that require grading, are assigned by the teacher and linked on the student Home Page within the calendar or the Assignments tab.

You will find specifications and guidelines for accessing **realidades.com** on home computers and mobile devices on MyPearsonTraining.com under the SuccessNet Plus tab.

---

realidades.com ⌄

For: Tips to Parents
Visit: www.realidades.com
Web Code: jce-0010

Check it out! At the end of the chapter, have your child tell you what his or her three favorite toys were when he or she was younger. Then have him or her describe himself or herself as a young child: for example, timid, well-behaved, or disobedient, etc.

Sincerely,

Videocultura Script

El Día de los Muertos

Spanish version:

Hace unos 3,000 años, los aztecas participaban en un ritual muy especial. Ellos usaban calaveras para simbolizar el regreso de los muertos a la vida.

Los indígenas creían que la muerte era una continuación de la vida.

En la modernidad, este ritual se llama el Día de los Muertos.

Hoy día es una combinación del antiguo ritual azteca con las prácticas de la religión católica.

Las familias se reúnen para recordar a familiares y amigos que han muerto. Ellos recuerdan su vida con alegría.

Un altar es construido en memoria a los muertos. Es decorado con velas y ornamentos y se exhibe la fotografía de la persona difunta.

Honrar la memoria de los muertos es una hermosa costumbre. Los mexicanos lo hacen de una forma muy especial durante la celebración del Día de los Muertos.

English version:

The Day of the Dead, or *El Día de los Muertos,* is celebrated in Mexico and countries in Latin America. It is a tradition that began 3,000 years ago.

Pre-Columbian civilizations displayed skulls as trophies and used them in rituals to symbolize death and rebirth.

The indigenous cultures believed that death was not the end of life, but rather a continuation of it.

On November first and second, people visit the graves of their departed relatives.

The modern celebration combines rituals from both Aztec and Catholic traditions.

At the cemetery, relatives usually clean and decorate the gravesite. They often build altars containing the favorite food and drinks of the departed as well as photographs and mementos. The graves are adorned with marigolds. These traditions are believed to encourage a visit by the soul of the departed.

The Day of the Dead celebrates the ancient belief that death is a continuation of life. On these two days in November, families remember and honor their departed loved ones.

Input Script

Presentation

Input Vocabulary 1: Place the transparency showing toys on the screen or bring actual toys to class and arrange them on a table at the front of the classroom with tags or signs showing the prices in the *A primera vista* toy store ad. Distribute copies of the Vocabulary Clip Art and have students cut them into individual images. Announce to students: *¡Vamos a hacer una guardería infantil en un rincón de la sala de clases! Tenemos 100 dólares para comprar juguetes. ¿Qué debemos comprar?* Tell students to hold up the Clip Art that most closely represents their favorite toy when they were younger. Then ask them if they collected anything: *¿Qué les gustaba coleccionar cuando eran pequeños?* Tell students to to hold up the Clip Art images that resemble what they collected. Next, have students decide which toys to buy for the day-care center by placing the Clip Art images in a pile on their desks. Remind them of the 100 dollar budget. Finally, ask who selected which toys: *¿Quién escogió la muñeca?* Have students hold up each Clip Art item and give its name in Spanish.

Input Dialogue: Perform the dialogue with a volunteer. Then ask individual students which toys they played with and what the toys were like. Also discuss any toy collections students might have had.

Input Day-Care Expressions: Place the transparency showing a day care center on the screen. Tell students that these are some of the expressions they will need to know before they can open the classroom day-care center. Ask for volunteers to pantomime the actions of the misbehaving children in the transparency. Reprimand them with the expressions given. Then ask for volunteers to practice reprimanding the "children." Once they demonstrate that they can keep the children in line, tell them they are ready to open the day care. (You might ask students with younger siblings to invite a parent and their siblings to class to make the presentation even more authentic. Allow the children to play with the toys and encourage students to use the day-care expressions on p. 187 if the situations arise in their day care. Students could also teach the children how to count in Spanish and the Spanish alphabet.)

Comprehension Check

- Tell students you bought toys for your niece and nephew and you want to make sure you spent the same amount of money on each one. Read a list of the toys you bought, with one list totaling much more than the other. Have students arrange the Clip Art toys in the order you mention them, add up the items, then tell you which items to take back to make the gift totals equal.

- Make logical and illogical statements about toys you are going to buy for children you know: *A Enrique le gustan los animales. Voy a comprar los bloques.* Have students raise their hand when they hear an illogical statement, and then hold up a more appropriate gift.

Realidades 2

Capítulo 4A

Audio Script

Audio DVD, Capítulo 4A

Track 01, *A primera vista, Cuando éramos niños*, Student Book, p. 186

Vocabulario y gramática en contexto
Lee en tu libro mientras escuchas el diálogo.

FEMALE TEEN 1: ¿Con qué jugabas de pequeña?

FEMALE TEEN 2: Tenía una muñeca favorita que se llamaba Pepita. Era muy bonita y rubia. ¿Y tú?

FEMALE TEEN 1: Me gustaba montar en triciclo y coleccionar osos de peluche. Tenía más de treinta en mi colección.

Vas a escuchar cada palabra o frase dos veces. Después de la primera vez hay una pausa para que puedas pronunciar la palabra o frase. Luego vas a escuchar de nuevo la palabra o frase.

el tren eléctrico	el dinosaurio
la muñeca	el pez
el triciclo	los peces
el oso de peluche	la tortuga
los bloques	

Más vocabulario

la moneda	el vecino
el mundo	la vecina

Track 02: *A primera vista*, Student Book, p. 187

Vocabulario y gramática en contexto
Vas a escuchar cada palabra o frase dos veces. Después de la primera vez hay una pausa para que puedas pronunciar la palabra o frase. Luego vas a escuchar de nuevo la palabra o frase.

la guardería infantil	la cuerda
el muñeco	saltar a la cuerda
el patio de recreo	

Lee en tu libro mientras escuchas el diálogo.

MALE ADULT: ¡Raúl! ¡Miguelito! ¡Basta! Los muñecos no deben pelearse así.

FEMALE ADULT 1: Margarita, no debes molestar a Juanito. ¡Estás muy traviesa hoy! No permitimos esto aquí.

FEMALE ADULT 2: Inés, ¿por qué no les ofreces a los otros un poco de tu pastel? Debes ser generosa y compartir con todo el mundo.

Track 03: *A primera vista*, Act. 1, Student Book, p. 187

Los juguetes favoritos
Escucha mientras unos chicos describen sus juguetes favoritos. Señala con tu dedo el juguete apropiado en la página 186. Vas a escuchar las frases dos veces.

1. Mi juguete favorito era un dinosaurio verde con dientes muy grandes.
2. Mi juguete favorito era un tren eléctrico.
3. Mi juguete favorito se llamaba Julia. Mi muñeca tenía pelo rubio y llevaba un vestido azul.

4. Mi juguete favorito era un oso de peluche. Dormía con él todas las noches.
5. Me gustaba montar en triciclo todos los días.
6. Mis juguetes favoritos cuando tenía tres años eran bloques de plástico de muchos colores.

Track 04: *A primera vista*, Act. 2, Student Book, p. 187

¿Cierta o falsa?
Escucha las siete descripciones de los niños en la guardería infantil y compáralas con el dibujo de arriba. Escribe el número de cada descripción en la columna apropiada para indicar si es cierta o falsa. Vas a escuchar las descripciones dos veces.

1. En la guardería infantil, los niños juegan en el patio de recreo.
2. Margarita es traviesa. Molesta mucho a Juanito.
3. Inés debe ser generosa y compartir con todo el mundo.
4. En la guardería infantil les permiten a los niños pelearse.
5. Una maestra salta a la cuerda en el patio de recreo.
6. Raúl y Miguelito se pelean con sus osos de peluche.
7. Inés debe ofrecerles pastel a los otros niños.

Track 05: *A primera vista*, Videohistoria, Student Book, pp. 188–189

¿Cómo era de niña?
¿Cómo se portaba Ana de niña?
¿Qué le gustaba a ella?

Lee en tu libro mientras escuchas la *Videohistoria*.

See Student Book pages 188–189 for script.

Track 06: *Manos a la obra*, Act. 6, Student Book, p. 190

Escucha y escribe
Víctor describe un animal que tenía cuando era niño. Escucha las cinco frases y escríbelas en una hoja de papel. Vas a escuchar las descripciones dos veces.

1. De niño tenía un perro muy divertido.
2. El nombre de mi perro era Julio.
3. Jugaba todos los días con Julio en el patio.
4. De vez en cuando iba al parque con Julio.
5. Julio era inteligente pero un poco travieso.

Track 07, Audio Act. 5, Writing, Audio & Video Workbook, p. 71

Do you remember your favorite childhood toy? Listen as each of the following people describes a favorite childhood toy. In the grid below, write what each person's favorite toy was and who gave the toy to him or her. You will hear each set of statements twice.

1. **ADULT MALE 1:** Soy Rogelio. De niño, mi juguete favorito era un triciclo. ¡En ese triciclo yo era el mejor policía de la cuadra! Mis abuelos me lo dieron cuando tenía tres años.

2. **ADULT FEMALE 1:** Yo soy Marta. Cuando tenía siete años, mi tía me dio una muñeca que se llamaba Julieta. Me gustaba vestirla con ropa bonita. ¡Cómo quería a esa muñeca!

3. **ADULT MALE 2:** Me llamo Andrés. De pequeño, yo quería mucho un tren eléctrico. Para mi cumpleaños de ocho años, mis padres me lo dieron. Jugaba con el tren por horas y horas. ¡De vez en cuando, ponía mis dinosaurios plásticos sobre uno de los carros!

4. **ADULT FEMALE 2:** Soy Lorena. Cuando era un bebé, mi hermano mayor me dio mi juguete favorito: mi primer oso de peluche. Todavía lo tengo. Voy a llevarlo conmigo a la universidad.

5. **ADULT MALE 3:** Mi nombre es Humberto. De pequeño yo jugaba mucho con mis bloques magnéticos. Mi mamá me los dio cuando yo tenía cinco años. Cada día, hacía una palabra nueva en el refrigerador con los bloques.

Track 08: Audio Act. 6, Writing, Audio & Video Workbook, p. 71

Ricardo, Susana, Marcos, and Julia haven't seen their preschool teacher, Señorita Rosi, since they were four years old. Now that they are teenagers, Señorita Rosi can't believe how they've grown. Listen as Señorita Rosi reminisces about their childhood, and write the name of each child under the corresponding picture. You will hear each statement twice.

1. ¡Qué gusto verlos! ¡Qué muchachos tan guapos y grandes ya! Susana, qué niña tan bien educada y obediente eras tú. Siempre decías "gracias" y "por favor," y prestabas tu muñeca favorita sin problema. Te portabas muy bien.

2. Y aquí está Marcos, el experto en dinosaurios. Siempre llevabas la colección de esos juguetes contigo y podías contar la historia de cada dinosaurio de la época jurásica.

3. ¡Julia, mi estudiante más tímida! Siempre tenías tu oso de peluche en los brazos. Jugabas con él todo el tiempo. Te gustaba tomar el té con tu oso. Siempre eras tan consentida, pero muy buena estudiante.

4. Ay, mi querido Ricardo. ¡Tan desobediente y travieso! La cabeza me explotaba casi todos los días contigo. Siempre ponías tu tortuga en la comida de las niñas en la cafetería. Yo tenía que hablar por teléfono con tu madre muchas veces cada semana.

Track 09: *Pronunciación*, The letters *r* and *rr*, Student Book, p. 193

Except at the beginning of a word or after *l* or *n*, the sound of the letter "ere," *r*, is made as you raise the tip of your tongue and tap the roof of your mouth. The position of your tongue is similar to the position when you pronounce the *d* in the English word *Daddy*. The sound of the *rr* is made as you raise the tip of your tongue and tap the roof of your mouth several times very quickly. Listen to and say these pairs of words:

You will hear each word twice. After the word is

pronounced the first time, there will be a pause so you can pronounce it. Then you will hear the word a second time.

pero	moro
perro	morro
ahora	caro
ahorra	carro

When *r* is the first letter of a word or comes after *l* or *n*, it is pronounced like the *rr*.

¡Compruébalo! Listen to these two verses of a popular Spanish lullaby, then try to repeat them.

Track 10:

A la rorro niño
a la rorro ya,
duérmete mi niño,
duérmete mi amor.
Señora Santa Ana,
Señor San Joaquín
Arrullen al niño
que se va a dormir.

Track 11: *Manos a la obra*, Act. 13, Student Book, p. 194

Escucha y escribe

Lola y Lulú eran vecinas y muy buenas amigas, pero eran muy diferentes. Lola era muy bien educada, pero Lulú era desobediente. Escucha las seis descripciones de las niñas y escribe las frases. Indica si la descripción es de Lola, de Lulú o de las dos. Vas a escuchar las descripciones dos veces.

1. Mentía de vez en cuando.
2. Jugaban bien y nunca se peleaban.
3. Por lo general se portaba bien.
4. Vivían en la misma calle.
5. Siempre compartía sus juguetes y muñecas.
6. Molestaba a los otros niños.

Track 12: Audio Act. 7, Writing, Audio & Video Workbook, p. 72

Listen as Patricia listens to her favorite popular radio show *Yo no lo sabía* to find out things that she didn't know about some of her favorite movie and TV personalities. Match what you hear the DJ say about her favorite celebrities to the pictures below. Write the number of each piece of gossip underneath the picture it refers to. You will hear each piece of gossip twice.

Bienvenidos a nuestro programa, *Yo no lo sabía*. Hoy hablamos de las vidas de sus favoritas personas famosas. Primero…

1. ¿Saben Uds. que Lana López tenía que llevar su oso de peluche a todas sus audiciones? Ella pensaba que le traía buena suerte.

2. ¿Y saben Uds. que a Chachis Chávez le encantaba comer espaguetis para el desayuno en su guardería infantil? ¡Qué loca!, ¿no?

3. ¿Y Vigo Villa? Uds. no van a creerlo. ¡De niño, él coleccionaba fotos y dibujos de tortugas! En las paredes de su dormitorio había veinte fotos de su tortuga favorita.

4. ¡Increíble! Tenemos nueva información sobre Pepe Pedroso. Todavía le gustaba montar en triciclo cuando tenía quince años. ¡Qué horrible!

5. ¿Saben que a Lola Cienfuegos le gustaban tanto las muñecas que a menudo llevaba toda su colección a la escuela? ¡Madre mía! ¿En dónde las ponía?

6. ¡Les tengo una información explosiva! Linda Cabeza de Vaca, la cantante rebelde de rock, nos dijo que le llevaba manzanas a su maestra todos los días como una estudiante modelo. Muy simpática, ¿no?

7. Otro cantante de rock, Martín Alaridos, se peleaba muchas veces en el patio de recreo con otros estudiantes. Después saltaba a la cuerda con las niñas para divertirse.

8. Enrique Pecho Grande, el famoso actor de películas de acción, tenía una colección de dinosaurios que por lo general llevaba a todos los lugares que visitaba.

Track 13: Audio Act. 8, Writing, Audio & Video Workbook, p. 73

Listen as adults recall their childhood and how they used to role-play having different kinds of jobs when they grew up. Write the number of each description under the picture of the corresponding profession each person imagined as a child. You will hear each description twice.

1. **ADULT MALE 1:** Cuando yo era pequeño, a menudo montaba mi triciclo e imaginaba que era un policía muy estricto. Corría muy rápido en mi triciclo para buscar a la gente mala. Mi hermano me veía, pero no quería jugar conmigo.

2. **ADULT FEMALE 1:** Cuando yo era niña, siempre me gustaba ayudar a mis amigos en la escuela. Pensaba que era la mejor profesora de matemáticas y ciencias de la ciudad. Yo iba a las casas de mis amigos para enseñarles cosas nuevas. Leíamos muchos libros interesantes. Mis amigos decían que era una profesora muy buena.

3. **ADULT FEMALE 2:** Cuando yo era pequeña, muchas veces cantaba enfrente del espejo. Imaginaba que era una cantante muy famosa. Practicaba mis canciones favoritas cuando me duchaba y me preparaba para la escuela. Cuando mi mamá me veía, me decía que tenía voz de ángel.

4. **ADULT FEMALE 3:** Cuando yo era niña, por lo general dibujaba las caras de mis amigos cuando iba a mi clase de arte. Yo veía a mi maestro de arte como un pintor famoso. Él era muy paciente e inteligente.

5. **ADULT MALE 2:** Cuando yo era niño, de vez en cuando iba a muchos conciertos de rock con mi hermano mayor. Me encantaba la música. En casa, tocaba las mismas canciones del concierto en la guitarra.

6. **ADULT MALE 3:** Cuando yo era pequeño, por lo general iba al cine. Quería ver películas de acción. Me imaginaba que era el actor principal de la película. Estaba manejando un coche y buscando cosas perdidas.

Track 14: Audio Act. 9, Writing, Audio & Video Workbook, p. 73

There are no gift tags on the Christmas gifts that the Rodríguez family received from their friend Gonzalo.

Señor Rodríguez has to call him on the phone to find out which gift goes to whom. Complete the sentences below to describe what Gonzalo gave to each person. For example, you might write: *Gonzalo le dio unos aretes a la abuela.* You will hear this conversation twice.

ADULT MALE 1: Hola, Gonzalo. Soy yo, Andrés. Oiga. Hay un problema con los regalos que nos envió. No sabemos para quiénes son. ¿Puede ayudarme?

ADULT MALE 2: ¡Hombre!… ¡Feliz Navidad! Bueno. Los boletos de avión son para sus abuelos. Ellos siempre me contaban de sus viajes.

ADULT MALE 1: Bien. ¿Y la colección de tarjetas de béisbol?

ADULT MALE 2: Ah, sí. Eso es para Luis. Es mi colección personal. Cuando yo era pequeño, me las llevaba al patio de recreo. El dinero en efectivo es para su hija, Marta. No sabía qué debía comprarle.

ADULT MALE 1: Ah, yo quería el dinero. Bueno, ¿y los zapatos de golf?

ADULT MALE 2: Compré los zapatos para su esposa, Cristina. A ella le gusta mucho jugar al golf, ¿no? Y para Ud., mi colección de monedas españolas.

Vas a escuchar esta conversación otra vez.

Track 15: *La cultura en vivo*, Student Book, p. 204

A todos los niños les encanta cantar. Aquí están dos canciones populares que los niños en algunos países hispanohablantes cantan mientras juegan con sus amigos.

Track 16: *El columpio*

See Student Book page 204 for lyrics.

Track 17: *Los elefantes*

See Student Book page 204 for lyrics.

Track 18: *Repaso del capítulo*, Student Book, p. 208

Vocabulario y gramática

Escucha las palabras y expresiones que has aprendido en este capítulo.

See Student Book page 208 for vocabulary list.

Track 19: *Preparación para el examen*, Student Book, p. 209

Escuchar

Practice task

You volunteer your time after school at the Youth Center. To get to know your kids better, you ask them about their favorite toys when they were younger. See if you can understand: a) what the toy was; b) how old the child was when he or she used to play with it; c) where he or she used to play with it.

Mi juguete favorito era el tren eléctrico en nuestra guardería infantil. Cuando teníamos siete años, mis amigos y yo jugábamos muchas horas con aquel tren.

Video Script

A primera vista: ¿Cómo era de niña?

ELENA: ¿Y quién es ella?

ANA: Es mi tía Teresa. La hermana de mi padre.

ELENA: Parece muy joven…

IGNACIO: Hola.

ANA: Hola, Ignacio.

IGNACIO: Hola, ¿qué tal?

ANA Y ELENA: Bien.

IGNACIO: ¿Qué es esto tan grande?

ANA: El árbol genealógico de mi familia; para la clase de ciencias sociales.

IGNACIO: Y, ¿quién eres tú?

ANA: Ésta soy yo, de niña. Era muy tímida.

IGNACIO: ¿Tímida? ¿Tú? No.

MAMÁ: Aquí tenéis. Hola, Ignacio. ¿Cómo estás?

IGNACIO: Hola.

MAMÁ: Ana, ¿recuerdas aquel video, de cuando eras pequeña?

ANA: Ay, no. No me gusta mucho.

ELENA: Ana, ¿por qué no? Vamos a verlo.

ANA: No, mejor no…

IGNACIO: ¡Vamos! Será divertido.

ANA: No sé…

IGNACIO: Mira, mira, allí estás.

ANA: Mamá, ¿cómo era yo de niña? ¿Era desobediente?

MAMÁ: No, por lo general eras obediente, y bien educada.

MAMÁ'S V.O.: Bueno, un poquito traviesa…

MAMÁ: ¡Ay, pero siempre te levantabas tan temprano!

IGNACIO: ¿Ana? ¿Cómo es posible? Ahora siempre llegas tarde a clase.

ANA: Mientes, Ignacio. Eso no es verdad.

ANA: Ay sí. Me encantaba mi oso de peluche. Era mi juguete favorito.

MAMÁ: Sí, te lo llevabas siempre contigo… a la guardería infantil. Y hasta dormías con él.

IGNACIO: ¿También te gustaban las muñecas?

ANA: Sí. Ésa era mi muñeca favorita.

ELENA: ¿Y tantos animales de peluche?

ANA: Sí, también tenía una colección de peluches.

IGNACIO: ¡Qué consentida eras!

ANA: Bueno, un poco… Y tú, ¿cómo eras de pequeño?

IGNACIO: Pues, yo siempre me portaba bien, obedecía a mis padres… y siempre decía la verdad…

ELENA: ¿Ignacio? No. No te creo.

MAMÁ: ¡Ay, mira mi nena!

ANA: No. Ya no podemos ver más.

IGNACIO: ¿Por qué no?

ANA: Nadie va a ver esto.

GramActiva Videos
The imperfect tense

HOST: Hi there. Today we're going to talk about the imperfect tense of regular verbs.

TIME TRAVELER: Aha! I've done it! I've invented the perfect time-travel device. It's compact, it's convenient. It's…

HOST: Mmm. It's tasty.

TIME TRAVELER: Nooooo! What have you done? Now how am I going to talk about the salty past?

HOST: Well another way to talk about the past is with the imperfect tense. We use the imperfect tense to describe actions that used to happen, or that happened repeatedly in the past.

V.O.: So in English we might say:
Lisa used to jump rope, or Juan used to eat bugs.
In Spanish we would say:
Lisa saltaba a la cuerda, and Juan comía insectos.

HOST: Let's look at how to form the endings for the imperfect. It's real easy. Here's the deal with -ar verbs. Think of these as -aba endings. Let's look at jugar.

V.O.: Jugaba. Jugabas. Jugaba. Jugábamos. Jugabais. Jugaban.

V.O.: Él jugaba con ositos de peluche. Cindy jugaba con trenes.

V.O.: And now, random car chases. That's fun! What's more fun? Let's see how to form endings of -er verbs. Think of these as -ía endings. Let's look at hacer.
Hacía. Hacías. Hacía. Hacíamos. Hacíais. Hacían.
Here is the good news! The -ir verbs are the same as -er endings.

V.O.: Yo hacía bien la tarea.
Hacíamos la tarea todos los días.

V.O.: Now let's take a quick look at vivir.
Vivía. Vivías. Vivía. Vivíamos. Vivíais. Vivían.

V.O.: Ella vivía en México.
Vivían al lado de un lago.

HOST: So, you see you don't need a time machine to talk about the past.

TIME TRAVELER: Aha! I've got it. Good bye…

HOST: Alrighty then, let's take a look at the imperfect tense of some irregular verbs. But good news is that there are only three irregular verbs. Here you go.

V.O.: Ir: iba, ibas, iba, íbamos, ibais, iban.

V.O.: Íbamos a muchas fiestas.
Iban a la playa.

V.O.: Ser: era, eras, era, éramos, erais, eran.

V.O.: Era una casa grande.
Eran felices allí.

V.O.: Ver: veía, veías, veía, veíamos, veíais, veían.

V.O.: Los domingos veía a mis primos.

HOST: Notice that all conjugations of nosotros have accent marks.

V.O.1: *Iba a la casa de mi vecino después de la escuela.*

V.O.2: *Siempre veía a mi tío.*

V.O.3: *Eran tímidos.*

HOST: We've learned a lot about talking about the past, now it's time to test your knowledge.

TIME TRAVELER: I thought I understood time travel before, but now I've really got it. Ha, HA, HA!

Quiz

V.O.: Complete the sentences with the correct form of the imperfect.

(hablar) Juanita _____ con sus amigas.

Juanita hablaba con sus amigas.

(ver) Ellos _____ la tele los sábados por la mañana.

Ellos veían la tele los sábados por la mañana.

(ir) Cada domingo nosotros _____ a casa de nuestros abuelos.

Cada domingo nosotros íbamos a casa de nuestros abuelos.

Indirect object pronouns

COACH: OK! Let's get started with a quick review. Remember, an indirect object tells to whom or for whom an action is being performed. Let's say I gave a ball to Paul. Paul is the indirect object.

COACH V.O.: Now let's say we replace the name *Paul* with him. "I gave him a ball. *Him* is the indirect object pronoun. It replaces *Paul*. In Spanish we say *Le di la pelota a Pablo* or *Le di la pelota*.

HOST: Indirect object pronouns are used to replace or accompany an indirect object noun. In Spanish the indirect object pronoun comes right before the conjugated verb. So let's review the indirect object pronouns in Spanish.

V.O.: Use *me* (to/for) me:

Me da un juguete.

te (to/for) you (informal):

Te compro un triciclo.

le (to/for) him, her, you (formal):

Le traigo el dinosaurio.

nos (to/for) us:

Nos enseña la canción.

os (to/for) you familiar:

Os prepara la comida.

les (to/for) them, you (formal):

Les escribo una carta.

HOST: Because *le* and *les* have more than one meaning, you can make the meaning clear by adding *a* + name, noun, or pronoun.

V.O.1: You could say, *Le escribí una carta.*

V.O.2: But who does *Le* stand for?

V.O.1: Oops, our mistake. To make it clear you need to say *a mi prima*. So the sentence becomes *Le escribí una carta a mi prima*.

FOOTBALL PLAYER: Well I guess that's about it for indirect object pronouns…

COACH: No! There's one more play in the indirect object pronoun book. Indirect object pronouns are placed right before the verb, or are attached to the infinitive.

V.O.: *Le quiere comprar dulces a su hija* or *Quiere comprarle dulces a su hija*.

HOST: You got all that? Well here's a little something to test your knowledge we like to call a quiz.

Quiz

V.O.: Complete the sentences with the correct indirect object pronoun.

(nosotros) Los profesores siempre _____ daban mucha tarea.

Los profesores siempre nos daban mucha tarea.

(ellos) Sus abuelos siempre _____ daban regalos a los niños.

Sus abuelos siempre les daban regalos a los niños.

(yo) Ana nunca _____ prestaba su cuerda.

Ana nunca me prestaba su cuerda.

Videomisterio: *En busca de la verdad*, Episodio 3

ROBERTO'S V.O.: Ésta es mi abuela, Nela Toledo. Ella es la mamá de mi papá y todos la queremos mucho. Ella vive sola en San Miguel de Allende, que es una pequeña ciudad cerca de Guanajuato. Y mi abuelo… bueno, ni mi abuela ni mi papá querían hablar de él. Era un misterio para la familia. Mi abuela tiene muchísimos amigos y una de sus mejores amigas es su vecina Olga. A las dos les encanta pasear por la ciudad, ir de compras al mercado y hablar con los vecinos.

ABUELA: Sofía, eres toda una artista. ¡Qué bonitas son estas catrinas!

SOFÍA: Gracias, Sra. Toledo… también están muy ricas. Pruebe una.

ABUELA: Sí, riquísimas. Dame una docena, por favor.

OLGA: Y una docena para mí también.

ABUELA: Permíteme, Olga. ¿Bueno?

ROBERTO: Hola, Abuelita, ¿cómo estás?

ABUELA: ¡Roberto! ¡Qué gusto oírte! ¿Cómo están todos?

ROBERTO: Muy bien. Daniela y yo pensamos visitarte mañana. ¿Qué te parece?

ABUELA: Me parece estupendo. Sabes que Uds. son siempre bienvenidos en esta casa. Me encanta cuando vienen a verme.

ROBERTO: Gracias. Ah, pero hay una cosa más. Voy a invitar a una amiga de San Antonio, Linda Toledo.

ABUELA: No hay problema. Linda también es bienvenida… No se oye bien. ¿Dices que ella es de Toledo?

ROBERTO: No, no, de San Antonio, Tejas. Su apellido es Toledo. Su mamá está aquí arreglando un programa de intercambio con nuestra escuela. Linda es muy simpática.

ABUELA: Ah, de San Antonio.

ROBERTO: Mañana, pues… ¿a las dos?

ABUELA: Muy bien. Les voy a preparar una comida rica.

ROBERTO: Muchas gracias, Abuelita. Hasta mañana.

ABUELA: Hasta mañana, hijo.

OLGA: ¿Buenas noticias, Nela?

ABUELA: Claro, muy buenas noticias. Mañana vienen a comer Roberto y Daniela… con una amiga de los Estados Unidos. Estás invitada.

OLGA: Gracias, Nela, pero no puedo. Mañana viene el carpintero a reparar algunas cosas en mi casa.

ABUELA: Bueno, entonces, ayúdame a pensar en lo que puedo prepararles para la comida.

ROBERTO: Y ahora quiero decirles un secreto. A mi abuela le gustan mucho las computadoras.

ABUELA: Vamos a ver… ¿Qué hay de nuevo en el correo electrónico…?

BERTA: Hoy hablé con la maestra Toledo. Ella dice que todo está progresando muy bien para el intercambio.

TOMÁS: Puede ser bueno para todos, aquí y allá… para conocerse mejor.

DANIELA: Y yo le enseñé a Linda esta mañana la escuela. Le gustó mucho. También vimos a Julio.

ROBERTO: Qué bueno… Papá, necesito el coche mañana. Vamos a visitar a la abuela.

TOMÁS: Está bien. Bueno, tengo que volver a la clínica. ¡Mis pacientes me esperan!

BERTA: Dani, tengo un pastel para la abuela. No lo olvides. Ayúdame con los platos para el postre.

DANIELA: Sí, claro.

ROBERTO: Papá, quisiera hablar contigo por un momento.

TOMÁS: ¿Qué pasa, hijo?

ROBERTO: Vamos a hablar en el pasillo.

DANIELA: Roberto, ¿nos ayudas?

ROBERTO: Ya voy. Un momento.

ROBERTO: Con la llegada de Linda, empecé a pensar en el misterio sobre mi abuelo. ¿Era una coincidencia que los dos éramos Toledo? Decidí hablar con mi papá.

ROBERTO: Papá, el apellido de Linda también es Toledo.

TOMÁS: ¿Y qué?

ROBERTO: Nosotros somos Toledo… ¿Habrá una conexión? A propósito, tú nunca hablas del abuelo. Yo no sé nada de él.

TOMÁS: Tu abuelo se llamaba Federico Toledo. Es todo lo que puedo decirte. Si quieres saber más, habla con tu abuela. Ella sabe más que yo. Ahora, tengo que irme.

ROBERTO's V.O.: Siempre lo mismo. Papá nunca quería hablar del abuelo. ¿Por qué no quería decirme la verdad?

Realidades 2

Capítulo 4A

Nombre _____

Fecha _____

Communicative Pair Activity **4A-1**

Estudiante **A**

Answer the following questions about what you did as a child. Record your answers in the space provided. Example:

—Sí. De pequeño(a), yo coleccionaba dinosaurios.

1. ¿Tenías un perro de niño(a)? _____

_____

2. ¿Jugabas con un tren eléctrico de niño(a)? _____

_____

3. ¿Qué coleccionabas de niño(a)? _____

_____

4. ¿Jugabas con muñecos o muñecas de niño(a)? _____

_____

5. ¿Jugabas en el patio de recreo? _____

_____

6. ¿Y jugabas con los bloques de niño(a)? _____

Now, ask your partner the same questions about what he or she did as a child. Record the answers in the space provided.

1. _____

2. _____

3. _____

4. _____

5. _____

6. _____

Realidades 2

Capítulo 4A

Nombre _____

Fecha _____

Communicative Pair Activity **4A-1**

Estudiante **B**

Answer the following questions about what you did as a child. Record your answers in the space provided. Example:

—*Sí. De pequeño(a), yo tenía una tortuga.*

1. ¿Nadabas en la piscina cuando eras pequeño(a)? _____

_____

2. ¿Montabas en un triciclo cuando eras pequeño(a)? _____

_____

3. ¿Cuál era tu juguete favorito cuando eras pequeño(a)? _____

_____

4. ¿Jugabas con muñecas o muñecos cuando eras pequeño(a)? _____

_____

_____

5. ¿Coleccionabas monedas cuando eras pequeño(a)? _____

_____

6. ¿Y saltabas a la cuerda cuando eras pequeño(a)? _____

_____

Now, ask your partner the same questions about what he or she did as a child. Record the answers in the space provided.

1. _____

2. _____

3. _____

4. _____

5. _____

6. _____

Realidades ❷

Capítulo 4A

Nombre _____

Fecha _____

Write your answers to the following questions on line A. Then ask your partner the same questions and write the answers on line B.

1. ¿Eras muy consentido(a) cuando eras pequeño(a)?

   A. _____

   B. _____

2. ¿Eras un(a) niño(a) bien educado(a) cuando eras pequeño(a)?

   A. _____

   B. _____

3. ¿Eras desobediente a veces cuando eras pequeño(a)?

   A. _____

   B. _____

4. ¿Son generosos tus padres?

   A. _____

   B. _____

5. ¿Eras tímido(a) cuando eras pequeño(a)?

   A. _____

   B. _____

6. ¿Eras travieso(a) de niño(a)?

   A. _____

   B. _____

7. ¿Eres travieso(a) ahora (de grande)?

   A. _____

   B. _____

Situation Cards

2A   Realidades ❷

Capítulo 4A

Talking about animals and explaining your actions

You are a science teacher talking to an elementary school child.

— Ask the student if he or she knows what happened to the fish (*plural*) and turtles that were in the classroom this morning.

— Ask him or her why he or she took them outside.

— Respond to the student's question affirmatively and thank him or her for telling the truth.

2B   Realidades ❷

Capítulo 4A

Talking about animals and explaining your actions

You are an elementary school child talking to a science teacher.

— Answer affirmatively saying that you took them outside to the playground.

— Answer your teacher's question saying that you are obedient in general but that you wanted to feed the turtles and the fish (*plural*) while playing outside.

— Then, ask the teacher if it was wrong of you to take them outside.

1A   Realidades ❷

Capítulo 4A

Talking about things you used to do and describing what someone was like

You are reminiscing with an older brother or sister about each other's behavior when you were little.

— Ask him or her if he or she remembers the toys with which you both used to play.

— Respond to his or her answer with emotion saying, "Of course!" and ask if he or she remembers what happened to it.

— Tell your partner you do not remember ever fighting because you were always obedient and well-behaved.

1B   Realidades ❷

Capítulo 4A

Talking about things you used to do and describing what someone was like

You are reminiscing with a younger brother or sister about each other's behavior when you were little.

— Respond to your brother or sister that you remember the electric train that your parents gave him or her.

— Answer the question negatively by saying you do not remember, but you recall that you both used to fight over it.

— Respond by saying that he or she was well-behaved in general but mischievous once in a while.

GramActiva

Cuando éramos niños

¿Cómo eras de niño(a)?, p. 205

No me permitían . . .			
Tenía que . . .			
Me gustaba más . . .			
Jugaba con . . .			
¿Cómo era?			

Vocabulary Clip Art

Vocabulary Clip Art

Core Practice Answers

4A-A
1. abuelos
2. prima
3. primo
4. tíos
5. padre
6. hermanos
7. abuelo

B.
1. la sal y pimienta
2. las servilletas
3. los tenedores y los cuchillos
4. las cucharas
5. los vasos

4A-B
A.
1. decoran con las luces
2. abre los regalos
3. rompe la piñata
4. comen pizza
5. hace un video
6. saca fotos

B.
1. facilísima
2. hermanito
3. grandísimos
4. riquísima
5. pequeñito
6. abuelita

4A-1
A.
1. bloques
2. triciclo
3. oso
4. colección
5. saltar
6. generosa
7. vecino
8. tren

B.
1. permitir
2. ofrecer
3. el mundo
4. todo el mundo
5. tímido

4A-2
1. muñecos
2. los peces
3. los dinosaurios
4. patio de recreo
5. la guardería infantil

6. a la cuerda
7. traviesa
8. tortuga

4A-3
A.
1. obediente
2. tímida
3. consentido
4. educada
5. travieso

B.
1. pelean
2. obedece
3. miento
4. portan
5. molestar
6. coleccionar

4A-4
1. Tiene una colección de muñecas.
2. Juega con su tren eléctrico.
3. Siempre duerme con su oso de peluche.
4. Les gusta saltar a la cuerda.
5. Se portan mal.
6. Sabe montar en triciclo.
7. Le gusta jugar con bloques.
8. Siempre se pelean.

4A-5
1. Mario saltaba a la cuerda.
2. Lorenzo y Alberto se portaban bien.
3. Tú le escribías cartas.
4. Yo coleccionaba dinosaurios.
5. Tú y yo montábamos a caballo.
6. Tú jugabas al tenis.
7. Nosotras nos peleábamos.
8. Luis y Sergio coleccionaban monedas.
9. Yo cuidaba a los niños.

4A-6
era / eran / éramos / íbamos / veías / iba / era / eras / eras / iba / iban / íbamos / veían / éramos

4A-7
1. Nosotros le damos un oso de peluche a Mónica.
2. Yo les doy bloques a los niños.
3. Mis padres me dan un gato a mí.
4. Mi hermana le da una corbata a mi padre.

5. Tus padres te dan libros a ti.
6. Nuestros amigos nos dan discos compactos a nosotros.
7. Yo le doy una pulsera a mi novia.

Crucigrama (4A-8)
Horizontal:
3. jugaba
5. general
8. obediente
13. obedezco
14. dinosaurio
16. consentido
17. muñeca
19. molesta
20. tren
22. cuerda
23. pelean
24. travieso
25. patio

Vertical:
1. peluche
2. era
4. guardería
6. mundo
7. vecino
9. bloque
10. porta
11. pez
12. les
15. iba
17. miente
18. tortuga
21. educado

Organizer (4A-9)
I. Vocabulary Answers will vary.
II. Grammar
1. **jugar:**

jugaba	jugábamos
jugabas	jugábais
jugaba	jugaban

permitir:

permitía	permitíamos
permitías	permitíais
permitía	permitían

ser:

era	éramos
eras	érias
era	eran

ir:

iba	íbamos
ibas	íbais
iba	iban

2. indirect object; me, te, le, nos, os, les

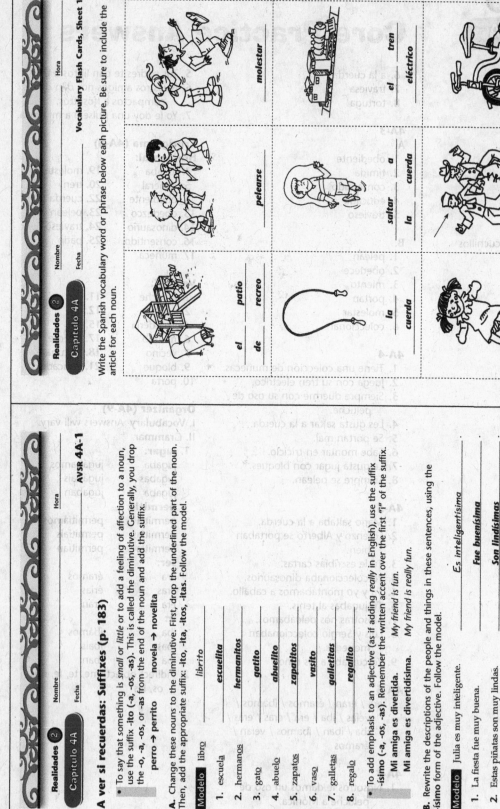

Nombre _____ Hora _____

Fecha _____

Vocabulary Flash Cards, Sheet 1

Write the Spanish vocabulary word or phrase below each picture. Be sure to include the article for each noun.

molestar

el tren eléctrico

el triciclo

pelearse

saltar a la cuerda

el muñeco

el patio de recreo

la cuerda

la muñeca

128 Guided Practice Activities ● Vocabulary Flash Cards 4A

Nombre _____ Hora _____

Fecha _____

AVSR 4A-1

A ver si recuerdas: Suffixes (p. 183)

• To say that something is *small* or *little* or to add a feeling of affection to a noun, use the suffix -ito (-a, -os, -as). This is called the diminutive. Generally, you drop the -o, -a, -os, or -as from the end of the noun and add the suffix.

perro → perrito   novela → novelita

A. Change these nouns to the diminutive. First, drop the underlined part of the noun. Then, add the appropriate suffix: -ito, -ita, -itos, -itas. Follow the model.

Modelo libro   librito

1. escuela   escuelita
2. hermanos   hermanitos
3. gato   gatito
4. abuelo   abuelito
5. zapatos   zapatitos
6. vaso   vasito
7. galletas   galletitas
8. regalo   regalito

• To add emphasis to an adjective (as if adding *really* in English), use the suffix -ísimo (-a, -os, -as). Remember the written accent over the first "i" of the suffix.

Mi amiga es divertida.   My friend is fun.
Mi amiga es divertidísima.   My friend is really fun.

B. Rewrite the descriptions of the people and things in these sentences, using the -ísimo form of the adjective. Follow the model.

Modelo Julia es muy inteligente.   Es inteligentísima

1. La fiesta fue muy buena.   Fue buenísima
2. Estas piñatas son muy lindas.   Son lindísimas
3. Los globos son muy preciosos.   Son preciosísimos
4. Mi mamá estuvo muy ocupada hoy.   Estuvo ocupadísima
5. Las fotos son muy graciosas.   Son graciosísimas

realidades.com
● Web Code: jdd-0401

A ver si recuerdas — 4A-1   127

Nombre _____ Hora _____

Capítulo 4A   Fecha _____   **Vocabulary Flash Cards, Sheet 3**

Copy the word or phrase in the space provided. Be sure to include the article for each noun.

obedecer	mentir	de vez en cuando
obedecer	mentir	de ___ vez ___ en ___ cuando
por lo general	permitir	ofrecer
por ___ lo ___ general	permitir	ofrecer
la verdad	de pequeño, de pequeña	todo el mundo
la ___ verdad	de ___ pequeño , de ___ pequeña	todo ___ el ___ mundo

130 Guided Practice Activities — Vocabulary Flash Cards 4A

Nombre _____ Hora _____

Capítulo 4A   Fecha _____   **Vocabulary Flash Cards, Sheet 2**

Write the Spanish vocabulary word below each picture. If there is a word or phrase, copy it in the space provided. Be sure to include the article for each noun.

el ___ pez	el ___ dinosaurio	la ___ guardería infantil
el ___ oso de ___ peluche	la ___ moneda	de ___ niño , de ___ niña
la ___ tortuga	los ___ bloques	el ___ vecino

Guided Practice Activities — Vocabulary Flash Cards 4A   **129**

Realidades ②

Nombre _____ Hora _____

Fecha _____ **Vocabulary Flash Cards, Sheet 5**

Capítulo 4A

These blank cards can be used to write and practice other Spanish vocabulary for the chapter.

Realidades ②

Nombre _____ Hora _____

Fecha _____ **Vocabulary Flash Cards, Sheet 4**

Capítulo 4A

Copy the word or phrase in the space provided. Be sure to include the article for each noun.

consentido, consentida

___consentido___ ,
___consentida___

desobediente

___desobediente___

generoso, generosa

___generoso___ ,
___generosa___

obediente

___obediente___

tímido, tímida

___tímido___ ,
___tímida___

travieso, traviesa

___travieso___ ,
___traviesa___

coleccionar

___coleccionar___

el mundo

___el___
___mundo___

portarse bien/mal

___portarse___
___bien/mal___

Sheet 2

Realidades 2

Nombre _____

Hora _____

Capítulo 4A

Fecha _____

Vocabulary Check, Sheet 2

Tear out this page. Write the Spanish words on the lines. Fold the paper along the dotted line so you can check your work.

blocks	*los bloques*
collection	*la colección*
rope	*la cuerda*
dinosaur	*el dinosaurio*
doll	*la muñeca*
action figure	*el muñeco*
teddy bear	*el oso de peluche*
electric train	*el tren eléctrico*
tricycle	*el triciclo*
fish	*el pez*
turtle	*la tortuga*
daycare center	*la guardería infantil*
playground	*el patio de recreo*
neighbor	*el vecino, la vecina*

Sheet 1

Realidades 2

Nombre _____

Hora _____

Capítulo 4A

Fecha _____

Vocabulary Check, Sheet 1

Tear out this page. Write the English words on the lines. Fold the paper along the dotted line so you can check your work.

los bloques	*blocks*
la colección	*collection*
la cuerda	*rope*
el dinosaurio	*dinosaur*
la muñeca	*doll*
el muñeco	*action figure*
el oso de peluche	*teddy bear*
el tren eléctrico	*electric train*
el triciclo	*tricycle*
el pez	*fish*
la tortuga	*turtle*
la guardería infantil	*daycare center*
el patio de recreo	*playground*
el vecino, la vecina	*neighbor*

Nombre _____ Hora _____

Fecha _____ **Vocabulary Check, Sheet 4**

Tear out this page. Write the Spanish words on the lines. Fold the paper along the dotted line to see the correct answers so you can check your work.

to collect	*coleccionar*
to bother	*molestar*
to fight	*pelearse*
to jump (rope)	*saltar (a la cuerda)*
to lie	*mentir*
to obey	*obedecer*
to permit, to allow	*permitir*
to behave well/badly	*portarse bien/mal*
as a child	*de niño, de niña*
once in a while	*de vez en cuando*

- Fold In ↓

To hear a complete list of the vocabulary for this chapter, go to www.realidades.com and type in the Web Code jdd-0489. Then click on Repaso del capítulo.

Nombre _____ Hora _____

Fecha _____ **Vocabulary Check, Sheet 3**

Tear out this page. Write the English words on the lines. Fold the paper along the dotted line to see the correct answers so you can check your work.

coleccionar	*to collect*
molestar	*to bother*
pelearse	*to fight*
saltar (a la cuerda)	*to jump (rope)*
mentir	*to lie*
obedecer	*to obey*
permitir	*to permit, to allow*
portarse bien/mal	*to behave well/badly*
de niño, de niña	*as a child*
de vez en cuando	*once in a while*

- Fold In ↓

Nombre _____ **Hora** _____

Capítulo 4A **Fecha** _____ **Guided Practice Activities 4A-2**

The imperfect tense: regular verbs (continued)

C. Write the correct endings for the -er and -ir verbs below. Follow the model.

Modelo Por lo general, yo obedec _ía_ a mis padres.

1. Mis primos me ofrec _ían_ sus bloques de vez en cuando.

2. A menudo mis tíos me permit _ían_ comer unas galletas.

3. Generalmente, mamá pon _ía_ la mesa.

4. Mis hermanos y yo hac _íamos_ la cama todos los días.

5. Tú viv _ías_ en la misma ciudad que yo.

D. Complete the sentences below to describe what people used to do. Use the drawings and the verbs in parentheses as clues. Follow the model.

Modelo   Mario _saltaba_ a la cuerda. (saltar)

1. Ellos _coleccionaban_ dinosaurios en la escuela primaria. (coleccionar)

2. Ellas _se_ _peleaban_ todos los días. (pelearse)

3. Nosotros _jugábamos_ al tenis los domingos. (jugar)

4. Tú _leías_ en la biblioteca los fines de semana. (leer)

Nombre _____ **Hora** _____

Capítulo 4A **Fecha** _____ **Guided Practice Activities 4A-1**

The imperfect tense: Regular verbs (p. 194)

- The imperfect tense is used to talk about actions that happened repeatedly in the past.

  Rafael caminaba y Ramiro corría en el parque.
  Rafael used to walk and Ramiro used to run in the park.

- Here are the regular forms of **-ar, -er,** and **-ir** verbs in the imperfect tense:

	jugar	hacer	vivir
yo	jugaba	hacía	vivía
tú	jugabas	hacías	vivías
usted/él/ella	jugaba	hacía	vivía
nosotros/nosotras	jugábamos	hacíamos	vivíamos
vosotros/vosotras	jugabais	hacíais	vivíais
ustedes/ellos/ellas	jugaban	hacían	vivían

- Note the accents on jugábamos and throughout the conjugations of the -er and -ir verbs.

- These expressions can cue you to use the imperfect: **generalmente, por lo general, a menudo, muchas veces, de vez en cuando, todos los días, nunca.**

A. Write the infinitive form of each conjugated verb. The first one is done for you.

1. jugaba _jugar_

2. molestaba _molestar_

3. coleccionaban _coleccionar_

4. obedecías _obedecer_

5. ofrecía _ofrecer_

6. permitían _permitir_

7. corríamos _correr_

8. vivíamos _vivir_

B. Fill in the blanks with the correct form of the **-ar** verbs in the imperfect tense. Follow the model.

Modelo   Tú habl _abas_ con mucha gente.

1. Alicia siempre molest _aba_ a su hermana.

2. Mis tíos nunca nos regal _aban_ nada a nosotros.

3. Pedro le d _aba_ agua al perro muchas veces.

4. Yo siempre me port _aba_ bien enfrente de mis padres.

5. A menudo nosotros jug _ábamos_ en el parque.

Capítulo 4A

Fecha _____ **Guided Practice Activities 4A-3**

The imperfect tense: irregular verbs (p. 196)

• There are only three irregular verbs in the imperfect tense: **ir**, **ser**, and **ver**. Here are their forms:

	ir	ser	ver
yo	iba	era	veía
tú	ibas	eras	veías
usted/él/ella	iba	era	veía
nosotros/nosotras	íbamos	éramos	veíamos
vosotros/vosotras	ibais	erais	veíais
ustedes/ellos/ellas	iban	eran	veían

• Note that only the **nosotros** forms of **ir** and **ser** carry accents.

• **Ver** uses the exact same endings as regular **-er** verbs, and is only irregular because of the added "e".

A. Choose the correct verb in parentheses to complete each sentence. Circle your choice. Use the chart above to help you. Follow the model.

Modelo Clara y Nubia (**eran**/ iban) mis amigas.

1. Por lo general, yo (era /**veía**) a mis primas.

2. Mis primos nunca (veían /**iban**) conmigo al mercado.

3. Mis hermanos y yo (**éramos**/ íbamos) muy traviesos.

4. ¿Tú (ibas /**veías**) muchas películas?

B. Complete the following sentences using the imperfect form of the verb in parentheses. Follow the model.

Modelo Nosotros (ir) _____**íbamos**_____ a la escuela todos los días.

1. ¡Mi mamá (ser) _____**era**_____ muy traviesa de niña!

2. Nosotros generalmente (ver) _____**veíamos**_____ la tele en casa.

3. De niña, yo (ir) _____**iba**_____ a la casa de mis tíos de vez en cuando.

4. La familia de mi mamá (ver) _____**veía**_____ a la abuela durante las vacaciones.

5. Juana y yo (ser) _____**éramos**_____ muy buenas amigas.

Capítulo 4A

Fecha _____ **Guided Practice Activities 4A-3a**

The imperfect tense: review

A. Below are two paragraphs about Christopher Columbus. As you read, fill in the blanks with the appropriate imperfect form of the verbs given. The first one has been done for you.

Cuando Cristóbal Colón _____*tenía*_____ (tener) diez años, le _____*gustaba*_____ (gustar) mucho navegar (to sail) con su papá. Cristóbal y sus amigos _____*imaginaban*_____ (imaginar) lugares distantes y exóticos que ellos _____*iban*_____ (ir) a visitar algún día. Sus padres siempre _____*decían*_____ (decir): "Es importante imaginar y descubrir (discover)". Cristóbal _____*pensaba*_____ (pensar) mucho y realmente _____*quería*_____ (querer) buscar un lugar nuevo.

Cuando _____*era*_____ (ser) mayor, él _____*hablaba*_____ (hablar) de vez en cuando con los reyes (kings, rulers) de España para pedirles dinero para sus exploraciones. Los reyes _____*decían*_____ (decir): "Cristóbal, tú _____*eras*_____ (ser) un buen explorador de niño con tu padre. Tú _____*veías*_____ (ver) muchos lugares nuevos. Es importante ahora descubrir una nueva ruta a la India". Cristóbal siempre _____*exploraba*_____ (explorar) y _____*veía*_____ (ver) muchos lugares nuevos, pero nunca encontró la ruta a la India.

Nombre _____ Hora _____

Fecha _____ **Guided Practice Activities 4A-4**

Indirect object pronouns (p. 199)

- An indirect object tells to *whom* or *for whom* something is done.
  Julio escribió una carta a Susana. *Julio wrote a letter to Susana.*
- Indirect object pronouns can replace an indirect object.
  Julio le escribió una carta. *Julio wrote her a letter.*
- Indirect object pronouns, especially **le** and **les**, can also be used with an indirect object.
  Julio le escribió una carta a Susana. *Julio wrote a letter to Susana (to her).*
- Here are the forms of the indirect object pronouns:

Singular	Plural
me (to/for) me	nos (to/for) us
te (to/for) you (familiar)	os (to/for) you (familiar)
le (to/for) him, her, you (formal)	les (to/for) them, you (formal)

A. Circle the indirect object pronoun in each sentence. Follow the model.

Modelo   Tú (le) escribías cartas a tu amigo boliviano Carlos.

1. Yo (le) pedía a mamá una muñeca.
2. Mi abuela (me) daba muchos besos.
3. Carlos y yo (te) ofrecíamos unos chocolates.
4. Claudia (nos) iba a comprar ropa.
5. Roberto (les) ofrecía el triciclo a sus hermanas.

B. Circle the appropriate indirect object pronoun in parentheses to complete each sentence. Then, underline the part of the sentence that indicates *to whom* the pronoun refers. The first one is done for you.

1. Generalmente mi abuela ((nos)/ me) compraba muchos juguetes a nosotros.
2. Mamá y yo siempre ((le)/ nos) dábamos tarjetas bonitas a la tía.
3. Yo ((te)/ le) ofrecía dulces a ti en la escuela primaria.
4. Tú siempre ((les)/ te) dabas osos de peluche a mis hermanas.
5. Mis padres no ((me)/ les) permitían a mí llevar gorra a la iglesia.

realidades.com
• Web Code: jdd-0406

Nombre _____ Hora _____

Fecha _____ **Guided Practice Activities 4A-4a**

Indirect object pronouns (continued)

C. Look at each of the following sentences. First, underline the indirect object noun. Then, in the space provided, put the indirect object pronoun that corresponds to the noun you underlined. Follow the model.

Modelo   Nuestros padres siempre ___nos___ decían la verdad a nosotros.

1. Por lo general, mis amigos ___me___ prestaban a mí sus juguetes.
2. Los abuelos de Alicia siempre ___le___ querían dar a ella buenas cosas.
3. La profesora ___les___ permitía a los estudiantes jugar en el patio de recreo.
4. Yo no ___te___ daba dinero a ti para ver las películas.
5. Tío Leo ___le___ compraba a mi hermano las vías (*tracks*) para su tren eléctrico.

- Indirect object pronouns can be placed before the verb or attached to the infinitive.
  Mi abuela nunca me quería dar dinero en mi cumpleaños.
  Mi abuela nunca quería darme dinero en mi cumpleaños.

D. Look at the sentences below and write a new sentence with the same meaning, placing the indirect object pronoun differently. Follow the model.

Modelo   Tía Lisa me quería llevar a la guardería infantil.
Tía Lisa quería llevarme a la guardería infantil

1. Yo no les podía mentir a mis padres.
Yo no podía mentirles a mis padres

2. Los tíos siempre nos tenían que decir que éramos niños traviesos.
Los tíos siempre tenían que decirnos que éramos niños traviesos

3. Mis primos malos siempre me querían molestar.
Mis primos malos siempre querían molestarme

4. A veces mis hermanos y yo no les queríamos obedecer a nuestros padres.
A veces mis hermanos y yo no queríamos obedecerles a nuestros padres

realidades.com
• Web Code: jdd-0406

Realidades 2

Capítulo 4A

Nombre _____

Fecha _____

Hora _____

Guided Practice Activities 4A-6

Presentación oral (p. 205)

Task: Describe what you were like when you were a small child and draw a series of pictures that illustrate your sentences.

A. Think about what you were like when you were a small child, what things you used to do, and what things you weren't allowed to do. Then, complete the following sentences.

1. Cuando era niño(a), era **Answers will vary.** _____ y _____

2. Yo jugaba con _____

3. Me gustaba jugar _____

4. Yo tenía que _____

5. Mis padres no me permitían _____

B. On a separate sheet of paper, make a drawing or cut out pictures from a magazine to illustrate each of your sentences from **part A**. Number your pictures 1 to 5.

C. Use your sentences from **part A** and your drawings from **part B** to prepare your presentation. You can practice your presentation with a partner. Make sure that:

- your sentences describe the pictures in order
- you use complete sentences
- you speak clearly so that you can be understood

D. Now, talk about what you were like when you were a child. Hold up your pictures in order during the presentation as you say your sentences to describe them. You can follow the model.

Cuando era niño(a), yo era obediente. Yo jugaba con mis amigos. Me gustaba jugar con mi triciclo. Yo tenía que portarme bien. Mis padres no me permitían saltar en la cama.

E. Your teacher will probably grade you on the following:

- the amount of information you communicate
- how easy it is to understand you
- the quality of visuals

Realidades 2

Capítulo 4A

Nombre _____

Fecha _____

Hora _____

Guided Practice Activities 4A-5

Lectura: El grillo y el jaguar (pp. 202–203)

> Making predictions is a useful strategy to help prepare you for a reading.

A. The reading in your textbook is a fable from Mexico. Look at the title of the reading and the pictures. Then, using the fables you know as guides, like *Aesop's Fables*, list three things that you think might happen in this fable.

1. **Answers will vary.** _____

2. _____

3. _____

B. In the following paragraph from the reading, the jaguar challenges the cricket to a race. Read the paragraph and then circle the option below that describes what you think will happen. **Answers will vary.**

—*Vamos a hacer una carrera (race) hasta aquella roca enorme que está por donde empiezan las montañas. Si llegas primero, te perdono todo y puedes seguir cantando, pero si llego primero yo, te prohíbo cantar.*

1. The cricket wins the race and can continue singing.
2. The jaguar wins the race and the cricket can't sing.

C. After you have read *El grillo y el jaguar*, write the letter of the answer that best completes each sentence.

1. Los personajes principales (*main characters*) de esta fábula son: **a**
   a. el grillo y el jaguar
   b. el jaguar y el jardín
   c. el grillo y el lago

2. El problema de esta fábula es: **c**
   a. El grillo quiere correr tan rápidamente como el jaguar.
   b. El jaguar quiere cantar.
   c. Al jaguar no le gusta la canción del grillo.

3. La moraleja (*moral*) de esta fábula es: **c**
   a. El grillo gana porque corre más rápidamente.
   b. El grillo gana porque el jaguar es simpático.
   c. El grillo gana porque es más inteligente.

realidades.com
• Web Code: jdd-0407

Nombre _____ Hora _____

Fecha _____

VIDEO

Antes de ver el video

Actividad 1

What were you like when you were younger? Think of several words that describe you. Then, use them in sentences about yourself. One has been done for you.

Palabras descriptivas	Oración sobre mí
generoso(a)	Era muy generoso(a) con mis hermanos pequeños.
Answers will vary.	Era
	Era
	Era

¿Comprendes?

Actividad 2

Do you remember the conversations from the video about Ana as a little girl? Fill in the blanks below with the words that describe Ana in each of the scenes shown.

1. ¿Cómo era Ana de niña?
Era muy _____tímida_____.

2. ¿Qué dice Ignacio de Ana?
Ignacio dice que era _____consentida_____.

3. Según su mamá, ¿Ana era _____desobediente_____ de niña?
No, por lo general era muy _____obediente_____ y muy bien _____educada_____.

4. ¿Ana era siempre bien educada de niña?
No, a veces era un poquito _____traviesa_____.

Actividad 3

All of the following sentences contain incorrect information. Rewrite each sentence to match what you learned in the video.

VIDEO

1. Ana, Elena e Ignacio trabajan en un proyecto para la clase de matemáticas.

   Ana y Elena trabajan en un proyecto para la clase de ciencias sociales.

2. De niña, Ana no tenía un juguete favorito.

   El oso de peluche era el juguete favorito de Ana.

3. Ana solamente tenía un animal de peluche, su oso.

   Ana tenía una colección de animales de peluches.

4. De niña, Ana siempre se levantaba tarde.

   De niña, Ana siempre se levantaba temprano.

5. Elena cree que Ignacio siempre obedecía a sus padres y que siempre decía la verdad.

   Elena cree que Ignacio no obedecía a sus padres.

Y, ¿qué más?

Actividad 4

Draw a family tree of your immediate family. Next to each person, write a word to describe him or her. Then, write three sentences about your favorite relatives.

VIDEO

Answers will vary.

Actividad 7

Listen as Patricia listens to her favorite popular radio show "**Yo no lo sabía**" to find out things that she didn't know about some of her favorite movie and TV personalities. Match what you hear the DJ say about her favorite celebrities to the pictures below. Write the number of each piece of gossip underneath the picture it refers to. You will hear each piece of gossip twice.

8   5   3

2   7   1

4   6

Actividad 5

Do you remember your favorite childhood toy? Listen as each of the following people describes a favorite childhood toy. In the grid below, write what each person's favorite toy was and who gave the toy to him or her. You will hear each set of statements twice.

	Juguete	Persona que le dio el juguete
Rogelio	triciclo	sus abuelos
Marta	muñeca	su tía
Andrés	tren eléctrico	sus padres
Lorena	oso de peluche	su hermano
Humberto	los bloques	su mamá

Actividad 6

Ricardo, Susana, Marcos, and Julia haven't seen their preschool teacher, Srta. Rosi, since they were four years old. Now that they are teenagers, Srta. Rosi can't believe how they've grown. Listen as Srta. Rosi reminisces about their childhood, and write the name of each child under the corresponding picture. You will hear each statement twice.

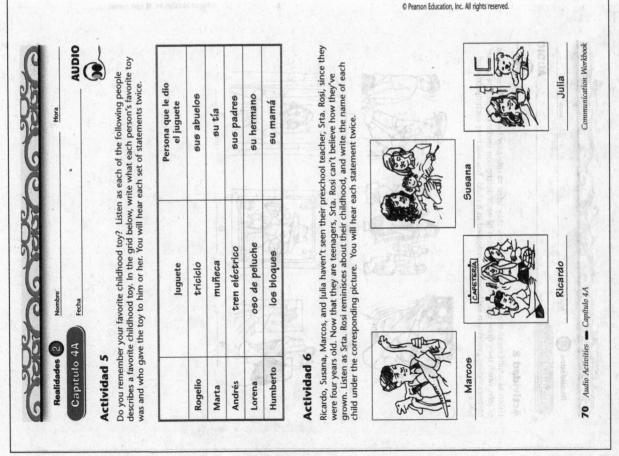

Marcos   Ricardo   Susana   Julia

Realidades 2
Capítulo 4A
Nombre
Hora
Fecha
AUDIO

Actividad 9

There are no gift tags on the Christmas gifts that the Rodríguez family received from their friend Gonzalo. Sr. Rodríguez has to call him on the phone to find out which gift goes to whom. Complete the sentences below to describe what Gonzalo gave to each person. For example, you might write, **"Gonzalo le dio unos aretes a la abuela."** You will hear this conversation twice.

1. Gonzalo __les__ dio unos boletos de avión a __los abuelos__
2. Gonzalo __le__ dio su colección de tarjetas de béisbol a __Luis__
3. Gonzalo __le__ dio dinero en efectivo a __Marta (la hija)__
4. Gonzalo __le__ dio unos zapatos de golf a __Cristina (la esposa)__
5. Gonzalo __le__ dio una colección de monedas al __señor Rodríguez__

Realidades 2
Capítulo 4A
Nombre
Hora
Fecha
AUDIO

Actividad 8

Listen as adults recall their childhood and how they used to role-play having different kinds of jobs when they grew up. Write the number of each description under the picture of the corresponding profession each person imagined as a child. You will hear each description twice.

1   2   3

4   5   6

Realidades 2
Nombre
Hora
Capítulo 4A
Fecha
WRITING

Actividad 11

You are at your best friend's family reunion, and all of the relatives are reminiscing about their childhood. Look at the pictures and tell what everyone did as children. Follow the model.

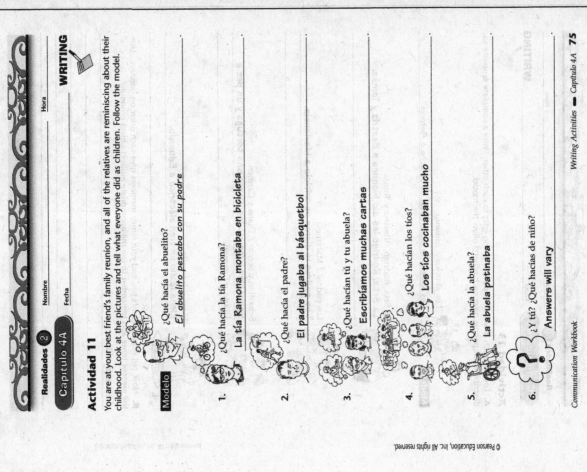

Modelo ¿Qué hacía el abuelito?
El abuelito pescaba con su padre

1. ¿Qué hacía la tía Ramona?
La tía Ramona montaba en bicicleta

2. ¿Qué hacía el padre?
El padre jugaba al básquetbol

3. ¿Qué hacían tú y tu abuela?
Escribíamos muchas cartas

4. ¿Qué hacían los tíos?
Los tíos cocinaban mucho

5. ¿Qué hacía la abuela?
La abuela patinaba

6. ¿Y tú? ¿Qué hacías de niño?
Answers will vary

Realidades 2
Nombre
Hora
Capítulo 4A
Fecha
WRITING

Actividad 10

Look at the scenes of children playing at a day care center. Then, write a sentence to tell what each child is doing.

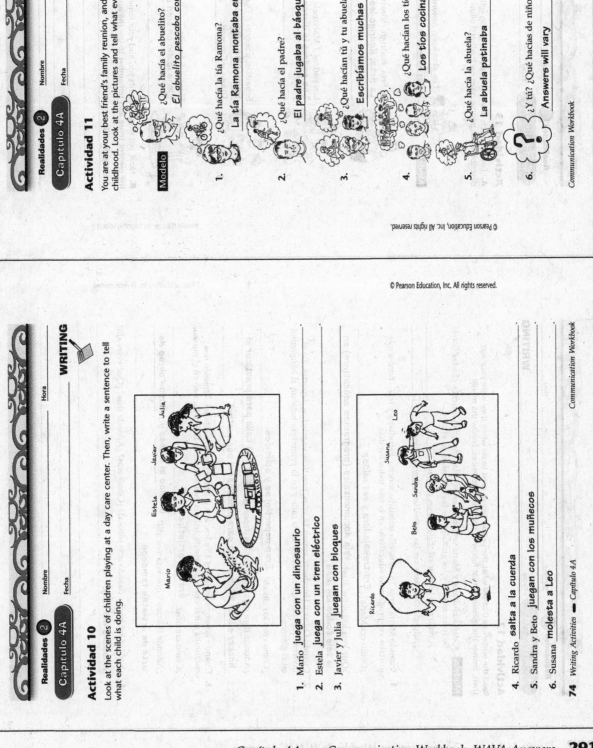

1. Mario juega con un dinosaurio

2. Estela juega con un tren eléctrico

3. Javier y Julia juegan con bloques

4. Ricardo salta a la cuerda

5. Sandra y Beto juegan con los muñecos

6. Susana molesta a Leo

Nombre _____ Hora _____

Fecha _____

WRITING

Actividad 12

Read the sentences that tell what the people below used to do when they were your age. Then, answer the questions that follow in complete sentences. Follow the model.

Modelo: Cuando Juliana y María tenían 14 años, ellas contaban muchos chistes (jokes). Se reían mucho y les gustaba ver las comedias en el cine.
¿Cómo eran las chicas? *Ellas eran cómicas*
¿Adónde iban para ver las comedias? *Iban al cine*

1. Cuando Marta tenía 16 años, ella trabajaba mucho. Estudiaba y leía. También le gustaba ver programas educativos en la tele todos los días.
¿Cómo era Marta? *Era trabajadora y estudiosa*
¿Qué veía todos los días? *Veía documentales (programas educativos) en la tele todos los días*

2. Cuando Óscar y Humberto tenían 14 años, practicaban muchos deportes. En el invierno practicaban el hockey en la calle y en la primavera jugaban al básquetbol en el gimnasio.
¿Cómo eran los chicos? *Eran deportistas y atléticos*
¿Adónde iban para practicar sus deportes? *Iban a la calle para practicar el hockey e iban al gimnasio para practicar el básquetbol*

3. Cuando nosotros teníamos 15 años, nos gustaba pintar y dibujar. También nos encantaba mirar obras de arte de artistas famosos como Dalí y Picasso en el museo.
¿Cómo éramos? *Éramos artísticos*
¿Adónde íbamos y qué veíamos allí? *Íbamos al museo y veíamos obras de arte de artistas famosos*

4. ¿Y tú? ¿Qué hacías cuando eras niño(a)? ¿Cómo eras? ¿Adónde ibas? ¿Qué veías allí?
Answers will vary.

Nombre _____ Hora _____

Fecha _____

WRITING

Actividad 13

A. Look at each drawing of people giving gifts to each other. Write a complete sentence to describe what people gave each other. Follow the model.

Modelo: Los abuelos / Antonio
Los abuelos le dieron osos de peluche a Antonio.

1. La Srta. Rodrigo / Beatriz y Tomás
La Srta. Rodrigo les dio bloques a Beatriz y Tomás.

2. Los padres / Marianela
Los padres le dieron un triciclo a Marianela.

3. Sebastián y Sergio / Diana y Carmen
Sebastián y Sergio les dieron una tortuga y un pez a Diana y Carmen.

4. Elena / Eduardo
Elena le dio un tren eléctrico a Eduardo.

B. Now, tell what presents you and your family members give each other on holidays. Use the present tense and remember to use the appropriate indirect object pronouns.
Answers will vary.

Test Preparation Answers

Reading Skills
p. 238 2. **A**
p. 239 2. **B**

**Integrated Performance
  Assessment**
p. 240
Answers will vary.

School-to-Home Connection

Dear Parent or Guardian,

The theme of our current unit is *Recuerdos del pasado* (Memories). This chapter is called *Celebrando los días festivos* (Celebrating holidays).

Upon completion of this chapter students will be able to:

- describe holiday celebrations
- talk about family and relatives
- describe people, places, and situations in the past
- talk about how people interact
- understand cultural perspectives on holidays and special events

Students will also explore:

- prefixes

Our textbook, *Realidades,* helps with the development of reading, writing, and speaking skills through the use of strategies, process speaking, and process writing. In this chapter, students will:

- read about *Los Reyes Magos* (the gift-giving occasion in January in many countries)
- write an e-mail describing an event from childhood

To reinforce and enhance learning, students can access a wide range of online resources on **realidades.com**, the personalized learning management system that accompanies the print and online Student Edition. Resources include the eText, textbook and workbook activities, audio files, videos, animations, songs, self-study tools, interactive maps, voice recording (RealTalk!), assessments, and other digital resources. Many learning tools can be accessed through the student Home Page on **realidades.com**. Other activities, specifically those that require grading, are assigned by the teacher and linked on the student Home Page within the calendar or the Assignments tab.

You will find specifications and guidelines for accessing **realidades.com** on home computers and mobile devices on MyPearsonTraining.com under the SuccessNet Plus tab.

For: Tips to Parents
Visit: www.realidades.com
Web Code: jce-0010

Check it out! At the end of the chapter, have your child describe how he or she customarily says hello and good-bye to his or her friends. Then have your child tell you what his or her favorite special event is.

Sincerely,

Realidades 2
Capítulo 4B
Videocultura Script

El Día de los Muertos

Spanish version:

Hace unos 3,000 años, los aztecas participaban en un ritual muy especial. Ellos usaban calaveras para simbolizar el regreso de los muertos a la vida.

Los indígenas creían que la muerte era una continuación de la vida.

En la modernidad, este ritual se llama el Día de los Muertos.

Hoy día es una combinación del antiguo ritual azteca con las prácticas de la religión católica.

Las familias se reúnen para recordar a familiares y amigos que han muerto. Ellos recuerdan su vida con alegría.

Un altar es construido en memoria a los muertos. Es decorado con velas y ornamentos y se exhibe la fotografía de la persona difunta.

Honrar la memoria de los muertos es una hermosa costumbre. Los mexicanos lo hacen de una forma muy especial durante la celebración del Día de los Muertos.

English version:

The Day of the Dead, or *El Día de los Muertos*, is celebrated in Mexico and countries in Latin America. It is a tradition that began 3,000 years ago.

Pre-Columbian civilizations displayed skulls as trophies and used them in rituals to symbolize death and rebirth.

The indigenous cultures believed that death was not the end of life, but rather a continuation of it.

On November first and second, people visit the graves of their departed relatives.

The modern celebration combines rituals from both Aztec and Catholic traditions.

At the cemetery, relatives usually clean and decorate the gravesite. They often build altars containing the favorite food and drinks of the departed as well as photographs and mementos. The graves are adorned with marigolds. These traditions are believed to encourage a visit by the soul of the departed.

The Day of the Dead celebrates the ancient belief that death is a continuation of life. On these two days in November, families remember and honor their departed loved ones.

Input Script

Presentation

Input Vocabulary 1: The day before class, ask for a volunteer to help you with the next day's presentation. Find a time to practice with the student the roles of mad scientist (you) and his or her creation: a cyborg robot who is uncannily human (the student). Use a clicker or other noisemaker to practice activating and deactivating the cyborg. Also, record the dialogues on p. 212 in a robot voice.

The day of the presentation, place the transparency showing greetings and leave-takings on the screen. Tell students that you are not really a Spanish teacher, but a scientific genius who has created the first cyborg robot who can pass as a human being without being detected. Use the clicker to activate the cyborg student. Gesture for the volunteer to stand up. Tell the class to say hello to your "invention." The cyborg will give an illogical response over and over in a very robot-like voice: *¡Hasta luego! ¡Hasta luego! ¡Hasta luego!* Deactivate the cyborg and explain that you will have to do a diagnostic test on him or her. Call out actions and have the cyborg do wrong ones: *¡Sonreír!* (the cyborg frowns) *¡Dar(se) la mano!* (the cyborg waves goodbye), and so forth. Deactivate the cyborg.

Input Dialogue 1: Explain that you will have to reprogram the cyborg. Take out a calculator and a large wrench and act as if you are programming the student. Reactivate the cyborg. Play the recording of the dialogue. The student will open and close his or her mouth as if the recording is coming from within. Stop the recording after each section and demonstrate the actions and point to them on the transparency. Then state the actions again and have the cyborg and the rest of the students act them out correctly.

Input Vocabulary 2 and Dialogue 2: Place the transparency showing celebrations on the screen. Tell students that you received a letter and these photos from your pen pal when you were first learning Spanish. Read the dialogue text and use the transparency, gestures, and pantomime to convey meaning. Next, distribute copies of the Vocabulary Clip Art and have students cut them into individual images. Then describe a fictional surprise party to celebrate a friend's birthday and wedding anniversary which share the date with Mexican Independence Day. Use the expressions from *A primera vista* in your description. In your story tell how things went disastrously wrong when someone accidently put fireworks instead of candles on the cake!

Comprehension Check

- Place the Clip Art images of actions showing good manners in a paper bag. Give pairs of volunteers one minute in which to draw each Clip Art image out of the bag and act it out for their classmates to guess.

- Describe fictional celebrations that were fun (*Mi hermano contaba chistes.*) and some that were not so fun (*Mis hermanas se pelearon.*), using the expressions from *A primera vista*. Have students tell you if the people at the parties *se divertían* or *no se divertían*.

Audio Script

Audio DVD, Capítulo 4B

Track 01: *A primera vista, Celebrando los días festivos,* **Student Book, p. 212**

Vocabulario y gramática en contexto

Lee en tu libro mientras escuchas la narración.

Recuerdos del pasado: Los buenos modales

MALE TEEN: Mis papás me enseñaron la importancia de los buenos modales. Es importante ser sociable y sonreír cuando se reúne con las personas.

Cuando saludas o te despides es costumbre siempre dar la mano.

Para saludar a los amigos puedes decir '¡Hola!,' '¿Qué tal?' o '¿Cómo estás?'

Cuando dos personas se conocen muy bien generalmente se besan para saludarse y despedirse.

Muchos hombres se abrazan cuando se saludan en la calle o cuando se despiden.

Debes saludar a los mayores con una expresión como 'Buenos días, señora,' o '¿Cómo está Ud.?'

Mi papá me dijo que una persona siempre debe saludar a todas las personas en una reunión o en una fiesta. Cuando sales, debes despedirte de cada persona también.

Vas a escuchar cada palabra o frase dos veces. Después de la primera vez hay una pausa para que puedas pronunciar la palabra o frase. Luego vas a escuchar de nuevo la palabra o frase.

sonreír	besarse
dar la mano	abrazar
darse la mano	abrazarse
besar	los mayores

Track 02: *A primera vista,* **Student Book, p. 213**

Vocabulario y gramática en contexto

Lee en tu libro mientras escuchas la narración.

Cómo celebrábamos los días festivos

MALE TEEN: El 10 de agosto fue el cumpleaños de mi papá. Celebramos con una fiesta de sorpresa. Cumplió cuarenta y seis años. Durante la fiesta, mi abuela habló de cuando él nació y ella empezó a llorar. Dijo que era un bebé grande y guapito. ¡Mi familia y yo le regalamos una cámara digital!

Mis abuelos celebraron su aniversario el 23 de octubre. Se casaron hace cincuenta años. Todos nuestros parientes, mis tíos y primos, y muchos amigos asistieron para felicitarlos. Todos cantamos: ¡Felicidades! Les regalamos un reloj antiguo muy bonito. Durante la fiesta los niños no se pelearon—todos se llevaban bien porque era un día muy especial.

Frecuentemente, durante los veranos, nosotros íbamos a un parque enorme donde hacíamos un picnic. Mientras los mayores charlaban, nosotros jugábamos. Mi tío, que es

muy cómico, siempre nos contaba chistes y todos nos reíamos mucho. Para días muy especiales, como el Día de la Independencia, había fuegos artificiales por la noche. Todas las personas alrededor del parque se divertían.

Vas a escuchar cada palabra o frase dos veces. Después de la primera vez hay una pausa para que puedas pronunciar la palabra o frase. Luego vas a escuchar de nuevo la palabra o frase.

los fuegos artificiales

Track 03: *A primera vista,* **Act. 1, Student Book, p. 213**

Los buenos modales

Trabaja con otro estudiante. Van a escuchar ocho frases sobre los buenos modales. Tienen que representar en pareja cada una de estas acciones. Vas a escuchar las frases dos veces.

1. Los jóvenes sonríen a sus amigos.
2. Los amigos se abrazan.
3. Los bebés lloran mucho.
4. Los compañeros se dan la mano.
5. Los niños besan a sus padres y a sus abuelos.
6. La joven se despide de su amigo.
7. Cuando escuchan los chistes, todos se ríen.
8. Siempre saludamos a los mayores.

Track 04: *A primera vista,* **Act. 2, Student Book, p. 213**

Vamos a celebrar

Vas a escuchar ocho frases. Escribe las letras *a, b* o *c* para indicar cuándo ocurrió cada actividad. Vas a escuchar las frases dos veces.

    a. durante la fiesta de cumpleaños
    b. durante la fiesta de aniversario
    c. durante la celebración del Día de la Independencia

1. Siempre veíamos los fuegos artificiales.
2. Le regalamos una cámara digital.
3. Mi tío contaba chistes y todos nos reíamos.
4. Celebramos el día cuando mis abuelos se casaron.
5. La celebración fue una sorpresa.
6. Hacíamos un picnic en un parque enorme.
7. Les regalamos un reloj antiguo.
8. Celebramos el día en que mi papá nació.

Track 05: *A primera vista, Videohistoria,* **Student Book, pp. 214–215**

La fiesta de San Pedro

¿Por qué es especial la fiesta de San Pedro?

Lee en tu libro mientras escuchas la *Videohistoria.*

See Student Book pages 214–215 for script.

Track 06: *Manos a la obra,* **Act. 5, Student Book, p. 216**

Escucha y escribe

Escucha las descripciones de diferentes personas que están presentes en la celebración de una boda. Escribe las frases. Después indica si las personas tienen buenos o malos modales. Vas a escuchar las frases dos veces.

1. Saluda y sonríe a las otras personas.
2. Se ríe del vestido de la madre del novio.
3. Se lleva mal con los parientes de los novios.
4. Felicita y abraza a los novios.
5. Les regala unos vasos bonitos a los novios.
6. Cuenta chistes sobre la madre de la novia.

Track 07: Audio Act. 5, Writing, Audio & Video Workbook, p. 81

Mrs. Lena is taking her third grade class to visit a group of senior citizens tomorrow. In order to make sure that all the children behave well at the Senior Center, she uses puppets named *Marco el malo* and *Bruno el bueno* to illustrate good and bad manners. Listen as she describes what each puppet does, and decide if the actions are most likely those of *Marco el malo* or *Bruno el bueno*. Put an X in the appropriate box in the grid below. You will hear this conversation twice.

TEACHER: Buenos días, niños. Mañana vamos al centro de ancianos. Esta mañana voy a hablar con Uds. de los buenos modales. Quiero presentarles a Marco. Él tiene muy malos modales… Marco, ¿quieres saludar a los niños?

PUPPET 1: ¡NO!

TEACHER: Y tú, Bruno. ¿Quieres saludar a los niños?

PUPPET 2: Sí, Señora Lena. Buenos días, niños.

TEACHER: Voy a describirles a Uds. como se portan Marco y Bruno. Tienen que decidir si describo a Marco o a Bruno. Recuerden… Marco tiene malos modales y Bruno tiene buenos modales. ¿Listos para el número uno?

ALL KIDS: ¡Sí!

1. Él no es sociable y nunca sonríe a la personas mayores.
2. Él siempre le da la mano a otra persona cuando la conoce por primera vez.
3. Mientras los mayores charlan, él quiere hablar con sus padres y no juega con los otros niños.
4. Él nunca besa a su abuela, ni para saludarla ni para despedirse.
5. Él levanta la mano cuando quiere hablar durante la clase de español.
6. Él no dice ni "mucho gusto" ni "encantado" cuando conoce a una persona por primera vez.
7. Cuando va al Café Latino, espera en la línea para comer.
8. Él siempre habla con la boca llena de comida durante la cena.

Vas a escuchar esta conversación otra vez.

Track 08: Audio Act. 6, Writing, Audio & Video Workbook, p. 81

Listen as four people talk about their favorite time to

spend with their families. Write the number of the description under the corresponding picture. You will hear each description twice.

1. Siempre celebramos el cumpleaños de mi abuelo con una fiesta de sorpresa. Nosotros sabemos que no es una sorpresa en realidad, pero a él le gusta la idea de una sorpresa. Este año cumple sesenta años.
2. Todos los años celebramos el cuatro de julio en un parque muy bonito. Mi familia hace un picnic con mucha comida. Los fuegos artificiales son lo mejor de la fiesta. Siempre hay muchos colores en el cielo. Es nuestro día festivo favorito.
3. Todos mis parientes celebraron el aniversario de mis abuelos hace tres semanas. Fue una fiesta sensacional. Ellos se casaron hace cincuenta años, pero todavía se quieren mucho. Mis abuelos estaban muy contentos durante su fiesta de aniversario. La celebramos en un restaurante mexicano muy bonito.
4. Me encantan las reuniones familiares. Este año, nuestra reunión familiar fue muy buena. Tuvimos mucha comida. Mis parientes trajeron pan, pollo, hamburguesas, ensaladas y muchas cosas más. Fue un picnic lleno de alegría. Mi abuelo hizo muchos chistes muy graciosos y nos reímos mucho.

Track 09: *Manos a la obra,* **Act. 13, Student Book, p. 222**

Escucha y escribe

En el cuadro *Tamalada*, la niña que está en la puerta recuerda el día, hace muchos años, cuando entró en la cocina con su padre y vio esta escena. ¿Recuerda ella la escena correctamente? Escucha las seis descripciones y escríbelas. Después, si la información es falsa, escribe la información correcta. Vas a escuchar cada descripción dos veces.

1. Entré en la cocina con mi papá.
2. Había tres personas alrededor de la mesa.
3. Todos ayudaban a hacer galletas.
4. Todos mis parientes tenían el pelo negro.
5. Las personas tenían diferentes trabajos.
6. Las paredes de la cocina eran amarillas.

Track 10: Audio Act. 7, Writing, Audio & Video Workbook, p. 82

When José Ignacio's mother returned from grocery shopping, she was shocked by some of the things her children and their friends were doing! Listen as she later tells José Ignacio's father what was going on when she got home. Based on what she says, fill in the grid below to tell how they were behaving. You will hear each set of statements twice.

1. Javier, no vas a creerlo. Había cinco chicos en la casa cuando regresé del supermercado. Cuando abrí la puerta del dormitorio de Miguelito, estaba dibujando en las paredes con muchos colores.
2. Cuando fui a la cocina, nuestra hija Lourdes y su amiga cocinaban la cena. ¡Qué sorpresa! Ellas no me oyeron cuando entré porque hablaban de sus novios y de sus problemas con ellos.

3. Luisa no hacía sus quehaceres cuando entré en su dormitorio. Grabada un disco compacto y no tenía idea de que yo estaba en casa.

4. Esta tarde cuando entré al dormitorio de José Ignacio, él tenía toda su ropa por todas partes. ¡Qué horrible! Era como una montaña enorme. No se veía ni el piso.

5. Javier, estoy muy contenta. Marcos tenía la música a un volumen normal cuando llegué a la casa. Él podía oírme cuando lo llamé.

6. ¡Este niño es horrible! Cuando llegué del supermercado, saltaba en el sofá mientras miraba la tele.

Track 11: Audio Act. 8, Writing, Audio & Video Workbook, p. 82

Some best friends like to do everything together, while others prefer to spend some time apart. Listen as some teenagers talk about whether they prefer to do certain things separately or together. Then put an X in the appropriate box in the grid. You will hear each set of statements twice.

1. **TEEN MALE 1:** Mi mejor amigo y yo somos buenos estudiantes y estudiamos mucho. Nos respetamos mucho. Él sabe más de matemáticas y yo entiendo mejor la historia. Siempre nos ayudamos con la tarea de estas clases.

2. **TEEN FEMALE 1:** Kiki es mi amiga de Costa Rica. Yo prefiero charlar por computadora. Pero ella es diferente. No tiene computadora. Entonces no podemos ni escribirnos ni hablarnos al mismo tiempo porque tampoco tiene teléfono.

3. **TEEN MALE 2:** Armando y yo nos reunimos en el cine todas las semanas, pero vemos películas diferentes. Nos saludamos y vamos a nuestra película preferida. Yo prefiero las películas de ciencia ficción y él prefiere las de horror.

4. **TEEN FEMALE 2:** Mi mejor amiga Margarita y yo nos divertimos mucho cuando salimos. Siempre la llamo cuando quiero ir al cine o de compras.

5. **TEEN FEMALE 3:** María, mi mejor amiga, es un poco exagerada. No vamos a restaurantes porque nunca estamos de acuerdo en qué tipo de comida queremos comer. Creo que es mejor despedirnos cuando tenemos hambre.

6. **TEEN MALE 3:** Jorge y yo siempre nos reunimos para ir a todos los partidos de fútbol de Las Chivas Rayadas. Es nuestro equipo favorito. Nos pintamos las caras de rojo y blanco para que la gente vea que somos de las Chivas. ¡Arriba, Chivas!

7. **TEEN FEMALE 4:** Rosa y yo vamos al lago a nadar todos los fines de semana. Rosa es mi mejor amiga. Nos divertimos mucho en el lago porque nos gusta hacer la misma cosa.

Track 12: Audio Act. 9, Writing, Audio & Video Workbook, p. 83

Listen as parents tell their children about their childhood memories of family celebrations and traditions. As you listen, match each conversation to the pictures below by writing the number of the conversation under the appropriate picture. You will hear each conversation twice.

1. **ADULT FEMALE 1:** Recuerdo bien que mi madre, tu abuelita, preparaba un pan de muertos para el Día de los Muertos. Cada año, el 2 de noviembre, visitábamos el cementerio para recordar a los parientes muertos.

2. **ADULT MALE 1:** De pequeño, mi familia siempre iba al País Vasco para celebrar la fiesta de San Pedro. Había un gran desfile con mucha gente bailando y tocando instrumentos como el *txistu* y el *tamboril*. Luego comíamos paella y salchichas vascas.

3. **ADULT FEMALE 2:** Mi tía siempre me contaba de una fiesta única que se llamaba la Tamborrada. Se celebraba en San Sebastián, una ciudad del País Vasco, el 20 de enero. Era un desfile de hombres vestidos de cocineros que tocaban el tambor mientras caminaban de noche por las calles. Una cosa muy graciosa, pero una verdadera noche festiva.

4. **ADULT MALE 2:** Todos los años mis padres y yo íbamos a San José para celebrar el Día de la Raza, o, como muchos lo llamaban, el Día de las Culturas. Había un gran desfile donde caminaba mucha gente vestida de los colores de su país de origen. Por ejemplo, el grupo de los Estados Unidos llevaba blanco, rojo y azul.

5. **ADULT FEMALE 3:** Un año tuve la oportunidad de visitar Sevilla durante la Semana Santa. Cada año había un desfile, que llaman una *procesión*, que terminaba en la catedral. En la procesión había estatuas enormes, que llaman *imágenes*, de varias iglesias de la ciudad.

Track 13: *Repaso del capítulo*, Student Book, p. 234

Vocabulario y gramática

Escucha las palabras y expresiones que has aprendido en este capítulo.

See Student Book page 234 for vocabulary list.

Track 14: *Preparación para el examen*, Student Book, p. 235

Escuchar

Practice task

To celebrate "Grandparents' Day," your teacher invited Spanish speakers from the community to talk about their favorite childhood memories. Listen as one of them describes one of their favorite family celebrations. See if you understand; a) the reason for the gathering; b) who was there; c) what people used to do at the celebration.

OLDER ADULT FEMALE: Buenos días. Me encanta hablar con los jóvenes. Recuerdo bien los domingos con mi familia. Cada domingo nos reuníamos en la casa de nuestra abuela para comer. Cuando los mayores hablaban, los niños jugaban con el perro y el gato.

Video Script

A primera vista: *La fiesta de San Pedro*

IGNACIO: A ver, tengo que preparar todo para mañana. Los vaqueros, la camiseta… y la ropa típica, por supuesto: una camisa blanca, y un pañuelo rojo también. Ah, y un paraguas… Siempre llueve, pero no importa.

JAVIER: Pero, Ignacio, ¿adónde vas con todo esto?

IGNACIO: Pues, mañana por la mañana voy a ir a Alsasua, el pueblo de mi madre. Ella nació allí. Este fin de semana se celebra la Fiesta de San Pedro.

JAVIER: ¿Vas a pasar el fin de semana en un pueblo?

IGNACIO: Pues, claro. Esta fiesta se celebra sólo una vez al año, el 29 de junio. Va a reunirse mucha gente y todo va a ser muy divertido.

JAVIER: ¿Y tú cómo lo sabes?

IGNACIO: Pues, porque de niño, mi familia y yo íbamos todos los veranos allí.

JAVIER: ¿Ah sí…?

IGNACIO: Sí, mira, lo recuerdo todo muy bien. La fiesta comenzaba por la mañana, con un desfile. Toda la familia se reunía allí.

IGNACIO's V.O.: Había bailes y músicos, que tocaban instrumentos típicos y antiguos.

IGNACIO: Me gustaba mucho la música. Es un tipo de música típica del lugar. Y los instrumentos musicales que tocan son tradicionales. Mira. Éste es el *txistu*, y éste, el *tamboril*.

JAVIER: ¿El qué?

IGNACIO: Sí, mira. Te, equis, i, ese, te, u. *Txistu*. Es una palabra vasca.

JAVIER: ¿Lo sabes tocar?

IGNACIO: Pues, un poco. Mi abuelo me enseñó cuando yo era pequeño.

JAVIER: Bueno, mejor no. ¿Y después? ¿Qué se hacía después?

IGNACIO: Pues, generalmente, íbamos a la iglesia.

JAVIER: ¿A la iglesia?

IGNACIO: Sí, es una tradición. Y la iglesia es muy bonita.

IGNACIO's V.O.: Generalmente hablan en español y en vasco.

JAVIER: Y tú, ¿hablas vasco?

IGNACIO: No, la verdad, no. Mis abuelos hablaban vasco, pero yo, no.

JAVIER: Oye, ¿y la comida? ¿Había comida especial?

IGNACIO: Ah sí, por supuesto. Mientras los jóvenes bailaban, los mayores preparaban la comida. ¡Y qué comida tan deliciosa!…

JAVIER's V.O.: A ver, ¿qué comían?

IGNACIO: Pues mira, paella y algo típico de allí, un tipo de salchicha que se llama *txistorra*. Todos comíamos muchísimo.

JAVIER: ¿Es otra palabra vasca?

IGNACIO: Sí, *txistorra*.

JAVIER: Oye, pues, ya tengo hambre.

IGNACIO: Después de comer, la gente charlaba, contaba chistes y se reía.

JAVIER: ¿Y los jóvenes?

IGNACIO: Los jóvenes seguían bailando.

JAVIER: Oye, Ignacio, tienes razón. Parece que va a ser muy divertido. ¿Puedo ir contigo?

IGNACIO: Está bien. Puedes venir aquí mañana, a las siete en punto, y luego nos vamos a la estación de tren.

JAVIER: ¡Vale! ¡Hasta mañana!

JAVIER: Aquí estoy. ¡Cómo llueve!

IGNACIO: Perfecto,… pero ahora tenemos que comprarte una boina.

GramActiva Videos
Reciprocal actions

FORTUNE TELLER: Ahh, you're back. Wait! Don't say anything, I can sense what you're here for. You're here to remember the reflexive pronouns *se, nos,* and *os.* Hold on! I'm getting more. You also want to learn about reciprocal actions.

BOY: What's reciprocal actions?

FORTUNE TELLER: Wait, I'm getting something. Let's help each other.

KID ON COMPUTER: *Nos escribimos*

FORTUNE TELLER: A-ha! So that's what it means! What else can you tell us?

V.O.: In English you could say, "They talk to each other for hours." This is a reciprocal action. The reciprocal action is "talk to each other." In Spanish you would say, *Ellos se hablan por horas y horas.*

HOST: Now let's use the reciprocal action with *nos* in a sentence. *Por lo general nos saludamos con un abrazo. También nos damos la mano.*

V.O.: *Los novios se abrazan y se besan.*

FORTUNE TELLER: You will remember what you have just learned. I see it now. Your future is bright with reciprocal actions. But first! You must take the challenge! *¡Nos vemos!*

Quiz

V.O.: Complete the sentences with the correct reciprocal pronoun.

Los amigos _____ saludan en la escuela.
Los amigos se saludan en la escuela.

Marta y yo _____ escribimos por correo electrónico todos los días.
Marta y yo nos escribimos por correo electrónico todos los días.

The imperfect tense: Describing a situation

HOST: Let's do a quick review of how to use the imperfect tense to say what someone used to do.

MAN: *Cuando era niño, siempre cantaba.*
La cucaracha, la cucaracha,
ya no quiere caminar,
porque no tiene, porque le falta
dinero para gastar.

HOST: The imperfect tense is also used to describe people, places and situations in the past.

V.O.: *La casa de mis abuelos era grande. Tenía cinco dormitorios.*

HOST: The imperfect tense is also used to talk about a past action when no beginning or end is specified.

V.O.: In Spanish if you want to say "there was" or "there were" you say *había.*
Había una tortuga en mi sopa.
Había dos tortugas en mi sopa.

EXCLAMATION MAN: You want more situations? You got it!

HOST: You often use both the preterite and the imperfect together to describe a situation that was going on when something else happened. In this case the situation is described using the imperfect tense, and what happened is in the preterite tense.
Here's a good way to visualize it.
"I was walking along when a teddy bear fell from the sky." How cute.
The situation is interrupted by an event.
The situation is in the imperfect.
The event is in the preterite.

KID V.O.: Give me my teddy back!

V.O.: *Hacía sol cuando llegamos a la piscina. Hacía sol* was the situation and *cuando llegamos a la piscina* was the event.

HOST: Now let's test your knowledge of how to say things about the past.

Quiz

V.O.: Fill in the the correct form of the imperfect.
(ser) La anciana _____ muy simpática.
La anciana era muy simpática.
(estar) Mis abuelos _____ muy felices en su aniversario.
Mis abuelos estaban muy felices en su aniversario.
And now, complete this sentence using the preterite and imperfect form of the verb as needed.
(comer/llegar) Mis parientes _____ cuando nosotros _____.
Mis parientes comían cuando nosotros llegamos.
(mirar/llamar) Yo _____ la tele cuando _____ María.
Miraba la tele cuando llamó María.

Videomisterio: *En busca de la verdad*, Episodio 4

ROBERTO'S V.O.: Al día siguiente, mi hermana Daniela y yo fuimos a recoger a Linda a su hotel. Íbamos a ir a San Miguel de Allende, a visitar a nuestra abuela Nela.

LINDA: Muchas gracias por invitarme a ir con ustedes.

ROBERTO: ¿Cómo se llamaba tu abuelo?
LINDA: Freddie.
DANIELA: Federico en español, ¿no?
LINDA: Sí, Federico Toledo. ¿Por qué?
ROBERTO: No sé… sólo curiosidad.
ROBERTO: ¿Bueno? Es Julio. Nos está siguiendo como un detective… Sí, hombre, aquí está… Quiere hablar contigo.
JULIO: Linda, ¿qué tal? Sé que tienes planes para la comida hoy, ¿no?
LINDA: Sí, con la abuela de Roberto…
JULIO: ¿Quieres comer mañana conmigo? Podemos vernos en el hotel.
LINDA: ¿El hotel? No sé… quizás. Mira, ¿por qué no me llamas mañana por la mañana?
JULIO: De acuerdo. Hasta mañana.

ROBERTO'S V.O.: Por fin llegamos a la casa de la abuela. Los tres estábamos muy contentos de estar allí.

ABUELA: Hola, bienvenidos.
ROBERTO: Abuela, te presento a Linda… Linda Toledo. Linda, nuestra abuela Nela.
ABUELA: Ah sí, de San Antonio. Mucho gusto en conocerte. Pero pasen, por favor.
LINDA: Mucho gusto, Señora.
ABUELA: Y aquí las fotos de la familia.
DANIELA: Aquí estamos con la abuela.
LINDA: Y… ¿su esposo?
LINDA'S V.O.: Qué extraño. ¿Por qué no había ninguna foto del abuelo de Roberto y Daniela?

ABUELA: Cuando mi esposo y yo llegamos aquí, San Miguel era un pueblo muy pequeño y muy lindo.
ROBERTO: Todavía es muy bonito, ¿no te parece?
LINDA: Sí.
DANIELA: Abuelita, este mole te salió riquísimo.
ROBERTO: Linda, ¿qué te parecen las quesadillas?
LINDA: Deliciosas.
ABUELA: El secreto está en las tortillas…
DANIELA: ¡Y en la salsa!
ABUELA: Y de postre tenemos el pastel de Berta y una gelatina que me ayudó a preparar mi vecina Olga…

ROBERTO: Abuela, el abuelo de Linda también se llamaba Federico… Federico Toledo. ¿Qué coincidencia, no? ¿Será posible? ¿Federico Toledo y Federico Toledo?

ABUELA: No te preocupes, hijo. Es… es imposible.

ROBERTO: ¿No tienes alguna foto del abuelo?

ABUELA: Sí… tanto tiempo, tanto tiempo…

ABUELA: Mira, éste es tu abuelo.

ABUELA's V. O.: Eran tiempos difíciles. Federico, tu abuelo, salió hacia el norte, en busca de oportunidades.

FEDERICO: Nela, cuídate mucho. Aquí tienes todo el dinero que tengo. Eres lo más importante para mí. Quédate con tu familia; yo volveré lo más pronto posible.

NELA: Querido, no tardes mucho. Tú sabes, nuestro bebé…

ROBERTO: "Federico Zúñiga y Chato Montesinos…" ¿Federico Zúñiga? No entiendo…

ABUELA: Así se llamaba tu abuelo. Cuando se fue con Chato y no volvió, me quedé con mi apellido de soltera, el de mi padre. Por eso nos llamamos Toledo.

ROBERTO: Y este Chato Montesinos, ¿quién es?

ABUELA: Sólo sé que era un amigo de Federico. Creo que era de Dolores Hidalgo o vivía allí.

ROBERTO: Dolores Hidalgo…

ROBERTO's V.O.: Ya tenía mi primera pista. Dolores Hidalgo y Chato Montesinos.

FEDERICO: Nela, querida Nela… ¿Cómo estás?

ABUELA: ¡¡¡Federico!!! Pero, ¿dónde estás?

FEDERICO: Nela… Nela… te puedo explicar todo…

OLGA: Nela, ¿estás ocupada? ¿Quieres tomar un café?

ABUELA: Sí, Olga…

Realidades 2

Capítulo 4B

Nombre _____

Fecha _____

Communicative Pair Activity **4B-1**

Estudiante **A**

Imagine that you are asking a friend questions about what his or her birthday parties were like as a child. Ask your partner the following questions. Write the answers in the spaces provided. Example: *Mis padres me felicitaban con regalos en mi cumpleaños.*

1. ¿Había mucha gente en la fiesta de cumpleaños? _____

_____

2. ¿Qué hacía tu mamá? _____

3. ¿Qué hacías tú? _____

4. ¿Qué hacían tus amigos? _____

5. ¿Qué hacía tu papá? _____

6. ¿Qué hacían los mayores? _____

Imagine that you are telling your friend about what you, your family, and your friends used to do at picnics as a child. Answer your partner's questions about your childhood following the cues below. Then write the full answer on the space provided. Follow this model:

Mis padres/contarme chistes

Cuando era pequeño(a), mis padres me contaban chistes.

1. Mi familia y yo/hacer un picnic al lado de un lago

_____

2. Mis amigos/saludarse a mí

_____

3. Yo/divertirse con mis amigos

_____

4. Mis parientes/reunirse con nosotros

_____

5. Mis abuelos/charlar al lado del lago

_____

6. Nosotros/despedirse al final del día

_____

Realidades 2

Capítulo 4B

Nombre _____

Fecha _____

Communicative Pair Activity **4B-1**

Estudiante **B**

Imagine that you are telling your friend about what your birthday parties were like as a child. Answer your partner's questions about your childhood following the cues below. Then write the full answer on the space provided. Follow this model:

Mis padres/felicitarme

Cuando era pequeño(a), mis padres siempre me felicitaban el día de mi cumpleaños.

1. Había/mucha gente

_____

2. Mi mamá/charlar con mis amigos

_____

3. Yo/divertirse con mis amigos

_____

4. Mis amigos/regalar muchas cosas

_____

5. Mi papá/sonreír

_____

6. Los mayores/contar chistes

_____

Imagine that you are asking a friend questions about what he or she used to do at picnics as a child. Ask your partner the following questions. Write the answers in the spaces provided. Example: *Cuando era pequeño(a), veíamos un desfile antes del picnic.*

1. ¿Dónde iban a hacer un picnic tu familia y tú? _____

2. ¿Qué hacían tus amigos? _____

3. ¿Qué hacías tú? _____

4. ¿Qué hacían tus parientes? _____

5. ¿Qué hacían tus abuelos? _____

6. ¿Qué hacían ustedes al final del día? _____

Realidades 2

Nombre _____

Capítulo 4B

Fecha _____

Communicative Pair Activity **4B-2**

Estudiante **A**

Read aloud the story below about Marta's surprise birthday party to your partner. Read it once for general comprehension. Then repeat the key words or phrases up to three times if needed. Read the story a second time for your partner to write down the key words and phrases he or she might recognize in the context of the story. Allow him or her enough time to write. Finally, ask your partner to tell the story back to you to see how well he or she remembers it. Answer any questions your partner may have to complete the story.

La fiesta sorpresa de cumpleaños de Marta

Ayer Marta (1) <u>cumplió 14 años</u> y sus amigos hicieron una (2) <u>fiesta de sorpresa</u>. Todos saludaron y (3) <u>felicitaron</u> a Marta cuando ella llegó. (4) <u>No había mucha gente</u>, pero charlaron, (5) <u>contaron chistes</u> y (6) <u>se rieron</u> mucho. Ella (7) <u>se divirtió</u> en su fiesta de cumpleaños.

Your partner will read aloud to you a story about Gerardo's family picnic. You will hear it once for general comprehension. Then your partner will repeat key words and phrases up to three times. He or she will read the story once more, and as you recognize the key words or phrases, write them in the space provided below. Tell the story back to your partner to see how well you remember it. Ask questions if necessary to complete the story.

1. _____

2. _____

3. _____

4. _____

5. _____

6. _____

7. _____

Talk!

Realidades 2

Capítulo 4B

Nombre _____

Fecha _____

Communicative Pair Activity **4B-2**

Estudiante **B**

Your partner will read aloud to you a story about Marta's surprise birthday party. You will hear it once for general comprehension. Then your partner will repeat key words and phrases up to three times. He or she will read the story once more, and as you recognize the key words or phrases, write them in the space provided below. Tell the story back to your partner to see how well you remember it. Ask questions if necessary to complete the story.

1. _____

2. _____

3. _____

4. _____

5. _____

6. _____

7. _____

Read aloud the story below about Gerardo's family picnic to your partner. Read it once for general comprehension. Then repeat the key words or phrases up to three times if needed. Read the story a second time for your partner to write down the key words and phrases he or she might recognize in the context of the story. Allow him or her enough time to write. Finally, ask your partner to tell the story back to you to see how well he or she remembers it. Answer any questions your partner may have to complete the story.

El picnic de Gerardo y su familia

La semana pasada, Gerardo fue a (1) <u>hacer</u> un picnic con su familia (2) <u>al lado de un lago</u> para celebrar un día (3) <u>festivo</u>. Había mucha gente (4) <u>alrededor</u> del lago (5) <u>enorme</u>. Su hermanita es una bebé y ella (6) <u>lloraba</u> mientras preparaban la comida porque ella tenía hambre. Cuando terminaron de prepararlo todo, su hermanita dejó de llorar y todos (7) <u>se divirtieron</u>.

2A

Capítulo 4B   **Realidades 2**

Talking about people, manners, and customs

You are with a friend talking about your family reunions when you were younger.

— Tell your friend that your family has a tradition of having a family reunion once a year with all the relatives. Ask your friend if his or her family has big gatherings also.

— Respond by telling your friend that it was fun but that your cousins had bad manners. Ask your friend if everyone gets along in his or her family.

2B

Capítulo 4B   **Realidades 2**

Talking about people, manners, and customs

You are with a friend talking about his or her family reunions when he or she was younger.

— Answer negatively saying that you have a small family and that almost all your relatives live far away. Ask your friend what he or she remembers and if he or she used to have fun at those gatherings.

— Answer your friend's question affirmatively saying that your family gets along very well.

1A

Capítulo 4B   **Realidades 2**

Talking about family and relatives, and describing special events in the past

You are reminiscing with an older brother or sister about his or her wedding last summer.

— Tell him or her that you remember when he or she got married last summer. Ask him or her if he or she remembers how many friends and relatives were at the party.

— Respond to his or her question affirmatively with emotion saying, "Of course!" and tell him or her that you laughed a lot when your friends told jokes about when they were students.

1B

Capítulo 4B   **Realidades 2**

Talking about family and relatives, and describing special events in the past

You are reminiscing with a younger brother or sister about your wedding last summer.

— Respond to your younger brother or sister saying that you do not remember exactly how many people were at the party, but you remember it was a huge party. Tell him or her that there were many old friends.

— Ask him or her if he or she remembers how much fun everybody had.

GramActiva

Celebrando los días festivos

Mi celebración favorita, p. 231

¿Por qué te gustaba?	¿Quiénes estaban?	¿Cómo era?	¿Dónde se reunían?	¿Qué hacían?

Vocabulary Clip Art

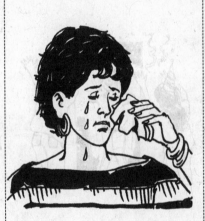

Vocabulary Clip Art

Vocabulary Clip Art

Core Practice Answers

4B-1
1. reunión
2. se ríen
3. nació
4. se reúnen
5. fiesta de sorpresa
6. fuegos artificiales
7. parientes
8. lloran
9. antiguo
10. cumplió

4B-2
A.
1. mayores
2. saludar
3. divertirse
4. enorme
5. frecuentemente

B.
1. abrazan
2. despide
3. besan
4. da la mano
5. saludan
6. sonríe

4B-3
1. festivos
2. cuenta
3. Felicidades
4. modales
5. bebé
6. llevan
7. un picnic
8. alrededor
9. recuerdo
10. charlan

4B-4
1. Sí, le gustan los días festivos. El cuatro de julio (el Día de la Independencia) es su día favorito.
2. Hay gente que espera el desfile en el parque, gente que hace picnics y otras personas, como la familia de Isabel, que se reúnen y van al centro.
3. Durante el desfile hay bandas musicales y carrozas que pasan por la Gran Vía. También hay mucha gente importante del pueblo caminando con el desfile, saludándole y sonriéndole a la gente. Los espectadores se ríen y se divierten mucho.

4. No, toda la gente se va al parque para reunirse con otra gente conocida (o algunas veces no conocida).
5. Una vez las personas que encienden los fuegos artificiales le permitieron a Isabel encender unos pequeños.

4B-5
era / se reunían / preparaba / ayudaban / jugaba / nos llevábamos / nos divertíamos / almorzábamos / contábamos / nos reíamos / traía / tocaba / gustaba / cantábamos / nos quedábamos (se quedaba) / regresábamos

4B-6
1. se saludan
2. se dan la mano
3. se abrazan
4. se besan
5. se hablan por teléfono
6. se escriben por correo electrónico
7. se pelean
8. se felicitan

4B-7
A.
Paragraph 1: I, P, I, P, P, P
Paragraph 2: I, I, I, P, I, P, P, P, I, I, P, P, P

B.
1. hacía
2. decidimos
3. contaban
4. encontramos
5. puso
6. Nos reunimos
7. Había
8. charlaban
9. jugaban
10. llegamos
11. se divertían
12. vinieron
13. Empezó
14. corrió
15. se reía
16. jugaban
17. empezaron
18. nos despedimos
19. terminó

Crucigrama (4B-8)
Horizontal:
2. casaron
3. picnic
4. modales
8. regalaron
10. nació
11. cumples
12. días
13. bebé
14. alrededor
19. desfile
22. aniversario
23. sonríe
24. contaron

Vertical:
1. frecuentemente
5. antigua
6. felicidades
7. costumbres
9. fiesta
15. reunión
16. ríe
17. mayores
18. besaron
20. charlamos
21. divierte

Organizer (4B-9)
I. Vocabulary Answers will vary.
II. Grammar
1a. describe people, places, and situations in the past
1b. talk about a past action or situation when no beginning or end is specified
1c. describe the situation or background information when something else happened or interrupted the ongoing action
2. reciprocal
3. Answers will vary, but should include six of the following: abrazarse, besarse, casarse, darse (la mano), despedirse, llevarse (bien/mal), pelearse, saludarse, verse

Realidades 2

Capítulo 4B

Nombre

Hora

Fecha

Vocabulary Flash Cards, Sheet 2

Write the Spanish vocabulary word or phrase below each picture. Be sure to include the article for each noun.

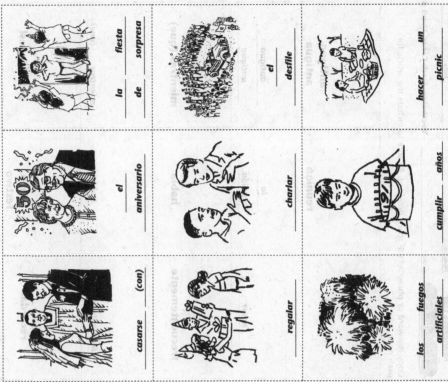

la fiesta de sorpresa

el desfile

hacer un picnic

el aniversario

charlar

cumplir años

casarse (con)

regalar

los fuegos artificiales

Realidades 2

Capítulo 4B

Nombre

Hora

Fecha

Vocabulary Flash Cards, Sheet 1

Write the Spanish vocabulary word or phrase below each picture. Be sure to include the article for each noun.

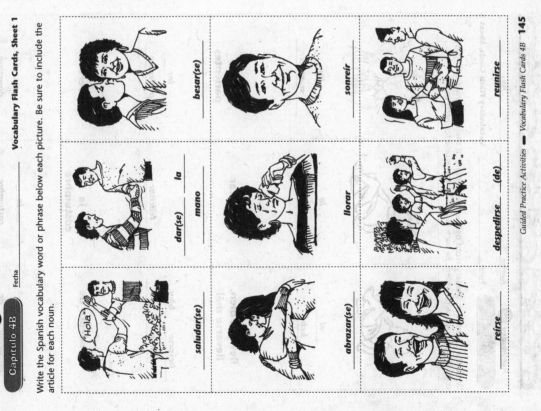

besar(se)

sonreír

reunirse

dar(se) la mano

llorar

despedirse (de)

saludar(se)

abrazar(se)

reírse

Sheet 4

Realidades 2
Capítulo 4B

Nombre _____ Hora _____

Fecha _____ Vocabulary Flash Cards, Sheet 4

Copy the word or phrase in the space provided. Be sure to include the article for each noun.

antiguo, antigua	la reunión	nacer
antiguo / antigua	la / reunión	nacer

mientras (que)	había	frecuentemente
mientras (que)	había	frecuentemente

¡Felicidades!	el día festivo	recordar
¡Felicidades!	el / día festivo	recordar

148 Guided Practice Activities — Vocabulary Flash Cards 4B

Sheet 3

Realidades 2
Capítulo 4B

Nombre _____ Hora _____

Fecha _____ Vocabulary Flash Cards, Sheet 3

Write the Spanish vocabulary word below each picture. If there is a word or phrase, copy it in the space provided. Be sure to include the article for each noun.

los mayores	la bebé	el bebé
los / mayores	la / bebé	el / bebé

los parientes	felicitar	llevarse bien, llevarse mal
los / parientes	felicitar	llevarse bien / llevarse mal

divertirse	la costumbre	alrededor de
divertirse	la / costumbre	alrededor de

Guided Practice Activities — Vocabulary Flash Cards 4B 147

Sheet 2

Tear out this page. Write the Spanish words on the lines. Fold the paper along the dotted line to see the correct answers so you can check your work.

baby	*el bebé, la bebé*
anniversary	*el aniversario*
custom	*la costumbre*
parade	*el desfile*
holiday	*el día festivo*
surprise party	*la fiesta de sorpresa*
fireworks	*los fuegos artificiales*
gathering	*la reunión*
grown-ups	*los mayores*
manners	*los modales*
to hug	*abrazar(se)*
to kiss	*besar(se)*
to shake hands	*dar(se) la mano*

Sheet 1

Tear out this page. Write the English words on the lines. Fold the paper along the dotted line to see the correct answers so you can check your work.

el bebé, la bebé	*baby*
el aniversario	*anniversary*
la costumbre	*custom*
el desfile	*parade*
el día festivo	*holiday*
la fiesta de sorpresa	*surprise party*
los fuegos artificiales	*fireworks*
la reunión	*gathering*
los mayores	*grown-ups*
los modales	*manners*
abrazar(se)	*to hug*
besar(se)	*to kiss*
dar(se) la mano	*to shake hands*

Realidades 2

Capítulo 4B

Nombre _____

Hora _____

Fecha _____

Vocabulary Check, Sheet 4

Tear out this page. Write the Spanish words on the lines. Fold the paper along the dotted line to see the correct answers so you can check your work.

- Fold In ↓

to say goodbye (to)	*despedirse (de)*
to greet	*saludar(se)*
to smile	*sonreír*
to tell (jokes)	*contar (chistes)*
to cry	*llorar*
to laugh	*reírse*
to meet	*reunirse*
to get married (to)	*casarse (con)*
to chat	*charlar*
to have a birthday	*cumplir años*
to have a picnic	*hacer un picnic*
to be born	*nacer*
to give (a gift)	*regalar*
to remember	*recordar*

To hear a complete list of the vocabulary for this chapter, go to www.realidades.com and type in the Web Code jdd-0499. Then click on Repaso del capítulo.

Realidades 2

Capítulo 4B

Nombre _____

Hora _____

Fecha _____

Vocabulary Check, Sheet 3

Tear out this page. Write the English words on the lines. Fold the paper along the dotted line to see the correct answers so you can check your work.

- Fold In ↓

despedirse (de)	*to say goodbye (to)*
saludar(se)	*to greet*
sonreír	*to smile*
contar (chistes)	*to tell (jokes)*
llorar	*to cry*
reírse	*to laugh*
reunirse	*to meet*
casarse (con)	*to get married (to)*
charlar	*to chat*
cumplir años	*to have a birthday*
hacer un picnic	*to have a picnic*
nacer	*to be born*
regalar	*to give (a gift)*
recordar	*to remember*

The imperfect tense: describing a situation (p. 219)

• The imperfect tense is also used to describe people, places, and situations in the past:

La casa de mis abuelos era pequeña. Tenía dos dormitorios.
My grandparents' house was small. It had two bedrooms.

Mi abuelo era muy generoso.
My grandfather was very generous.

Las fiestas en la casa de mis abuelos eran muy divertidas.
The parties at my grandparents' house were a lot of fun.

A. Read the following paragraph and draw a line underneath all the verbs used to describe the situation. The first one has been done for you.

Cuando <u>era</u> niño, mi familia y yo siempre <u>íbamos</u> al lago. Mis abuelos <u>tenían</u> una

casa de verano que <u>estaba</u> cerca del lago. El lago <u>era</u> muy grande y bonito. <u>Había</u>

árboles alrededor del lago. Generalmente <u>hacía</u> mucho calor y por eso nos <u>gustaba</u>

nadar en el lago porque <u>era</u> más fresco (*cool*).

B. Read the following sentences about the paragraph in exercise A. Write **cierto** if they are true or **falso** if they are false. The first one is done for you.

1. La familia siempre iba al océano durante el verano.   *falso*

2. Los tíos tenían una casa de verano cerca del lago.   *falso*

3. Era un lago grande con árboles alrededor.   *cierto*

4. Hacía mucho calor en el verano.   *cierto*

5. No podían nadar en el lago.   *falso*

The imperfect tense *(continued)*

C. Complete the following sentences by writing the correct form of the verbs in parentheses using the imperfect tense. Use the the pictures to help you with the meaning of the sentences. Follow the model.

Modelo   El tío Pepe (contar) ___*contaba*___ chistes.

1. Nosotros (charlar) ___*charlábamos*___ con los parientes.

2. Mis padres (hacer) ___*hacían*___ picnics.

3. Yo (pasar) ___*pasaba*___ tiempo con mis amigos.

4. Mis hermanos (jugar) ___*jugaban*___ al fútbol.

5. Andréa (tener) ___*tenía*___ buenos modales.

6. Tú (divertirse) ___*te*___ ___*divertías*___ en las fiestas.

The imperfect tense (continued)

- The imperfect is also used to talk about a past action or situation when no beginning or ending time is mentioned.

  Había mucha gente en la fiesta para el aniversario de mis padres.
  There were many people at the party for my parents' anniversary.

D. Look at the scene to start thinking about what is happening. Then, read the paragraph below it and fill in the missing form of the verbs in parentheses that describe the situation in the past. The first one is done for you.

Cuando yo _**era**_ (ser) niña, mis parientes _**se**_ _**reunían**_ (reunirse) los domingos en casa de mi abuela. Mi abuela _**preparaba**_ (preparar) mucha comida y mis tías la _**ayudaban**_ (ayudar). Yo _**jugaba**_ (jugar) con mis primos. Todos nosotros _**nos**_ _**llevábamos**_ (llevarse) muy bien, y _**nos**_ _**divertíamos**_ (divertirse) mucho. Nosotros _**almorzábamos**_ (almorzar) juntos (together) y _**nos**_ _**reíamos**_ (reírse) mucho contando chistes todo el tiempo.

realidades.com
• Web Code: jdd-0413

Guided Practice Activities — 4B-2 **155**

The imperfect tense (continued)

- The imperfect tense is also used to tell what someone was doing when something else happened (preterite):

  Mis parientes *charlaban* cuando mi mamá *entró*.
  My relatives were chatting when my mother came in.

E. Read the sentences below about a party. Circle the action that was taking place in the description. Then, underline the action that stopped it. The first one is done for you.

1. Yo hablaba por teléfono cuando la fiesta empezó.

2. Mis parientes y yo charlábamos cuando la fiesta empezó.

3. Cuando llegaron sus padres, Luz contaba chistes.

4. Marta comía un pastel cuando le dieron los regalos.

5. La bebé jugaba cuando su abuela entró.

6. Cuando llegó Ana, los primos bebían refrescos.

7. Luisa y Mariana bailaban cuando la fiesta terminó.

8. Cuando se fueron todos, yo escribía sobre la fiesta.

9. Tú sacabas la basura cuando volvieron tus primos para celebrar más.

10. Cuando los primos y yo nos reunimos en el sótano, tú llamabas a la policía.

realidades.com
• Web Code: jdd-0413

156 Guided Practice Activities — 4B-3

Reciprocal actions (p. 224)

• You can use **se** and **nos** to express the idea "(to) each other":

Luis y Jorge se veían con frecuencia.
Luis and Jorge used to see each other frequently.

Mis primos y yo nos escribíamos a menudo.
My cousins and I used to write each other often.

A. Choose the correct reciprocal verb to describe each picture. Then, write the correct form of the verb using the imperfect tense in the blank. Follow the model.

Modelo Elena y María **se** ___**pelean**___ (pelearse / besarse)

1. Alicia y yo **nos** ___**besamos**___ (saludarse / besarse)

2. Gregorio y Andrés **se** ___**dan la mano**___ (darse la mano / abrazarse)

3. Daniel y Susi **se** ___**despiden**___ de Tomás. (pelearse / despedirse)

4. Gloria y yo **nos** ___**saludamos**___ (saludarse / darse la mano)

5. Antonio y Clara **se** ___**abrazan**___ (abrazarse / verse)

realidades.com • Web Code: jdd-0414

The imperfect tense (continued)

F. Look at the drawing below of a surprise 50th anniversary party. Then, read the paragraph and fill in the blanks with the correct form of the verbs in parentheses using the imperfect tense. The first one is done for you.

Feliz Aniversario

La semana pasada ___*era*___ (ser) el aniversario de mis abuelos. Todos nuestros parientes ___**estaban**___ (estar) en la casa de mis tíos. Las mujeres ___**charlaban**___ (charlar) y los hombres ___**contaban**___ (contar) chistes. ___**Había**___ (Haber) un pastel muy grande en la mesa. El pastel ___**tenía**___ (tener) flores muy bonitas. Nosotros ___**nos divertíamos**___ (divertirse) mucho.

G. Now, read the paragraph that tells what happened when the couple entered in the room. Fill in the blanks with the correct form of the verbs in parentheses using the preterite tense. The first one is done for you.

Cuando mis abuelos ___*llegaron*___ (llegar) todos les ___**felicitaron**___ (felicitar) a ellos. Las personas que charlaban antes, ahora ___**saludaron**___ (saludar) a los abuelos, y algunas personas los ___**besaron**___ (besar). Mis abuelos ___**sacó**___ (sacar) los regalos de otro cuarto. Mamá ___**entraron**___ (entrar) y luego la fiesta ___**empezó**___ (empezar).

realidades.com • Web Code: jdd-0413

Nombre _____

Fecha _____   Hora _____

Guided Practice Activities **4B-6**

Presentación escrita (p. 231)

Task: Some friends want to learn more about your favorite celebration or holiday. Write a brief paragraph describing such an event from your childhood.   ***Answers will vary.***

A. Read the names of the following celebrations. Then, circle three of your favorite celebrations.

¿Qué celebrabas con tu familia?		
El Día de San Valentín	El Día de la Madre	La Navidad (*Christmas*)	La Semana Santa (*Easter week*)
El Año Nuevo	Halloween	El Día del Padre	El Día de Acción de Gracias

B. Which of the celebrations or holidays from **part A** was your favorite when you were younger? Why was this your favorite celebration or holiday? Name the celebration and then give two reasons below.

_____ era mi celebración favorita porque _____

y _____

C. Use the chart below to think about what happened during your favorite celebration. What did you use to do? Where did you get together? Who was there? Circle all the expressions that describe the celebration.

¿Qué hacían?	¿Dónde se reunían?	¿Quiénes estaban?
bailábamos	en nuestra casa	mis primos y parientes
había muchos regalos	en casa de los abuelos	los amigos
comíamos mucho	en casa de mis tíos	muchos niños

D. Now, write a brief paragraph about your favorite celebration or holiday. Use your answers from **parts B** and **C.** You may also follow the model below. Remember to use the imperfect in your description.

El Día de los Reyes Magos era mi celebración favorita porque lo celebraba con mi familia. Nosotros íbamos a la casa de los abuelos. Me gustaba mucho porque había muchos regalos. Siempre jugaba con mis primos.

E. Read your paragraph and check for correct spelling and vocabulary use. Share your paragraph with a partner, who should check the following:

_____ Is the paragraph easy to understand?

_____ Is there anything you should add?

_____ Are there any errors?

160 *Guided Practice Activities* ━ 4B-6

Nombre _____

Fecha _____   Hora _____

Guided Practice Activities **4B-5**

Lectura: El seis de enero (pp. 228–229)

A. *El seis de enero*, or Three King's Day, is one of the most beloved holidays for children in the Hispanic world. Before this holiday arrives, children write letters to the **Reyes Magos** (Three Kings or Wise Men), just as many children in the U.S. write to Santa Claus before Christmas. Put an X next to the things you would expect to find in a letter to the **Reyes Magos**.

1. Los niños dicen sus nombres. _____ **X**

2. Los niños dicen que se portan bien. _____ **X**

3. Los niños dicen que se portan mal. _____

4. Los niños dicen qué juguetes quieren. _____ **X**

B. Now, read the following letter to the **Reyes Magos.** Answer the questions that follow.

4 de enero

Queridos Reyes:

Yo soy Carolina y quiero decirles que me porto bien con mami, papi y la maestra. Les escribo para pedirles una bicicleta rosada. Muchas gracias. Feliz año nuevo.

Les quiere,

Carolina

1. See if you can find in the letter any of the things that you marked in **part A.** List three of them in English.

Her name. _____ , *She behaves well.* _____ , **She wants a bicycle.**

2. ¿Qué regalo pide Carolina?   **She behaves well.**   *una bicicleta*

3. ¿De qué color es la bicicleta?   *rosada*

C. Imagine that you are writing a letter to the **Reyes Magos** or to Santa Claus. Write about two gifts that you would like to have and tell why you want each one. You may follow the model.   ***Answers will vary.***

Yo quiero _____ y _____ porque _____

Yo quiero _____ porque _____

Yo quiero _____ porque _____

⊙ realidades.com
• Web Code: jdd-0416

Guided Practice Activities ━ 4B-5 **159**

Antes de ver el video

Actividad 1

Do you have a favorite holiday or celebration? What is it? Why? Name three special things about it. Follow the model.

Modelo Mi día favorito es *el Día de los tres Reyes Magos.*
Los Reyes Magos nos traen muchos regalos. Comemos cosas ricas ese día. La familia se reúne a celebrar.

Mi día favorito es _____ *Answers will vary.*

¿Comprendes?

Actividad 2

In a letter, Javier explains his plans for the weekend to a friend, but he has left out certain details. Help him by writing the missing words in the blanks. Use the pictures to help you.

Estimado Salvador,

Este fin de semana me voy con mi amigo Ignacio al pueblo de su madre, *Alsasua, España*. Ignacio me dice que siempre llueve y necesitamos llevar un paraguas. Durante el fin de semana, ellos celebran la *fiesta de San Pedro*.

De niño, él siempre pasaba los veranos allá. Todos los años, la fiesta comienza con un *desfile*. Hay bailes y músicos, y ellos tocan instrumentos *típicos*

27 de junio

y *antiguos*. Algunos de los instrumentos son el txistu y el tamboril.

El txistu es una palabra vasca para una *flauta*. Ignacio sabe tocar el txistu, pero no sabe hablar *vasco*, como sus *abuelos*. Luego todos se reúnen en la iglesia, donde celebran una misa en español y en vasco. Esto es una *tradición*. Bueno, Salvador, te cuento más al regresar.

Tu amigo, *Javier*

Actividad 3

Match each word or phrase on the left with its corresponding sentence on the right.

1. __i__ la fiesta de San Pedro
2. __c__ txistu
3. __h__ txistorra
4. __a__ ropa típica
5. __g__ una boina
6. __d__ vasco
7. __b__ desfile
8. __f__ antiguos
9. __e__ paraguas

a. En la maleta pongo una camisa blanca, un pañuelo rojo y una boina roja.
b. Comienza en la mañana, cuando todos nos reunimos en esta marcha ordenada, generalmente para celebrar la fiesta.
c. Mi abuelo me enseñó a tocar este instrumento cuando yo era pequeño.
d. Este idioma lo hablan los abuelos de Ignacio.
e. Me llevo esto para la lluvia porque siempre llueve, pero no importa.
f. Los músicos tocan instrumentos típicos y muy viejos, o _____.
g. Javier no tiene una gorra redonda, o un tipo de sombrero típico.
h. Tienen hambre, y quieren comer este tipo de salchicha.
i. Esta fiesta siempre se celebra el 29 de junio.

Y, ¿qué más?

Actividad 4

Your cousin invited you this past weekend to spend it with his/her family, for a special celebration. Where did you go and what did you do? In a simple paragraph, explain your weekend. Use your imagination and follow the model.

Modelo *El fin de semana pasado fui a la casa de mi primo favorito, para celebrar su cumpleaños. La fiesta fue en un centro comercial. Allí jugamos a los bolos. Luego comimos un pastel de chocolate y bebimos refrescos. También cantamos y bailamos mucho. Finalmente, regresamos a su casa y dormí allá. Al día siguiente, mis padres volvieron por mí.*

Answers will vary.

_____

_____

_____

_____

_____

_____

_____

_____

Actividad 5

Mrs. Lena is taking her third grade class to visit a group of senior citizens tomorrow. In order to make sure that all the children behave well at the Senior Center, she uses puppets named **Marco el malo** and **Bruno el bueno** to illustrate good and bad manners. Listen as she describes what each puppet does, and decide if the actions are most likely those of **Marco el malo** or **Bruno el bueno**. Put an X in the appropriate box in the grid below. You will hear this conversation twice.

	1	2	3	4	5	6	7	8
(Marco el malo)	X		X	X		X		X
(Bruno el bueno)		X			X		X	

Actividad 6

Listen as four people talk about their favorite time to spend with their families. Write the number of the description under the corresponding picture. You will hear each description twice.

1 _____ 2 _____

3 _____ 4 _____

Actividad 9

Listen as parents tell their children about their childhood memories of family celebrations and traditions. As you listen, match each conversation to the pictures below by writing the number of the conversation under the appropriate picture. You will hear each conversation twice.

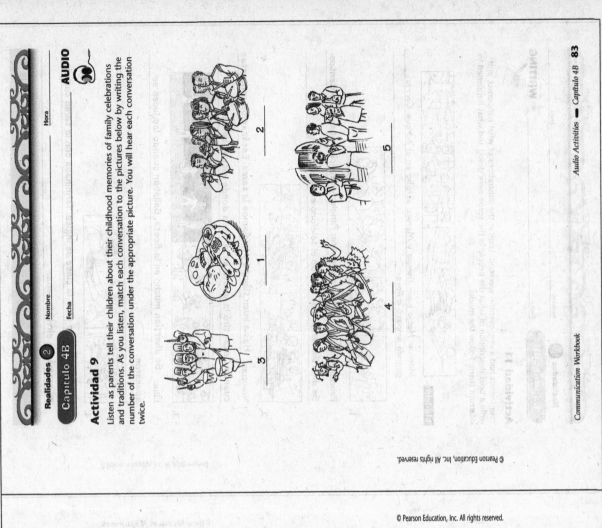

_3_ _1_ _2_

_4_ _5_

Actividad 7

When José Ignacio's mother returned from grocery shopping, she was shocked by some of the things her children and their friends were doing! Listen as she later tells José Ignacio's father what was going on when she got home. Based on what she says, fill in the grid below to tell how they were behaving. You will hear each set of statements twice.

	1	2	3	4	5	6
Se portaban bien		X	X		X	
Se portaban mal	X			X		X

Actividad 8

Some best friends like to do everything together, while others prefer to spend some time apart. Listen as some teenagers talk about whether they prefer to do certain things separately or together. Then, put an X in the appropriate box in the grid. You will hear each set of statements twice.

	1	2	3	4	5	6	7
Juntos (together)	X			X		X	X
Solo		X	X		X		

Page 84

© Pearson Education, Inc. All rights reserved.

Realidades 2

Capítulo 4B

Nombre _____

Hora _____

Fecha _____

WRITING

Actividad 10

Josephine is an exchange student in Spain and wants to make sure she acts appropriately when greeting people. Help her by answering her questions about what people tend to do in the situations she describes. Follow the model.

Modelo ¿Qué hago para saludar a una persona que conozco bien?
Uds. se besan o se abrazan para saludarse.

1. ¿Qué hago cuando encuentro a una persona que no veo con frecuencia?
   Answer should be in complete sentences using Uds. forms of
   abrazarse, saludarse, or besarse.

2. ¿Qué digo cuando una persona se casa o se gradúa de la universidad?
   Answers may vary but should include decir ¡Felicidades!

3. ¿Qué hago cuando conozco a una persona por primera vez?
   Answers may vary but should include darse la mano.

4. ¿Qué hago cuando salgo de un lugar o de la casa por la mañana?
   Answers may vary but should include despedirse.

5. ¿Qué hago cuando no veo a una amiga por mucho tiempo y quiero verla?
   Answers may vary but should include reunirse.

6. ¿Qué hago cuando paso a una persona a quien no conozco en la calle?
   Answers may vary but should include sonreír.

Page 85

Realidades 2

Capítulo 4B

Nombre _____

Hora _____

Fecha _____

WRITING

Actividad 11

Your friends had a very eventful weekend. Look at the illustrations of what happened, and write a brief description of what the people in the scene were doing and what happened to interrupt them. Follow the model.

Modelo

Mónica: *Hacía buen tiempo y Mónica estaba en el parque. Corría cuando empezó a llover.*

1.

Pancho y Patricia: Possible answers: Pancho y Patricia estaban contentos. Se divertían en el cine cuando el teléfono empezó a sonar.

2.

Nosotras: Hacía buen tiempo y hacíamos la tarea. Estábamos contentas cuando Óscar tiró la pelota en la mesa donde estudiábamos.

3.

Ellos: Se divertían mucho en la fiesta. Bailaban cuando las luces se apagaron.

4. Yo: Leía mi libro para la clase de inglés. Terminaba con la tarea cuando mi mamá me sirvió la cena.

© Pearson Education, Inc. All rights reserved.

Actividad 12

A. Lolis and Teresa are cousins who live quite far away from each other. Look at the pictures below and write complete sentences about what they do. Follow the model.

Modelo   *Las primas se quieren mucho y se llevan muy bien.*

1. Las primas se escriben por correo electrónico.

2. Las primas se ven una vez al año.

3. Las primas se saludan.

4. Las primas se abrazan.

5. Las primas se despiden.

B. Now, write about a cousin or other relative you like who lives far away. Follow the model.

Modelo   *Mi prima Cristina y yo nos vemos una vez cada dos años.*

Answers will vary.

Communication Workbook

Actividad 13

Pablo's family has just returned from a family reunion and he is writing in his diary about the day's events.

A. First, look at the picture of the party and write several sentences to describe the scene.
Answers will vary.

B. Next, tell what everyone at the party did when they were first reunited.
Answers will vary.

C. Finally, help Pablo write his diary entry using the phrases that you wrote above and any connecting words you may need to make your paragraph smooth.

Querido diario:

Hoy fui a la reunión de mi familia en San Juan.   Answers will vary.

Communication Workbook

Test Preparation Answers

Reading Skills
p. 241 2. **D**
p. 242 2. **D**

**Integrated Performance
 Assessment**
p. 243
Answer will vary.

Practice Test: El parque
p. 245

1. B
2. H
3. D
4. G
5. Answers will vary.
6. Las respuestas variarán, pero
   deben incluir recuerdos de
   personas cuando eran ninos,
   jóvenes y adultos.

Lecturas Teacher's Guide

Level 2

CAPÍTULO 1

Por qué pican los mosquitos

Prereading
Answers will vary. Possible answers: Little Red Riding Hood; Aesop's Fables

You might want to present some of the following terminology used in discussing literature: *ambiente* (atmosphere); *antagonista* (antagonist); *argumento* (plot); *desarrollo* (development); *desenlace* (resolution); *efecto* (effect); *escenario* (setting); *al final* (at the end); *motivo* (motive); *personaje* (character); *personificación* (personification); *al principio* (at the beginning); *protagonista* (protagonist); *punto culminante* (climax); *punto de vista* (point of view); *punto decisivo* (turning point); *representar* (represent); *significado* (meaning); *simbolizar* (symbolize); *símbolo* (symbol); *tema* (theme); *tono* (tone).

Answers to ¿De qué se trata?
1. Answers will vary. Possible answers: The fox symbolizes laziness, irresponsibility, and deceit; the mosquito symbolizes cunning and resourcefulness. *(El zorro simboliza a las personas perezosas, irresponsables y mentirosas o engañosas; el mosquito simboliza a las personas listas e ingeniosas.)*
2. Answers will vary.
3. Answers will vary. Possible answers: These tales are popular because there are good and bad characters, and the good ones know how to triumph over the bad. *(Estos cuentos son populares porque hay personajes buenos y malos, y los buenos saben cómo ganar a los malos.)*

For futher discussion
You may want to ask students the following questions:
1. Can you think of a tale in English that is similar to this one? *(¿Puedes pensar en un cuento en inglés como éste?)* ("The Tortoise and the Hare." You may want to tell students that the story in this reading is a variant of a tale from Chile. Stories of races between the clever and the stupid, whether animals or people, are a common type of tale found in all parts of the world.)

2. Do you think there are a lot of people who, just like the fox, say they will do something but then don't do it? Why do you think this happens? *(¿Crees que hay muchas personas, como el zorro, que dicen que van a hacer algo pero que no lo hacen? ¿Por qué crees que ocurre esto?)* (Possible answers: Yes, there are people like that. It probably happens because they like to appear helpful or give the impression that they can do something when in reality they don't know how to do it; they might be lazy; they might think that the person to whom they promised something will forget about it.)
3. When someone does something bad or unjust to you, how do you react? *(Cuando alguien te hace algo malo o injusto, ¿como reaccionas?)*

CAPÍTULO 2

Mi Tío Mundo

Prereading
Answers will vary.

Answers to ¿De qué se trata?
1. Because Tío Mundo changes jobs every six or seven months. *(Porque Tío Mundo siempre cambia de trabajo cada seis o siete meses.)*
2. Answers will vary.

For futher discussion
You may want to ask students the following questions:
1. Why do you think the main character, Raimundo, is called "Mundo"? *(¿Por qué crees que el protagonista, Raimundo, se llama "Mundo"?)* (Possible answers: It's the second part of the name Raimundo; *mundo* means "world," so it could be a play on words on the part of the narrator, who means his uncle is worldly since he's had so many jobs; he's done a little of everything.)
2. Why do you think the narrator's mother says that Tío Mundo is only ten years old? *(¿Por qué crees que la madre del narrador dice que Tío Mundo tiene sólo diez años?)* (Possible answers: He seems immature because he doesn't seem to want to settle down to one job; he has a childlike attitude toward life.)

3. Do you agree with Tío Mundo's philosophy about learning something from every job? Why or why not? (¿*Estás de acuerdo con la filosofía de Tío Mundo de que en todos los trabajos uno aprende algo? ¿Por qué sí o por qué no?*)

4. Of the jobs listed in the story, which one appeals to you most? Why? (*De los trabajos que se mencionan en el cuento, ¿cuál te gusta más? ¿Por qué?*)

CAPÍTULO 3

La invasión de las iguanas moradas

Prereading
Answers will vary. Possible answers: Yes, because everybody either reads the paper, or listens to the radio, or watches television. The media can have a lot of influence. (*Sí, porque todo el mundo lee periódicos, o escucha la radio, o mira la televisión. Los medios de información pueden tener mucha influencia.*)

Answers to ¿De qué se trata?
1. Answers will vary. Possible answers: They could be the dictators of a country; the heads of an institution; they could also symbolize a way of thinking. (*Pueden ser los dictadores de un país; los jefes de alguna institución; también pueden simbolizar una manera de pensar.*)

2. Answers will vary. Possible answers: Yes, life is better because everything is very orderly and organized; no, life is worse because people have to do whatever the iguanas say and don't have to think, or cannot think for themselves. (*Sí, la vida es mejor porque todo está muy ordenado; no, la vida es peor porque la gente tiene que hacer lo que dicen las iguanas y no tiene que pensar, o no puede pensar independientemente.*)

3. Answers will vary. Possible answers: Life is going to be the same as it is now; the iguanas are going to control everything; the next generation will be a mixture of humans and iguanas; humans may rebel and become independent again. The girl may change her mind in the future, because she will see that the iguanas may not allow her to do many things.

(*La vida va a ser igual que ahora; las iguanas van a controlar todo; la próxima generación puede ser una mezcla de humanos e iguanas; los humanos pueden rebelar y ganar su independencia. La muchacha puede cambiar d idea en el futuro, porque va a ver que las iguanas no la van a permitir hacer muchas cosas.*)

For further discussion
You may want to ask students the following questions:

1. Do you think an "invasion" like the one in th story is desirable in certain situations? Why or why not? (¿*Crees que una "invasión" como la de este cuento es necesaria en ciertas situaciones? ¿Por qué sí o por qué no?*) (Possible answers: Yes, when there has been chaos under the old rule; no, people should never be dictated to in that way.)

2. Imagine that you are the writer of this story. Would you change the ending? Explain your answer. (*Imagínate que eres el escritor de este cuento. ¿Cambias tú el final? Explica tu respuesta.*) (Possible answers: Yes, I would change the ending and have the people eventually rise up against the iguanas; no, I wouldn't change the ending, and this way the people can symbolize those who are too lazy o passive to do anything.)

3. Do you agree with the iguanas' philosophy that *todo en la vida es sólo cuestión de tiempo* Why or why not? (¿*Estás de acuerdo con la filosofía de las iguanas de que "todo en la vida es sólo cuestión de tiempo"? ¿Por qué sí o por qué no?*) (Possible answers: Yes, because people can adapt to anything, given time; no, because those who cannot accept change or those who perceive something to be unfair or a restriction of their freedom, will rebel sooner or later.)

4. What is the tone of the narrator of the story' Explain your answer with an example from the reading. (¿*Cómo es el tono del narrador del cuento? Explica tu respuesta con un ejemplo a la lectura.*) (Possible answers: Ironic or sarcastic; enthusiastic. The narrator says in the end: *Qué maravilla, ¿verdad?*—line 70.)

5. You might want to ask students if they have ever read the novel *1984* by George Orwell, an if so, ask them in what ways it is similar to this reading. (If students have never read the book, you may want to provide a synopsis of it: it deals with a totalitarian society, where the population's activities are constantly monitored by an entity called "Big Brother," and any signs of rebellion or independent thinking are instantly corrected or eliminated.)

CAPÍTULO 4

La pensión de doña Flor

Prereading
Answers will vary.

Answers to ¿De qué se trata?
1. Answers will vary. Possible answers: No, because he has a bad attitude; yes, because he is an interesting person. (No, porque no tiene una actitud buena; sí, porque es una persona interesante.)
2. Answers will vary. Possible answers: She learned not to be so afraid of Julia; she learned to be comfortable in a new country; she learned to understand people from a different culture; she got to know different people. (Aprendió a no tener tanto miedo de Julia; aprendió a estar cómoda en un nuevo país; aprendió a comprender a la gente de una cultura diferente; conoció a personas diferentes.)
3. Answers will vary. Possible answers: I could introduce him/her to my friends, to the places I know, and to life in this country. (Puedo presentarlo/la a mis amigos; puedo llevarlo/la a los lugares que conozco; puedo explicarle cómo funciona la vida de este país.)

For further discussion
You may want to ask students the following questions:
1. Would you like to live in a boardinghouse like doña Flor's? Why or why not? (¿Te gustaría vivir en una pensión como la de doña Flor? ¿Por qué sí o por qué no?)
2. Imagine that you are the narrator of this story. Would you include other types of experiences? Which ones? (Imagínate que eres la narradora de este cuento. ¿Incluyes otros tipos de experiencia? ¿Cuáles?) (Possible

answers: How she adapts to the weather and the way it affects living conditions there; how she learns to dance flamenco; fellow tenants' quirks.)
3. Imagine that you can live anywhere for three months in order to further your education. Where would you like to go and why? (Imagínate que puedes vivir en cualquier lugar por tres meses para continuar con tus estudios ¿Adónde te gustaría ir y por qué?)
4. You may want to ask students to make a list of the exchange students in your school, identifying where they are from, how long they have been in this country, how long they are going to be here, and with whom they are staying.

CAPÍTULO 5

Sara María Dolores Sánchez Papillón

Prereading
Answers will vary.

Answers to ¿De qué se trata?
1. Answers will vary. Possible answers: Take care of and help that person; try to do something fun or entertaining for him/her. (Cuidar a y ayudar a esa persona; tratar de hacer algo divertido para ella.)
2. Answers will vary.

For further discussion
You may want to ask students the following questions:
1. Which lines in the poem indicate to us that something unusual is happening? (¿Qué versos del poema nos indican que pasa algo extraordinario?) (Lines 30-33.)
2. When was the last time you had to stay in bed for a week due to an illness? What did you do? What can a person who has to stay in bed for a long time do? (¿Cuándo fue la última vez que te quedaste en cama por una semana a causa de una enfermedad? ¿Qué hiciste? ¿Qué puede hacer una persona que tiene que quedarse en cama por mucho tiempo?)
(Answers will vary. Possible answer: You can catch up on doing things that you normally wouldn't have time to do.)

3. Why do you think Sara imagines that a circus has come to visit her? Why do you think some people tend to live in a dream world rather than in the real one? (*¿Por qué crees que Sara se imagina que un circo la viene a visitar? ¿Por qué crees que alguna gente prefiere vivir en un mundo imaginario en vez de en el real?*) (Possible answers: Sara probably likes circuses. Some people prefer to live in a dream world because they don't want to deal with reality and life's problems.)

CAPÍTULO 6

El dueño del Sol

Prereading
Answers will vary. Possible answers: That person will not be happy, or will want more, or will not have any ambition to work. (*Esa persona no va a estar contenta; va a querer más; no va a tener ambición para trabajar.*)

Answers to ¿De qué se trata?
1. Answers will vary. Possible answers: Miguelito's parents give him too many things; Miguelito has too much and won't be a happy adult because he will always want more; he will think that the world will give him everything. (*Los padres de Miguelito le dan demasiadas cosas; Miguelito tiene demasiadas cosas y no va a ser un adulto feliz, porque siempre va a querer más; siempre va a pensar que el mundo le va a dar todo.*) (If students ask, you might want to tell them that the expression "to spoil someone" is *mimar* in Spanish.)
2. Answers will vary. Possible answers: We want something because others have it; because we want to be the first to have it; because we want to impress someone; because we like it; because it works well. (*Queremos algo porque otros lo tienen; porque queremos ser los primeros en tenerlo; porque queremos impresionar a alguien; porque nos gusta; porque funciona bien.*)
3. Answers will vary. Possible answers: In general, having something means being responsible for it; often we don't appreciate something once we have it. (*Por lo general, tener algo significa ser responsable de esa cosa; a menudo no apreciamos algo una vez que lo tenemos.*)

For further discussion
You may want to ask students the following questions:
1. What else could Miguelito want to own that might cause as many problems as his owning the sun did? (*¿De qué otra cosa puede ser el dueño Miguelito que puede causar tantos problemas como ser el dueño del Sol?*) (Possible answers: The moon; the seas and the oceans.)
2. When you were ten, what did you most desire to have? Did you ever get it? Do you still have it? If you didn't get what you wanted, what do you think you would do with it if you got it now? (*Cuando tenías diez años, ¿qué fue lo que más querías tener? ¿Lo conseguiste? ¿Lo tienes todavía? Si no conseguiste lo que querías, ¿qué crees que harías con esa cosa si la consiguieras ahora?*)
3. The expression "Do unto others as you would have them do unto you" is found in many parts of the world in various forms. Do you agree with this saying? Do you believe that if others treat you badly, someday they will be unlucky or will also be treated badly? Why do you think some people believe in this? (*El dicho "No hagas a otros lo que no quieras que te hagan a ti" se encuentra en muchas partes del mundo de varias formas. ¿Estás de acuerdo con esto? ¿Crees que si otros te tratan mal, algún día ellos van a tener mala suerte o se los van a tratar mal también? ¿Por qué crees que algunas personas creen en esto?*)
4. If everybody were to have what they most wanted, what do you think the world would be like? (*Si todo el mundo tuviera lo que más quisiera, ¿cómo sería el mundo?*) (Possible answers: There might be conflicts, boredom, chaos.)

CAPÍTULO 7

Luisita "la distraída"

Prereading
Answers will vary.

Answers to ¿De qué se trata?
1. Luisita learned that natural sounds are more pleasant than rock music. (*Luisita aprendió que los sonidos naturales son más agradables que la música rock.*)

2. Answers will vary.

3. Answers will vary.

For further discussion
You may want to ask students the following questions:

1. Do you think someone like Luisita is always going to be absent-minded, or can he/she change? Explain your answer. (*¿Crees que una persona como Luisita va a ser siempre distraída o puede cambiar?*) (Possible answers: Yes, someone like Luisita can change; Luisita, for example, stopped listening to her radio. No, people like Luisita cannot change; they will probably find something else to be absent-minded about.)

2. In Luisita's case, her liking for music causes her absent-mindedness. Can you think of some other reasons for being absent-minded? (*En el caso de Luisita, su afición a la música causa su distracción. ¿Puedes pensar en algunas otras razones por ser distraído/a?*) (Possible answers: Living in a dream world; being too talkative; being too preoccupied about something.)

3. In your opinion, which is worse: to be too absent-minded like Luisita, or to be too watchful and suspicious? Why do you think so? (*En tu opinión, ¿cuál es peor: ser demasiado distraído/a como Luisita, o estar siempre vigilando y sospechoso/a de otros? ¿Por qué crees eso?*)

4. What are your favorite kinds of comic strips? (*¿Cuáles son las clases de historietas que prefieres?*)

CAPÍTULO 8

El maíz de la roca

Prereading
Answers will vary. Possible answers: I feel uncomfortable; I don't like to share my things with anyone; I like to share what I have with others. (*Me siento incómodo/a; no me gusta compartir mis cosas con nadie; me gusta compartir lo que tengo con otros.*)

You may want to tell students that this story is a variant of a Mayan myth. This kind of tale is called an *ejemplo,* which means a tale that sets an example. This tale is one of the most widely reported among Mayan stories.

Answers to *¿De qué se trata?*
1. Answers will vary. Possible answers: I would try to get the corn out and keep it; I might try to grow the corn. (*Trato de sacar y guardar el maíz; puedo tratar de cultivar el maíz.*)
2. Answers will vary. Possible answers: Yes, when people do something bad with what they have; no, people have a right to keep what they have, since it's their property. (*Sí, cuando esa persona hace algo malo con lo que tiene; no, cada persona tiene derecho a quedarse con lo que ella tiene, porque es su propiedad.*)

For further discussion
You may want to ask students the following questions:

1. Look at the paragraph about the woodpecker. Based on that paragraph, can you think of another title for this tale? (*Mira otra vez el párrafo sobre el pájaro carpintero. Basándote en ese párrafo, ¿puedes pensar en otro título para este cuento?*) (Possible answer: "How the woodpecker got its red crest.")
2. Imagine that you are the narrator of this tale. Would you have the fox punished in some way for what she did? Why or why not? (*Imagínate que eres la narradora de este cuento. ¿Castigarías a la zorra de alguna manera por lo que hizo? ¿Por qué sí o por qué no?*)

CAPÍTULO 9

Isabel y el nuevo alumno (primera parte)

Prereading
Answers will vary.

Answers to *¿De qué se trata?*
1. They are afraid that Isabel's parents might not accept Emilio because he's disabled. (*Tienen miedo de que los padres de Isabel no acepten a Emilio porque es minusválido.*)
2. Answers will vary. Possible answers: For their personality; because they are intelligent/clever; because they are good-looking; because they are nice or have a good sense of humor. (*Por su personalidad; porque son inteligentes/listos; porque son guapos; porque son agradables o tienen un buen sentido del humor.*)

For further discussion

You may want to ask students the following questions:

1. Isabel says in the story: *Siempre me duele la cabeza cuando tengo que crear composiciones originales,* and Emilio says the same thing happens to him with his math homework. Which subjects do you have a hard time with? How can you overcome this problem? *(Isabel dice en el cuento: "Siempre me duele la cabeza cuando tengo que crear composiciones originales," y Emilio dice que lo mismo pasa con él con sus tareas de matemáticas. ¿Con qué clases tienes tú más dificultad? ¿Cómo puedes resolver el problema?)*

2. What do you think will happen next in the story? *(¿Qué crees que va a pasar después en el cuento?)*

CAPÍTULO 10

Isabel y el nuevo alumno (segunda parte)

Prereading

Answers will vary. Possible answers: Because parents do not always have the same views as their children; because parents have one lifestyle and their children another. *(Porque los padres no siempre tienen el mismo punto de vista que los hijos; porque los padres tienen un estilo de vida y los hijos otro.)*

Answers to *¿De qué se trata?*

1. Answers will vary. Possible answers: Yes, because it's better to prepare her parents; no, it's better for them to see Emilio and react naturally. *(Sí, porque es mejor preparar a sus padres; no, es mejor que vean a Emilio y que reaccionen naturalmente.)*

2. Answers will vary.

3. Answers will vary. Possible answers: Modern-day society accepts the disabled better now than the society of a generation or two ago did. Our society has the technology to improve the life of the disabled; for example, we can provide them with many kinds of jobs. *(La sociedad moderna acepta más a los minusválidos ahora que la sociedad de hace una o dos generaciones. Nuestra sociedad tiene la tecnología para poder mejorar la vida de los*

minusválidos; por ejemplo, podemos darles varias clases de trabajo.)

For further discussion

You may want to ask students the following questions:

1. Did you expect the story to end this way? Explain your answer. *(¿Esperabas esta clase de final al cuento? Explica tu respuesta.)*

2. Imagine that you are Isabel. How would your parents react to Emilio? *(Imagínate que eres Isabel. ¿Cómo reaccionarían tus padres hacia Emilio?)*

3. How do you think Emilio felt when he arrived at Isabel's house for dinner: *(¿Cómo crees que se sintió Emilio cuando llegó a la casa de Isabel para la cena?)* (Possible answers: nervous; uncertain.)

4. Think about Marta's role in the story. Do you think she was right in being doubtful about Isabel's parents' reaction, and in telling Isabel about her doubts? *(Piensa en el papel de Marta en el cuento. ¿Crees que ella tenía razón al ser tan dudosa de la reacción de los padres de Isabel, y al contarle a Isabel sus dudas?)*

5. Do your friends generally give you good advice? What is your definition of a good friend? *(Por lo general, ¿te dan buenos consejos tus amigos? ¿Cuál es tu definición de un/a buen/a amigo/a?)* (Possible answers: Someone you can rely on and trust; someone who can sympathize with you and make you laugh; someone who will be there when you need him/her.)

CAPÍTULO 11

El extraño caso del mosquito

Prereading

Answers will vary. Possible answers: Yes, I need someone or something to help me with tests and exams; no, because I'll never learn anything. *(Sí necesito a alguien o algo para ayudarme en los exámenes; no, porque nunca voy a aprender nada.)*

You may want to tell students that this story is

Make sure students understand the following terminology used in discussing plays: *personaje* (character); *acto* (act); *escena* (scene).

answers to ¿De qué se trata?

Answers will vary. Possible answers: Its plan could be successful, but sooner or later it would fail; the mosquito can die and Eduardo will realize that he never learned anything, and he doesn't know anything. *(Su plan puede tener éxito, pero tarde o temprano va a ser un fracaso; el mosquito puede morir y Eduardo va a saber que nunca aprendió nada, y no sabe nada.)*

Answers will vary. Possible answers: I prefer to study with the radio on because I like music and I don't have to hear other noises; I don't like to study with the radio on because I can't pay attention; I prefer to study in silence. *(Prefiero estudiar con el radio encendido porque me gusta la música y no tengo que escuchar otros ruidos; no me gusta estudiar con el radio encendido porque no puedo prestar atención; prefiero estudiar en silencio.)*

Answers will vary. Possible answers: You shouldn't depend on others to do what you should do. *(Tú no debes depender de otros para hacer lo que tú debes hacer.)*

or further discussion

You may want to ask students the following questions:

Imagine that Alfonso did not kill the mosquito and Eduardo lets him in on the secret. What do you think they would do with the mosquito? *(Imagínate que Alfonso no mató al mosquito y que Eduardo le cuenta el secreto. ¿Qué crees que harían con el mosquito?)* (Possible answers: They might take turns having the mosquito help them; they might go into business and rent out the mosquito to other students, or exhibit the mosquito and have people pay to see him; they might write a book about him.)

Instead of the mosquito, what kind of animal or insect would you choose to help or accompany you? Why? *(En lugar del mosquito, ¿qué animal o insecto escogerías para ayudarte o acompañarte? ¿Por qué?)*

Do you think that someday in the future we will be able to communicate with most animals? What would the world be like then? *(¿Crees que algún día en el futuro podremos comunicarnos con la mayoría de los animales?*

¿Cómo sería el mundo entonces?) (Possible answers: Yes. Human beings might learn many things from animals, and vice-versa; the hierarchy of intelligent beings might change.)

CAPÍTULO 12
"El encuentro"

Prereading
Answers will vary. Possible answers: Sometimes they don't get along because of jealousy; because they don't understand each other; because they are very different. *(A veces no se llevan bien porque tienen celos; porque no se entienden; porque son muy distintos.)*

Answers to ¿De qué se trata?
1. Answers will vary. Possible answers: He might have gone to another country; he might not have played the flute in public anymore. Other titles could be "Los hermanos"; "Los rivales"; "Alejandro y Miguel"; "El éxito"; "La suerte." Because the story deals with the life of and rivalry between two brothers. *(Se fue a otro país; dejó de tocar la flauta en público. Otros títulos pueden ser "Los hermanos"; "Los rivales"; "Alejandro y Miguel"; "El éxito"; "La suerte." Porque el cuento trata de la vida de y la rivalidad entre dos hermanos.)*
2. Answers will vary.

For further discussion
You may want to ask students the following questions:
1. Do you think it was right for Alejandro to leave Miguel after his brother's success? What else could he have done? *(¿Crees que Alejandro tenía razón al dejarlo a Miguel después del éxito de su hermano? ¿Qué más podía haber hecho?)* (Possible answers: He could have stayed on with Miguel and eventually shared in his success. They might have separated later since they had different styles, but they could have achieved fame together in the beginning.)
2. Luck, whether good or bad, can sometimes change people's lives drastically. Do you know someone whose life has been changed in this

way? How did it happen? *(La suerte, ya sea buena o mala, a veces puede cambiar radicalmente la vida de las personas. ¿Conoces a alguien cuya vida haya sido cambiada de esta manera? ¿Cómo ocurrió?)*

3. Have your parents influenced you greatly in music or art? Does your own taste reflect this influence? In what way? *(¿Has tenido mucha influencia de tus padres en cuanto a la música o al arte? ¿Esto se muestra en tus propios gustos? ¿De qué manera?)*

4. You may want to ask students to rewrite the story as a play, starting from the second recital of the brothers.

CAPÍTULO 13

El gato negro

Prereading
Answers will vary. Possible answers: A story about superstition, magic, or witches. *(Un cuento sobre la superstición, la magia o las brujas.)*

Answers to ¿De qué se trata?
1. Answers will vary. Possible answers: Yes, she's also the black cat that scared the narrator in the forest; both have the same twisted smile and the cold, penetrating look; no, it's pure coincidence that she limps. *(Sí, es también el gato negro que le asustó al narrador en el bosque; los dos tienen la misma sonrisa torcida y la mirada penetrante y fría; no, cojea por pura coincidencia.)*
2. Answers will vary.
3. Answers will vary. Possible answers: It's common because ever since the Middle Ages in Europe, black cats have been associated with witches. Cats, in general, are old women's companions, and if an old woman was considered a witch, it was also thought that she could change herself into a (black) cat. Hence the belief that black cats are witches' companions or familiars. *(Es común porque desde la Edad Media en Europa, se ha asociado el gato negro con las brujas. Los gatos, por lo general, son compañeros de las viejas, y si una vieja fuera considerada una*

bruja, se pensaba también que ella podía convertirse en un gato. De allí viene la creencia de que los gatos negros son los compañeros de las brujas.)*

For further discussion
You may want to ask students the following questions:
1. Why do you think some people believe in witches and magic? Do you think it's possible that they might exist? Why or why not? *(¿Por qué crees que algunas personas creen en las brujas y la magia? ¿Crees que es posible que existan? ¿Por qué sí o por qué no?)* (Possible answers: People are fascinated by mysteries, things they can't understand or explain; yes, it's possible that witches and magic might exist, because there have been stories through the ages about witches and magical powers; no, it's not possible, because things like witches and magic cannot exist in our enlightened, practical world.)
2. Can you think of some other animals that are associated with witches? *(¿Puedes pensar en otros animales que se asocian con las brujas?)* (Possible answers: Newts, frogs, spiders, owls, crows/ravens, toads, bats, wolves, goats.)
3. Why do you think some people are believed to be witches? *(¿Por qué crees que se sospechan a algunas personas de ser brujas?)* (Possible answers: Because they look and act strange, or claim to have vivid dreams and illusions, or give the others the "evil eye"; people who are gullible therefore brand them witches.)

CAPÍTULO 14

El Iztaccíhuatl y el Popocatépetl

Prereading
Answers will vary.

You may want to tell students that Iztaccíhuatl and Popocatépetl are the names of two snow-covered volcanoes near Mexico City, which was formerly the ancient Indian capital of Tenochtitlán. The taller peak, which has a sharp volcanic cone, is Popocatépetl; the lower peak, which resembles the outline of a woman lying on her back, is Iztaccíhuatl, or the "Sleeping Lady." They are often called Popo and Izta for short.

This legend, one of the best-known of the central region of Mexico, is a variant of "The Love of a Mexican Prince and Princess," and it explains how the lovers were converted into the two famous peaks.

Answers to ¿De qué se trata?
1. Answers will vary. Possible answers: This legend is similar to Romeo and Juliet in that there are two lovers whose families don't want them to get married because the families are rivals in some way, but the lovers want to be together because they can't live without each other. In the end the lovers die together. A modern version: West Side Story. (Esta leyenda se parece a Romeo y Julieta en que hay dos enamorados cuyas familias no quieren que se casen porque las familias son rivales de alguna manera, pero los enamorados quieren estar juntos porque no pueden vivir separados el uno del otro. Al final los enamorados se mueren juntos. Un cuento moderno: West Side Story.)
2. Answers will vary. Possible answers: Yes, they have another choice. They could try to survive until they get to another civilization, and live together there. (Sí, tienen otra opción. Pueden tratar de sobrevivir hasta llegar a otra civilización, y vivir juntos allí.)
3. Answers will vary. Possible answers: It's pessimistic because the lovers die; it's optimistic because they think they are going to be together in the next world. (Es pesimista porque los enamorados se mueren; es optimista porque ellos piensan que van a estar juntos en el próximo mundo.)

For further discussion
You may want to ask students the following questions:
1. Do you know any couples whose families didn't want them to get married, but who ended up marrying and having a happy life? Can you tell what happened? (¿Conoces a parejas cuyas familias no querían que se casaran, pero quienes se casaron al final y tuvieron una vida feliz? ¿Puedes contar lo que pasó?)

2. What are some reasons for a family's being opposed to a son's or daughter's marriage? (¿Cuáles son algunos motivos por los que una familia se oponga al matrimonio de un hijo o una hija?) (Possible answers: They may think that the young couple are too different or too young; they might not want the couple to suffer through hardships they could avoid by not getting married to each other.)
3. Imagine that your parents don't want you to marry a certain person. What do you do? What do you think you would do if your best friend wanted to marry someone you didn't like? (Imagínate que tus padres no quieren que te cases con cierta persona. ¿Qué haces tú? ¿Qué crees que vas a hacer si tu mejor amigo/a quiere casarse con alguien que no te cae bien?)

CAPÍTULO 15
Jicotea / Por qué el mono es mono

Prereading
Answers will vary.

You may want to tell students that Jicotea is a popular character in Afrocuban fables. Jicotea usually symbolizes cunning and wisdom, winning over brute strength and simplicity. Jicotea could be described as the equivalent of the fox in some European folk tales. The first tale is a variant of other fables about Jicotea.

Answers to ¿De qué se trata?
1. Answers will vary. Possible answers: Yes, it was fair, because Jicotea didn't keep her promise; she didn't buy Ochún the gifts she promised her; no, it wasn't fair, because Ochún should have punished her another way and not left the marks on her back. (Sí, fue justo, porque Jicotea no cumplió con su promesa; no le compró a Ochún los regalos que le prometió; no, no fue justo, porque Ochún debió castigarla de otra manera y no dejarle las marcas en la espalda.)
2. Answers will vary. Possible answers: Both contain three of the same characters: the monkey, Jicotea, and Obatalá. Both stories deal

with the theme of someone who is granted a favor, but who doesn't know how to make the most of it and be grateful for it. *(Los dos tienen tres de los mismos personajes: el mono, Jicotea y Obatalá. En los dos cuentos se trata el tema de alguien a quien se le hacen un favor, pero que no sabe aprovecharlo y agradecérselo.)*
3. Answers will vary.

For further discussion
You may want to ask students the following questions:
1. What does *cuando las gallinas dormían y las estrellas estaban prendidas en el cielo* (lines 33-34) mean? *(¿Qué quiere decir "cuando las gallinas dormían y las estrellas estaban prendidas en el cielo"?—líneas 33-34)* (At night.)
2. Which fable do you prefer: "Por qué pican los mosquitos" in Chapter 1 of this book, "Jicotea" or "Por qué el mono es mono" in this chapter? What similarities can you find among the three fables? *(¿Qué fábula prefieres: "Por qué pican los mosquitos" del capítulo 1 de este libro, "Jicotea" o "Por qué el mono es mono" de este capítulo? ¿En qué se parecen las tres fábulas?)* (Answers will vary. Possible answers: The main characters are all animals; Jicotea did not keep her word and neither the fox nor the monkey kept theirs; all of the fables have a moral about being punished for not keeping one's word.)
3. Is it always easy to keep one's promise? Why or why not? *(¿Es siempre fácil cumplir con una promesa? ¿Por qué sí o por qué no?)* (Possible answers: No, it isn't always easy to keep one's promise, because something else might happen that causes you to break the promise; yes, it's easy because you have to remember to honor your promises if you expect other people to do the same.)

CAPÍTULO 16
Dos leyendas de México

Prereading
Answers will vary.

You may want to tell students that the *flor de la Nochebuena* (Christmas Eve flower, or poinsettia) was originally found in Mexico

during the time of the Aztecs. They called it *cuetlaxóchitl*, the "flower of purity." It grew only in December, and coincided with the holiday of Huitzilopochtli, the god of the Aztecs. When the Spaniards arrived in Mexico, they noticed that there were similarities between Christmas and the Aztecs' Huitzilopochtli celebration. The Indians liked the solemn festivities of Christmas, and they adopted it and celebrated it with the *cuetlaxóchitl* flower. The Spaniards, upon seeing the exquisite scarlet flower which grew only in December, began to use the flower to decorate the nativity scenes in their homes and churches.

It was Dr. Joel Roberts Poinsett, the United States ambassador to Mexico, who brought the flower to the U.S. He was an amateur botanist, and was fascinated by the flower whose petals seemed to be the color of fire. He sent some roots to his greenhouse in the U.S. and the flower was named the "poinsettia" in his honor.

The tale of *La flor de la Nochebuena* is one of the many variants on the legend of the Christmas Eve flower.

You may also want to tell students about the origins of the *ojo de dios*, or "god's eye." It came from the Huichol Indians of Jalisco and Nayarit, west of the Sierra Madre; these Indians are the purest indigenous group from Mexico. The *ojo de dios* is made by stretching strands of yarn onto bamboo crosses to form lozenge shapes through which the gods can see their followers and keep them from harm. The Huichols believe in the gods of nature and the bamboo cross symbolizes the four elements: earth, fire, water, and air. The *ojo de dios* is also used to bring about a long and healthy life for children. When a child is born, the central eye is woven by the father. An additional eye is added for each year of the child's life until the child reaches the age of five, when the *ojo* is completed. A prayer arrow is thrust within the eye in order to channel and direct the prayers of the people. Many South American Indians have also used the *ojo de dios* as a good-luck charm, and for protection against evil.

Answers to *¿De qué se trata?*

1. Answers will vary. Possible answers: Stories about the apparition of the Virgin of Guadalupe to an Aztec Indian, Juan Diego. *(Cuentos sobre la apariencia de la Virgen de Guadalupe a un indio azteca, Juan Diego.)*

2. Answers will vary.

For further discussion

You may want to ask students the following questions:

1. Which of the two stories in this reading has Christian elements, and which has indigenous elements? *(¿Cuál de los dos cuentos de esta lectura tiene elementos cristianos y cuál tiene elementos indígenas?)* (Christian elements: *La flor de la Nochebuena*; indigenous elements: *El ojo de dios.*)

2. Do you know anyone who has had what they consider to be a supernatural experience? What happened? *(¿Conoces a alguien que ha tenido lo que considera una experiencia sobrenatural? ¿Qué fue lo que ocurrió?)*

3. You may want to ask students to write a story about a seemingly supernatural experience that they themselves have had, or that they have heard of, or that they have seen in a movie or read about in a book. You might want to have the stories read to the class and then take a poll on which one students thought was most believable.

Notes

Notes

Notes